NEOLIBERALISM, URBANIZATION, AND ASPIRATIONS IN CONTEMPORARY INDIA

Neoliberalism, Urbanization, and Aspirations in Contemporary India

Edited by

SUJATA PATEL

OXFORD
UNIVERSITY PRESS

Oxford University Press is a department of the University of Oxford.
It furthers the University's objective of excellence in research, scholarship,
and education by publishing worldwide. Oxford is a registered trade mark of
Oxford University Press in the UK and in certain other countries

Published in India by
Oxford University Press
22 Workspace, 2nd Floor, 1/22 Asaf Ali Road, New Delhi 110002, India

© Indian Sociological Society 2021

Copyright of the individual essays rests with respective contributors

The moral rights of the author have been asserted

First Edition published in 2021

All rights reserved. No part of this publication may be reproduced, stored in
a retrieval system, or transmitted, in any form or by any means, without the
prior permission in writing of Oxford University Press, or as expressly permitted
by law, by licence or under terms agreed with the appropriate reprographics
rights organization. Enquiries concerning reproduction outside the scope of the
above should be sent to the Rights Department, Oxford University Press, at the
address above

You must not circulate this work in any other form
and you must impose this same condition on any acquirer

ISBN-13 (print edition): 978-0-19-013201-9

ISBN-10 (print edition): 0-19-013201-9

ISBN-13 (eBook): 978-0-19-099431-0

ISBN-10 (eBook): 0-19-099431-2

DOI: 10.1093/oso/9780190132019.001.0001

Typeset in Minion Pro 10/13
by Newgen KnowledgeWorks Pvt. Ltd., Chennai, India

Printed in India by Rakmo Press Pvt. Ltd

Preface and Acknowledgements

Since the early 1990s, the government in India has promoted the idea that 'the market' delivers benefits better than what is achieved through state planning. Termed neoliberalism, this idea has endorsed a developmental model and an academic paradigm that promotes, in addition to economic policies, the use of digital technologies to speed up the expansion and circulation of commodities and of the money market in order to ensure efficiency and rationality of the system. In the last four decades, the state has introduced new institutions while dismantling old ones, changed legal instruments, initiated privatization of the tertiary sector, such as in electricity, roads, transport, and communication, in construction and housing, as well as in hospitality and tourist businesses, and the professional/service sector, such as education and health. A new economy of real estate and land market as also of natural resources, such as water and its subsequent privatization, has been supported.

As a cultural project, neoliberalism encourages new lifestyles for the aspiring classes. It considers the 'middle classes' as key to the expansion of the market. No wonder that it promotes urbanization and projects urbanism as a way of being modern and global. As a consequence, social scientists are now assessing how maps, plans, models, and architectural designs are representing and producing space together with cultures of middle-class modernities. They are asking questions regarding the discourses, policies, and processes organizing the making of new towns and cities and how the digitalization of governance of existing cities (through smart city projects) has simultaneously promoted and disrupted lives, affected received democratic processes, displaced settled populations, created conflicts with peasants and farmers, encouraged local, regional, and transnational migration, expanded informalization of work, furthered inequalities in the distribution of housing and urban services, disturbed the ecological balance, and constituted new forms of exclusions in urban areas. Scholars have enquired into the recent forms of mobilization by the poor and assessed the nature of this politics and through these queries have evaluated the nature of contemporary conflicts in urban India. They have also investigated how these conflicts in turn affect the nature of individual and collective violence in towns and

vi PREFACE AND ACKNOWLEDGEMENTS

cities while creating demands to enhance social, cultural, and ecological securities.

The chapters in this volume present a bird's-eye view of the aforementioned themes. These are presented by sociologists, anthropologists and demographers, economists and political scientists who participated in the plenaries convened during the 43rd All Indian Sociological Conference from 9 to 12 November 2017, organized by the Indian Sociological Society (ISS) at the University of Lucknow. The conference created an opportunity to hold an interdisciplinary dialogue between experts on urban studies with those who studied inequalities and exclusions and assessed cultures of power, domination, and hegemony in place in India.

I would like to take the opportunity to thank the organizing secretary of the conference, Professor D. R. Sahu, together with Professor Sukanta Chaudhury and colleagues in the Department of Sociology of the University of Lucknow for their help and support during the days of conference deliberations. Fulsome backing and institutional assistance provided by the then Vice Chancellor and other officers of the university were important for the conference's success. They together with the then secretary and treasurer of ISS, Professors Abha Chauhan and Biswajit Ghosh, the members of the ISS Managing Committee, 2016–17, and the staff of ISS, ensured that the conference made an intellectual contribution so that we were able to bring out this volume.

Sujata Patel
Pune, December 2020

Contents

List of Contributors	ix
Endorsements	xiii

1. Introduction: Comprehending Neoliberal India:
   Sujata Patel — 1

PART ONE: NEOLIBERALIZATION: A CONTEMPORARY SNAPSHOT

2. Democracy in Smart Times: Neoliberalism, Populism, and Instant Communication:
   Maitrayee Chaudhuri — 29

3. On Demographic and Gender Dividend in India:
   K. S. James — 48

4. Growth and Consumption in Uttar Pradesh under 'Neoliberalism': **Ravi Srivastava** — 64

5. The Urban Experience in Contemporary India:
   Sujata Patel — 89

PART TWO: THE URBAN PROCESS AND NEOLIBERALIZATION

6. New Urbanism and the Remaking of Citizenship, Class, and 'Community': **Sanjay Srivastava** — 109

7. Rural Real Estate: Empty Urbanization and the Agrarian Land Transition: **Carol Upadhya** — 132

8. Political Centrality of 'Capital' Cities: A Case of Amaravati, Gurgaon, and Rajarhat: **Purendra Prasad** — 153

9. India's Emerging Risk Urbanism: Cities, Commons, and Neoliberal Transformations: **D. Parthasarathy** — 175

viii CONTENTS

PART THREE: BECOMING MIDDLE CLASS, BEING DEPRIVED, AND HAVING ASPIRATIONS

10. Dalits in Neoliberal Economy: A Discussion on Most Marginal Communities: **Badri Narayan** — 197

11. From Social Justice to Aspiration: Transformation of Lower Caste Politics in Uttar Pradesh in the 2000s: **Sudha Pai** — 212

12. Markets and Aspirations: **Aseem Prakash** — 233

13. The Muslim Middle Class: Structure, Identity, and Mobility: **Tanweer Fazal** — 257

Index — 279

Contributors

Maitrayee Chaudhuri has been teaching at the Centre for the Study of Social Systems (CSSS), Jawaharlal Nehru University (JNU) since 1990. She has written widely on feminism, media, academia, and pedagogy. Her key publications include *The Women's Movement in India: Reform and Revival* (1993); *The Practice of Sociology* (ed.) (2003); *Feminism in India* (ed.) (2004); and *Sociology in India: Intellectual and Institutional Trends* (ed.) (2010). Her most recent books are *Refashioning India: Gender, Media and Public Discourse* (2017) and *Doing Theory* (co-ed) (2018).

Tanweer Fazal is Professor of Sociology at the University of Hyderabad. Earlier he taught at the Centre for the Study of Social Systems, Jawaharlal Nehru University, New Delhi and at Nelson Mandela Centre for Peace and Conflict Resolution, Jamia Millia Islamia, New Delhi. His interests lie in the history and theory of nationalism, minority studies, and the study of state practices and collective violence. He is the author of *The Minority Conundrum: Living in Majoritarian Times* (ed.) (Penguin, 2020); *Nation-State' and Minority Rights in India: Comparative Perspectives on Muslim and Sikh Identities* (Routledge, 2015); and *Minority Nationalisms in South Asia* (ed.) (Routledge 2012). His forthcoming book is tentatively titled 'Muslims, Law and Violence: Reflections on the Practices of the State' (Three Essays, 2020).

K. S. James is Director and Sr. Professor, International Institute for Population Sciences (IIPS), Mumbai, India. He holds his PhD degree from Jawaharlal Nehru University, New Delhi and was a postdoctoral fellow at the Harvard Centre for Population and Development Studies, Harvard University, USA. He worked extensively on demographic changes with focus on population and development. He has published widely on demographic transition and demographic dividend in India in journals such as *Science, Lancet, BMC Public Health, Ageing International, Brown Journal of World Affairs, Maternal and Child Health Journal, Journal of Ageing and Health, Social Science and Medicine, Economic and Political Weekly*, etc. He has been a visiting fellow in many prestigious institutes and universities including Harvard University, USA; London School of Economics, UK; University of Southampton, UK; University of Groningen, The Netherlands; and International Institute of Applied System Analysis (IIASA), Austria.

Badri Narayan is a social historian and cultural anthropologist. He is Director, G. B. Pant Social Science Institute, Allahabad. His interests lie in popular culture, social and anthropological history, Dalit and subaltern issues, and the relationship between power and culture. Besides having written a number of articles in both English

X CONTRIBUTORS

and Hindi, he has recently authored *Fractured Tales: Invisibles in Indian Democracy* (Oxford University Press, New Delhi). His other critically acclaimed books are *Kashriram* (Penguin, 2014); *The Making of the Dalit Public in North India: Uttar Pradesh 1950–Present* (Oxford University Press, 2011); *Women Heroes and Dalit Assertion in North India* (Sage, New Delhi, 2006); *Fascinating Hindutva – Saffron Politics and Dalit Mobilisation* (Sage, New Delhi, 2006).

Sudha Pai retired as Professor and Pro-Vice Chancellor (2011–15) at the Centre for Political Studies of Jawaharlal Nehru University. She was National Fellow, ICSSR New Delhi (2016–17) and Senior Fellow at the Nehru Memorial Museum and Library Teen Murti, New Delhi (2006–9). Currently, she is heading PRAMAN (Policy Research and Management Network) a research institute that undertakes investigation of such areas as Health, Agriculture, Foreign Policy, and Education at Gurgaon. Some of her well-known books include *Dalit Assertion and the Unfinished Democratic Revolution: The BSP in Uttar Pradesh* (Sage, 2002); *Developmental State and the Dalit Question in Madhya Pradesh: Congress Response* (Routledge, 2010); *Indian Parliament: A Critical Appraisal* (ed. with Avinash Kumar, Orient Blackswan 2014, 2017); and more recently *Everyday Communalism: Riots in Contemporary Uttar Pradesh* (co-authored with Sajjan Kumar, Oxford, 2018) and *Constitutional and Democratic Institutions in India: A Critical Analysis* (ed.) (Orient Blackswan, 2019).

D. Parthasarathy is with the Department of Humanities and Social Sciences, Indian Institute of Technology (IIT) Bombay. He is also Associate Faculty of the Inter-Disciplinary Program in Climate Studies and the Centre for Policy Studies at IIT Bombay. He is the author of *Collective Violence in a Provincial City* (1997), and has co-edited *Cleavage, Connection and Conflict in Rural, Urban and Contemporary Asia* (2013). He has carried out research projects and published widely in the areas of urban studies, law and governance, climate studies, gender and development, and disaster risk and vulnerability. His current research interests include urban informality, urban commons, transnational urbanism, legal pluralism and resource governance, coastal conflicts, climate uncertainty, and disaster governance.

Sujata Patel is Distinguished Professor at Savitribai Phule Pune University and Kerstin Hesselgren Visiting Professor at Umea University (2021–22). Earlier she was National Fellow at the Indian Institute of Advanced Study, Shimla and has been a teacher of sociology at the Universities of Hyderabad, Pune, and SNDT (Shreemati Nathibai Damodar Thackersey) Women's University. Her work combines a historical sensibility with four perspectives—Marxism, feminism, spatial studies, and post- structuralism. She has authored, edited, and co-edited thirteen books and published more than sixty-six peer reviewed papers/book chapters. She is Series Editor of *Oxford India Studies in Contemporary Society* (Oxford, India) and *Cities and the Urban Imperative* (Routledge, India) and in between 2010 and 2015 edited *Sage Studies in International Sociology and Current Sociology Monographs* (Sage,

CONTRIBUTORS xi

London). Her latest edited text is *Exploring Sociabilities in Contemporary India. New Perspectives* (Orient Blackswan, 2020). The papers in this volume were presented in the plenaries of All India Sociological Conference which she organized as President of the Indian Sociological Society in November 2017.

Aseem Prakash is Professor of Public Policy at School of Public Policy and Governance, Tata Institute of Social Sciences, Hyderabad. His research interests include the interface between the state and markets; regulation and institutions; sociology of markets; social discrimination; and human development. Currently, Aseem's research efforts are focused on two research projects: "Regulation of Small-Town Capitalism" and "Cities, Social History and Muslim Entrepreneurs". His most recent books are titled *Dalit Capital: State, Markets and Civil Society in Urban India* (Routledge, 2015) and *The Indian Middle Class* (co-authored with Surinder Jodhka) (Oxford University Press, 2016).

Purendra Prasad is Professor and currently head of department of Sociology at University of Hyderabad. His research interests include urban studies, political economy of health, agrarian studies, development and disasters. He has published widely in these areas. His publications include *Equity and Access: Health Care Studies in India* (co-ed.) (Oxford University Press, 2018). He is on the academic and ethical advisory boards of several universities and institutions in India.

Ravi Srivastava is Director, Centre for Employment Studies, Institute for Human Development, Delhi. He is a former Professor of Economics, Centre for the Study of Regional Development, Jawaharlal Nehru University, New Delhi and a full-time member of the erstwhile National Commission for Enterprises in the Unorganised Sector. He has published several books and more than one hundred papers in national and international journals in the areas of agriculture, rural development and rural poverty, the informal sector, regional development, decentralization, human development, land reforms, social protection, labour and employment, and migration. His book (with G. K. Lieten) on decentralization and development in Uttar Pradesh (UP) *Unequal Partners* (Sage, New Delhi, 1999) has been widely acclaimed. He co-authored a book (*Uncaging the Tiger: Financing Elementary Education in India* (Oxford University Press, New Delhi, 2005) on the access to and financing of Elementary Education in UP and India.

Sanjay Srivastava is British Academy Global Professor in the Department of Geography, University College London, and Professor of Sociology, Institute of Economic Growth, Delhi. An anthropologist by training, his research spans themes of masculinities and sexualities, consumerism, middle-class cultures, and new urbanism in India. His publications include *Constructing Post-Colonial India. National Character and the Doon School* (Routledge, 1998); *Passionate Modernity. Sexuality, Class and Consumption in India* (Routledge, 2007); *Entangled Urbanism: Slum, Gated*

xii CONTRIBUTORS

Community and Shopping Mall in Delhi and Gurgaon (Oxford University Press, 2015); *Key Theme in Indian Sociology* (Sage, 2019); and *(Hi)stories of Desire: Sexualities and Culture in Modern India* (Cambridge University Press, 2019). He is currently completing a manuscript entitled *Gender and Power in the Post-National City: Masculinity, Consumerism and Urbanism in India* (Cambridge University Press).

Carol Upadhya is Professor in the School of Social Sciences at the National Institute of Advanced Studies (NIAS), Bangalore, India, where she leads the Urban and Mobility Studies Programme. Prof Upadhya is currently co-director of an international collaborative research project, *Speculative Urbanism: Land, Livelihoods, and Finance Capital*, a comparative study of real estate-led urbanization in Jakarta and Bangalore. She is the author of *Reengineering India: Work, Capital, and Class in an Offshore Economy* (Oxford University Press, New Delhi, 2016) and co-editor of *Provincial Globalization in India: Transregional Mobilities and Development Politics* (co-edited by C. Upadhya, M. Rutten, and L. Koskimaki) (Routledge, 2018).

Endorsements

This volume is an important addition to already proliferating literature on the phenomenon of neoliberalism. By being sensitive to subtle and changing nuances of the plethora of inextricable ties between state, market, and civil society, it unravels the evolution of political economy in India over the past few decades. Into the bargain, this oeuvre presents a critical analysis of a wide variety of themes including the very functioning democracy, the changing nature of state and social movements, the role of the middle classes, the status of marginalized Dalit groups, growth and consumption in Uttar Pradesh, the demographic and gender dividend, and the growing challenges of urbanization in India. Serious and stimulating in its engagement, this study should be a starting point for a fresh debate on the impact of neoliberalism on state and society in India.

Rajen Harshe, Former Vice Chancellor, Central University of Allahabad.

Both in popular usage and in academic discourse, 'neoliberalism' has always been one of those words where the 'ought' dominates the 'is'. This means that disputes (or assertions) about what our attitude towards neoliberalism ought to be tend to displace (or distort) attempts to describe its empirical content. This volume is a welcome effort to reclaim the space that description has lost to pre-emptive praise or condemnation. It has a stellar line-up of authors who focus on the content of neoliberalism in contemporary India, covering a wide variety of fields from urban planning through demography to caste relations. Because it pays careful attention to the specific Indian contexts that have been re-formed by, and have in turn reshaped, a global phenomenon, this book will be especially useful to students of the social sciences who are beginning to imagine a future beyond neoliberalism. *Neoliberalism, Urbanization, and Aspirations in Contemporary India* is a well-crafted and timely collection; may its tribe increase.

Satish Deshpande, Professor of Sociology, University of Delhi.

1
Introduction
Comprehending Neoliberal India

Sujata Patel

Neoliberalism is both easy and hard to define. On one hand most scholars would agree that it is the contemporary version of laissez-faire economic principles or free market perspective promoted by European economists of the nineteenth century and that its programmes attempt 'to re-establish the conditions for capitalist accumulation and to restore the power of economic elites' (Harvey 2005, 19).[1] Beyond an agreement with this position, scholars would disagree regarding its many details. Connell and Dados (2014) have provided an explanation for these disagreements. They suggest that not only is there a variation in the neoliberal policies and programmes between countries but that these variations can be grouped into two: neoliberalism in the Global South versus the Global North. They argue that the existing literature on neoliberalism has been skewed towards a critique of neoliberal policy interventions made by the elites of the Global North in the late 70s while neoliberalism's origin can be traced to the economic programmes initiated in Chile and other countries of the Global South in the mid-70s (much before it became popular as an economic strategy in the North). Based on an analysis of neoliberal policies in countries of the Global South, they contend that the orientation and content of neoliberalism in the latter is significantly different. However, the lack of engagement with these policies and programmes has led scholars to valorize the literature on neoliberalism in the Global North and universalize it as being organized around privatization, de-industrialization, welfare state rollback, and their consequences. The latter literature, that is, that of the Global North, they suggest can be broadly divided into two major

---

[1] Specifically, Harvey (2005) defines neoliberalism as 'a theory of political economic practices proposing that human well-being can best be advanced by the maximization of entrepreneurial freedoms within an institutional framework characterized by private property rights, individual liberty, unencumbered markets, and free trade. The role of the state is to create and preserve an institutional framework appropriate to such practices'.

Sujata Patel, *Introduction* In: *Neoliberalism, Urbanization, and Aspirations in Contemporary India.*
Edited by: Sujata Patel, Oxford University Press. © Oxford University Press 2021.
DOI: 10.1093/oso/9780190132019.003.0001

2 SUJATA PATEL

perspectives though several other scholars such as Pinson and Journel (2016) have suggested a fivefold division of approaches.

The first approach to neoliberalism in the literature of the Global North examines it as a system of ideas (the ruling ideas of our time), a set of propositions incorporated in various texts starting with David Harvey (2005), Stiglitz (2002), and that of Naomi Klein (2007). This perspective also connects to the thesis of governmentality. These texts ground the origin of neoliberal ideas to the period after the Second World War when the right wing economists contested Keynesian principles. Over time, their ideas became part of the majority position and were incorporated in economic policies promoted in the UK by Margaret Thatcher and in the USA by Ronald Reagan. The second point of view within the Global North perceives the growth of neoliberalism as part of the crisis of capitalism and the intervention of the capitalist class to expand the capitalist system to offset this crisis. Neoliberalism is considered in this literature as a new stage in the growth of the global capitalist system with financialization as its key programme. This point of view is represented in Dumenil and Levy (2004), Hardt and Negri (2000), and in Robinson (2014).

Connell and Dados (2014) assert that unlike what the above-mentioned literature argues, the goal of neoliberal policies in the Global South is to present neoliberalism as a development strategy superior to earlier strategies such as import replacement industrialization and/or state-centred command economies. Thus, neoliberalism in the South countries, more often than not, has three functions: first, that of fulfilling the role of being a development model; second, that of integrating the country's economy with global and international trade flows; and third, that of adopting and adapting global inclusion through the use of Information and Communication Technologies (ICT). In addition, as mentioned earlier, the key to the success of the programme is the expansion of the middle class. In terms of policies, in most South countries, neoliberalism is focused on converting agriculture and agriculture-based land into new agro-industrial complexes and integrating the latter with transnational corporations and the world economy. Such policies do not indicate an end to subsidies; rather it may mean an end to land reforms and structural assistance to small farmers and/or peasants, and pushing them to migrate to urban areas and become part of urban informal economies and giving them aid and hope of becoming economically mobile. Also, the neoliberalism programme may not initiate an attack on the welfare state. Rather some neoliberal programmes incorporate welfare provisions to offset negative impacts on the poor. However, these programmes are conceptualized to

COMPREHENDING NEOLIBERAL INDIA 3

target individuals and incorporate them into the market. One such example is self-help groups. Lastly, neoliberalism programmes demand new organizational forms, such as export processing zones, tourist sites, business parks, and the creation of new townships and other novel forms of urban reorganization. It thus rescales the state, which now redefines its objective vis-à-vis the society in terms of market rationalities and subsequently reorganizes its institutions. The state thus mobilizes and aligns itself with new groups and organizations to provide legitimacy to its new ideology (Joseph 2007).

In the following, I discuss the specifics of the last four decades of the neoliberal process in India in order to provide the background to the questions being addressed by this volume.

Neoliberalism in India

It has been argued that India's economic reforms were introduced by 'stealth' (Jenkins 1999). In this context, it is imperative to assess the way the Indian regimes introduced neoliberal reforms and describe its interventions and its actions in order to understand how India's economy changed fundamentally from being an import-substitution model of development led through state-intervention and couched and represented in socialist ideas to its present avatar as a neoliberal economy. Further it is also vital to evaluate what have been the implications of this policy to Indian society and polity. Particularly it is essential to comprehend how expansive consumerism, the growth of the IT sector, and changes in political culture have impacted the excluded groups, households, and individuals.

By now there is extensive literature in the public domain that equates the changes initiated through the structural adjustment programme in 1991 with the neoliberal policy and programme. Atul Kohli (2006, 2009) who has been researching and writing on this theme for the last many years has pushed the date of its initiation backwards, to the second term of Indira Gandhi and pinpointed 1980 as the date of its launch. Kohli has argued that Indira Gandhi regime during its second tenure downplayed redistributive concerns and abandoned her regime's earlier left-leaning, anti-capitalist rhetoric and policies, such as *garibi hatao* and bank nationalization. Instead she prioritized economic growth; sought an alliance with big business; adopted an anti-labour stance; put brakes on the growth of public sector industries; and demoted the significance of economic planning and of the Planning Commission. He has also argued that India's neoliberal programme can be best characterized as

4 SUJATA PATEL

being pro-indigenous business rather than pro-market[2] as the latter orientation within the Indian programme was limited to the opening of the global market. After the end of Indira Gandhi's regime, the Rajiv Gandhi regime not only continued with this programme but also speeded up the pro-big business interventions by introducing the telecom and computer revolution and encouraging the establishment of the ICT-led industries. The regime of the two Gandhis according to Kohli (2006, 1255) institutionalized three components as its neoliberal programme model for economic growth which he argues continues till date: a) prioritization of economic growth as a state goal; b) supporting big business (rather than small and medium business) to achieve this goal; and c) taming labour as a necessary aspect of this strategy.[3]

What was the origin of this model? Kohli (2006) has argued that this model drew from but did not replicate the East Asian experiment of neoliberalism.[4] The critical aspect of this model was the nature and quality of state intervention in executing the neoliberal programme. The East Asian experiment used the state to promote and facilitate the availability of capital, labour, technology, and even entrepreneurship. These regimes introduced new supply side policies that enhanced tax collection and investment; pushed public banks to give credit to preferred private firms and sectors; shifted resources from agriculture and urban labour to private industrialists; provided supply of cheap, 'flexible', and disciplined labour and ensured that it obeyed its commands through repression. On the demand side the East Asian states pursued policies for growth such as expansionist monetary and fiscal policies and tariffs and exchange-rate policies and also encouraged production for both domestic and foreign consumption.

The Indian state's imitation of the East Asian experiment, according to Kohli (2006, 1253–4), was not 'always self-conscious'. The Indian regime could not 'replicate the cohesion, effectiveness, or the brutality of a Japanese or a Korean state' nor was the Indian state managerially efficient to provide

---

[2] A pro-market strategy rests on the idea that free play of markets will lead to efficient allocation of resources, as well as promote competitiveness, hence boosting production and growth. It also implies bringing governmental expenditures more in line with revenues on the one hand, and opening the economy with the hope of promoting exports on the other hand, as well as privatizing public sector enterprises, cutting public subsidies, reducing the public role in setting prices, devaluation, reduction of tariffs, and opening the economy to foreign investors.

[3] Kohli (2006, 1361) also says that import quota reduction, currency devaluation, and liberalization of the foreign investment regime together with easing of external financial transactions did not benefit businesses.

[4] Atul Kohli (2006, 1365) unlike Connell and Dados has argued that there are three models: the neoliberal model of Anglo America, the social democratic model of Scandinavia, and the statist model of Japan and South Korea.

COMPREHENDING NEOLIBERAL INDIA   5

education to many of its poor nor to control and repress and/or reskill its labour. Thus, the regime merely used the model in terms of its self-conscious orientation to economic growth and in associating with big Indian capital in various ways that promoted these firms and enhanced their profits and their personal wealth. Capital which until now had only veto power over policies started slowly setting the economic agendas for the neoliberal regime (Jaffrelot et al. 2019, 286). In these circumstances, the state initiated the neoliberal process slowly and steadily, honed a strategy of political dexterity, and changed rules and regulations and various clauses within laws one by one rather than altogether in order to ensure that it could camouflage as best as it can the decisions that were being made. Commentators have argued that such skills became necessary because on one hand the legacy of rent-seeking by the elite and the top-heavy state of the pre-liberal period did not allow for drastic changes and on the other the democratic process in the form of elections and control of parties by various castes having different and competing interests curtailed the freedom for the government to intervene drastically. Thus, the changes towards neoliberalism were not only slow but also not clearly discernible in the initially first decade. There were no drastic privatization of public sector units and budget deficits remained an issue for successive governments; public expenditures were hard to limit and corporate taxes could not be increased given its impact on investment. New strategies had to be evolved to create revenues given that further IMF loans could not be availed as a consequence of the criticism against it while an increase of indirect taxes in all situations was difficult. Also, the competition for resources from the deprived increased pressures while subsidies could not be eliminated because of its impact on elections.

Though the neoliberal programme is now almost four decades old, it took the central government up to 2014 to remove the last item from the list of items reserved for production in the small-scale sector and up to 2002 to dismantle most of the government's controls over private investment. By that time the entire system of government's industrial licensing had been nearly abolished and the list of industries reserved solely for the public sector had been drastically reduced. The Indian state restrictive trade policy, which was said to protect inefficient domestic production, was also gradually dismantled. As early as 1993, import licensing for capital goods and intermediates was abolished and India introduced a flexible exchange-rate regime and allowed foreign institutional investors to purchase shares of listed Indian companies in the stock market leading to the simplification of procedures for foreign direct investment. However, it was only in 2001 that import

6 SUJATA PATEL

restrictions on consumer goods and agricultural products were removed and since 1999, the privatization of public sector entities has been encouraged.

Kohli (2006) has argued that the Indian programme of neoliberalism is quite revolutionary though it did not make drastic changes to the country's economy as did other countries of the globe.[5] For example, the number of private companies increased five times from 1991 to 2014; in 1991, India had only 2 lakh companies (Chandra 2015, 48). There was also a change in the social composition of the business groups. The narrow caste, ethnic, and language base of the business community that India inherited from the colonial times was slowly dismantled with new first-generation players from artisan, agricultural, and bureaucratic families entering the market leading in turn to the growth of new business and political party networks. But India's programme also emphasized major continuities with the earlier forms of organizing state–market relationships through business. Though the state dismantled the centralized system of licensing policy and regulations, in some cases new regulations were introduced in various deregulated sectors, such as electricity, railways, airports, roads, ports, and telecommunications.

Chandra (2015) argues that a new system of licenses, leases, concessions, permits, and contracts was established to regulate infrastructural industries in which the Indian state earlier had monopoly and that the Indian state also created similar instruments for obtaining inputs such as raw material and credit, water and electricity, and land (Chandra 2015, 46). (On how these regulations create new risks, see Parthasarthy in this volume.) Though some of these instruments were made in collaboration with the newly emerging elite, others such as the law on land acquisition involved social movements and civil society actors as well as the business interests (Jenkins 2019). Overall, these new regulations have created more ambiguity, complexity, and many layered and distributed jurisdiction (Chandra 2015, 48) leading according to some to 'development deadlocks' (Nielson and Oskarsson 2016, 67). Also, in certain situations, there has been a failure of the state to provide any regulatory frameworks of governance which Corbridge has called 'state scarcity' (see Ravi Srivastava in this volume on Uttar Pradesh [UP]). Such a process, mainly seen in poor states of the country, has invited private players to introduce 'unplanned urban and industrial processes'. (On the role of developers and real estate agents, see in this volume Upadhya and Prasad.)

---

[5] Though tariffs came down significantly, Kohli (2006, 1362) argues these were still 30% at the end of the 1990s which he states was lowest in the world at that time while foreign trade was only 25% of GDP.

COMPREHENDING NEOLIBERAL INDIA   7

Chandra (2015) affirms that these instruments did not change drastically the nature of the state structure which it had inherited from its pre-liberal days. Instead the inauguration of these changes and the increase of multiple state actors boosted the discretion of bureaucrats and allowed them to deepen patronage structures and escalate rent seeking. The new plural character and big business involvement was thus not only the distinctive attribute of this 'new Indian state' under the Congress neoliberal regime. Rather according to Chandra (2015) it was the continuation of the patronage system[6] built during the pre-liberal period that was its most significant attribute and since the 90s it has increased the power of family-based dynasties in politics (Chandra 2016). The latter characteristic was critically important in legitimizing the relationship between the state and capital. Thus, if the dismantling of regulations led to the diffusion of power from the centre to the state and onward to the district, the growth of new local and regional players allowed new patronage relationships based on caste, language and ethnicity to be constituted leading to new networks between business and political elites and between the latter and the bureaucracy to be created through the newly constituted ministries and administrative departments. These new networks allowed business to work in an organic way with the political parties and influence party ideologies and election manifestos. Members of the business communities became party members and represented these parties in the state legislatures and in the parliament and through this process actively intervened in framing legislative bills and administrative rules in their favour. In turn, party leaders also started businesses making possible an organic link between them (Sinha 2019).[7]

Curiously the state in India has made little formal efforts (until recently[8]) to deregulate employment. This has led Rina Agarwala (2019) to

[6] Chandra (2015, 46) defines patronage as 'the individualized allocation of state-controlled resources by state official to citizens'. This is part of what she calls a 'dominant state' syndrome, that is, the use of discretionary powers by state officials in allocating goods and services (Chandra 2016, 33).

[7] Sinha's data indicate that since 1991 the share of business interests represented in the Lok Sabha in Congress and BJP parties increased from 14.20% in 1991 to 26.33% in 2014 (BJP) and that their representation is also increasing across state assemblies with between 50% and 70% in Goa and Maharashtra and the poor states of the north-east and the left party states of Kerala and West Bengal having less than 20%.

[8] The central government introduced labour reforms to convert forty-four labour legislations into four codes. The code on wages was passed by the parliament while that on occupational safety, health, and working conditions has gone to the Standing Committee (*Economic Times*, 29 December 2019). Available at https://economictimes.indiatimes.com/news/economy/policy/with-four-labour-codes-2020-to-be-a-year-of-reforms-santosh-gangwar/articleshow/73027335.cms?utm_source=contentofinterest&utm_medium=text&utm_campaign=cppst, accessed 18 May 2020.

8   SUJATA PATEL

argue that the state has used this silence to encourage irregular and contract work in the manufacturing industry and in new infrastructure industries. Consequently, she suggests, the structure of employment has changed. There has been a decline in agricultural employment and an increase in employment for men and women with higher education in the urban domain (Kannan and Raveendran 2019). While the number of informal labourers in registered organized industry has increased by three times as compared to formal employment, contract labour has escalated from 12 per cent to 23 per cent between 1985 and 2002 (Agarwala 2019, 111). Similarly, there has been an increase of informal work in government and public sector jobs. These developments have led Agarwala to argue that informal employment (which in India was always high; Jha (2016, xiv) estimates that it constitutes 82 per cent of all workers while the Economic Survey of 2018–19, released on 4 July 2019, says 'almost 93%') has shifted from the so-called traditional unorganized sector to the modern organized sector. Informal and unregulated work has become the openly acknowledged new normal for India's modern economy. Kannan and Ravindran also argue that the biggest job loss of workers in this sector has been for Muslims, Other Backward Classes, and women in rural areas. Agarwala thus asserts that there is defeminization of Indian labour and that this is a consequence of a drop of 1.4 per cent in women's employment from 1999 to 2011. This trend relates to the decrease in woman's contract work which fell by 10.4 million between 1999 and 2011 (NSS 2012).[9] (See James in this volume on the impact of this trend on the gendered demographic dividend.) These trends have got complicated in the context of the Covid-19 crisis which recognized the presence of about 35 to 40 per cent short-term circulatory/seasonal migrants in the urban informal (Srivastava 2020).

It seems that despite the above-mentioned changes, the Indian experience of neoliberalism has leaned heavily on continuities (except during the present regime of the BJP government) and reproduced existing structures of state power. Certainly, one part of the answer for these continuities lies in the cautious approach that has organized the programme's launch and its organization. However, there are two other processes that have aided this process

---

[9] Agarwala contends that women may have taken up alternate employment in the construction industry where they have a significant presence (30%) and have found work in other invisible occupations such as paid domestic work in which the numbers range from 3.9 million according to the 2011 NSSO statistics, to 10 million according to the 2009 Labour Bureau statistics (Agarwala 2019). However, since the start of the Covid pandemic it seems more women than men have lost jobs (Swaminathan 2020).

COMPREHENDING NEOLIBERAL INDIA 9

which are of equal significance. The first is the character of the polity from 1989 onwards and the second is the nature of the middle class. The neoliberal project was launched at a time when the rent-seeking and patronage-based upper caste-led 'Congress Party System' that had earlier used factions and factionalism to negotiate pressures from various deprived interest groups to redistribute resources had disintegrated. By the late 70s, ferment among backward peasants had yielded to the growth of a new backward caste alliance in North India (called the AJGAR[10]). This backward caste upsurges led the then central government to agree to accept the recommendations of the Mandal Commission report and provide reservation of 27 per cent[11] to the Other Backward Classes.[12]

In the same period a new dalit movement emerged in north India which had an impact in the State of Uttar Pradesh. This movement, led by Kanshi Ram, aimed to integrate all oppressed castes which they called the Bahujans under its leadership. Later this movement became a party called the Bahujan Samaj Party (Badri Narayan in this volume indicates how the latter has not been able to provide opportunities to its constituency). Given this political fragmentation and its impact on the Congress party's traditional vote banks, the latter experimented to create its own majoritarian bloc of lower caste and minority groups, as it did in Gujarat through the experiment of KHAM.[13] However, this experiment did not help it to retain its vote banks for more than a term as slowly and steadily the upper castes shifted their affiliations to the developing Hindutva movement led by the Bharatiya Janata Party (BJP) and the latter created new political alliances with regional parties. The impetus for the consolidation of this movement came through the anti-reservation agitation which soon refashioned itself to become a Hindu majoritarian

---

[10] Ahirs, Jats, Gujars, and Rajputs.

[11] Until then reservation was limited to 15% for Scheduled Caste and 7.5% for Scheduled Tribes. (Thirteen states had already provided this extension to OBCs.) Jayal (2015, 120–1) suggests that the reservation for OBC took place when there was already a judicial review of the system of quotas. Second, there were administrative challenges related to identifying the eligible, fake certificates, and other malpractices leading to under-representation of the Scheduled Castes and Scheduled Tribes in Class I and II jobs. There was little or no presence of lower castes in government that could make upper castes feel threatened.

[12] Over the years since then the state has consistently devolved the legitimacy of social and cultural exclusions for giving benefits of reservation and upended those of economic backwardness as in the 10% reservation for economically weaker castes in government jobs passed in early 2019. This change introduced the notion that economic backwardness has equal relevance with the earlier accepted principle of historically constituted social and cultural discrimination, exploitation, and domination on which basis both Scheduled Castes and Scheduled Tribes were given reservation.

[13] Khastriya, Harijan, Adivasi, and Muslim.

10   SUJATA PATEL

movement after the Hindu zealots destroyed the Babri mosque and took up the issue of building the Ram temple.

Political commentators have thus suggested that the period from 1989 to 2014 should be characterized as the third-party system which brought with it competitive politics, political fragmentation of traditional vote banks, and the emergence of new regional parties leading to the federalization of national politics together with the slow consolidation of a Hindu bloc (Yadav 1999). Given the fragmentation of both the Congress- and BJP-led blocs, the Indian state governed by these coalitions has also used another strategy of designing economic programmes for the poor as one of its important developmental goals. During the 2004–9 UPA regime redesigned Maharashtra's Employment Guarantee Scheme to pass it in a new avatar called the National Rural Employment Guarantee Act[14] which gave provision a of 100 days' work for one member of all poor families and the right to information that helped to question the patronage-oriented governance system that was biased towards the dominant castes locally. Though in early 2019, the BJP passed a policy of cash transfers and extended reservation to economically backward families it has not been so positive about the MGNREGA and other programmes and legislations of the earlier government. Rather it has used the ideology of aspirations (as Sudha Pai and Aseem Prakash argue in this volume) to mobilize the poor. Thus, when Kohli (2006) argue that anti-poverty programmes in the name of economic growth have aided the conviction among many supporters of the Indian state that it remains committed to its earlier pro-poor orientation, he may mean the Congress-led coalitions.

However, since 2014, the BJP-led coalition has travelled on a new path and their economic management has shown little to no understanding of the system that has been constituted since independence and the deep processes that have been at work to organize the same. The Congress-led coalition, aware of this, at first deflected the discussions on neoliberal interventions, then articulated these as development programmes, and later rode these policies in adjunct with social welfare programmes for the poor. The BJP's ideological proclivity against these policies has led them to take arbitrary and random and sometimes uninformed policy interventions. More generally, the present government has been perceived as having little sensitivity for the poor and thus it is no surprise to note that any engagement with the concerns of the poor has been rare. Nor has the BJP government incorporated the

[14] Later renamed Mahatma Gandhi National Rural Employment Guarantee Scheme.

COMPREHENDING NEOLIBERAL INDIA   11

latter's representatives to discuss inclusive policy interventions. In these circumstances, commentaries have argued that the policy of 'shocks' to the system, such as demonetization and GST and recently, during the Covid-19 crisis, the complete shutdown of the economy has created not only strangulated the economy but has created an all-embracing hardship and survival problems for the large mass of India's poor. As a consequence, and as mentioned above, not only has unemployment increased[15] but also have inequalities. If four decades of neoliberalism policies decreased absolute poverty in India, there is a likelihood of this trend being reversed henceforth.

In addition, neoliberalism has increased regional divides within the country. Political fragmentation and growth of strong regional parties in the last decade of the twentieth century and in the beginning of this century allowed for the expansion of neoliberal programmes in India's various rich states. In these states, the dominant caste which supported these regional parties used its capital to invest in new projects, allowing for new business actors to emerge. Kohli suggests that poor states were further deprived as they not only did not obtain private investment but lost out on public investment (see Ravi Srivastava in this volume on how history, inter-regional unevenness, and governance issues affected economic growth in the state of UP). Additionally, given that land was the main resource of these dominant castes it was natural for some of these rich states to create opportunities for investment in agro-based industries as also through giving concessions for converting agricultural land into commercial land or for constructing townships and gated communities. In these circumstances, development came to be redefined as urbanization or industrialization or infrastructure creation (Chandra 2015, 50). Contemporary urbanization in India is all about land acquisition and greenfield development. (See in this volume, Patel for an overview of the neoliberal urbanization process; Sanjay Srivastava, on how DLF township was made, Upadhya on the 'empty urbanization' and Prasad how the Andhra Pradesh state assessed land for the new city of Amravati.)

This political milieu was extremely significant for the inauguration of the state's ideological project to create a new middle class and related to it, its efforts to promote ICT-oriented service industries that could use the country's English-educated, technically trained human resources for its

---

[15] India's unemployment rate increased 14.8 percentage points, rising to 23.5% in April 2020, according to a survey conducted by the Centre for Monitoring Indian Economy (CMIE). Available at https://www.livemint.com/news/india/unemployment-increased-14-8-pct-points-rose-to-23-5-in-apr-2020-cmie-survey-11588316116699.html.

12 SUJATA PATEL

expansion. It was during the Rajiv Gandhi term that the state presented this ideological project when it argued that India is poised to emerge as a massive consumer market for both Indian and global businesses in which the key role would be played by the country's middle class. To this effect, the regime involved its statistical organization, the National Centre for Applied Economic Research (NCAER), to start computing the numbers of the middle classes which it did on the basis of income. At one point, it was argued that this middle class was larger than that of USA and would cover 100 to 300 million individuals. The hype about the middle class since then has been scaled down and depending on the measures used, the estimated size of this middle class ranges between 78 million (*Economist* 2018) to 604 million (Krishnan and Hatekar 2017).[16] The latter has used the income criteria to argue that the new middle class in India (that is, those spending between US$2 and $10 per capita per day) has doubled in size between 2004–5 and 2011–12 and that it amounts to nearly half of India's population. They have also indicated that the middle class is stratified into three sections. The lower middle class who work in mainly poor occupations such as construction and farm work and have presence across most of the rural and urban areas of Indian states. This group, consisting of lower castes and ethnic and religious minorities, can quite quickly slip into poverty and precarity.[17] On the other hand, the upper middle class is mainly composed of the upper castes. They are in traditional services and as well in new IT- and media-related occupations. In the middle are the comfortable middle class who are in salaried occupations.[18]

Both Leela Fernandes (2004, 2012) who has written extensively on the new middle class and Sanjay Joshi (2017) who has written in the colonial middle class have argued that this class is not new. Rather the upper segments of this class have been part of the old middle class of India; these being the English-educated upper castes, mainly male, bureaucratic, managerial,

---

[16] Maryam Aslany (2019) uses a composite indicator-based income, skills and credentials, social networks, housing (ownership and access to sanitation), and lifestyle (consumption and purchasing power) to define the middle class. Using data from the India Human Development Survey (2011–12) 28% of India's population is middle class-of which 14% is lower middle class and about 3% is upper middle class.

[17] See the employment data presented above.

[18] Fernandes (2006) also divides the middle class into three groups: the dominant faction having cultural capital and recognized authority positions with interests close to the bourgeoisie; the petty bourgeoisie such as small business owners, merchants, and farmers having some economic independence; and last the subordinate middle class who are salaried workers and may have educational capital but little or no authority positions.

COMPREHENDING NEOLIBERAL INDIA   13

and intellectual elite who at one point of time supported constitutionalism, developmentism, and modernism (Joshi 2017) and affirmed a pro-poor agenda to resolve the country's problems (Fernandes 2004). Both Fernandes and Joshi contend the newness of the contemporary middle class with regard to the cultural and political role that it is playing in contemporary polity as against what it had played earlier. Fernandes whose focus on the contemporary middle class sees the dominant fraction of this class acting as a reference group for other fractions. This fraction articulates public discourses in English language and represents life style in consumption practices.[19] These discourses become standards against which 'aspirations of other fractions of the middle class are measured' (Fernandes and Heller 2006, 501). As a consequence, this group holds out itself as a model for mobility, of inclusion and yet it represents ways in which hierarchies and exclusions are constituted that aids it to secure its dominance. (See Aseem Prakash and Tanweer Fazal on the aspirations of dalits and Muslims in this volume and how their mobility is blocked because of their lack of cultural capital.) Joshi argues that this tendency has a colonial location given that old middle class was caught in trying to find an authentic identity for itself while simultaneously emulating the British and using the English language as cultural capital to mark its superiority against the subalterns. Joshi provides extensive evidences to indicate how this search for authenticity reflected itself in the imaginaries of the many nationalist leaders. The latter according to Joshi, espoused Hindu religious concerns and practices while simultaneously propounding modern values. As a consequence, Joshi contends the old middle class could not build hegemony with the country's subaltern groups and thus used patronage politics to create for themselves a nationalist bloc.

Similar arguments are provided by Fernandes (2012) regarding the new middle class. She argues that the new middle class not only represents 'pre-existing forms of inequality, it also generates inequality' (Fernandes 2012, 76). Thus, Fernandes and Heller (2006) contend that the new middle

---

[19] Chancel and Picketty (2019) have analysed data based on household surveys, national accounts, and tax data to understand inequality in India from 1922 to 2015. They argue that the share of national income accruing to the top 1% is at its highest since the creation of the Indian Income Tax Act in 1922. The top 1% of earners captured less than 21% of total income in the late 1930s, before dropping to 6% in the early 1980s and rising to 22% in the recent period. Over the 1951–80 period, the bottom 50% group captured 28% of total growth, and incomes of this group grew faster than the average, while the top 0.1% incomes decreased. Over the 1980–2015 period, the situation was reversed; the top 0.1% of earners captured a higher share of total growth than the bottom 50% (12% vs 11%), while the top 1% received a higher share of total growth than the middle 40% (29% vs 23%).

14 SUJATA PATEL

class in India has taken the choice of being illiberal and reactionary and has moved towards Hindu nationalism. They suggest that the middle class can sponsor both radical and reactionary ideologies and that the choice it takes depends on the alliances that it makes and the support it gives to the civil society groups and political parties. These choices affect the nature of democracy and the polity (see Chaudhury in this volume on how social media is used in this context). The Hindutva project, Fernandes and Heller argue, becomes a mechanism to incorporate the various middle-class fractions into its fold as it allows a unifying nationalist ideology to be constituted that does not disturb the dominant fraction's pre-eminent position. Given that the Congress is perceived as being pro-lower castes and minorities, it has become easy for this section to shift to the Hindutva political project. This project allows the deep material differentiation that characterizes the middle classes to be transcended by an identity with a political-religious agenda which is linked to casteism and majoritarianism. In turn, it also helps to create a network of collective business interests legitimized by dynastic politics to aid and support this bloc. Fernandes and Heller argue that this class is now being reimagined at the level of habitus[20] (see Sanjay Srivastava in this volume and his conceptualization of 'moral consumption' in this context) and the reaffirmation of caste, language, and religious resources, practices, and identity are furthering inequalities and differentiation within the middle class which the Hindutva ideology tries to displace through a collective appeal for politico-religious issues (see Sudha Pai on how the BJP has formulated this aspirational ideology to mobilize the weaker sections in UP). Like Joshi they also argue that despite a strong attempt by the dominant fraction of the middle class to hegemonize the middle-class fractions and the subalterns, the latter has not been able to be successful thereby promoting the continuance of the strategy of patronage.

This is the background on which the twelve chapters in this volume are presented, though the authors do recognize that significant changes have taken place in almost all the processes that they are investigating since the Covid 19 crisis started and their papers need updating. But the implications of this crisis will take some time to analyse.

---

[20] Fernandes and Heller (2006, 509) quote Pierre Bourdieu in this context. A class can be imagined 'at a deepest level of habitus, to the tastes and distastes, sympathies and aversion, fantasies and phobias which, more than declared opinions, forge conscious unity of class'.

Introducing This Volume

This volume has twelve chapters written by scholars in the disciplines of sociology, anthropology, political science, political economy, and demography. They use their scholarship to engage with various trends occurring in contemporary India regarding neoliberalism in the context of the rise of the Hindu majoritarian movement and an assertion of upper-caste patriarchal cultures. The authors agree that neoliberal changes in India have created a challenge to social scientists and that they now need to construct a new language to comprehend the present and design new interdisciplinary perspectives to narrate analytically these contemporary changes. No longer is neoliberalism indiscernible, as argued by Jenkins and Kohli and mentioned above. It is there upfront and is impacting everyday lives of individuals and is determining the structuring of new contemporary sociabilities. Authors have used a combination of methodologies and methods, from ethnography to surveys, from analysis of aggregate data, interviews and life history narratives, participant observation, and content analysis of newspapers to analyse how it is doing so.

The chapters in this volume capture trends in neoliberalism that have taken place since the beginning of this century and particularly in the last decade. The chapters are divided into three sections: The first section contains four chapters on four distinct themes associated with neoliberalism—an assessment of the negative impact of social media on democracy; gender implications of demographic dividend; an assessment of the neoliberal programmes in the State of Uttar Pradesh and the roles played by history, regional inequalities, and governance in it; the attributes of the neoliberal processes of urbanization. The second and third sections of this volume consisting of four chapters each are focused on two specific themes. The first assesses the interface of neoliberalism with urbanization an area which has not received enough attention by scholars in the near past and the last section starts with an evaluation of the aspirations of the deprived groups and how the Hindutva party of BJP in UP has mobilized them. The last two chapters in this volume analyses the constraints that are faced by dalits and Muslims due to the lack of cultural capital which is defined today by the Hindu upper-caste communities. This volume reasserts a contention made by previous scholars that contemporary neoliberal economic policy has increased inequalities and exclusions while providing opportunities to the upper sections of society. In turn, it has also creating new risks and challenges to everyday lives of the lower middle classes, the marginalized,

16 SUJATA PATEL

and the excluded in India. Subsequently, I present the key ideas explored by the authors of this volume.

Neo Liberalization: A Contemporary Snap-Shot

The first four chapters are reflective essays and assess the impact of neoliberalism on democracy, on demographic, gendered dividend, in Uttar Pradesh, a large but poor state of India and on urbanization. The first chapter in this volume is by Maitrayee Chaudhury, titled 'Democracy in Smart Times'. It analyses the nature of contemporary media system in India which is fuelled by ICT technology and argues that this technology has reinforced neoliberal ideas and these together derail the received democratic political culture of the country. This chapter analyses WhatsApp messages and indicates how these have affected social networks and inclusive sociabilities in the country. Neoliberal ideas, Chaudhuri argues, bring market rationality into all aspects of life. On the economic front, it maximizes competition, encourages free trade through deregulation, and promotes monetary and social policies favourable to business. This perspective seeps through the political and the cultural domains and reconstitutes the individual self. Neoliberalism, she argues, is a form of governmentality and 'reaches out to define the soul of human beings'. Human beings are encouraged to become homo economicus and subject all dimensions of life to market rationality. By making an individual responsible for herself Chaudhuri states, neoliberal ideas equate rationality with morality. Therefore, the citizen becomes a consumer and an individual's moral autonomy is measured by her capacity of 'self care'. In these circumstances, the individual has little to no interest in being concerned with the larger public and forging ideological solidarities across groups. S/he can be instigated to believe whatever media circulates to oneself as the truth.

The next paper by K.S. James titled 'On Demographic and Gender Dividend in India' maps out the debate on gender-oriented demographic dividend. As mentioned earlier, there is a decrease in Female Work Participation Rate (FWPR) in India for women aged 15–59 by more than 10.9 per cent. In this context how is it possible to understand the issue of gender dividend? James suggests that if scholarship equates gender dividend only with an increase of FWPR, then India does not have this dividend. However, he contends a rethinking the concept in context to contemporary trends is necessary. Surely, he asks household-based production, quality of care for the children and for the old are also important productive activities and for these reasons should women not remain at home to do them? This conclusion by James will surely elicit a debate given that the feminist social anthropologists such as Hannah Papanek have examined women's increased involvement in the home as 'status production' while other scholars have termed it 'home production'. Feminist scholars have suggested that women are trained or socialized to produce and reproduce the home. Their labour is deployed to enhance the status and mobility of the family as a whole. At home, they involve themselves in a basket of tasks and roles including income generation but also childcare, housework, networking with extended kin and community, meeting obligations, nurturing relationships. James' arguments make one ask whether the increase of women's involvement in the home implies that neoliberalism reproduces patriarchy in new ways.

The next chapter in this section is by Ravi Srivastava is titled, 'Growth and Consumption in Uttar Pradesh under "Neoliberalism". As mentioned earlier, UP is India's largest state in terms of population size has not given any rewards from neoliberalism to its people. Srivastava argues that UP has suffered because political regimes which has not been able to negotiate with competitive interests in order develop policies and administer governance. UP is a prime example of 'scarcity of state'. Srivastava gives us some reasons to understand what has happened in UP. He suggests that a) there is a long history of regional variations in the state with in turn is related to its political elite not having created programmes that would benefit these sub-regions and their population; b) there has been since 1989 chronic government instability. From 1991 until today, there have been twelve governments in power; c) the impact of the demolition of Babri Masjid in 1992 has led to the deep fissures between the Muslims and Hindus and in turn UP's growth; d) given that the rule of law is weak in UP, it has led parties to favour crony capitalism, discretionary, and ad hoc decisions. Regimes have been characterized by rampant corruption. The chapter analyses agriculture growth, industrial stagnation and consumption in UP and makes assessments of contemporary inequalities among social groups in terms of education, land, and jobs. It concludes that in UP, neoliberalism has led to slow growth, increasing gap with national economy, and spatial concentration of industry while data suggest a significant gap in terms of consumption with the all India average figures. The author suggests that UP did not create sufficient jobs for all and today the existing jobs are mainly held by upper-caste

18 SUJATA PATEL

Hindus. The political and economic scenario of last twenty-five years has been has indeed been dismal. Unfortunately, neoliberalism as a development strategy has not succeeded in UP. The last chapter in this section makes an overall assessment of India's contemporary urbanization process. This chapter by Sujata Patel, titled 'The Urban Experience in Contemporary India', argues that contemporary urbanization in India is fuelled by the state through the creation of physical infrastructure, that is, roads, transport facilities and communication, encouragement of private investment in construction and housing, in hospitality and tourist businesses, in professional/service sector education and health. Today's urbanization has benefitted from changing legal instruments and by creating an economy of real estate and land market as also of other services, such as electricity, sanitation, roads, education, and health. These trends have allowed a few elite groups, the upper-caste middle classes to reside in high-value residential complexes with privatized infrastructure facilities and a concomitant life style. The chapter suggests that neoliberal interventions have deprived a large segment of the population from access to basic physical infrastructure: portable water, sanitation, housing, and transport and communication services. With the privatization of social infrastructure such as health and education, this population has been deprived of the same leading to increasing discrepancy between upper caste and marginal groups in access to services. This has led to spatial segregation based on class, caste, and ethnic groups. Contemporary urbanization the chapter argues bolstered the organization of informal work and labour in small and large commercial industries and activities as also through self-employment. These economies have integrated individuals in semi-independent peasant households with urban informal work and allowed them to migrate across these activities. This chapter suggests that there has been a growth of individual, collective, and state violence in the context of these changes.

The Urban Process and Neoliberalization

For neoliberalism to succeed there is a need for the middle classes to remake their imaginaries. Sanjay Srivastava's paper titled 'New Urbanism and the Remaking of Citizenship, Class and "Community"' is an ethnographic study of the Delhi Life Finance Company (DLF) township which he argues promoted a new understanding between state–people–capital. In the case of DLF the developer used a combination of strategies, such as caste and community

COMPREHENDING NEOLIBERAL INDIA   19

bonds with famers whose land they took on credit and political patronage to change and/or dilute planning measures to acquire agricultural land for building urban residences. These practices allowed a perceptional change in the notion of role of the state, now perceived to be corrupt and subservient to capital. In this context the middle classes who lived in these townships developed new notions of their rights and demanded that the state fulfill their needs through the de-regulation of the economy, lessen the role of the public sector and ensure easy loans for consumer purchases. When the state did not acquiesce, these middle classes initiated protests. Srivastava calls this politics 'post nationalist' as it shifts the idea of the nationalist solidarity to middle-class solidarity and the reorients the nationalist family to the nuclear family. This 'post national' domesticity, Srivastava argues, is the site of the new culture of consumption. The middle-class subjectivity is constituted in the context of 'transnational consumerist modernity where the bedroom is the window to the world'. At the same time, this middle class needs to affirm its authenticity of being Indian. Srivastava suggests that women are made guardian of Indian traditions and a new discourse of control which he calls 'moral consumption' is articulated. This discourse organizes the family life through the valourization of festivals such as *Kadva chauth* and such like. This Indianness again is expressed when 'ethnic villages' are made sites for leisure, spirituality, health, and aesthetics. Srivastava contends that these spatial classes represent a 'simulacra of separate spheres' of the modern and the traditional.

The next two chapters discuss ways in which agrarian land has been converted into real estate to promote urbanization. The chapter by Carol Upadhya titled, 'Rural Real Estate: Empty Urbanization and the Agrarian Land Transition' is on land and its conversion as real estate. Land, she argues, is no longer a factor in production but it is used for creating a market and for accumulation of capital. Its conversion from its earlier 'use value' to 'exchange value' has been buttressed by the neglect of agriculture, lack of support to small and marginal farmers and thus increasing non-sustainability of cultivation. The state has become a land broker by acting for the interests of capital in appropriating land for private use. First it initiated this process through Special Economic Zone (SEZ) and now it is being done in new forms: through the extension of city's boundaries or by creating new infrastructure projects or announcing the establishment of a new city. Such interventions drive up land prices and enables the interlinking of different circuits of capital and spheres of value, as capital moves through formal and informal credit markets and mutates between different forms such as land, real estate, financial investments, and other assets such as gold. The chapter

20 SUJATA PATEL

also argues that complex caste network patterns have emerged as and when brokers, moneylenders, real estate agents, or rentiers organize the sale of land. She also notes that once land is acquired, this does not imply that it would develop immediately. It is possible that for some time it will remain unoccupied or 'undeveloped' and barren. Therefore, today it is possible to note a new form of urbanization in India, which she calls 'empty urbanism'. This consists of open plots of fallow land, ready for 'development', half-built small apartment buildings giving us a visual representation of a country and a nation that is half finished or completed.

The next chapter in this section titled 'Political Centrality of "Capital" Cities: A Case of Amaravati, Gurgaon and Rajarhat' by Purendra Prasad uses an ethnographic approach to comprehend the process described earlier by Upadhya. In his chapter, Prasad looks at this history of the building of capital cities in India and in this context analyses Amravati, a project that the Chandrababu Naidu government initiated and which since then has been redesigned to include two other cities by the new Jagmohan Reddy government. The chapter explains how the state is playing a critical role in shaping the conditions for capital accumulation and circulation and thereby representing certain political interests. Prasad assesses the rescaling strategies used by the state to reorganize capital cities and examines how physical space, political power, and the logic of accumulation play out in the neoliberal context. The focus of the chapter is the implications of the shift from one city to three cities by the present government. If Amravati, the new capital city to be built on 50,000 acres of land appropriated through the land pooling method and displacing the inhabitants of twenty-nine villages displaced and dispossessed farmers, would impact on the ecology of this land area and increase the problems faced by citizens of this new city to access basic infrastructure such as water, electricity, and sanitation, the making of the capital city into three parts would. Prasad draws three conclusions from this study. Such cities he argues consolidate a community that links upper classes and castes in order to organize what he calls 'corporate urbanism' and secondly it will not accommodate with the labouring poor who give services to the city. These two chapters affirm that neoliberal urbanism in India is about converting agricultural land into real estate for creating new roads or infrastructure, or to create new townships for the middle classes as discussed by Sanjay Srivastava earlier. It is no longer directed towards involving labour for productive uses and nor for creating homes for them.

The theme of ecology is also the focus of the last chapter in this section. This chapter by D. Parthasarthy is titled 'India's Emerging Risk Urbanism:

COMPREHENDING NEOLIBERAL INDIA 21

Cities, Commons and Neo Liberal Transformations'. This chapter addresses three issues. The first relates to the definition of the concept of risk urbanism which Parthasarthy coins by extending the discussion of risk society to neoliberal urban processes of cities of India. Parthasarthy argues that almost all cities of India are facing risks due to natural disasters and hazards. Risk urbanism according to Parthasarthy occurs when citizens, state agencies, markets, and stakeholders perceive and recognize risks and have to change their behaviours in order to create techniques of coping or not coping with these risks. Parthasarthy questions the theories that have argued that neoliberal economic interventions have led the dispossession and displacement of those who were dependent on natural resources. Rather he argues that because of lack of proper implementation of neoliberal principles communities have been facing dispossessions. Theories should give equal significance to how the practices of governance affect risks given that a large part of urban economies are organized around non-capitalized production systems and employ large groups of informal workers. Environmental impacts of these small-scale household-based economies also promote risks.

Becoming Middle Class, Being Deprived, and Having Aspirations

The last section of this volume analyses the question of aspirations of the deprived groups in the context of increasing intolerant Hindu majoritarian polity. Aseem Prakash in this volume argues for a need to change the terms of discussion from the size of the middle class to an assessment of its aspirations. The section starts with a paper by Badri Narayan titled, 'Dalits in Neo liberal Economy: A Discussion on Most Marginal Communities'. He uses historical narratives and ethnographies to understand the economic and social conditions affecting the most marginal Dalit communities in UP. The chapter focuses on groups who are artists, artisans, and those who use forest resources to make crafts. The second part of the chapter argues that these Dalit caste groups have not been able to transit from being self-employed to becoming entrepreneurs in this market economy despite the organization of self-help groups by the government which build 'capacity to aspire'. Consequently, they have been dispossessed from their livelihoods and become deskilled. Only five to six of the sixty-six Dalit communities in UP have benefitted, given their association with the ruling BSP party. Narayan argues that the culture of finding alternatives has become routinized today.

22 SUJATA PATEL

Sudha Pai's chapter 'From Social Justice to Aspiration: Transformation of Lower Caste Politics in Uttar Pradesh in the 2000s' picks up the story from here. It discusses how in UP the growth of political parties of the lower castes, the BSP and SP mobilized the deprived groups for social justice, dignity, and self-respect created an aspiration among these groups to improve their status. However, the constant instability of government (as mentioned earlier by Srivastava), the corruption and political patronage given to a few favoured groups of the lower castes led the remaining to shift to a rightist party, the BJP. The first part of this chapter analyses the socio-economic and political changes responsible for the shift from the politics of identity in the 1990s, to aspiration and the revival of the BJP under a new generation leadership in UP in the 2000s. The second part analyses how the BJP took advantage of these changes through its new, socially inclusive and developmental strategy of mobilization and was able to gain the support of the OBCs and the dalits leading to its massive victories in the 2014 and 2019 national and 2017 assembly elections making it the dominant party in UP and the country.

Aseem Prakash's chapter titled 'Markets and Aspirations' reports the finding of a study that traced and surveyed groups of aspirational individuals from two cities, the first in Pune and the second in Hyderabad. These were divided in terms of religious community and upper, OBC, and dalit castes, as the goal was to comprehend how they realized their aspirations. Though all those who were interviewed were desirous of deepening their market relationship, participate in high-consumption activities, access material goods and buy homes, acquire health and educational capabilities for the next generation, the study found that it was difficult to do so. Prakash argues that four informal networks and institutions intervene in this process. These are a) association with market peers to access informal credit and business opportunity; b) relationship with local state institutions and actors; c) relationship with kin and caste groups' and relationship with the wider community. Thus, while the upper castes were able to forge both vertical and horizontal networks these were not equally accessible to the OBCs and more so for dalits and Muslims, given the history of discrimination faced by them. The chapter concludes by assessing the aspiration gap: the difference between claim and realized aspirations leads to frustration, vulnerability, and insecurity. If aspirations are about attaining dignity and respect from state, civil society and kin, education, and health for oneself and family, dalits and Muslim lose out due to the lower level of social and cultural capital.

The last chapter in this volume is by Tanveer Faizal's chapter titled 'The Muslim Middle Class: Structure, Identity, and Mobility' argues for a need

COMPREHENDING NEOLIBERAL INDIA 23

to contextualize the middle class in the Muslim community. This chapter is based on triangulation of quantitative data sets with narratives gathered through long interviews (done in Delhi). The quantitative data indicate that by 2011–12, a little less than half of the Muslim population could be counted among the middle class, a large number of them being new entrants of Muslim OBCs. The chapter asks whether this group is homogenous ideologically and can it have political solidarity and if so what is its content? The author suggests that in the case of Muslims it is not middle-class occupational locations, in professions, software industries, self-employed, and entrepreneur but it is social capital, cultural networks, the historicity, and route of middle-class formation that plays a significant role in the shaping of values and norms of Muslim middle-class households. Most of the interviewees were extremely conscious of the outside, mainly hostile world (given the rise of Hindu majoritarianism); the changing relationship between the state and the Muslims in the country; the family's history of dispossession of property, migration, and mobility in the last one or two generations; their understanding of what constitutes a Muslim identity, and their changing political outlook. The author concludes that middle-class identity in the case of Muslims and the deprived groups retains tensions, anxieties, and is full of contradictions.

References

Agarwala, Rina. 2019. 'The Politics of India's Reformed M odel'. In *Business and Politics in India*, edited by C. Jaffrelot, A. Kohli, and K. Murali, 95–123. Delhi: Oxford University Press.

Aslany, Maryam. 2019. 'The Indian Middle Class, Its Size, and Urban-Rural Variations'. *Contemporary South Asia* 27 (2): 196–213.

Chancel, l and T. Picketty. 2019. 'Indian Income Inequality, 1922–2015. From British Raj to Billionaire Raj?' World Inequality Lab, Paris School of Economics. Available at https://wid.world/document/chancelpiketty2017widworld/, accessed 10 Oct 2019.

Chandra, K. 2015. 'The New Indian State. The Relocation of Patronage in the Post-Liberalisation Economy'. *Economic and Political Weekly* 50 (41): 46–58.

Chandra, K. 2016. 'Democratic Dynasties: State, Party and Family'. In *Democratic Dynasties. State, Party and Family in Contemporary Indian Politics*, edited by K. Chandra, 12–55 Delhi: Cambridge University Press.

Connell, R. and N. Dados. 2014. 'Where in the World Does Neolibersalism Come From? The Market Agenda in Southern Perpective'. *Theory and Society* 43 (2): 117–38.

Duménil, G. and Lévy, D. 2004. *Capital Resurgent: Roots of the Neoliberal Revolution.* Cambridge, MA: Harvard University Press.

24 SUJATA PATEL

Fernandes, L. 2004. 'India's Middle Classes in Contemporary India'. In *Routledge Handbook on Contemporary India*, edited by Knut A. Jacobsen, 232–42. London: Routledge.

Fernandes, L. 2012. 'Hegemony and Inequality. Theoretical Reflections on India's "New" Middle Class'. In *Elite and Everyman. The Cultural Politics of India's Middle Classes*, edited by A. Baviskar and R. Ray, 58–82. Delhi: Routledge.

Fernandes, L. and P. Heller. 2006. 'New Middle Class Politics and India's Democracy in a Comparative Perpective'. *Critical Asian Studies* 38 (4): 495–522.

Hardt M. and A. Negri. 2000. *Empire*. Cambridge, MA: Harvard University Press.

Harvey, D. 2005. *A Brief History of Neoliberalism*. New York: Oxford University Press.

Harvey, D. 2007. 'Neoliberalism as Creative Destruction'. *ANNALS of the American Academy of Political and Social Science* 610 (21): 22–44.

Jaffrelot, C., A. Kohli, and K. Murali. 2019. 'Conclusion'. In *Business and Politics in India*, edited by C. Jaffrelot, A. Kohli, and K. Murali, 282–99. Delhi: Oxford University Press.

Jayal, N. G. 2015. 'Affirmative Action in India: Before and after the Neoliberal Turn'. *Cultural Dynamics* 27 (1): 117–33.

Jenkins, R. 1999. *Democratic Politics and Economic Reforms in India*. Cambridge: Cambridge University Press.

Jenkins, R. 2019. 'Business Interests, the State and the Politics of Land Policy'. In *Business and Politics in India*, edited by C. Jaffrelot, A. Kohli, and K. Murali, 124–50. Delhi: Oxford University Press.

Jha, Praveen. 2016. *Labour in Contemporary India* (Oxford India Short Introductions series). Delhi: Oxford University Press.

Joseph, S. 2007. 'Neoliberal Reforms and Democracy in India'. *Economic and Political Weekly* 42 (31): 3213–18.

Joshi, Sanjay. 2017. 'India's Middle Class'. In *Oxford Research Encyclopedia of Asian History*, edited by David Ludden. Oxford University Press. Available at https://oxfordre.com/asianhistory/view/10.1093/acrefore/9780190277727.001.0001/acrefore-9780190277727-e-179?rskey=BrF512&result=1, accessed 10 Sept 2019.

Kannan, K. P. and G. Raveendran. 2019. 'From Jobless to Job-Loss Growth. Gainers and Losers during 2012–2018'. *Economic and Political Weekly* 54 (44): 38–44.

Klein, N. 2007. *The Shock Doctrine: The Rise of Disaster Capitalism*. London: Penguin.

Kohli, A. 2006. 'Politics of Economic Growth in India, 1980–2005 Part I: The 1980s; Part II: The 1990s and Beyond'. *Economic and Political Weekly* 1251–59, 1361–70. Reprinted in Atul Kohli. 2014. *Democracy and Development in India. From Socialism to Pro Business*, 140–85. Delhi: Oxford University Press.

Kohli, A. 2009. 'States and Economic Development'. *Brazilian Journal of Political Economy* 29 (2): 212–227.

Krishnan, S. and N. Hatekar. 2017. 'Rise of the Middle Class in India and Its Changing Structure'. *Economic and Political Weekly* 52 (22): 40–8.

Nielson, K. B. and O. Oskarsson. 2016. 'Development Deadlocks of the New Indian State'. *Economic and Political Weekly* 51 (4): 67–9.

Pinson, G. and C. M. Journel. 2016. 'The Neoliberal City—Theory, Evidence, Debates'. *Territory, Politics, Governance* 4 (2): 137–53, doi: 10.1080/21622671.2016.1166982

Robinson, William I. 2014. *Globalization and the Crisis of Humanity.* Cambridge: Cambridge University Press.

Sinha, A. 2019. 'India's Porous State. Blurred Boundaries and the Evolving Business-State Relationship'. In *Business and Politics in India*, edited by C. Jaffrelot, A. Kohli, and K. Murali, 50–94. Delhi: Oxford University Press.

Srivastava, R. 2020. 'Migrant Labour in the Shadow of the Pandemic'. Webinar, 2 May 2020. Available at https://www.youtube.com/watch?v=8y5MOaqN9SY

Stiglitz, J. E. 2002. *Globalization and Its Discontents.* London: Penguin.

Swaminathan, M. 2020. 'Reset Rural Job Policies, Recognize Women's Work'. The Hindu, 4 July 2020. Available at https://www.thehindu.com/opinion/lead/reset-rural-job-policies-recognise-womens-work/article31984168.ece, accessed 13 July 2020.

Yadav, Y. 1999. 'Electoral Politics in the Time of Change: India's Third Electoral System'. *Economic and Political Weekly* 34 (34–5): 2393–99.

PART ONE
NEOLIBERALIZATION: A CONTEMPORARY SNAPSHOT

PART ONE

2

Democracy in Smart Times

Neoliberalism, Populism, and Instant Communication

Maitrayee Chaudhuri

The Paradoxes of Instant Communication and Split Publics

We live in times where the rapidity of change has changed. This is perhaps most evident in the transient nature of contemporary media headlines. For things have sped up: 'markets shift faster, products evolve quicker, customers are more fleeting. . . .'[1] I cite this quote from a consultancy firm of intelligence professionals knowingly, for evident in our voluble public discourse is the story of how a corporate managerial discourse has increasingly pervaded media discussion, political campaigns, policy formulations, and even everyday middle-class conversation. This managerial language lends itself well to smart one-liners, buzzwords, and acronyms. The complexities of the world are now captured and 'managed' through these aphorisms.[2] This change has acquired new intensities and scales in a world where communication is big, smart, and instant.

India is a leader in many respects of this.[3] This is a world of communicative abundance: a world of 24×7 breaking news; Twitter fights; barrage of WhatsApp messages; Facebook posts, Instagram, and Bots. General Election of 2014 was a first wherein social media was used extensively.[4] Seven years

---

[1] India is the third largest user of Twitter after Japan and USA https://www.statista.com/statistics/242606/number-of-active-twitter-users-in-selected-countries/, accessed 7 March 2021.

[2] Prime Minister Modi has an unusual penchant for acronyms.

[3] India has overtaken the USA as the second-largest smartphone market during July–September as shipments touched a record high of 40 million units, said Singapore-based analyst firm Canalys. Available at http://www.business-standard.com/article/companies/india-overtakes-us-as-smartphone-shipment-touches-record-high-in-q2-117102700358_1.html, accessed 29 Oct 2017.

[4] See Chaudhuri 2017, ch. 12.

Maitrayee Chaudhuri, *Democracy in Smart Times* In: *Neoliberalism, Urbanization, and Aspirations in Contemporary India*. Edited by: Sujata Patel, Oxford University Press. © Oxford University Press 2021.
DOI: 10.1093/oso/9780190132019.003.0002

30   MAITRAYEE CHAUDHURI

later, social media is a pervasive presence in our lives. We now live in times of media convergence.[5] The list is long, and we witness new technological innovations almost every other day, making possible for us to connect and communicate instantly.[6] These have transformed the way we run our lives. They have broken language barriers and made possible much larger participation of people across different groups to be a part of public discourse. It has redefined the way business is done, personal relationships built, and politics conducted.

The nature of an interactive media where everyone is in some sense empowered to 'like' and 'dislike', post their views and opinions on social media, forward images and texts on WhatsApp of often virulent anti-democratic content makes the paradoxes of our times both dramatic and tragic. For what we encounter is the potent paradoxes of: *one*, instant access and unequal knowledge; and *two*, of a global internet whose use which is often confined within bounded groups living in their echo chambers. I try and very quickly elaborate on both these sets of paradoxes and proceed to argue that a world of split publics (who do not speak to each other) works for, indeed, is mutually constitutive of both neoliberal common sense and populism.

By instant access one is referring to the flood of information which beams right into our rooms and into our phones. It is instant, ready, and creates a sense of being equal, on par—that is unparalleled in history. A snippet of a conversation that I had with an Uber driver in the last month of 2017 captures the impossibility of a conversation in a context defined by instant access and unequal knowledge. As I settled down in the car inside the university I taught in, he first confirmed that I was a 'Professor' and then asked me whether I knew who the first prime minister of the country was. Taken aback I answered 'Nehru'. Anticipating my answer, he said: (like TV quiz masters whom both he and I would have been spectators to) 'wrong'! He continued that political parties had spread this falsity but this could no longer hold for 'Google' now offers people the truth directly. It was Patel who was

---

[5] Media convergence is a phenomenon involving the interconnection of information and communications technologies, computer networks, and media content. With the World Wide Web, smartphones, tablet computers, smart televisions, and other digital devices, people access media content that was once tied to specific communications media (print and broadcast) or platforms (newspapers, magazines, radio, television, and cinema). Available at https://www.britannica.com/topic/media-convergence/Transmedia-storytelling, accessed 20 Oct 2019.

[6] 'WhatsApp testing group video and voice calls, official roll out soon'. Available at http://indiatoday.intoday.in/technology/story/whatsapp-testing-group-voice-and-video-calling-and-recall-messages-feature-roll-out-expected-soon/1/1073155.html, accessed 29 Oct 2017.

NEOLIBERALISM, POPULISM, AND COMMUNICATION   31

the first prime minister. The other piece of 'knowledge' that he provided was that Gandhiji of the Congress party had got Bhagat Singh, the founder of Bharatiya Janata Party (BJP) killed. After the initial sense of shock I tried to counter his 'view' or was it 'information' with little success. I felt shaken and helpless as I struggled to explain the ways data were uploaded on the internet. It was with a quiet sense of calm and accomplishment that he witnessed my flustered response. He continued speaking, recounting how he constantly gathers knowledge from the computer and converses with his diverse passengers. Knowledge he said was his passion. The challenges of a paradox marked by instant access and unequal knowledge are formidable.

Both the content and style of his communication are typical of populism. A populist vision of democracy basically separates society into two homogeneous and antagonistic groups, 'the good people' versus 'the bad elite', and postulates the unrestricted sovereignty of the people. According to Kriesi (2018) the use of these key messages is part of a political strategy that manifests itself in broader communication patterns characterized by elements such as 'emergency rhetoric', 'emotionalization' as well as 'assertive/absolutist' and 'colloquial' language, among others. Approaching populism from a communications perspective inevitably involves considerations of style as well as ideology (Sorensen 2017, 139).

The other paradox that looms large over our everyday lives is that the internet is global but that its use is not. Seen from afar, the globalization of information and communication technologies might appear to be leading to uniformity. The form indeed is uniform but the content is not. It has been observed that countries, governments, and populations shape the way the internet is used to suit themselves. Scholars have shown how though the 'Internet' is everywhere the same, the 'internets' are everywhere different (Martel 2018).

In some sense, this split is akin to the argument that Arvind Rajagopal made in his seminal work on politics after television (Rajagopal 2001). He had argued that the meteoric rise of Hindutva has to be linked in the context of the burgeoning market and media of the late 1980s and 1990s. That was a specific historical moment 'wherein a different relationship between communication and public participation was made possible by three factors: the growth of new media; the expansion of the market; and the legitimation crisis of political authority' (Rajagopal 2001, 273). Hindu nationalists, taking advantage of a structural set of mutual misperceptions between English-language elites and those of regional languages, seized upon the split public, which the new media environment exhibited. Rajagopal argues that while for

32 MAITRAYEE CHAUDHURI

the English-language press, Ram Janmabhumi was essentially inexplicable; the Hindi papers' proximity to religious symbolism demonstrated a more direct emotional engagement with the movement. The story line has moved a long way since then. The content of English language television and those of Indian languages is not very different. The format is the same. Hinglish is used across channels and anchors; women and men, dress in western clothes. Most significantly, media content whether of television, Facebook Posts, or WhatsApp is delivered onto our smartphones. Different languages of politics no longer circulate in *incomplete* overlapping spheres. The possibility of different meanings being appropriated is severely curtailed. A convergent media has consolidated majoritarian politics. In some sense there is only one sphere. The other has been rendered illegitimate; labelled anti-national; and communicated so 24x7. The split is now complete; the spheres do not even incompletely overlap. In evidence is the 'emergency rhetoric', the 'emotionalization', an 'assertive/absolutist' and 'colloquial' language that defines populism. Illustrative of this is few of the slogans and memes that have marked Modi-led BJP's campaign.

Ma-bete ki sarkar (the government of mother and son) or Damaad Shree (referring to Robert Vadra, Sonia Gandhi's son-in-law, accused of land scams)

Shahzada (prince, referencing Rahul Gandhi and the Gandhi dynasty, who were enemies of democracy)

Mamooli chai wala/gareeb ma ka beta (Modi as ordinary tea vendor; son of a poor mother, contrasting with the Gandhis)

Dand/Sazaaa do. (Punish them!)

Sickular. Vote bank politics. (Congress and other parties that used secularism cynically for votes only)

Mar Jawan Mar Kisan (death to the solider, death to the farmer)—a highly emotive inversion of an old Congress slogan jai jawan jai kisan ("Victory to the soldier, victory to the farmer"), which invokes gruesome killings of Indian soldiers from Pakistani territory and farmer suicides.

Unke liye Ganga ek nadi hai, mere liye Ganga ma hai. (For them the Ganges is a mere river. For me, Ganga is Ma.)

Mujhe Ganga Maiyya ne bulaya hai. (I have been called by Mother Ganges.) (Sinha 2017, 4166)

Apart from its raw emotive connect, this is a language that has worked for the media market. It is effective just as commercial advertisements are. Indeed,

NEOLIBERALISM, POPULISM, AND COMMUNICATION 33

Modi used a PepsiCola slogan, 'ye dil mange more' ('this heart desires more') to address this social category he named 'the neo-middle class' (Jaffrelot 2013). I address the key tenets of neoliberalism and populism later in the chapter, arguing that the two together with the new communication apparatus erodes the very substance of democracy.

In such a context, what happens to the idea of a public sphere? In Nancy Fraser's (1990) words, the public sphere designates a theatre in modern societies in which political participation is conducted through a medium of talk. It is the arena where citizens deliberate about their common affairs and therefore what Fraser calls an 'institutionalized arena of discursive interaction'. (http://my.ilstu.edu/~jkshapi/Fraser_Rethinking%20the%20Public%20Sphere.pdf accessed 15 February 2018.) Critics of public sphere have often pointed out the inadequate and skewed access of different sections of people to this public sphere. In the smart and instant times that we live in, the challenges are further compounded. What happens when the Uber driver and I, citizens of the same state, and now equal in 'knowledge', in a world of communicative abundance are face-to-face but unable to have a conversation?

The Argument

We in contemporary India now live in times of communicative abundance, a point that I have dealt with extensively elsewhere (Chaudhuri 2017). I draw from John Keane who argues that modern communications media since the invention of the printing press have been dominated by images of scarcity. Time lags, transportation difficulties across geographic space, and high production and distribution costs, frustrated the circulation of opinions and information among individuals, groups, and organizations (Keane 1991).

Today, the old language of scarcity is being superseded by images of abundance; talk of information overload, and cornucopias of communication. This change of intellectual climate is overdetermined by a variety of cultural, organizational, and market-driven forces. Technical factors—such as electronic memory, tighter channel spacing, new frequency allocation, direct satellite broadcasting, digital tuning, and new compression techniques—certainly play their part.

Communication today is global and instant. The internet is global but its use is not. Most often it is used for accessing and sharing news of interest within a group of people—not necessarily ascribed but 'bounded'. They may consist of members of an upper-class residential complex reflecting

34 MAITRAYEE CHAUDHURI

both the dominant class, caste, and religious composition that defines such complexes; or of members of a religion-based community of a village or region; or members of a region; or a diasporic community; or followers of political parties or fans of a football club. What is common is that they are bounded groups and these 'publics' consume 'media content' that cater to them and most often affirm the beliefs that they already hold. The terms of discourse are set and difficult to break.

This I argue is akin to the way advertisements are made. Apart from the logic of a managerial discourse, it is the logic of advertisement making and consuming that appears to have become a dominant model in all spheres of society. What defined the logic of commercial advertisement is its 'closed circle of ideas'. It is this magic system, which has over time suffused public discourse. Today, common sense—wisdom of the 'ordinary' person, knowledge so self-evident that it is beyond debate—has become a powerful political ideal globally (Chaudhuri and Thakur 2018). We thus have a paradox of greater 'choice', wider 'participation'; instant SMS polls; antagonistic sound bites; on one hand and concomitantly less investigative reportage coupled with complete innocence of the social sciences on the other.

It is in such times that we need to think about the state of our education and our inability to analyse or see beyond the obvious. This is where our media and management professionals are trained. The decline of liberal education[7] and the new dominance and legitimacy of extant common sense work well in these times. Both the media and the academia which in modern, liberal times rested on the crucial and theoretical distinction between the taken for granted knowledge and knowledge based on set protocols of investigation appears to have succumbed to the lure and affectivity of common-sense knowledge. If the core of social sciences was to explore beyond the obvious, to de-familiarize the self-evident, the dominant way of doing journalism or academic research today appears to do the contrary. They reaffirm the common sense. In some instances, they bolster extant prejudices.

Within what one can term as high-end academia we have witnessed the influence of theoretical approaches that strongly argues against what could be seen as a political economic determinist position. For instance, in media theory, the concept of the rhizome, stemming from the theories of Gilles Deleuze and Felix Guattari has been offered as an explanatory framework for

---

[7] That liberal studies, in a transformed sense, have got an unexpected boost in these times is a story that will be explored another time.

NEOLIBERALISM, POPULISM, AND COMMUNICATION 35

network theory. Put simply, the rhizome is non-hierarchical, heterogeneous, multiplicitous, and acentred. It is posited against the tree metaphor as an in adequate explanation of multiplicity. A political implication of the tree is that it reinforces notions of centrality of authority, state control, and dominance. The argument therefore is that since the rhizome is both heterogeneous and multiplicitous, it can be entered from many different points, all of which connect to each other. The rhizome does not have a beginning, an end, or an exact centre. (Gilles and Guattari 1987, 21)

I argue that a comparison of the Web as non-hierarchical is deeply flawed. For, the characterization of the Web as a rhizome leaves out aspects of the concept described by Deleuze and Guattari. As Tim Berners-Lee et al. originally explained, 'the common URI syntax reserves the "/" as a way of representing a hierarchical space'(Berners-Lee et al. 1994, 907–12).[8] In addition, the Web operates on the internet, itself a structure with a tree-like root whose centralized features have been cited as ripe for domination.[9] This aspect of the internet as a locus of political power was widely acknowledged in recent objections to continuing U.S. control of the internet.[10] These are disanalogies to the idea of Web as rhizome, the former example shows the hierarchical nature of the Web, while the latter reminds us of the traditional institutions that lay beneath the interfaces of the internet. Indeed, studies on the rise of Modi and BJP show careful organized planning and use of new media. Critics have suggested, therefore, that 'network technologies have reinforced existing power structures by allowing them to become "nomadic"'. (https://lucian.uchicago.edu/blogs/mediatheory/keywords/rhizome/ accessed 14 February 2018).

My argument is that the logic of the broader political economic context of neoliberalism works well with the new forms of communication. Both exude certainty and brook no space for either dialogue or critique. They corrode democracy even as they speak of choice, selfhood, and ascribed identity—fertile grounds for populism. Hence, I would like to spend a little time on the basic tenets and modes of operation of neoliberalism before I return to the new communication technologies.

---

[8] (For example, the URI http://chicagoschoolmediatheory.net/projectsglossary.htm actually describes a tree-like structure, with http://chicagoschoolmediatheory.net/ at the base.)

[9] Several books address this subject, including: Mueller 2002; Lessig 1999.

[10] For example see T. K. Maloy, 'Net Control at Question', *United Press International*, 9 February 2006, 16 February 2006. Available at http://www.upi.com/Hi-Tech/view.php?StoryID=20060208-062823-2265r.

Neoliberalism and Democratic Politics

Neoliberalism is the reigning ideology—the dominant common sense. In ordinary parlance, neoliberalism refers to the repudiation of Keynesian welfare state. In popular usage, neoliberalism is equated with a radically free market: maximized competition and free trade achieved through economic deregulation, elimination of tariffs, and a range of monetary and social policies favourable to business (https://www.dissentmagazine.org/blog/booked-3-what-exactly-is-neoliberalism-wendy-brown-undoing-the-demos accessed 16 February 2018).

Neoliberalism is not simply a set of economic policies; it is not only about facilitating free trade, maximizing corporate profits, and challenging welfarism. It involves extending and disseminating market values to all institutions and social action, even as the market itself remains a distinctive player. This has serious political implications for liberal democracy.

The political sphere, along with every other dimension of contemporary existence, is also submitted to an economic rationality. All dimensions of human life are cast in terms of market rationality. In contrast with the laissez-faire of classical economic liberalism, neoliberalism does not conceive of either the market itself or rational economic behaviour as purely natural. Both are constructed—organized by law and political institutions, and require political intervention and orchestration; the latter is most effectively done by a new convergent media for the dissemination of social norms designed to facilitate competition, free trade, rational economic action, consumption, indulgence on the part of every member and institution of society. Embedded in the neoliberal ideology is the centrality of the individual, a self-propelled selfhood that can carve itself with no help from either the state or the 'public'. My study of the dominant mediatized discourse in India after the new economic policies of the 1990s shows that state, market, media, and academic theories in circulation acted in tandem in the making of the individualized self. There was a disdain of collective movements based on progressive ideals such as equality, liberty, fraternity of all people (Chaudhuri 2017). Importantly, this disdain did not extend to collective movements based on one's 'own' ascribed identities—a natural extension of the self.

It may be productive to explore whether neoliberal rationality is, in important ways, compatible with that of an affirmation of primordial identities. It is not simply that both have an innate individualism. Only those who are like yourself and therefore of the same identity matter. Others do not. This is the unstated ground for the rise of majoritarian politics. The potent point where neoliberalism as ideology appears to converge with the logic of managerialism and its buzzwords is that both hinge on reconfiguring cultural individualism in economic terms. The citizen as we know is the consumer. The public is now the target group of advertising firms and state policies alike. Not surprisingly customized news and feeds that pop up in our phones sit well with cultural individualism and identity affirmations. Choice is the buzzword (Chaudhuri 2017).

A fully realized neoliberal citizenry would be the opposite of public-minded; indeed, it would barely exist as a public. The body politic ceases to be a body but is rather a group of individual entrepreneurs and consumers, which is, of course, exactly how voters were addressed in most American campaign discourse and increasingly so in India. The Prime Minister's celebration of the pakora maker is not a happenstance. https:// thewire.in/217826/watch-pakoda-wallahs-respond-to-modis-employment/, accessed 14 February 2016. There is nothing in liberal democracy's basic institutions or values—from free elections, representative democracy, and individual liberties equally distributed to modest power-sharing or even more substantive political participation—that inherently meets the test of serving economic competitiveness or inherently withstands a cost-benefit analysis. The dissemination of neoliberal norms through an overcommunicative media has engulfed us to an extent that it is difficult to speak outside the contours of the logic that it has laid out and that which has become a natural taken-for-granted world. The split is absolute.

The media had to redefine itself from an institution that ought to play the role as the fourth pillar of liberal democracy to a site that became a key instrument for propagating neoliberal values of the utility seeking individual; replacing the citizen with the consumer; redefining constitutional principles of rights to market rhetoric of choice. In the 1990s, we see a concerted move within the media to move to what was described as sunny-side journalism (Chaudhuri 2017). From the 1990s, the academia had to redefine itself as a site for 'useful' knowledge, of skill enhancement, and market competitiveness. Empirically we saw the decline of humanities, even science, and the rise of commerce and management (Chaudhuri 2010).

Liberal education is a key component for a functioning democracy. In a recast academia this is eroded. The four practices that distinguish a liberal arts education, namely: critical thinking, examination of life, encounters with difference, and free exchange of ideas are sure victims of this new vision. A liberally educated person should be capable of principled judgement, seeking to understand the origins, context, and implications of any area of

38 MAITRAYEE CHAUDHURI

study, rather than looking exclusively at its application. Our education system has faltered on all accounts. There are schools that do not teach children to read and write. Then we have the top of the heap management graduates who are trained within a framework that shuts of any serious engagement with the liberal arts. They are trained to offer solutions to given problems. It is not surprising therefore to meet highly successful corporate executives, comfortable in global circuits, whose views would be marginally different from the Uber driver whose story I recounted early in the chapter. It is in this vein that I return to the discussion on Whatsapp subsequently.

WhatsApp and Its Challenges Today

Murderous attacks on helpless victims have now become routine in India, with numerous and varied grounds for killing the victims. In recent years, two men were murdered in Assam after being suspected as child kidnappers. However, in the last couple of years, the grounds for murdering innocent people have mainly been cow slaughter and cattle smuggling. The religious and ethnic identities of victims too have varied. Attacks on suspected child lifters have been usually by local villagers against 'strangers-outsiders'. Ideologically driven cow vigilantes have targeted Muslims, terming them outsiders and dangerous 'others'.

The antipathy towards 'outsiders' and 'others' is not the only pattern. In all these instances, rumours fuelled by Facebook and WhatsApp have been the immediate triggers. But what is far more ominous and important to recognize is that these triggers rest on an ecosystem of fear and hate, which has been nurtured with care and clear intent. There is clear purpose and careful dissemination of such messages (text message forwards) in the works. The rhizome model obfuscates the determined resolve and operation of BJP's strategies.

Hate has been the central message. Old grievances, prejudices, and fear of 'other' people have been invigorated in a time where media ensures instant access and amplification. It is this hydra-headed messaging that demands attention. Mobs have bayed for blood and left only after the victim was beaten to death with a ferocity that hate alone can propel. Bystanders watched on, unmoved. Or perhaps they videotaped the spectacle of unbelievable cruelty and humiliation so those absent could vicariously participate in this moment of 'triumph'. For, the broader message that has taken over our country is that 'hate' is for the brave; 'love' the hallmark of the chicken-hearted. We live in muscular and mean times. The BJP, which learned early on that the media is a communication tool for PR, uses it deftly and ruthlessly. As the reigning ideology states, it is all about perceptions. Amit Shah had famously urged

NEOLIBERALISM, POPULISM, AND COMMUNICATION 39

his party workers not to spread fake news though it does create a 'mahaul' (an atmosphere). 'This is something worth doing but don't do it! (Crowd laughs) Do you understand what I am saying? This is something worth doing but don't do it! We can do good things too. We are capable of delivering any message we want to the public, whether sweet or sour, true of fake. We can do this work only because we have 32 lakh people in our WhatsApp groups. That is how we were able to make this viral.' https://thewire.in/politics/amit-shah-bjp-fake-social-media-messages.

People find distinguishing fake news from facts redundant in such climes (Chaudhuri 2018 https://thewire.in/society/if-hate-has-been-normalised-can-whatsapp-triggered-lynchings-be-far-behind).

A media piece highlights the conundrum that WhatsApp poses. It writes how a colleague received a message which said that the recent stoning on a school bus ferrying children was carried out by five Muslim men at a time when the anti-*Padmaavat* protests were in full swing. The message on WhatsApp had named all the five 'accused' and was spread widely on WhatsApp and later on Facebook and Twitter. It was used to spread anti-Muslim hysteria and several people shared that message to make political gains. (http://indianexpress.com/article/opinion/columns/the-whatsapp-conundrum-fake-news-rumors-kasganj-violence-5051441/ accessed 5 February 2018).

The rapidity of change has changed was the note I began on. This has acquired new virulence and power as recent events show. New media technologies have aggravated divides of 'publics' instead of constructing new communities of solidarities. The story since 2019 has been a dismantling of every institution that acted as checks and balances in a democracy. In this new imagination, both media and academia are supposed to be cheer leaders of the regime in power; advertising the sunny stories of the day.

WhatsApp messages played a crucial role in the communal clashes in Kasganj, Uttar Pradesh, after a 'Tiranga Yatra' motorcycle rally was taken out to celebrate Republic Day. The rally was chanting *Vante Mataram* and *Bharat Mata Ki Jai*. A newspaper report writes that '[w]hen they reached a minority community-dominated locality, some "anti-social elements" pelted stones and opened fire. In this firing, Chandan was killed and two others were injured.' The report writes how the threat WhatsApp can pose in such fragile times. After the death of a youth, Chandan Gupta, in the violence, rumours were spread claiming the death of another person—Rahul Upadhyay. These rumours were circulated on Twitter, Facebook, and WhatsApp groups, among other social media platforms. Upadhyay later clarified to the media that 'the rumours of his death were greatly exaggerated, and were being used by people spreading hate and paranoia on social media' (http://indianexpress.com/

40 MAITRAYEE CHAUDHURI

article/opinion/columns/the-whatsapp-conundrum-fake-news-rumors-kasganj-violence-5051441/ accessed 5 February 2018).

The most distressing part of these developments is that people believe a 'news' or 'information' on the basis of who they are. Veracity is of little consequence. On a visit to Kashmir in the summer of 2016, just before the most recent turmoil broke out one repeatedly met people who shared Facebook posts. Most were provocative and intensely emotive. Passionate speeches were shared on YouTube. But no one knew who had made them and when. However, it was the ongoing context that facilitated the reception and the meaning that was derived. There was a passionate speech made in the colonial period against the colonial rulers that invoked the resistance and sacrifices of Kashmiris. The speech was read as a contemporary one, made in current Kashmir.

The situation is worrying because there is no apparent solution of the problem that WhatsApp poses for law enforcement agencies, and society at large. The issue of checking 'fake news' and misinformation on WhatsApp has never become part of popular discourse. Unlike Facebook or Google, the messaging service did not play a role in allegedly 'influencing' the US elections and is not as popular in the West. The story in India is however quite different. The challenge it poses is both immense and complex.

In India, according to Satista, a leading statistics company, the number of monthly active WhatsApp users in India in February 2017 was 200 million—exponentially greater from August 2013, when it was just 20 million. The messaging application is being used more and more by rural and older populations, who are often new to the internet and less tech-savvy. In July 2019 WhatsApp announced that it now has more than 400 million users in India (https://techcrunch.com/2019/07/26/whatsapp-india-users-400-million/ accessed 20 October 2019).

WhatsApp works in a way that is fundamentally different from Facebook and Twitter. In the latter, it is comparatively easier to check fake news and prevent the spread of misinformation. It is possible to view Facebook posts if one is a friend of a user. WhatsApp (the app is owned by Facebook) messages, on the other hand, are encrypted end-to-end—a feature that is great from the perspective of privacy of users. Facebook newsfeeds are regulated by algorithms, which can be tweaked by the social media platform. WhatsApp's rationale for its security is a viable one: The encryption helps messages, photos, videos, voice messages, documents, status updates, and so on from falling into the wrong hands and can be controlled by users. There is no way to turn off the end-to-end encryption.

WhatsApp's end-to-end encryption ensures only you and the person or group you're communicating with can read and see what is sent, and nobody

NEOLIBERALISM, POPULISM, AND COMMUNICATION 41

in between—interestingly even WhatsApp does not have access to the media and messages. When a message leaves a person's phone, it is assigned a cryptographic lock, and only the person receiving the message has the key to this lock. These keys change with every single message that is sent (https://faq. whatsapp.com/en/android/28030015/ accessed 14 February 2018). The story as it has unfolded appears more complex.[11]

The challenge, however, is not only that it can and has been inciting violence and killings, not just that the apparent security measures intended for ensuring privacy makes cross checking for fake news more difficulty but that it has very serious implications for mainstream media. For the 'problem of fake news and misinformation being spread via WhatsApp has become a trend across the globe' and 'media organisations and fact-checkers face a problem every time they get a message on WhatsApp with something that is potential news'. And this is the danger:

> [A]s passionate journalists, we always get excited by information that can make a news story. The problem with what we receive on WhatsApp is that often we cannot confirm the source of the message. Many messages are shared on groups, where you might not have the contact of the person who has shared the message saved on your phone. (http://indianexpress.com/article/opinion/columns/the-whatsapp-conundrum-fake-news-rumors-kasganj-violence-5051441/ accessed 5 February 2018)

What can be done? The spread of fake news through WhatsApp is something we might not be able to control directly, and its encryption does protect the privacy of its users.[12] This puts the responsibility of stopping this spread of misinformation on citizens and the media. But how will that happen when we are all prisoners of Echo Chambers, when we seek news and consume it because they reaffirm our increasingly prejudiced common-sense beliefs?[13]

---

[11] If we blame end-to-end encryption of WhatsApp for the Israeli spyware Pegasus that affected 1,400 select users of the Facebook-owned messaging app globally, including 121 in India, we will be barking up the wrong tree, say experts. Available at https://www.livemint.com/technology/apps/is-encryption-to-blame-for-whatsapp-snooping-11574049392267.html.

[12] The BJP had used WhatsApp on a major scale. Available at https://thewire.in/politics/amit-shah-bjp-fake-social-media-messages, accessed 20 Oct 2019.

In more recent times there have been some efforts to see whether the encryption can end. The issue of traceability has been a flashpoint between the government and WhatsApp, and the Facebook-owned messaging platform has so far resisted India's demand for identification of message originators, arguing that doing so would undermine its policy on privacy and end-to-end encryption. Available at https://prime.economictimes.indiatimes.com/news/71367088/technology-and-startups/battle-for-privacy-and-encryption-whatsapp-and-government-head-for-a-showdown-on-access-to-messages, accessed 21 Oct 2019.

[13] Research shows that WhatsApp was used extensively in the 2019 General Elections in India. https://www.cjr.org/tow_center/india-whatsapp-analysis-election-security.php.

42 MAITRAYEE CHAUDHURI

The threat is ominous and my plea for critical social sciences and liberal education stem from this.

Common Sense and Its Hegemony in the Academia and Media

Robert Park in his 1940 piece on News as Knowledge distinguished between 'knowledge by acquaintance' and 'knowledge about'. The greatest threat today for the public sphere is that the boundaries between the two have blurred. It is perhaps in order that one explicates what the distinction is. 'Acquaintance with sort of knowledge is one which we acquire in the course of one's personal and firsthand encounters. "It is the knowledge, which comes with use and wont rather than through any sort of formal or systematic investigation". . . . It is the sort of personal and individual knowledge which makes each of us at home in the world in which he elects or is condemned to live' (Park 1940, 670).

These are characters, which individuals acquire in informal and unconscious ways, but, once acquired, they tend to become private and personal possessions—something, at any rate which cannot well be formulated or communicated from one individual to another by formal statements (Park 1940, 670). In contrast, 'knowledge about' is formal, rational, and systematic. It is based on observation and fact but on fact that has been checked, tagged, regimented, and finally ranged in this and that perspective, according to the purpose and point of view of the investigator (Park 1940, 672). This is knowledge, which has achieved some degree of exactness and precision by the substitution of ideas for concrete reality and of words for things (Park 1940, 672).

In this world of ready downloads and instant access a different kind of convergence between the media and academia is taking place. If the media world is suffused with over communicative abundance, instant likes, and hyper-visibility, we in the academia are not left untouched. The Google Baba as the search engine as is often called within media circles is our source too.[14] Glossy Power Point Presentations is not the preserve of the corporate world. We too are 'Smart' now.

---

[14] A wide range of interviews and discussions with journalists between 2015 and 2017 suggests this. See Maitrayee Chaudhuri, Unpublished Report on Mediatization for ICSSR, 2017.

NEOLIBERALISM, POPULISM, AND COMMUNICATION 43

My contention, as I mentioned a short while ago, is also that the academia and media have played a crucial role in the making of the new hegemony. There are two reasons for this: (i) They are both central sites of knowledge production and circulation in any modern society; (ii) And they are, as I mentioned before, both centrally involved in communication. This in itself is nothing new.

What is new is that both the academia and media have undergone significant changes in the last few decades. They have expanded and, in some senses, have become more inclusive. They have expanded in size and scale. They have greater representation today than before of different sections from our unequal and diverse society. Though needless to say it is a project that has a long way to go. My focus, however, is not on exclusions. For I argue that even as there are greater diversities we have greater 'uniformities' for here too conversations across sections become limited. There are affirmations of views within groups much like the way we choose to hear the TV channel that appears to be closest to our views.

This development further occurs in a world where common sense has acquired a new legitimacy. There are at least two dimensions to the way we can understand common sense in this context: the first being found 'in the wild' so to speak, and the second, the discursively construed (and often constructed) mediatized appeals to common sense. It would be simple to think that it is a fissure between the two that has opened-up in recent times, where the political commentariat is simply out of touch with 'real' common sense. But this would fail to grasp the mechanisms by which common sense operates, particularly regarding the way in which both forms are shaped by power, and potentially leads to the reified abuse of opinion polls, and the dangerous idea that a 'new common sense' has already been reached.

As such, accounting for common sense is somewhat tricky, since its sedimentation and construction occur at the level, not of discursive rules, but of assumptions, habits, and dispositions. Common sense is not the sort of thing that can be discursively elaborated, being composed of attitudes that are open-ended, differential responses to each other and to contexts, emotions, and embodied actions. But, since this social background of norms shapes the meanings within which our lives are formed, it is also the central site in which our local interactions and contexts are tied to broader structures, practices, and sanctions. It is on this terrain in which common sense is continuously formed and reformed, as part-and-parcel with the material and embodied practices of our lives, where these are sculpted

44 MAITRAYEE CHAUDHURI

by the specific socio-economic conditions in which we are inextricably located. It is also for this reason that common sense can neither be disparaged as misguided or intrinsically conservative, nor can it be upheld as a single monolithic and static 'reality' outside of the conditions of power in which it is sculpted.

Neoliberalism, on this sort of story, cannot be adequately approached as if imposed as an ideological set of principles, but neither can it be fully captured in its objective and infrastructural forms—it is neither merely discursive nor merely material-determinative. Rather, the power of neoliberalism is that it is a massive-scale, and complex, engineering project, which has required multiple mutations over time, and constant reinforcement at all levels—from common sense to economic policy; from higher-education timetabling systems to detention-centres. Appeals to common sense are part of much wider processes requiring already entrenched meanings regarding, in this case, individual competitiveness, work, gender, populism, and nationhood. These interests are then used to underpin substantial socio-political and material effects, looped into institutions and practices that serve to enact and enforce policy decisions, which then feed-back into media to further embed those social norms as if reality. The task to challenge common sense has thus become extremely difficult and unless we return to the business of thinking through at what has happened to the two key institutions of knowledge—the academia and media, we appear to be facing a losing battle for democracy. For in this new celebration of common sense we in India have the rise of populism and majoritarian rule as democracy. In the *Indian Express*, Varshney (2017) writes that Ram Madhav, a national general secretary of the BJP, summed up Modi's appeal thus: 'The mob, humble people of the country, are behind Modi . . . They are enjoying it' (https://indianexpress.com/article/opinion/columns/india-prime-minister-narendra-modi-a-populist-populism-democracy-donald-trump-pro-hindu-4901786/ accessed 20 October 2019).

Quite clearly distinctions between populism and democracy have blurred. Murder and violence are routinely defended today on the grounds that sentiments of 'people' have been hurt. The meaning of 'people' bears no resemblance to the spirit of our Constitutional Pledge[15] which begins with a solemn affirmation of by 'we the people' constituting a sovereign India committed the principles of secularism, socialism, and democracy. 'We the

---

[15] Available at https://www.constitution.org/cons/india/preamble.html, accessed 20 Oct 2019.

'people' now means 'people from the Majority community'. A populist sees no wrong in celebrating mob rule or a majoritarian rule. A democrat can. We know that neither the majority nor the mobs are always right. Sati was popular in parts of India, and so was untouchability. It was popular for blacks to be lynched in the American south. That is why all modern democracies constrain mob sentiments with constitutions and laws. Populism and democracy are not to be confused. A conflation of mobs and democracy only leads to frequent vigilante violence. The undermining of the press and judiciary has weakened law-based governance. The question that has moved to India's political centrestage is: 'Would that be good for the country?' (http://indianexpress.com/article/opinion/columns/india-prime-minister-narendra-modi-a-populist-populism-democracy-donald-trump-pro-hindu-4901786/ accessed 16 February 2018).

In a polarized world where mob rule is understood as democratic rule knowledge is threatened. Robert Merton (1972) many decades ago had argued that the growth of knowledge depends upon complex sets of social relations based on a largely institutionalized reciprocity of trust among scholars and scientists. In an ideal free society each person would have perfect access to the truth: truth in science, in art, religion, and justice, both in public and in private life. But this is not practicable; each person can directly know very little of truth and must trust others for the rest. Indeed, to assure this process of mutual reliance is one of the main functions of society. The academia and media as social institutions have a key role to play in this. But as cleavages deepen between groups, social strata, or collectivities of whatever kind, the social network of mutual reliance is at best.

In place of the vigorous but intellectually disciplined mutual checking and rechecking that operates to a significant extent, though never of course totally, within the social institutions of science and scholarship, there develops a strain towards separatism, in the domain of the intellect as in the domain of society. Partly grounded mutual suspicion increasingly substitutes for partly grounded mutual trust. There emerge claims to group-based truth: Insider truths that counter Outsider untruths and Outsider truths that counter Insider untruths. We are privy to this today.

References

Berners-Lee, Tim et al. 1994. 'The World Wide Web'. *Communications of the ACM* 37 (8): 907–12.

Chaudhuri, Maitrayee. 2010. *Sociology in India: Intellectual and Institutional Practices.* Jaipur: Rawat.

Chaudhuri, Maitrayee. 2017. *Refashioning India: Gender, Media and a Transformed Public Discourse.* New Delhi: Orient Blackswan.

Chaudhuri, Maitrayee. 2018. 'If Hate Has Been Normalised, Can WhatsApp-Triggered Lynchings Be Far Behind?'. Available at https://thewire.in/society/if-hate-has-been-normalised-can-whatsapp-triggered-lynchings-be-far-behind, accessed 20 Oct 2019.

Chaudhuri, Maitrayee and Thakur Manish. 2018. *Doing Theory: Locations, Hierarchies and Disjunctions.* Hyderabad: Orient Blackswan.

Deleuze, Gilles and Félix Guattari. 1987. *A Thousand Plateaus: Capitalism and Schizophrenia.* Minneapolis, MN: University of Minnesota Press.

Fraser, Nancy. 1990. 'Rethinking the Public Sphere: A Contribution to the Critique of Actually Existing Democracy'. *Social Text* 25/26: 56–80. Available at https://www.jstor.org/stable/466240?seq=1#page_scan_tab_contents, accessed 15 Feb 2018.

Gilles Deleuze and Felix Guattari. 2013. *A Thousand Plateaus.* London: Bloomsbury Revelations.

Jaffrelot, C. 2013. 'Gujarat Elections: The Sub-Text of Modi's "Hattrick"—High Tech Populism and the Neomiddle Class'. *Studies in Indian Politics* 1 (1): 79–96.

Keane, John. 1991. *The Media and Democracy.* Cambridge: Polity Press.

Kriesi, H. 2018. 'Revisiting the Populist Challenge'. *Politologický Časopis/Czech Journal of Political Science* 25: 5–27.

Lessig, Lawrence. 1999. *Code and Other Laws of Cyberspace.* New York: Basic Books.

Martel, Frederick. 2018. *Smart: The Digital Century.* Translated by Sindhuja Veeraragavan. India: Harper Collins.

Merton, Robert K. 1972. 'Insiders and Outsiders: A Chapter in the Sociology of Knowledge'. *American Journal of Sociology* 78 (1): 9–47.

Mueller, Milton L. 2002. *Ruling the Root: Internet Governance and the Taming of Cyberspace.* Cambridge, MA: MIT Press.

Park, Robert E. 1940. 'News as a Form of Knowledge: A Chapter in the Sociology of Knowledge'. *American Journal of Sociology* 45(5): 669–686.

Rajagopal, Arvind. 2001. *Politics after Television: Hindu Nationalism and the Reshaping of the Public in India.* Cambridge: Cambridge University Press.

Sinha, Subir. 2017. 'Fragile Hegemony: Modi, Social Media and Competitive Electoral Populism in India'. *International Journal of Communication* 11: 4158–80.

Sorensen, L. N. 2017. 'Populism in Communications Perspective: Concepts, Issues, Evidence'. In *Handbook on Political Populism*, edited by R. Heinish, C. Holtz-Bacha, and O. Mazzoleni, 137–51. Baden-Baden: Nomos.

Varshney, Ashutosh. 2017. 'Is Narendra Modi a Populist? The old narrative about India's Prime Minister is not dead, but a new one is emerged'. *The Indian Express*, 23 October 2017 Available at http://indianexpress.com/article/opinion/columns/india-prime-minister-narendra-modi-a-populist-populism-democracy-donald-trump-pro-hindu-4901786/, accessed 16 Feb 2018.

http://indianexpress.com/article/opinion/columns/the-whatsapp-conundrum-fake-news-rumors-kasganj-violence-5051441/, accessed Feb 2018.

https://lucian.uchicago.edu/blogs/mediatheory/keywords/rhizome/, accessed 14 Feb 2018.

https://faq.whatsapp.com/en/android/28030015/, accessed 14 Feb 2018.

https://www.dissentmagazine.org/blog/booked-3-what-exactly-is-neoliberalism-wendy-brown-undoing-the-demos, accessed 16 Feb 2018.

Wendy Brown Booked #3: What Exactly Is Neoliberalism? https://www.dissentmagazine.org/blog/booked-3-what-exactly-is-neoliberalism-wendy-brown-undoing-the-demos

3

On Demographic and Gender Dividend in India

K. S. James

Demographic changes are often valorized due to their potential to create a strong middle class. The demographic transition inevitably leads to age structure transformation leading to relatively higher proportion of working age population. As large majority of the population falls in the productive age group during the period of demographic dividend, it is expected to create a strong middle class in any society, because, each age structure creates its own unique impact on the economy. A rapid growth of working age population in relation to child population can generate considerable economic benefits in distinct ways, such as swelling of labour force, diverting resources from investing in children to investing in physical capital, increased female work participation due to fertility decline, and increased household saving (Bloom and Canning 2011). While the notion that the age structure has the potential to create a strong middle class has been widely accepted, the pathways through which this apparently strong relationship operates in different contexts are not explored in detail.

India has been experiencing rapid demographic changes in recent years with large expected economic benefits. Even while the demographic dividend potential is well recognized in the country, there are many pessimistic views expressed on the ability of the country to take advantage of demographic changes due to several constraints such as illiteracy, unskilled labour force, poverty, and so forth. Of these, the lack of significant increase in the female labour force participation despite faster fertility transition has attracted wide attention in recent times (Desai 2010; Klasen and Pieters 2012). Among the pathways to achieve demographic dividend, increase in female labour force participation, undisputedly, plays an important role in any context (Bloom et al. 2009).

As the age structure change is a direct outcome of faster decline in fertility, it is expected that women will increasingly enter the labour market, resulting

K. S. James, *On Demographic and Gender Dividend in India* In: *Neoliberalism, Urbanization, and Aspirations in Contemporary India*. Edited by: Sujata Patel, Oxford University Press. © Oxford University Press 2021.
DOI: 10.1093/oso/9780190132019.003.0003

in larger economic benefits. The age at first birth still remains low and stopping of births takes place at relatively young age in India (James 2011). This results in women spending longer periods of time away from child bearing and rearing responsibilities during their adult ages. Hence there is large potential for women's labour force participation.

At the same time, a lack of major improvement in female work participation rates, despite rapid economic changes and lower fertility, has been a matter of concern in India. It has been argued that India is unlikely to realize its demographic dividend to the fullest extent due to very low work participation of females (Desai 2010; Klasen and Pieters 2012; Afridi et al. 2016). In other words, the major lacuna of the Indian demographic changes is that the gender dividend is nearly absent in India. Perhaps, all these arguments point towards the lack of benefits for females due to demographic changes. Thus, a general pessimism exists on the impact of demographic changes on female labour force participation in India, thus contributing to demographic and gender dividend.

This chapter examines the demographic dividend in India through a gender lens. The impact of demographic changes on females particularly on the work participation is examined in detail. The chapter is divided into three sections. First, it reviews the demographic dividend literature in India by considering its impact on gender dividend. Second, it examines demographic change and its impact on female labour force participation over the last thirty years. Third, it presents the implications of the result to understand the demographic and gender dividend in India.

Demographic Dividend: Rhetoric and Reality

India is experiencing rapid changes in the age structure of its population, particularly in the last two decades. India's fertility transition has quickened during the same period. The total fertility rate (TFR) was 2.4 children per women in 2011, close to the replacement level. For the first time, the child population (aged 0–6 years) has recorded a decline in absolute terms during the last decade, according to the 2001 and 2011 census results. The decline has been to the tune of 0.3 per cent per annum. The proportion of child population has also come down substantially among states which achieved replacement level fertility; among major states in 2011, the proportion varies from around 10 per cent in Tamil Nadu to 19 per cent in Bihar. The proportion of adult population (15–59 years) has increased substantially and stands around 63 per cent in 2011.

Figure 3.1 presents the projected ratio of working to non-working age population in India from 2000 to 2100. The proportion aged 0–14 years is currently on a rapid decline and will continue to decline over the next forty years. Moreover, the percentage of population in the sixty plus years age group is modest at present, although increasing at a rapid pace. As a result, the percentage of adult population will remain high for a few more decades. Therefore, India, undoubtedly, will have a demographic dividend advantage for a few more decades.

Although India has an age structure with greater potential to contribute to economic growth, there are serious concerns on the ability of the country to take advantage of its demographic dividend. As already pointed out, the major concern has been the lack of sufficient progress in the facilitating factors of the demographic dividend. Bloom and Canning (2011) considered five distinct forces facilitating demographic dividend. These forces can be divided into two broad groups: (a) accounting and (b) behavioural. The swelling of adult population, which is the age group associated with prime years of saving, provides an accounting benefit during the stages of demographic dividend. But more important benefits accrue through the behavioural mechanism. The behavioural forces consist of (1) incentive to save for a longer period with the expansion of life expectancy, (2) reallocation of resources from investing in children to investing in physical capital, and

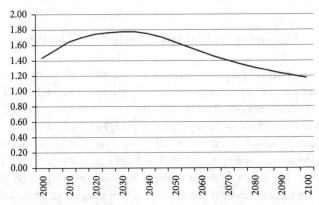

Figure 3.1 Ratio of Working Age (15–59) to Non-Working Population, India, 2000–2100

Source: UN Population Projection (Revision, 2012); (http://esa.un.org/wpp/)

DEMOGRAPHIC AND GENDER DIVIDEND   51

(3) increase in women's work participation resulting from fertility decline (Bloom and Canning 2011).

The behavioural forces, therefore, have large potential to take the country forward in realizing the demographic dividend. However, there has always been a concern about the progress of three behavioural forces as far as India is concerned. Although the household saving rate shows an increasing trend, it is uncertain how much of this can be attributed to demographic factors. Moreover, India does not have good data on household saving rate at the state level for a detailed analysis. On the other hand, the cross-country aggregate-level panel data show that demographic factors have a strong and statistically significant effect on aggregate savings (Bloom et al. 2003; Deaton and Paxson 2000; and Kelly and Schmidt 2007). This is found to be true to some extent for India as well (James 2008).

The other key behavioural force—reallocation of resources away from children—is not possible in India, especially from public spending as the health and educational status of children leaves a lot to be desired, and the current policy pronouncements aim at enhancing the allocation of resources towards the health and education sectors. The educational levels of the adult population are dismal with nearly 36 per cent remaining illiterate according to the 2001 census result. Using data from a global panel of countries, Cuaresma et al. (2012) observed that improvements in educational attainment are the key to explaining productivity and income growth and that a substantial portion of the demographic dividend is an education dividend. It is, therefore, argued that the educational deficit of the working age population will be an obstacle in harnessing the demographic dividend for the country (Chandrasekhar et al. 2006).

There has always been a concern in the country on female labour force participation. India has one of the lowest female work participation rates in the world. According to the International Labour Organisation (ILO), India ranks 11th from bottom in female labour force participation rate out of the 131 countries with available data (ILO 2013). The National Sample Survey Organisation (NSSO) data also showed a sharp decline in female work participation in the last decade. As a result, once work participation rates are factored in, the real dependency ratio in India turns out to be far higher and this hardly provides a reason to be sanguine about the potential for realizing the demographic dividend (Desai 2010).

It is generally argued that to take advantage of the demographic dividend appropriate policies to boost economic growth need to be put in place (Bloom 2012). The sheer increase in the size of working age population, without the

52   K. S. JAMES

backing of favourable policy measures, can lead to more underemployment and unemployment than economic progress. According to Bloom (2012: 462–497) 'this scenario would be a "demographic disaster" instead of a demographic dividend, in some instances promoting state fragility and failure, potentially with adverse political, social, economic, and ecological spillovers to other countries'.

India's capacity to reap the benefits of its demographic dividend has been questioned on the basis of the above reasoning. It is argued that the economic growth potential of the larger workforce is nearly absent in India. Thus, perception on the likelihood of realizing the demographic dividend has been rather pessimistic. It is argued that India's demographic dividend will turn out to be more of a burden (Mitra and Nagrajan 2005; Chandrasekhar et al. 2006; Desai 2010; Basu 2011; Mitra 2011; Upadhyay 2012). Such writings have filled the pages of several leading newspapers across the country in recent years.

However, understanding the long-term relationship between demographic changes and economic progress necessitates rigorous empirical analysis. Many of the writings on demographic dividend have involved more rhetoric than thorough empirical examination of the data. There are several ways to empirically scrutinize the impact of age structure change on the economy. Findings from such empirical examination would provide a clearer understanding of the demographic benefits due to age structure transition. In the past few years, there were many attempts to estimate the effect of demographic change on economic growth. These statistical estimates clearly brought out that those states achieving fertility transition are also able to enhance their per-capita income growth substantially. Table 3.1 presents the major empirical studies providing estimates of the demographic dividend in India.

Although concerns have been raised on the effect of demographic changes on the economy, the statistical estimates invariably indicate a large positive effect of demographic changes on the economy. The results are often very optimistic on the demographic dividend despite several constraints. For instance, Aiyer and Mody (2011) observed that substantial fraction of the 'growth acceleration that India has experienced since the 1980s—sometimes ascribed exclusively to economic reforms—is attributable to changes in the country's age structure'. They estimated that the demographic dividend could add nearly 2 percentage points to India's per-capita GDP growth in the next two decades. Although other studies have been less optimistic on the magnitude of growth, the conclusions remained nearly the same that age structure

Table 3.1 List of Major Studies Estimating the Effect of Demographic Change on the Per-Capita Growth Rate of Income in India

Studies	Method	Indicator	Result
James (2008)	State level panel data	Growth of working age population	Positive
Bloom et al. (2010)	India-China time series	Growth of working age population	Positive
Kumar (2010)	State level panel data	Percentage of working age population	Positive
Aiyer and Mody (2011)	State level panel data	Percentage of working age population	Positive
Ladusingh and Narayana (2011)	National Transfer Account	Age allocation of income	Potentially positive

changes have significant positive impact on the current growth pattern of the Indian economy.

Thus, there appears to be a disconnect between statistical estimates and general perception on India's demographic dividend (James 2011). This discordance is partly due to the result of lack of considerable changes in the facilitating factors of demographic changes on the economy. In what follows, we consider one of the important facilitating factors of demographic dividend, the female labour force participation, and examine how far this factor has contributed to the economic change.

Female Work Participation

As already pointed out, one of the important benefits expected from fertility transition is increased work participation of women. With the decline in family size, a woman spends a relatively short period of her adult ages on child bearing and rearing. The additional time available can be effectively utilized in the labour market. Bloom et al. (2009) show that a reduction in fertility increases female labour force participation and results in positive economic changes. However, this relationship remains complex as there is also an expected endogeneity between woman's work participation and fertility (Bloom et al. 2009; Browning 1992). One of the major reasons for the fertility transition in developing countries is considered to be the increased female labour force participation (Standing 1983). Moreover, this relationship is also confounded by several other economic, social, and cultural factors (Olsen and Mehta 2006; World Bank 2010; Mazumdar and Neetha 2011; Mehrotra and Sinha 2017).

The work participation of females has been generally quite low in the south Asian region. In India, not only is women's work participation relatively very low, it has also displayed an erratic trend over the last two decades despite rapid economic and demographic transformation. The NSSO quinquennial employment survey provides information on the trends in female work participation in India. While NSSO data in 2004–05 reported a considerable increase in the work participation of women compared to the previous round in 1999–2000, it recorded a sharp decline between 2004–05 and 2009–10. The latest data from NSSO indicate further sharp decline in the female work participation for the period 2017–18. The work participation rate of women (principal status and subsidiary status) declined from 28.7 per cent in 2004–05 to 22.8 per cent and further dipped to 16.5 per cent in 2017–18 (Ministry of Statistics and Programme Implementation 2019). The decline was visible in both rural and urban areas, and was especially steep in rural areas during the same period.

The 2011 census result also portrays near-stagnancy in the work participation rate among females in the last decade. Figure 3.2 presents work

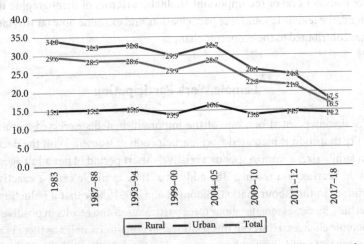

Figure 3.2 Work Participation Rate (5) by Usual Status (Principal Status and Subsidiary Status), India, 1983 to 2017–18
Source: Ministry of Statistics and Programme Implementation (2019)

participation rate among women by place of residence in various NSSO rounds since 1983. Several interesting observations can be gauged from this figure. First, only less than one-fifth of women in the country participate in the labour market. Second, work participation among women has showed a drastic decline in the recent period compared to earlier rounds of NSSO. The rate remained nearly same in urban areas between the different rounds but with a very low participation. Third, even with low fertility in urban India, the female work participation remains very low. Perhaps, the service sector has turned out to be a boon for female workers in urban areas in recent years resulting in not sharp decline from the existing low rate in urban areas. Both young and middle-aged female workers increased their share of regular jobs, particularly in the service industry (Ramaswamy and Agrawal 2012).

Figure 3.3 presents the number of working females as a percentage of all females in individual states based on the 2001 and 2011 census results. The female work participation rate varies substantially across states; the highest work participation rate is observed in Himachal Pradesh with 45 per cent of women working while at the other extreme in Punjab only 14 per cent of the women participate in the labour market in 2011. The states of Punjab, Haryana, and Uttar Pradesh traditionally have low work participation of women, consistent with the poor status of women in these places. The states of Haryana, Punjab, and Gujarat recorded a sharp decline in work participation rates, in spite of being traditionally low-fertility regions. This underscores the role which larger cultural factors play in the level of female work participation in India.

The figure also indicates that all the four southern states—Andhra Pradesh, Karnataka, Kerala, and Tamil Nadu—showed an upward trend in female work participation between 2001 and 2011. These states have recorded below replacement level fertility in the last decade. However, there has been significant variation in the levels of work participation among the southern states, with Kerala recording only about half the rate of Andhra Pradesh and Tamil Nadu. Himachal Pradesh which tops the work participation rate is also among the states with below replacement level fertility. Odisha and Maharashtra with low fertility also recorded an increase female work participation rates in the last decade. States like Rajasthan, Madhya Pradesh, and Chhattisgarh recorded relatively higher work participation rates than other regions, but in the two latter states female work participation declined between 2001 and 2011. At the same time, the pattern appears to be rather mixed in other parts of the country. Thus, the data suggest mixed findings as far as the relationship between fertility transition and work participation of women are concerned, and do not provide the basis for a definite conclusion. Therefore, it is important that the data are scrutinized more carefully before drawing any final conclusion.

India's slow progress in female work participation has been a matter of intense debate for a long time. Several possible explanations have been provided for the lack of significant progress. First, there is a well-known U-shaped relationship between economic changes and female labour force participation. Therefore, with an increase in the household income, it is possible that women withdraw from the labour market initially, as many of them are engaged in the agricultural sector. There are, however, disagreements on the nature of this relationship in many contexts. Gaddis and Klasen (2011) concluded that the U hypothesis has little relevance to developing countries of today. According to them, it is not necessary that every economy passes through a declining and later increasing phase of female work participation in the course of economic development. Similar findings were observed by Lahoti and Swaminathan (2013) in the Indian context. Contrary to this, Neff et al. (2012) found a strong U-shaped pattern in the rural women's work participation in India; this study also found that the rural women's work participation falls with higher levels of household wage rate of men.

Second, there is a possibility that increasing levels of education lead to a postponement of female work participation as the early working ages are spent pursuing education, leading to a fall in work participation in these age

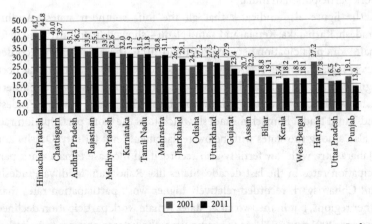

Figure 3.3 Crude Female Work Participation Rate across Major States in India, 2001 and 2011

Source: Census Figures 2001 & 2011

groups. Undoubtedly, there has been a steep rise in the education levels of women aged fifteen and above in recent years. For instance, between 2004–05 and 2009–10, the percentage of women attending educational institutions in the age group 15–19 has increased from 38 per cent to 52 per cent and that of 20–24 age group has increased from 6.8 per cent to 12 per cent according to the NSSO results. However, Neff et al. (2012) argued that education cannot be the main reason for the declining female labour force participation in the second half of the 2000s, as education could explain the decline only in rural areas but not in the case of urban areas.

Third, the lack of employment opportunities in India is considered another important reason for the poor work participation of females. Despite the rapid economic growth, the employment scenario did not improve due to 'jobless growth' in the economy (Chowdhury 2011; World Bank 2010). A significant number of females work as marginal workers who only occasionally participate in the labour market. According to the 2011 census data, nearly 40 per cent of female workers are marginal workers. The fall in female work participation rate was mainly due to a fall in the marginal workers rather than main workers, particularly in the rural areas. This may be an indication of either a lack of employment opportunities or a withdrawal from the rural labour market of those who were occasionally participating.

The above discussion indicates that the impact of fertility transition on female work participation is complex and cannot be established merely by considering the trends in work participation over time. Even though lower fertility rates may result in higher female labour force participation, the effect of women withdrawing from the labour market, especially in rural areas, can cause a net decline in female work participation rate. Perhaps, some of the concerns on the lack of association observed between fertility transition and work participation of women need further scrutiny as they were based on merely looking at the trends in the participation rate (Desai 2010).

Why No Gender Dividend?

The overwhelming perception, however, in India is that gender dividend is nearly absent due to lack of progress in work participation among women (Mehrotra and Sinha 2017). Alternatively, however, Afridi et al. (2016) argue that changes in demographic and socio-economic characteristics of married women can explain the fall in female labour force participation. They argue that with the demographic and socio-economic changes, the women's participation in domestic work enhances. Perhaps, it is natural that with the demographic changes, women automatically have more time to spent which will be utilized at the domestic front. As against such argument, there are also studies showing that the fertility transition has, indeed, helped women to achieve better work participation as well as led to better demographic dividend overall (James and Vani 2013).

There are two important questions that need to be answered in this context. First, why is the expected relationship between demographic change and female labour force participation absent in India? In other words, has fertility transition in India not helped females to be economically more independent? The second question: Is the gender dividend completely absent in India?

The concept of gender dividend is relatively new and has become a talking point under the demographic dividend concept (Miller et al. 2016). Undoubtedly, much of the demographic dividend can be realized through a harnessing gender dividend. To achieve gender dividend, the female population needs to productively contribute to the economy and society. But unfortunately, there are serious issues that encounter when it comes to measuring the contributions of females on the economy. Thus, the gender dividend as such remains obscured in many instances particularly in India.

Gender dividend naturally flows from a low-fertility regime where the time spent for child rearing and child caring become significantly less than during the period of a high-fertility regime. It is expected that the women will be able to enter into the labour market during this period creating gender dividend resulting in faster economic development. However, India's demographic transition has been different with a large majority of the illiterate women accepting small family norm as against the experience of Western countries where the socio-economic development has led to fertility changes (Bhat 2002; James 2011; James and Goli 2017). As a result, the productive employment of women has been much less than what generally would expect in a low-fertility setting. But it does not indicate that the contribution of women in economic development though the gender dividend has been absent in India.

Bhat (2002) estimated the effect of small family among illiterate mothers particularly in educating their children. The study found that when the family size is large, the children are not often sent to school but when the family size became small the children, invariably, are attending school. It means that the women are able to spend considerable amount of time to ensure the quality of the children improves during the low-fertility regime. Perhaps, it is also true in the case of other care giving at the household level particularly for the elder care. Normally, the demographic changes also lead to higher instance of purchasing of elder care due to reduction in family size, increased life expectancy, and women not available at the household. But, in the Indian context, this burden is also taken over by the non-working women although it has not been measured appropriately by any survey.

The studies based on the national transfer account (NTA) methodology also bring out the contribution of women both for the household economy (Ladusingh 2013). While the aggregate labour income from the women has been less than the overall consumption, the contribution to the household management as well as care for the child, sick, and elderly has been immense which are not measured as their contribution to the economy. In a typical country with demographic changes, these services would have been monetized as these services are to be bought from the market. Within family, most women would have been employed outside necessitating the purchase of these services. Therefore, the gender dividend although absent by the existing measures of women work participation cannot be ignored given the services they provide within the household which has considerable current and future implications for economic development.

***

It is now well recognized that demographic changes create a robust middle class with wide socio-economic implications. There has been considerable discussion on demographic dividend in recent years as it generates potential for any society to progress. More importantly, demographic changes also have the ability to benefit the women considerably with a potential gender dividend. This chapter dwells upon the implications of demographic change on female labour force participation and the gender dividend in India.

It has generally been argued that India is unlikely to harness the benefits of demographic opportunity due to several institutional constraints. One of the major constraints identified was the lack of opportunities for females to enter into the labour market. Moreover, it is often blamed that the education and skill levels of Indian women are relatively resulting in lack of employability. These arguments, thus, provide a pessimistic view on the gender dividend and women's contribution to the economic progress in India.

It is well known that the fertility changes itself are not in line with the conventional transition with a large number of uneducated or low-skilled women adopting small family norm. Therefore, a large number of females in the middle class also have only limited education and skill levels. All these keep

60 K. S. JAMES

limitations on achieving gender dividend to its potential capacity. The lack of progress of female work participation is also attributed to such constraints. At the same time, such changes do not also indicate that the gender dividend is completely absent in the country.

There is no doubt to the fact that the effect of demographic changes is to be realized majorly through gender dividend and by enhancing the productive contribution of females. The lack of significant changes in the female labour force participation, however, cannot solely be considered as a negative effect on gender dividend. There are many studies that suggests that even while withdrawing from the labour market, the women contributes significantly to the household productivity. It is also argued that with the demographic and educational changes, the household productivity of women is considerably changing which will ultimately result in gender dividend. There is a strong correlation between women's household contribution and children's achievements.

The invisibility of female employment has been a matter of serious concern for long. It is, perhaps, time to rethink on women's contribution in development by extending the framework of gender dividend. Although gender dividend is conceptualized only as income earning occupation outside home, it needs to be redefined expanding the productivity changes that are observable at the household level particularly on human capital formation and household level petty production. Such expansion will give a better idea of how gender dividend, in fact, is realized even when the work participation outside home is negligible.

The analysis, thus, brings out several important points to reflect on the gender dividend in India. First, against common perception, the demographic changes indeed created a gender dividend but outside the measure of female work participation. Second, the fertility transition has a major role in enhancing the quality of children and care provision within households which are not accounted when female work participation is measured. Third, although limited at present due to low levels of work participation among females, demographic changes would ultimately help in augmenting dividend and overall economic development.

References

Afridi, Farzana, Taryn Dinkelman, and Kanika Mahajan. 2016. 'Why Are Fewer Married Women Joining Workforce in India? A Decomposition Analysis over Two Decades'. IZA Discussion Paper Series No. 9722, Institute of Study of Labour, Bonn, Germany, February. Available at http://ftp.iza.org/dp9722.pdf.

DEMOGRAPHIC AND GENDER DIVIDEND 61

Aiyar, Shekhar and Ashoka Mody. 2011. 'The Demographic Dividend: Evidence from the Indian States'. IMF Working Paper, No. 11/38, February, New York: International Monetary Fund. Available at www.imf.org/external/pubs/ft/wp/2011/wp1138.pdf.

Basu, Alka Malwade. 2011. 'Demographic Dividend Revisited: The Mismatch between Age and Economic Activity Based Dependency Ratios'. *Economic and Political Weekly* 46 (39): 53–8.

Bhat, P. N. M. 2002. 'Returning a Favor: Reciprocity between Female Education and Fertility in India'. *World Development*, 30 (10): 1791–803.

Bloom, David E. 2012. 'Population Dynamics in India and Implications for Economic Growth'. In *The Oxford Handbook of the Indian Economy*, edited by Chetan Ghate, 462–497. New Delhi: Oxford University Press.

Bloom, David E. and David Canning. 2011. 'Demographics and Development Policy'. *Development Outreach*, 13 (1): 77–81.

Bloom, D.E., D. Canning, and B. Graham. 2003. 'Longevity and Life Cycle Savings'. *The Scandinavian Journal of Economics* 105 (3): 319–38.

Bloom, David E., David Canning, Günther Fink, and Jocelyn E. Finlay. 2009. 'Fertility, Female Labor Force Participation, and the Demographic Dividend'. *Journal of Economic Growth* 14: 79–101.

Bloom, David E., David Canning, Linlin Wu, Yuanli Liu, Ajay Mahal, and Winnie Yip. 2010. 'Demographic Change and Economic Growth: Comparing China and India'. *Journal of Comparative Economics* 38 (1): 17–33.

Browning, M. 1992. 'Children and Household Economic Behaviour'. *Journal of Economic Literature* 30 (3): 1434–75.

Chandrasekhar, C. P., Jayati Ghosh, and Anamitra Roychwdhury. 2006. 'The Demographic Dividend and Young India's Economic Future'. *Economic and Political Weekly* 9 (December): 5055–64.

Chowdhury, Subhanil. 2011. 'Employment in India: What Does the Latest Data Show?'. *Economic and Political Weekly* 34 (32): 23–6.

Cuaresma, Jesus Crespo, Wolfgang Lutz, and Warren Sanderson. 2012. 'Age Structure, Education and Economic Growth'. Interim Report, IR-12-011, International Institute for Applied System Analysis, Laxenburg, Austria.

Deaton, Angus and Christina H. Paxson. 2000. 'Growth, Demographic Structure, and National Saving in Taiwan'. *Population and Development Review* 26, Supplement: Population and Economic Change in East Asia: 141–73.

Desai, Sonalde. 2010. 'The Other Half of the Demographic Dividend'. *Economic and Political Weekly* XLV (40) (October): 12–14.

Gaddis, Isis and Stephan Klasen. 2011. 'Economic Development, Structural Changes and Women's Labour Force Participation: A Reexamination of the Feminisation U Hypothesis'. Discussion Paper No.71, University of Gottingen, Germany.

ILO (International Labour Organization). 2013. *Global Employment Trends 2013: Recovering from the Second Jobs Dip*. Geneva: International Labour Organization.

James, K. S. 2008. 'Glorifying Malthus: The Current Debate on Demographic Dividend in India'. *Economic and Political Weekly* XLIII (25) (June): 21–7.

James, K. S. 2011. 'India's Demographic Change, Opportunities and Challenges'. *American Association for the Advancement of Science* (AAAS) July: 29.

62 K. S. JAMES

James, K. S. and B. P. Vani. 2013. 'Female Work Participation and Demographic Dividend Prospects for India'. Paper presented at the seminar on '40 per cent of the World: Population Change, Human Capital and Development in China, India and Indonesia' organized by JY Pillay Comparative Asia Research Centre, National University of Singapore, Singapore, May 22–4.

James, K. S. and Srinivas Goli. 2017. 'Demographic Change in India: Is the Country Prepared for the Challenge'. *Brown Journal of World Affairs* XXIII (1): 169–87.

Kelley, A. and R. Schmidt. 2007. 'A Century of Demographic Change and Economic Growth: The Asian Experience in Regional and Temporal Perspective'. In *Population Change, Labor Markets and Sustainable Growth: Towards a New Economic Paradigm*, edited by A. Mason and M. Yamaguchi, 39–74. Amsterdam: Elsevier.

Klasen, Stephan and Janneke Pieters. 2012. 'Push or Pull? Drivers of Female Labor Force Participation during India's Economic Boom'. IZA Discussion Paper No. 6395, Institute for the Study of Labour, Germany, February.

Kumar, Utsav. 2010. 'India's Demographic Transition: Boon or Bane? A State Level Perspective'. MPRA Paper No. 24922. Available at SSRN: http://ssrn.com/abstract=1675278.

Ladusingh, Laishram. 2013. 'Gender Accounting of Consumption and the Life-Cycle Deficit for India'. *Asia-Pacific Population Journal* 28 (2): 27–49.

Ladusingh, Laishram and M. R. Narayana. 2011. 'Demographic Dividends for India: Evidence and Implications Based on National Transfer Accounts'. ADB Economics Working Paper Series No. 292, Asian Development Bank, Manila, December.

Lahoti, Rahul and Hema Swaminathan. 2013. Economic Growth and Female Labour Force Participation in India'. Working Paper No 414, Indian Institute of Management, Bangalore, June.

Mazumdar, Indrani and N Neetha. 2011. 'Gender Dimension: Employment Trends in India, 1993–93 to 2009–10'. *Economic and Political Weekly* 46 (43):118–26.

Mehrotra, Santosh and Sharmistha Sinha. 2017. 'Explaining Falling Female Employment during a High Growth Period'. *Economic and Political Weekly* 52 (39, Sept 30).

Miller, Tim, P. Saad, and C. Marinez. 2016. 'Population Ageing, Demographic Dividend and Gender Dividend: Assessing the Long Term Impact of Gender Equality on Economic Growth and Development in Latin America'. In *Demographic Dividends: Emerging Challenges and Policy Implications, Vol. 6, Demographic Transformation and Socio-Economic Development*, edited by R. Pace and R. Ham-Chande, 23–43. Heidelberg: Springer Cham.

MSPI (Ministry of Statistics and Programme Implementation). 2019. Annual Report: Periodic Labour force Survey (July 2017–June 2018), National Statistical Office, Ministry of Statistics and Programme Implementation, Government of India, May, http://mospi.nic.in/publication/annual-report-plfs-2017-18.

Mitra, Arup. 2011. 'Missing Demographic Dividend?, *The Economic Times*, July 4.

Mitra, Siddhartha and R. Nagarajan. 2005. 'Making Use of the Window of Demographic Opportunity: An Economic Perspective'. *Economic and Political Weekly*, December 10, 5327–32.

Neff, Daniel, Kunal Sen, and Veronika Kling. 2012. 'The Puzzling Decline in the Rural Women's Labour Force Participation in India: A Reexamination'. GIG Working Paper No.196, German Institute of Global and Area Studies, Germany, May.

Olsen, Wendy and Smita Mehta. 2006. 'A Pluralist Account of Labour Participation in India'. Working Paper No 42, Global Poverty Research Group, University of Manchester, May.

Ramaswamy, K. V. and Tushar Agrawal. 2012. Services-led Growth, Employment and Job Quality: A Study of Manufacturing and Service-sector in Urban India'. Working Paper-2012-07, Indira Gandhi Institute of Development Research, Mumbai, March.

Standing, Guy. 1983. 'Women's Work Activity and Fertility'. In *Determinants of Fertility in Developing Countries, Vol. 1, Supply and Demand for Children*, edited by Rodolfo A. Bulatao and Ronald D. Lee, 517–46. New York: Academic Press.

Upadhyay, Ashoak. 2012. 'India's Demographic Dividend May Turn into a Nightmare'. *Business Line*, May 13.

World Bank. 2010. *India's Employment Challenge: Creating Jobs, Helping Workers*. New Delhi: Oxford University Press.

4

Growth and Consumption in Uttar Pradesh under 'Neoliberalism'[*]

Ravi Srivastava

Neoliberal growth has delivered strong gains in income and consumption to the top deciles of the population in India with much smaller and more volatile changes occurring at the bottom (NCEUS 2007; Sengupta et al. 2006). The acceleration in growth that took place in the period of the global economic bubble, combined with certain social policies, also pulled up the income of wage earners in this period. However, rising inequalities income and wages are reflected in patterns of consumption, which the poor cannot afford to follow. Moreover, regional patterns of growth and accumulation have remained quite diverse in India with increasing inequality among states and regions. It is now clear that neoliberal growth has led to increasing divergence between states whereas the expected outcome was higher convergence (Ahluwalia 2000; Srivastava 2003; GoI 2017: Chapter 10). A number of explanations have been offered for the divergent conditions. These include initially favourable conditions (level of infrastructure, location), governance (which could include factors such ability to uphold rule of law and property rights; as well as cohesive policy regimes), and ability to maintain a pro-business policy regime. These factors are related to specific social, historical, and political factors in the states and have influenced the way political regimes negotiate with interest groups, build support, develop policies, and administer institutions of governance.

The adoption of a neoliberal growth regime by the central government in the early 1990s paved the way for provincial governments to fashion neoliberal agendas in the light of their own circumstances. Taken together with the factors mentioned above, this has influenced the deviation of regional

---

[*] An earlier version of this chapter was presented in the Regional Plenary of the 43rd All India Sociological Congress, held at Lucknow University between 9 November and 12 December 2017 on the theme of *Neoliberalism, Consumption and Culture.*

Ravi Srivastava, *Growth and Consumption in Uttar Pradesh under 'Neoliberalism'* In: *Neoliberalism, Urbanization, and Aspirations in Contemporary India.* Edited by: Sujata Patel, Oxford University Press.
© Oxford University Press 2021. DOI: 10.1093/oso/9780190132019.003.0004

UTTAR PRADESH UNDER 'NEOLIBERALISM' 65

trajectories from the national trajectory. The case of Uttar Pradesh (UP) is one where slower growth has increased the gap between the state and the all India levels of living. But at the same time, the greater integration of markets, especially labour markets, has had different implications for different groups in the state.[1]

This chapter focuses on specific features of UP's political economy, and how its pattern of liberalization impacted on the spread of economic opportunity in the post liberalization period, as measured by a few conventional indicators—incomes, private consumption, and jobs. UP has failed to deliver on a pattern of growth under which these could grow in a satisfactory manner. There has been a signal failure of successive governments, all of which have followed a broadly similar neoliberal paradigm, to accelerate growth in the state, build on its productive potential, and to provide the benefits of development equitably. This has happened despite the fact that parties in power in recent years have claimed marginalized social groups as their core support groups.[2] But at the same time, slow improvements in real income and consumption, even among a section of historically deprived social groups, and changing aspirations, specially of the youth, which are fuelled by global consumption patterns, provide a fertile basis for various, and often contradictory, socio-political dynamics.

---

[1] The impact of political economy factors and state-level political regimes has been the focus of a few other studies (Srivastava 1995; Kohli 2006, 2012; Pai 2007; Dreze and Sen 1997). Kohli (1987, 2007, 2009, 2012) has paid close attention to regime-types and developmental outcomes across countries. A number of his studies focus on India as well as regions within India and variations in the nature of growth process and its performance under neoliberal reforms. Compared to Gujarat, which he characterizes as developmental coalition, and West Bengal (social democratic), he characterizes politics in Uttar Pradesh (UP) as neo-patrimonial politics. He finds that a weak sense of public purpose in UP run by personalistic and clientelistic political leaders mainly based on social strata (that is, castes) significantly contributed to poor development performance in the state.

[2] UP experienced unbroken Congress rule for the first fifteen years (1952–67) under five of its chief ministers. The spell of Congress rule was broken in 1967 by the Bhartiya Kranti Dal, and between 1967 and 1980, the state oscillated between non-Congress and Congress governments, and president's rule and saw nine chief ministers. The state reverted to Congress rule between 1982 and 1989. Between 1989 and 1997, the state again oscillated between four unstable non-congress government formations and spells of president's rule. The thirteenth Assembly (1997–2002) saw a fragile alliance between the BSP and the BJP, with the BJP taking reigns for most of the period (four-and-a-half years). The fourteenth Assembly first saw the BSP assume power but the SP then engineered a majority and formed government from 2003–7 for a period of about three, years and nine months. Since 2007 the state has seen three stable majority governments, led by the BSP, the SP, and the BJP successively.

Neoliberalism's Attire in Uttar Pradesh

Although the basic features of the neoliberal economic framework under globalization can be articulated quite easily, neither the pace nor pattern of neoliberal economic change is wholly predictable, since they are determined by many mediating factors. Even within the framework of a national economy pursuing a neoliberal agenda, sub-national governments may follow their own specific strategies.

In the Indian case, many factors, including the force of circumstances, caused the central government to announce far-reaching reforms in the direction of liberalization in August 1991. The first Union budget incorporating principles of structural adjustment was presented in 1992. But meanwhile, on the political front the politics of identity and representation was being played out, engulfing the state, first on the issues relating to OBC reservation, and then the Ram Mandir at Ayodhya. Mr Advani emerged on the scene in 1990 as a Toyota riding warrior, marshalling forces for the Ram Mandir.

Powered by these events and the consequent communal polarization, the BJP formed its first government in UP in June 1991, and in 1992, the Babri Mosque was brought down by *karsewaks*. In UP's political dynamics, a focus on economic liberalization was backstage and far removed from the central agenda. We may add that the BJP was also part of two subsequent governments in UP, apart from the current one. Communal peace and the rule of law in the state remain tentative with numerous occurrences of communal disputes affecting the lives and activities of direct producers, particularly in the urban informal manufacturing sector who are both poor Muslims and Hindus.

UP's high industrial growth in the 1980s, to which reference has been made later in this paper, was driven by large doses of public investment (both central and state) and stimulation of the private sector, in a period, when for the most part, there were Congress governments in the state and the centre. These factors could not have been sustained in the 1990s since the earlier policy umbrella was withdrawn. The reforms at the centre set the stage for a more liberal economic environment and competition among states to attract private investment. Struggling with relative backwardness, and infrastructural, fiscal and governance constraints in the 1990s, UP tried to fall in line with the changed environment. Industrial policies, labour policies, and land policies were revised from time to time to facilitate market-led growth.

For the record, it was the Mulayam Singh government of 1994 which initiated some policy changes, and this was then followed by comprehensive policy statement by the BJP government under Kalyan Singh in 1998. Since then, industrial policies in the state have been revised in 2004, 2012, and in 2017. There were also Industrial Policy related decisions the governments led by Mayawati in 2002 (alliance government with BJP) and in 2008. Each of these changes aimed at making UP a more attractive destination for Indian and foreign capital and promoting more rapid growth of the different segments of industry, services and infrastructure, with some difference in emphasis. The 2012 Industrial Policy, for example, aimed at infrastructure-led industrial development. For details of the successive industrial policies, the reader may refer to Srivastava and Ranjan (2016).

In principle, the policy shifts ostensibly focused on creating a conducive market-based environment for industrial growth, and considered all types of industries, large, medium, and small. In practice, however, crony capitalism, lack of transparency, and adhocism characterized most major decisions. The SP government, under Mulayam Singh, formulated an industrial policy in 2004, but its major decision to attract investors was to put together a 'Development Council' comprising a number of well-known industrialists at the national level and a famous film-star, headed by Mr Amar Singh, a political figure very close to the chief minister and also to two of the industrialists nominated to the Council. Detailed analysis of the work of this Council has not been undertaken, but some of the decisions taken by the then government appeared to have bypassed competitive bidding procedures and amounted to passing benefits to some of the industrial groups considered close to the government (Tripathi 2004). In some cases, as in power and housing, policies formulated by the government appeared to benefit these industrialists at the cost of the public exchequer. Many of the decisions then taken, for example the move to privatize sugar factories when the world demand for sugar was booming, are still under scrutiny. The Council, a clear manifestation of crony capitalism, was disbanded on the first day that the new BSP government assumed office in 2012. But Mayawati's government was itself open to the charge of cronyism due to its alleged proximity to single industrial house and non-transparent procedures that were followed in contracts that were set up in this period.

The knee-jerk reactions of state governments and their failure to evolve transparent rules pointed to discretionary decision-making and rent-seeking without systematically seeking to overcome barriers to growth. Successive governments have taken on board the interests of industrialists only through discretionary policy rather than address the systemic issues. The failure of the successive regime's in UP to address constraints on industrial growth was

68 RAVI SRIVASTAVA

best typified by their neglect of the small sector and traditional industries. These industries involve a very large number of workers, mainly belonging to the 'backward castes' among both Hindus and Muslims. This happened despite the fact that at least two of the major parties in the state swear by the social base to which these small producers belong. One answer lies perhaps in the fact that these small producers are part of a production chain dominated by merchant capitalists with whom the political parties are able to strike a deal (Mishra and Srivastava 2004; Srivastava and Ranjan 2016).

The general argument being made here is that UP's economic agenda tried to free up space for capital, but as a matter of fact, crony capitalism prevailed and arbitrary decisions were taken and favours given selectively to a few large industrialists. There was no attempt to address systemic barriers to growth and accumulation for generally, leading to, as we shall see later in this chapter, a slow and distorted pattern of growth.

Neoliberalism can be expected to reduce the economic space within which political regimes, particularly those at the state level take up policies or programmes which involve pro-poor interventions, although some types of interventions, popularly called safety nets supplement the implementation of neoliberal strategies. However, parties in power will take up pro-poor policies or programmes for ideological or populistic reasons within fiscal or policy constraints which exist. In UP, the different regimes that have been in power since the 1990s have attempted to do the same.

The BSP which has been in power in UP five times since 1993 took up a few major programmes. These have included the Ambedkar Village Programme (AVP) in 1995 through which it converged development schemes to develop localities/villages with a large dalit population. The focus on distributive and effective possession of patta land was another important programmatic plank which had modest success (Pai 2005; Srivastava et al. 2006).

The SP's schemes were modest in scope except for its announcement of an unemployment allowance for unemployed educated youth in 2012. Towards the end of its last regime it upscaled allocations to several programmes, especially in pensions and housing.

But UP's regimes have been more in the news for publicized scams in recruitment and transfers, land acquisitions and sweet deals with developers, scams in the distribution of foodgrains meant for government programmes such as the JRY, Sampoorna Gramin Rozgar Yojana, the Antyodaya Anna Yojana (AAY), Mid-day Meal Scheme, the TPDS, and the Old Age Pensions. A major scam during the Mayawati government relating to the National Rural Health Mission allegedly involving an amount of Rs 9,400 crores.

UTTAR PRADESH UNDER 'NEOLIBERALISM' 69

A systematic review of the performance of public programmes for the poor in UP since 2000 shows that the state was a consistently poor performer in all the programmes reviewed, unlike several other low-income states which showed silver linings in terms of good performance in some of the programmes (Srivastava 2012a). This comparatively poor performance has dogged the state right up to the recent period with programmes like MGNREGA and the NFSA registering outcomes which put the state among the poorest performers (Srivastava and Ranjan 2016).

It could be asked whether there were any significant regime differences in this nearly three decade period during which the state was ruled by several coalitions and parties. While it is possible to go into greater detail and focus on specific differences which have existed, as a matter of fact, the political economy of UP's governance remained broadly the same in many essential features throughout this period.

Growth Performance under Neoliberalism

Having broadly outlined UP's political economy during in the period after economic liberalization, we will now focus on what neoliberal changes were able to deliver on the growth front. We will restrict ourselves to only three issues viz: UP's aggregate growth performance, impact of regions, and the state's industrial performance.

UP possessed some initial advantages at the time of independence.[3] But the state was not able to build a momentum of growth from the very beginning and steadily slipped back. The state's per capita income was 97 per cent of the national per capita income in 1951. This fell to 68 per cent in 1971–2, and remained close to this level till 1991–2 (67.5 per cent). This shows that UP's aggregate growth performance was almost on par with the national economy during the 1970s and 1980s. Between 1991–2 and 2014–15, this share fell to a further low of 40.5 per cent in 2014–15 (Srivastava and Ranjan 2016).

Comparative trends (UP and all India) for sectoral and aggregate net domestic product, as well as those for two major industry groups (agriculture and manufacturing), are presented below in Table 4.1 for the period up to

---

[3] These included its location in the fertile Indo-Gangetic belt, a modest background of land reforms, a legacy of a unified administration under British India, reasonably good physical and social infrastructure, a diversified base of traditional and modern industries, and a political leadership with substantial weight in the national political establishment after independence.

70 RAVI SRIVASTAVA

Table 4.1 Annual Growth Rates, UP and India

Sector	1961–2 to 1988–9		1989–90 to 2015–16	
	UP	India	UP	India
Agriculture and Allied	3.1	2.4	2.1	2.9
Primary	1.6	2.6	1.8	3.0
Manufacturing	7.1	5.1	3.8	6.6
Secondary	6.6	4.8	4.7	6.7
Tertiary	3.9	5.2	6.1	7.8
NDP/NSDP	3.8	4.0	4.9	6.5

Source: Computed from NDP/NSDP data provided by CSO

1998–89, and from 1989–90 till 2014–15. The so-called liberalization period has seen a remarkable slippage in UP's aggregate growth performance, as well in the performance of various sectors and sub-sectors.[4] The largest gap occurred in manufacturing, with an annual growth in UP of 3.8 per cent compared to 6.6 per cent at the national level.

The somewhat exceptional period in UP's growth story was in the 70s and 80s, during which a more interventionist public strategy led to faster agricultural growth in the agriculturally poor regions. Further, industry supported by incentives and public investment grew at a fairly high rate, although this growth was spatially more concentrated in the Western region (Srivastava and Ranjan 2016).

Moreover, contrary to what has been observed elsewhere (World Bank 2010), there are no major signs that this growth reduced the economic distance between UP's regions. Indeed, in some respects and in some sectors, growth is much more spatially concentrated today than it was at the beginning of the liberalization period.

As is well known, UP is a large state with several regions with distinct features and historical trajectories. The Western and the Eastern regions have a share of about 37 and 40 per cent, respectively, in the state population while about one-fifth of the population lives in the central region, and only 5 per

---

[4] This gap has continued to widen in more recent years. From 2014–15 to 2018–19, UP's Gross Value Added (GVA) at constant prices increased at an annual average rate of 6.22% while India's GVA rose at an annual rate of 7.33% a year.

Table 4.2 Region-Wise Percentage Share in Net State Domestic Product

Region	1980–1	1990–1	2013–14
Western	47.0	44.9	46.4
Bundelkhand	5.2	5.5	5.1
Central	16.4	18.2	17.8
Eastern	31.4	31.5	30.6

Source: Computed from Statistical Abstract of Uttar Pradesh, Various Years

cent is in Bundelkhand. The density of population in the Bundelkhand region is less than half of the population density of the state whereas the Eastern region has the highest population density with the lowest per capita availability of land. The economic distance between the different regions in UP has influenced both politics and policy. The Western region is relatively the most developed region of the state in terms of economic prosperity and leads in terms of agricultural and industrial performance. East UP and Bundelkhand are officially designated as backward regions. The characteristics of these regions in terms of development and poverty have been analysed at the district and region level in the two state Human Development Reports (GoUP 2003, 2007) and by a World Bank report (World Bank 2010).

The regions have largely retained their share of Net Domestic Product since the 1980s (see Table 5.2). The share of the Western region in Net Domestic Product declined in the 1980s but again picked up and was 46.4 per cent of the State Domestic Product in 2013–14. All the three other regions saw their share in Net State Domestic Product (NSDP) picking up marginally in the 1980s, but saw a drop in these shares in the subsequent twenty-four-year period.

As percentage of the Western region's per capita net product, the central region showed an improvement in 2013–14 over 1990–1 and 1980–1 (Table 4.3). The Bundelkhand and Eastern regions show a reduction in the gap in per capita net domestic product between 1980–1 and 1990–1, which was reversed thereafter. The Eastern region lags behind the most in per capita terms.

Analysis by broad sectors shows that tertiary sector growth is the most evenly spread between the regions, while secondary sector growth is the most spatially concentrated. In 2013–14, the Western region's share in Secondary,

Table 4.3 Per Capita Net Domestic Product as Percentage of the Western Region

Region	1980–1	1990–1	2013–14
Western	100	100	100
Central	78	81	86
Bundelkhand	80	88	85
Eastern	60	66	58

Source: Computed from Statistical Abstract of Uttar Pradesh, Various Years

Primary, and Tertiary Sector Net Domestic Product was 52.2, 48.8, and 43.5 per cent, respectively (Table 5.4).

Analysis of sectoral Ginis (analysing the concentration of domestic product within each region) shows a more varied picture. In the Western region, the spatial concentration increased for all sectors, with the secondary sector Gini increasing from 0.42 to 0.56 between 1980–1 and 2013–14, but in the other regions secondary sector Ginis were lower in 2013–14 compared to 1980–1. Tertiary sector Ginis increased in all regions, while primary sector Ginis fluctuated between the years but were lower in 2013–14 compared to 1980–1 in two regions (Eastern and Central) and higher in one (Bundelkhand) (Srivastava and Ranjan 2016).

The general picture, therefore, is that even with greater heterogeneity within the region, the Western region has more or less maintained its lead over the other regions, and in per capita terms, the gap between it and the Eastern region has not diminished over several decades.

Table 4.4 Regional Share in Sectoral GDP, 2013–14

Region	Primary	Secondary	Tertiary
Western	48.77	52.22	43.49
Bundelkhand	5.75	4.27	5.14
Central	15.48	16.74	19.14
Eastern	30.01	26.77	32.23

Source: Computed from Statistical Abstract of Uttar Pradesh, Various Years

Elusive Industrial Growth

Liberalization was not only expected to unleash growth potential of the Indian economy as a whole, but more specifically that of the industrial sector. However, as pointed out earlier, UP's industrial growth has been significantly lower than the national economy since the 1990s. The state's share in manufacturing income had increased from about 5.6 per cent in the early 1960s to about 9 per cent in the late 1980s, but has fallen to about 5 per cent currently. The share of manufacturing income in state income also more than doubled from about 7 per cent in the early 1960s to about 15 per cent in the late 1980s but is currently only at about 9 per cent.

A specific feature of UP's economy has been the significant presence of the unorganized industrial sector, ranging from family run enterprises (own account units) to small units working with a few hired workers. The state had about 22.34 lakh unregistered units with a gross output of Rs 37,024 crores (10 per cent of the national output) employing about 51.76 lakh persons (15 lakh people (12.66 per cent of persons employed nationally in this segment in 2006–7, Fourth Report of All India Census of Medium, Small and Micro Enterprises, 2006–7, Unregistered Sector). UP also has a massive presence of a large number of skill intensive traditional industries. These include handloom, zardosi, chikan work, perfume industry, brassware, pottery, glassware, lock-making, leatherwork, wooden toys, furniture carving, and so forth. The state has 1.1 lakh handloom worker households and about 2.2 lakh workers of whom 1 lakh were full time. Forty-two per cent weaver households were located in urban areas. More than 90 per cent of the workers belong to the OBC. Nearly three-quarter work with master weavers and a quarter are independent weavers. The cooperative sector covers a negligible proportion of units in the state (Census of Handlooms). The total unregistered manufacturing sector currently contributes about 49 per cent of manufacturing SDP.

In terms of the regional pattern of industrialization, industrial concentration was not markedly high at independence. The major industrial centre in Uttar Pradesh, Kanpur, was in Central Uttar Pradesh. Other well-known traditional industries, as well as modern industries such as sugar, were dispersed throughout the Western and Eastern parts of the state. The location of public sector industries in the post-independence period also did not favour the Western region.

However, the spatial pattern of industrialization in the state changed rapidly even in the first two decades after independence with higher

74 RAVI SRIVASTAVA

non-agricultural and industrial growth in the Western region. In 1970–1, the estimated gross value of industrial output per capita (Annual Survey of Industries) in the Western and Central regions was higher than the state average (which included the erstwhile Hill region) by 46 per cent and 40 per cent, respectively, and lower than the state average by 48 per cent and 88 per cent in the Eastern and Bundelkhand regions. But even in 1988–9, seven of the ten districts with the highest investments in these industries were not in Western UP, although the level of industrial development as well as its growth was the highest in this region, due its agro base, better infrastructure, and the proximity of the region to Delhi. However, between 1987–8 and 2010–11, the share of the Eastern, Central, and Bundelkhand regions in total NVA declined from 25.5, 20.1, and 2.1 per cent to 16.5, 19.9, and 1.5 per cent, respectively, while the share of the Western region increased from 61 per cent to 72.2 per cent. Over the same period, the share of the Eastern, Central, and Bundelkhand regions in total persons employed declined from 25.5, 20.1, and 2.1 per cent to 10.1, 14.2, and 2 per cent, respectively, while the share of the Western region increased from 52.2 per cent to 73.7 per cent (Srivastava and Ranjan 2016).

The policy shift has also not begun to bear results in terms of the objective of attracting large-scale investments. Between 2010 and 2015, the Indian Entrepreneur's Memorandum filed for investment in UP averaged Rs 21,524 crores, which was 2.1 per cent of the IEMs filed for the country as a whole. Between 2010 and March 2016, the actual investment was only Rs 8800 crores (less than an average annual investment of Rs 1500 crore) and only 2.2 per cent of the national figure.

Thus, UP's specific neoliberal paradigm has neither been able to build on the strengths on the state's industrial base in the handicraft/handloom sector, nor build the modern small/medium/large-scale sector. But in the name of developing industries and infrastructure, cronyism has been promoted and there have been numerous conflicts related to land acquisition (see Srivastava and Ranjan 2016).

Employment in the State

There is a strong recognition in state policy that rapid growth in industries and services in the state is required to create jobs for the new entrants into the workforce and it is quite clear the existing pattern of growth has failed to do that.

Further, an important issue is not only the creation of any type of job in industries and services but jobs which are good and could be attractive to young, educated people. Even though the national economy itself is not creating enough good jobs, the gap between UP and the country is simply huge. The state economy is not generating enough good jobs. Between 1993–4 and 2011–12, the percentage of regular workers in the country increased from 13.6 per cent of all workers to 18.5 per cent of all workers. But in UP, over the corresponding period, the percentage of workers with regular/salaried jobs only increased from 8.5 to 10.8. Over this period, the percentage of workers in the state in white-collar occupations increased from 12.8 to 16.7, while nationally the percentage of white-collar workers went up from 15.8 to 23.6.

The current employment situation summarizing the proportion of good jobs by the usual indicators is shown in Table 4.5. Only 10.79 per cent workers in UP have a regular wage or salaried employment in any sector of the economy, compared to 18.45 per cent workers in the country. This is not simply a reflection of the agrarian nature of UP's economy. Both within manufacturing and services, UP generates far fewer regular wage/salaried jobs. The formal sector is also much smaller in UP. Only 8.52 per cent workers in UP are employed in the formal/organized sector, compared to 13.4 per cent workers in the country. Further, the percentage of formal sector workers is smaller in both manufacturing and services. Using a definition of a formal worker as a worker with any kind of written contract, we find that only 4.17 per cent workers in UP had formal employment, compared to 6.7 per cent workers in India. Only 3.11 per cent workers employed in manufacturing in the state were formal workers and 8.65 per cent workers were formally employed in services. Finally, only 3.72 per cent of all workers, also employed in the organized sector were formally employed.

The slow rate of generation of good-quality jobs is getting reflected in higher levels of unemployment among the youth with tertiary levels of education. The unemployment rate among tertiary educated young men was as high as 23.6 per cent in 2011–12 compared to 19.2 per cent in India. The unemployment rate among young women was higher still at 32.7 per cent in UP compared to 29.4 per cent in India.

The generalized crisis of employment in the state which results in both lack of livelihoods and lack of jobs has been leading to large-scale emigration of workers from the state. The World Bank (2010) has argued that that the slow growth in urban wages and negligible increase in the number of regular salaried jobs compelled men, especially young men, to look for employment

76 RAVI SRIVASTAVA

Table 4.5 Employment Characteristics, UP and India, 2011–12

		In Manufacturing	In Services	In Total Employment
Regular Workers (%)	UP	23.15	22.16	10.79
	India	35.22	34.59	18.45
Formal Sector Workers (%)	UP	20.65	17.68	8.52
	India	29.36	25.44	13.40
% all Formal Workers to Total Workers	UP	3.11	8.65	4.17
	India	7.89	12.77	6.70
% Formal Workers in Formal Sector to Total Workers	UP	2.64	7.75	3.72
	India	6.41	10.80	5.67

Source: Computed from unit level data, Employment–Unemployment Survey, NSSO

elsewhere. About 2 million men left UP in the last decade and 70 per cent of them did so to look for employment as shown in Census 1991 and 2001 and World Bank (2010). Urban areas of Maharashtra, Delhi, and Gujarat are the top three destinations for those who migrate out of UP for economic reasons. The top three rural destinations are Haryana, Uttaranchal, and Delhi. Additionally, about 1.5 million men migrated to other destinations within UP.

These figures are rough estimates of decadal migration flows from UP. They ignore the shorter term flows due to seasonal or circular migration, and long-term migration which has contributed to the stock of UP out migrants. While most migrants from UP use social networks to migrate for work in various industries in the destination areas, and mostly to the urban informal sector, poorer migrants migrate through organized recruitment networks to work in construction, brick kilns, or other industries.

Large-scale out migration has important economic, socio-cultural, and political consequences, particularly for rural life in UP, particularly in those areas/regions in Eastern and Central UP and Bundelkhand where it is very widespread. Among other impacts, remittances and savings impact on the consumption of families left behind. We have no estimate of savings brought back by migrants when they return (and this is likely to be higher for poorer migrants). However, the NSS 64th Round (2007–8) provides an estimate of households receiving remittances and the amount of remittances received by them. As per these estimates, 17.1 per cent rural households and 5.9 per cent urban households received an estimated Rs 7.319 crore of remittances from long-term outmigrants. The percentage of households reporting the receipt of remittances did not vary much across consumption quintiles.

To sum up: Slow growth in wages, lack of rural employment and livelihoods, and slow growth in good quality jobs has resulted in a generalized crisis of employment, and emigration has been a major response, especially in rural areas. Emigration influences incomes, lifestyles, and cultural preferences of the returnees and migrants' families, with significant socio-political, cultural, and economic impacts. Remittances and savings are an important component of receipts of rural households, particularly in rural UP, influencing the level and pattern of consumption, as well as patterns of investment. We will have more to say on this in the following section.

Trends in Consumption and the Pattern of Consumption

Economists put more in store on measuring the level of consumption of households/individuals since consumption is likely to be more stable than incomes (although incomes remain the most important determinant of consumption). Neoliberal growth under globalization could affect both the level and pattern of consumption of both public and private goods, through impacts on employment and income, trade and relative prices, and consumer preferences.

Data on both income and consumption of public goods is scanty and economists have relied on patterns of private consumption (measured by consumption expenditure) to measure changes in welfare impact on various groups of households through changes in the incidence of 'economic poverty'. According to most estimates, real per capita consumption expenditure has been rising across all deciles, and irrespective of the benchmark expenditure level used for a 'poverty line', most economists argue that economic poverty has been declining. The major argument, however, is whether economic liberalization has speeded up the decline in poverty, that is, whether the elasticity of poverty decline to growth has increased post-liberalization. But this debate remains inconclusive since the benchmark level of poverty becomes very relevant for comparisons. One must also note that there is a counter-argument (Utsa Patnaik 2010) which gives primacy to calorie-deprivation as the core indicator of poverty and argues that this deprivation has actually increased after liberalization.

The argument in this section is pitched at a broad level. In the previous section, we have noted that consumption levels in UP, particularly in rural UP, could follow a different pattern from incomes due to large-scale emigration and remittances/savings of the migrants. We therefore analyse whether this has influenced relative consumption levels in UP vis-à-vis the country as a whole, and also whether this has impacted on inter-regional trends in consumption within the state. We then examine the trends in consumption inequality. Finally, we analyse the pattern of food and non-food consumption.

UP's overall Monthly Per Capita Consumption Expenditure (MPCE) is comparatively much closer to all-India level compared to PCY which we discussed earlier. As a matter of fact, rural MPCE had inched close to all-India levels (96.3 per cent of all India level in 1993–4). Urban MPCEs are comparatively lower than the all India levels. But in both cases, the relative gap has tended to increase in the post-liberalization period, and this gap increased fastest between 2004–5 and 2011–12. Rural MPCE as a percentage of all India MPCE fell from 96.8 in 1993–04 to 81.8 in 2011–12, and over the same period, urban MPCE in the state as a percentage of all India MPCE fell from 83.8 to 78.8. This reflects the rising gap between the state and all -India PCY over this period which other sources of income/consumption (such as remittances) have not been able to bridge to the earlier extent.

The regional differences in MPCE, which is also based on incomes originating outside the regions, reflect the same pattern as the PCY discussed earlier. The Western region has the highest MPCE throughout. The relative gap between the central and Bundelkhand regions and the Western region, shown in Table 4.6, reflects the pattern of the PCY. But Eastern UP's MPCE has remained at just over three-quarter of the level of Western UP throughout these years, a much smaller gap than that denoted by its PCY.

Broadly then, as one would expect, average consumption levels are less unequal between UP and the country as also between UP's regions. But there are other types of differences that should concern us.

First, as Figure 4.1 shows, rural to urban consumption disparities have steadily increased. Rural consumption was 76 per cent of the urban level in 1983. This fell to 71 per cent in 1993–4, and further to 62.2 per cent in 2004–5. By 2011–12, rural consumption was only 55.4 per cent of urban per capita consumption.

Second, analysis shows that while rural consumption inequality has been low (in comparison to urban inequality), the latter has increased

UTTAR PRADESH UNDER 'NEOLIBERALISM' 79

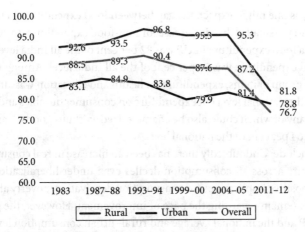

Figure 4.1 MPCE in UP as Percentage of All India MPCE

Table 4.6 Region's MPCE as Percentage of MPCE in Western UP

Region	1983	1993–4	2011–12
Central	79.8	80.3	83.8
Eastern	76.2	76.4	76.7
Southern	67.5	65.3	79.0

Source: Computed from NSS Consumption Expenditure data

significantly.[5] The Gini coefficient of MPCE remained at 0.25 for rural areas between 1993–4 and 2011–12. However, in urban UP, the Gini increased from 0.30 in 1993–4 to 0.35 in 2004–5 and further to 0.42 in 2011–12. As a result, total consumption inequality increased from 0.27 in 1993–4 to 0.31 in 2011–12. This pattern is reflected in UP's regions, all of which show rising urban inequality, although urban structures and economic activity differ across the regions.

---

[5] A longitudinal study of a village in Eastern UP (Srivastava 2016b) where different groups in the village access different segments of the urban job market through migration, remittance, and income flows has kept horizontal inequalities from rising in the village. At a macro level, migration and remittances, on the one hand, and the behaviour of rural wages from 2004–05 to 2011–12 has probably played a major role in checking the rise in rural inequality in consumption.

80 RAVI SRIVASTAVA

Third, as one might expect, the gap between food expenditure in the state and country is smaller than is the case for non-food expenditure. In 2011–12, per capita food expenditure in UP was 82 per cent of the all India level, while non-food expenditure was 74 per cent of the all India level. Among the various sub-group of items, expenditure on health and education was almost on par with the national level but expenditure on consumer durables and 'Other items', many of which could also be characterized as 'status goods', was 52 per cent and 64 per cent of the national level.

To conclude: Undoubtedly there has been an increase in real consumption expenditure across all consumption deciles even under liberalization. This has had positive implications for consumption deprivation/poverty although questions remain regarding the pace of improvement. However, the gap between UP and the national average and rural–urban consumption levels has increased, despite the favourable impact of remittances on rural consumption. Among various factors, rising wages and the pattern of remittances may have contributed to keeping rural consumption inequalities low and stable. But urban inequalities have steadily increased, and there is a large gap in non-food consumption of certain items.

Growth and Inter Social Group Equity

Have market- or state-mediated growth processes under liberalization reduced inequalities in consumption/income/ access to jobs among UP's social groups? The causal channels can be complex and bi-directional, but keeping this mind, we briefly discuss social groups' access to education, land, and jobs, and then to consumption-related outcomes.

In rural areas, access to land is still closely related to livelihood security and economic status. Neoliberal policies rely more on markets rather than on redistributive land policies and changes in land ownership are more likely to be result of autonomous economic processes and land transfers. But to some extent land transfer via distribution and repossession of pattas or its reverse viz. land acquisition by government has also played a role in UP. As noted in Srivastava and Ranjan (2016), data from the NSSO employment-Unemployment Round shows that OBC and General categories own more land than their share in population, whereas the reverse holds for SCs and Muslims. The former two categories owned 83.6 per cent land in 2011–12. However, there has been some accretion of land by SCs whose share in land owned was 8.2 per cent in 1993 and 10.4 per cent in 2011–12, and the

UTTAR PRADESH UNDER 'NEOLIBERALISM' 81

latter is marginally higher than the percentage of land owned in 1983 (10 per cent). The data are less unambiguous for Muslims since estimates how fluctuations between rounds and the trend is also less clear for other groups such as OBCs because of lack of long-term data. SCs and others who accumulate small surpluses through outmigration invest in land purchase. But land transfer via distribution and repossession of *pattas* was also a policy objective of the Mayawati government, and may have partly contributed to these changes.

Education is another key variable which influences access to job markets. The neoliberal economic regime demands greater spatial integration of labour markets inducing a greater competition for valuable jobs. Policy support to education in India shows a clear decline with higher levels of education, since neoliberal economics provides flawed argument that higher levels of education do not have a merit good character. As a result, privatization of higher levels of school education has been increasing. We have shown elsewhere that a secondary or higher secondary level of education constitutes a break point in the access to jobs (Srivastava 2008). In this scenario, we analyse the social-group attainment of a secondary level of education for Hindu SCs, OBCs, and Others, and for Muslims.

We have first carried out a comparison of the trends in social group-wise gap between all India and UP's performance. Indeed, there is a rising gap for all three major social groups. At the same time, the general castes among Hindus not only continued to out perform this category at the all -India level, but the relative gap in its performance increased. In 1983, SCs and Muslim were more or less at par with their counterparts in the country but in 2012, they had fallen behind with nearly 5 per cent gap for SCs (a similar gap also existed for OBCs) and 7 per cent gap for Muslims. On the other the general category of Hindus in the state outperformed the national counterparts by 1.6 per cent in 1999–2000 and this gap increased in their favour to 4.2 per cent by 2011–12.

Within the state also, the inter-group inequity in secondary school education has been rising. For SCs, while the gap between average attainment levels and SC attainment of secondary education was 6 per cent in 1983, it rose to 11.4 per cent in 2011–12. In the case of Muslims, whose attainment of secondary education is the least in UP, the gap was 3.3 per cent in 1983 and rose to 11.6 per cent in 2011–12. For OBCs, the gap persisted but reduced—from 4.8 per cent in 1999–2000 to only 1.1 per cent in 2011–12, and General category of Hindus outperformed the state average by an increasing percentage (21.1 per cent in 1999–2000 and 28.7 per cent in 2011–12).

Growth—particularly the spurt in growth in the first decade of this century—enabled a faster structural change in employment in terms of diversification out of agriculture. Yet for the rural poor and lower castes, this has been towards sectors such as construction with poor working conditions—a higher percentage of SC workers—23 per cent, compared to 17.4 per cent in India—were employed in the construction sector in UP.

Indeed most of the jobs in the non-farm sector are of poor quality. Fresh recruitments in the public sector are now mainly restricted to public security agencies and the social sector. These have been targeted by successive governments to garner jobs for their social base, which has repeatedly come under scrutiny. At the same time, the structural change and the growth of the services sector have brought about some changes towards highly skilled jobs as well as jobs which are salaried and white collar, even if other-wise these jobs have transformed into informal and poorer-quality jobs. One needs to examine the extent to which socially and economically deprived groups in UP have accessed such jobs.

One broad indicator of better (not good) quality jobs is the percentage of workers in regular wage/salaried jobs. This percentage has been improving overall but the percentage of such jobs remains smaller in UP. Between 1983 and 2011–12, the percentage of all workers with regular jobs went up from 8.8 to 10.8 per cent in UP and in the corresponding period, the percentage of regular to total jobs in the country went up from 13.6 to 18.5 per cent, widening the gap from 2 to 4.9 per cent. In fact, this gap has widened after 1993–4 for all major categories in the state.

However, interestingly, within UP, two of the groups that held a very low share of regular jobs—SC and Muslim—have been able to increase this share from a low base (share of OBC in regular jobs, however, still remains low and virtually stagnant).

Educated workers mainly aspire for white-collar jobs. The percentage share of white-collar workers among all workers increased in the state between 1993–4 and 2011–12 by 4 percentage points. The percentage share of white-collar jobs among SCs remains substantially lower than their share in the working population but also increased *paripassu* over this period by 4.7 percentage points. By 2011–12, 9.1 per cent SC workers held white-collar jobs. However, there is no distinct trend in the share of white-collar jobs among Muslims, although compared to the early 1980s or 1990s, the share of white-collar jobs among them increased slightly to 17.7 per cent by 2011–12. Further, while OBCs experienced a small improvement in their occupational status after 1999–2000, the general caste Hindus not only retain the

UTTAR PRADESH UNDER 'NEOLIBERALISM'   83

lion's share of such jobs but also experienced the most improvement in recent years (40.7 per cent general caste workers held white-collar jobs in 2011–12, as against 31.4 per cent in 1999–2000).

Finally, as pointed out earlier, consumption levels (measured by expenditure) are considered to be an important signifier of economic well-being. Growth since liberalization has improved the average real consumption levels for all social groups over time. This also implies that poverty levels, measured by benchmark levels, have been reducing over time. We will again not go into the relative rates of decline in poverty since this depends on the benchmark level (that is, the poverty line) used on which no consensus exists.

Instead, we will focus on relative consumption levels either by comparing average consumption, or the distribution of households across different quintile groups.

First, a comparison of the average per capita consumption levels of the major social categories, relative to the all India average, given in Figure 4.2, shows that in 1983, UP's per capita consumption was about 90 per cent of the country's average for Muslims and 90 per cent of the national level for SCs. Since the 1990s, however, the average MPCE for all these groups and OBCs has drifted downwards in comparison to the national level.

We have also analysed the changes in consumption within each group relative to the other social categories within the state to examine whether consumption distribution has become more equitable across these groups over time. This has been done by examining the percentage of each major social group among the bottom 40 per cent (the consumption poor) and the top 20 per cent (the consumption rich) of the population in terms of their MPCE. Among the bottom 40 per cent population, the share of both Muslims and SCs, shown in Figure 4.3 has increased quite systematically (except for one year—1999–2000 in the case of SCs), but the increase (showing a worsening in consumption distribution) is more significant for Muslims (from 14.2 per cent in 1983 to 20.8 per cent in 2011–12). The SCs form a larger share among the consumption poor and their share increased from 27.3 per cent in 1983 to 31.4 per cent in 2011–12. Till 1999–2000, separate data were not available for OBCs and upper caste Hindus, but their combined share shows a consistent decline (improvement) among the consumption poor. From 1999–2000 onwards, separate data are available for these two categories, and these results show an increase in the percentage of OBCs among the consumption poor, whereas the share of the upper castes declined. Only 5.5 per cent of general caste Hindus were among the consumption poor in 2011–12.

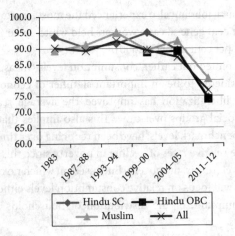

Figure 4.2 Average Monthly Per Capita Expenditure (MPCE) in UP to All India MPCE for Selected Social Groups

The trends in the share of social groups at the higher consumption end are less stable. But overall, the percentage of SC and Muslim households among the well-off households is much lower than their share in the population, particularly for SCs. The Muslim population's share in the top quintile has slowly drifted upwards while the share of the OBC/General population segment shows a small decline after 1993–4. The share of SC population in highest consumption quintile has fluctuated over the years, but remained lower at 11.6 per cent in 2011–12, compared to 13.3 per cent in 1983. The OBC/General share increased from 1983 to 1993–94 but has remained more or less stable at 72 per cent.

Thus, after economic liberalization, the consumption of the socially deprived groups has declined in UP relative to their national consumption levels. Within the state, a higher percentage of SC and Muslim households has joined the ranks of the consumption poor among the bottom 40 per cent. Among these groups, there is some evidence that consumption inequality has worsened since their representation in the top 20 per cent has either remained the same or increased slightly. A comparison of the Gini coefficient for 1993–4 and 2011–12 shows that intra social group inequality in consumption worsened for all social categories. Between these years, it increased from 0.29 to 0.32 among Muslims, 0.28 to 0.32 among (Hindu) SCs, and 0.33 to 0.38 among OBC/general caste Hindu.

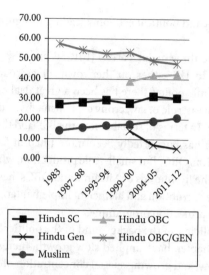

Figure 4.3 Percentage Share of Social Groups in the Bottom Two Quintiles in UP

To conclude: growth has undoubtedly resulted in some improvement in the status of SCs, Muslim, and OBCs in matters of education attainment, average levels of consumption, per cent accessing regular or white-collar jobs, and land ownership. But at the same time, the gap with the improvement made by the same social groups at the national level, and with upper castes within UP, has also grown on most indicators. Moreover, intra-group inequality among the deprived social groups has also increased over time.[6]

Ensuing Contradictions of Neoliberal Growth—A Concluding Note

Neoliberal policies adopted by the Union government in India since the early 1990s became the general prototype of changes pursued by provinces. Although liberalization and globalization have limited the autonomous policy sphere for states, these policies are refracted through specific

---

[6] Social group impacts and their link with political regimes and change have also been analysed by us in different papers (Srivastava 2007, 2012b, 2016).

state-level factors and political economy leading to significant variations in outcome.

Since 1989, the three major parties (BJP, SP, and BSP) have participated in governments in UP, either on their own, or as coalition partners. In matters of economic policy, there has been a great deal of continuity in the state marked by weak rule of law, crony capitalism, discretionary, and ad hoc decision-making. In terms of social policy, the BSP and the SP have followed an agenda which has purportedly been more tilted in favour of dalits and Muslims or Muslim/OBC. But small-scale production, which forms the economic basis for the livelihoods of Muslims and OBCs, has languished in the state. Large-scale corruption and inefficient implementation have limited the benefits of social protection programmes.

Neoliberal policies, in the background of the political economy characterized in this chapter, have implied slow growth, increasing gap with the national economy, and growing spatial concentration of industrial growth. The state economy has been unable to produce sufficient jobs accelerating outmigration across the spectrum of workers. Migration has significant impacts on consumption patterns and preferences, cultural values, socio-political and economic factors. Remittances have acted as a buffer for consumption. Nevertheless, the gap between consumption levels in the state and national level has grown and inequality between rural and urban consumption, and within urban areas has increased significantly. Given this pattern of growth, the upper castes remain highly over-represented among the consumption rich, the landed classes, and among those with better jobs. On the other hand, SCs and Muslims have now a higher weight among the consumption poor, with some evidence of an intra-group increase in consumption inequality. Indeed, although still grossly represented there is some improvement in their access to good-quality jobs and land. This should caution us with treating social categories as homogenous.

Globalization and neoliberal capitalism with its centrality of markets and consumerism, and the spread of communication technologies, have been impacting on cultural patterns and consumer preferences, particularly of the youth. In the case of UP, migration also reinforces these changes. But the real economy, which reinforces a hierarchy of access to jobs, incomes, and consumption produces a strong hiatus between real choices and virtual preferences. Given the outcome of neoliberal policies, this hiatus is exceptionally large for UP as a whole, and differs significantly across spaces, sectors, and social classes.

The combination of very limited improvements at the bottom combined with rising inequalities in jobs, incomes and patterns of consumption across, and even within, social classes are creating an aspirational pressure cooker, which we can hardly ignore.

References

Ahluwalia, Montek S. 2000. 'Economic Performance of States in Post-Reform Period'. *Economic and Political Weekly*, May 6.

GoI (Government of India). 2017. *Economic Survey 2016–17*. Economic Division. Department of Economic Affairs. Ministry of Finance.

Government of Uttar Pradesh, Planning Department. 2003. 'First Human Development Report of Uttar Pradesh'. Lucknow: Planning Department.

Government of Uttar Pradesh, Planning Department. 2007. 'Uttar Pradesh Human Development Report 2003'. Lucknow: Planning Department.

Kohli, Atul. 1987. *State and Poverty in India: Politics of Reform*. New York: Cambridge University Press.

Kohli, Atul. 2006. 'Politics of Economic Growth in India, 1980–2005. Part II: The 1990s and Beyond'. *Economic and Political Weekly*. April 8: 1361–70.

Kohli, Atul. 2009. 'States and Economic Development'. *Brazilian Journal of Political Economy*, 29 (2): 212–27, April–June.

Kohli, Atul. 2012. *Poverty amid Plenty in the New India*. New Delhi: Cambridge University Press.

Mishra, Nripendra K. and Ravi Srivastava. 2004. 'Technological Choice in Textile Industry Revisited: The Handloom-Powerloom Controversy'. *Artha Vijnana*, XLVI (3–4 Sept–Dec): 373–88.

NCEUS (National Commission for Enterprises in the Unorganised Sector). 2007. *Conditions of Work and Promotion of Livelihood in the Unorganised Sector*. New Delhi: Government of India.

Pai, Sudha, ed. 2007. *Political Processes in Uttar Pradesh: Identity, Economic Reforms and Governance*. New Delhi: Pearson Longman.

Patnaik, Utsa. 2010. 'A Critical Look at Some Propositions on Consumption and Poverty'. *Economic and Political Weekly* 45 (6, 6 Feb): 74–80. Available at https://www.epw.in/journal/2010/06.

Sengupta, Arjun, G Raveendran, K.P. Kannan. 2006. India's Common People: Who Are They, How Many Are They and How Do They Live? *Economic and Political Weekly* 43 (11, 15 Mar): 49–63.

Srivastava, Ravi. 1995. 'India's Uneven Development and Its Implications for Political Processes: An Analysis of Some Recent Trends'. In *Industry and Agriculture in India since Independence, Vol 2, Social Change and Political Discourse in India, Structures of Power, Movements and Resistance in India*, edited by T. V. Sathyamurthy, 219–47. New Delhi: Oxford University Press.

Srivastava, Ravi. 2007. 'Economic Change among Social Groups in Uttar Pradesh, 1983–2000'. In *Political Processes in Uttar Pradesh: Identity, Economic Reforms and Governance*, edited by Sudha Pai, 345–361. New Delhi: Pearson Longman.

Srivastava, Ravi. 2008. 'Education, Skills, and the Emerging Labour Market in India'. *The Indian Journal of Labour Economics* 51 (4, Oct.-Dec): 759–782.

Srivastava, Ravi. 2012a. 'Performance of Anti-Poverty Programmes in Indian States: Identifying the Achilles Heel'. *Indian Journal of Human Development* 6 (2): 149–74.

Srivastava, Ravi. 2012b. 'Economic Change and Social Inclusion in Uttar Pradesh, 1983–2010'. *UPEA Journal*, August 2012, Revised Presidential Lecture, Seventh Annual Conference of the Uttar Pradesh and Uttarakhand Economics Association, October 2011.

Srivastava, Ravi. 2016. 'Assessing Change: Land, Labour and Employment in an Eastern UP Village, 1994–2012'. In *Longitudinal Research in Village India: Methods and Findings*, edited by Praveen Jha Himanshu and Gerry Rodgers, 32–41. New Delhi: Oxford University Press.

Srivastava, Ravi and Rahul Ranjan. 2016. 'Deciphering Growth and Development—Past and Present'. *Economic and Political Weekly* 51, LI, (53, 31 Dec) (Special Issue on 'Uttar Pradesh: Vortex of Change'): 32–41.

Srivastava, Ravi S. 2003. 'India's Uneven Development: An Analysis of Some Recent Trends and Implications'. *The Indian Journal of Economics*, June.

Tripathi, P. 2004. 'Industry and Concerns, *Frontline*, February 14–27.

Drèze, Jean and Amartya Sen. 1997. *Indian Development: Selected Regional Perspectives*. New Delhi: Oxford University Press.

World Bank. 2010. 'India Living Conditions and Human Development in Uttar Pradesh: A Regional Perspective April 30, 2010'. Report No. 43573-IN, Poverty Reduction and Economic Management, South Asia.

5

The Urban Experience in Contemporary India[*]

Sujata Patel

Every day we note new buildings being constructed even if these become dilapidated almost immediately, new roads being dug which with one rainfall spurt potholes, new pipelines being laid, however badly. All such initiatives take place in what the contemporary state has designated as urban and rural areas. Our cities have become crowded and polluted with people jostling against hand carts, bicycles, motorcycles and cars, and negotiating potholes. In the midst of all this, there are broken pavements, homes and slums, street markets selling goods and processed food, as well agricultural activities. Urbanization is all over without our peasants becoming industrial working classes and discontinuing agricultural activities. This is accurate depiction of not only big and large cities or small and medium towns but also of villages which soon convert themselves into new satellite towns and merge with metropolitan ones creating a never-ending urban corridor.

But this visual record paradoxically does not match with the census data sets. Incredibly, the 2011 census data set gives us a different picture; it suggests that India is 31 per cent urban and indicates a sluggish growth of urbanization with the annual exponential growth of urban population almost similar to that of the decade back; the difference being a mere 0.03 per cent. Additional data available from the National Sample Survey (NSS) reinforces this trend. It suggests that migration from rural to urban has declined. The NSS data notes that the share of adult male migrants in the adult male population has declined from 32 per cent in 1999–2000 to 31 per cent in 2007–8

---

[*] This is the revised version of the Presidential Address at the 43rd All India Sociological Conference held at Lucknow University, Lucknow, Uttar Pradesh on 10 November 2017 and published as 'Rethinking Urban Studies Today' in *Sociological Bulletin* 67 (1): 1–19, 2018. The author wishes to acknowledge that sections of this article were presented in longer versions as the Satynendra Nath Sen Memorial Lecture for the Asiatic Society in January 2017, Kolkata, and as A. R. Desai Memorial Lecture at the University of Mumbai in March 2017.

Sujata Patel, *The Urban Experience in Contemporary India* In: *Neoliberalism, Urbanization, and Aspirations in Contemporary India*. Edited by: Sujata Patel, Oxford University Press. © Oxford University Press 2021.
DOI: 10.1093/oso/9780190132019.003.0005

90 SUJATA PATEL

and migration for economic reasons has gone down among the rural–urban migrants. The census together with other data sets informs us that except when it is discussing census towns (settlements which have more than 5,000 population wherein 75 per cent males are employed in non-agricultural activities and there is a density of more than 400 per square kilometre), which it notes has increased, there seems to be little to no exponential growth of urbanization (Kundu 2011). Additionally, secondary literature on returns on agriculture has noted that the latter is no longer an enticing activity for many of the non-urban population. Thus, we have an anomaly that we have to square up. While the census suggests stagnation in both urban growth and agricultural incomes, the visual documentation notes increasing building activities, roads and transport facilities, growth of gated communities, shopping malls and increasing movement of population to service these activities. It seems that the census data obfuscates the extent of organized and unorganized or informal urbanization in the country. Thus, the question: Where do we start our discussion when we think of the urban today and how is it related to growing and expanding urbanization process?

This chapter attempts to answer these questions in the next four sections. I start by suggesting a need for deconstructing the statistics on urban in order to understand the complex patterns organizing urban India. In the first section I present the debate on how to define the urban and deconstruct the statistics in the census. In the next section, I discuss the specific nature of urban inequalities and exclusions in India and assess recent material regarding spatial exclusions in context to caste, minorities, and gender. The third section examines the nature of work and labour and relates it with family, kin, and caste groupings. Lastly, in the fourth section, I examine the nature of urban policy, planning, and governance and explore how the aspirational middle classes of the country determine new spatial strategies of urbanization. The urban process in India I am arguing expresses itself in variegated spatial manners within these above-mentioned characteristics of urbanization.

Statistical Spin and Urbanization

Scholars in India have suggested that satellite data indicates that India's urbanization has increased to more than 40 per cent and if one used only one index, that of settlements having more than 5000 people, it would increase to 47 per cent, with its south and western regions having urban growth as high as 60 to 70 per cent. In order to comprehend the discrepancy between census and other data sources scholars have presented two sets of hypotheses to capture the nature of contemporary urban expansion. The first hypothesis is that of *rurbanization* (Kundu 2017) (settlements having urban characteristics while retaining rural socio-economic base) which while continuing to use census figures together with the formal definitions of city boundaries suggests that India has a unique pattern of urbanization and that this is developing new variegated urban geographies. It highlights three such processes. First, it suggests that there is a real expansion in the periphery of highly developed regions because large cities have become exclusionary (Kundu 2009). Consequently, there is relocation and outsourcing of enterprises to its outskirts, leading to migration and informalization of work and housing, and simultaneously and paradoxically, the growth of gated communities. These trends of peripheral rurbanization are evident in satellite cities and large urban agglomerations.

Second, there is a decrease in in-migration and increase in out-migration with declining investments in small and medium towns in backward regions of the country as part of policy initiatives of central and state governments. A large number of small and medium towns (except for a small minority which are university towns or are constituted around public-sector units) have sluggish growth, stagnation, and fluctuating agricultural economy (Kundu 2011). Their rurbanization is linked to regional integration. Third, there is a sharp increase of a number of census towns (almost 2500 more such have been declared in 2011 census) because these satisfy the demographic criteria, but many of these have not been given statutory status by their respective state governments. As a consequence, these have not been provided with urban infrastructure (that is, sanitation facilities, tarred roads, water supply, etc.) and these thus remain rurbanized. The census, it has been argued, has not been able to capture the complex diversities in urbanization processes and has proved inadequate in comprehending these processes.

The second hypothesis titled, subaltern urbanization has defined urbanization as 'autonomous, economically vital and independent of the metropolis' and is perceived to be a process that comprehends cities as a system of interrelationships (Mukhopadhyay et al. 2017). Re-emphasizing many of the processes highlighted earlier, that of morphological growth rather than population movement, that of small and medium town developments, that of growth due to transportation and historical reasons, the authors argue that subaltern settlements are those that have a significant population in cities just below Class 1. For example, about 41 per cent of India's urban population reside in small towns with less than 100,000 population. The spatial spread of

92 SUJATA PATEL

urbanization can be located not only in the increase of census towns but also in what it calls settlement agglomerations. These territories have emerged due to economic and historical reasons and whose developments have not been noted in the census. If these geographies are taken into account, the urban population may be pushed up by another 10 per cent, that is, India it declares is at least 39 per cent plus urban, if not more.

What do these perspectives tell us? First, this narrative suggests that one must use the census data with caution and certainly not initiate an assessment of the urban by limiting oneself to it. These analyses have also suggested that the urban is now encapsulated outside officially declared towns and cities and within what is may be officially called rural. In other words, official data have made invisible the urban as it has folded itself in villages and into the so-called rural.

The second point of significance is that the urban need not be about density, numbers of workers doing industrial/urban work nor about the existence of official institutions of urban governance, such as the municipalities. Additionally, today's economy does not have a strict distinction between work which is rural and that which is urban and thus it is possible that villages may have households where seasonal migrants may be employed in tertiary work and who may be also doing agricultural work. We all know that the Canadian geographer T.G. McGee has used Indonesian material to call this form of urbanization the 'desakota'.

The third point is related to policy. In a large number of cases, it is because of the state's classification system that many census towns have not been declared as statutory towns. This has had a negative impact on these settlements, for these have not been declared urban but consequently, they have not been provided full urban services and have been forced to remain 'rural'. Fourth, in these circumstances, it is important to accept that the present urbanization process is articulating variegated and segmented geographies across the country. Thus, there is spatial segmentation and inequalities between settlements within India. Thus, not only will one perspective not fit all, but it demands a particular and specific historiographical comprehension to understand these uneven and variegated patterns being articulated by capitalist urbanization. We thus need to ask: do we have tools to assess this? Fifth and lastly, it is difficult to continue to use the binary of urban as against rural any longer. Rather this discussion demands that we now have to reconstitute our deliberations regarding rural/agrarian/peasant societies in India. Unfree labour, casteism, and patriarchy in employment and popular forms of everyday culture related to these ideologies pervade the entire

THE URBAN EXPERIENCE   93

country and are being differently articulated given the variegated histories and geographies of settlements but they are and remain present in all parts of India.

Inequalities and Exclusions of Urban India

I have already highlighted the constraints in the existing data sets; these are related to conceptual incoherence. In these circumstances how do we fit the ground realities which we can observe with the conceptual and discursive universe which is pre-given? We need a starting point and thus let me initiate the discussion on urban inequalities with a description of the slum which is regarded by economists, geographers, and activists as the quintessential representation of the urban today and also of 'southern urbanism' (Rao 2006). UN documents giving data on urban growth immediately slip into a discussion on slums as the problem characterizing urbanism in the Global South. The slum is defined generally as an informal and a non-legal settlement of dense population, characterized by substandard housing, little to no services in the form of water, sanitation, and other infrastructure and a lifestyle of squalor (UN-Habitat 2003). Given this description, most academics and activists including those who are from the NGO sector have asked whether slums represent poverty and further whether data on number of slums, size, and regional spread will give us an idea of urban poverty in India and thus give us a peep into inequalities of living, housing, and social services in India.

Unfortunately, to answer this question, we have to again go back to the census data sets, because these do give numbers for slum settlements across cities and towns of India. The census started collecting information on slums in early 2000. The 2001 census states that 43 million (that is, 23 per cent) of India's urban population live in slums and by 2011 census, this number had increased to 93 million. Some cities such as Mumbai had, according to the census, nearly 50 per cent of its population living in slums while cities such as Chennai and Delhi had 19 per cent. However, the 2011 data does not record existence of slums in many cities and towns in India raising the question whether these have been enumerated and if so, whether these do not have slums. If it is the latter, then why do such cities not have slums? It seems that there is a problem in enumeration because on one hand a government report published in 2010 covering around 5,000 plus towns and cities gives the slum populations as being 75.3 million (26.3 per cent of India's urban population)

94 SUJATA PATEL

and on the other the UN-Habitat report of 2001 states that Indian's urban slum population was 158.4 million (55 per cent of its urban population). But despite these confusing data if we have to assess the vulnerabilities faced by the slum population then we need to match the above statistics with the information in government records, that more than 30 per cent of those who live in slums have no tenure (legal right) over their land and house. In this context one can comprehend the insecurities in which this population lives (Dupont 2011).

Further, if we incorporate slum or slum-like characteristics as an index for poverty, then it is possible that the numbers of poor may increase exponentially. For example, if we add the entire urban population living outside officially declared towns and cities then the number of such poor may be more. Also, analysts have pointed out these numbers miss households that may be poor, but which have not been designated slums. This has led some commentators to examine the number of households which do not have access to services such as water and sanitation and relate these to household assets to determine poverty levels. Others have distinguished one room households with or without kitchens and tabulate these with access to water and toilets to create a map of spatial inequalities across the country. But what about people who live in non-urban areas which house themselves in temporary, non-permanent, and non-serviceable shelters and have little to no access to sanitation, drainage, and potable water. Should we also not add these numbers? If we add these numbers to the general numbers mentioned earlier, the proportion of poor increases geometrically. No wonder, commentators (Jana and Bhan 2013) suggest a need to move beyond the slums and examine access to services, particularly toilets and potable water as criteria for defining poverty. This as we know has huge implications for women and relates to their body and its security. As a consequence, I shift the discussion away from poverty to exclusions in the form of spatial inequalities and segregation (Bhan and Jana 2015). In order to comprehend exclusions, we need to place the above analysis with information regarding group affiliation. If this is done, we get a peep into the nature of the discrimination that the contemporary urban process has propagated and simultaneously assess how spatial inequality is linked to segregation. There is evidence that a large number of SCs and STs who live in outer wards of the city may be suffering from segregation because of lack of access to urban services.

Does this imply caste and tribe discrimination? A recent study (Vithayathil and Singh 2012) suggests that caste and tribe segregation increases when equated with access to in-house drinking water and access to in-house

THE URBAN EXPERIENCE   95

latrines. This study also attests some mega cities such as Kolkata are more segregated than Chennai (almost 20 per cent more). Earlier, Roy (2008) had suggested that most of the urban poor stay in the urban periphery in Kolkata. It is important to note further that the degree of segregation increases in small and medium towns. Additionally, this study has suggested that in almost 60 per cent of Indian cities segregation has not lessened in the last two decades, rather it has worsened. This evidence alludes to the nature of post-1990s urban policies which I will discuss in the last section. Data on segregation of religious minorities is difficult to get though one study does suggest that the Muslim minority and Dalit groups occupy on average 12.6 and 19.8 per cent less floor area, respectively, compared with the majority of the population. Some in-depth ethnographic accounts have also suggested that the services and conditions of housing have dilapidated in case of Muslim localities particularly in the post-2002 period as a consequence of bias or lack of interest in these groups by municipal authorities. This study is of Kolkata but there may be evidence for other cities such as Ahmedabad and Bombay. Additionally, there is evidence that in a large number of cities rented places outside these segregated areas are not available for minorities and Dalit groups (Sidhwani 2015). Urbanization and modernity are supposed to filter pre-modern social affiliations such as caste and religiosities; in India these seem to be increasing.

Work, Labour, and Its In-securities

What is the nature of employment structure and how does this affect spatial inequalities and segregation? Scholars have recognized for some time now that Indian economy has not transited towards industrial manufacturing and that a significant part of Indian work force—almost 85 per cent (Jha 2016) are laboring as informal workers. Studies of increasing informalization and casualization of the workforce in the manufacturing sector together with other studies that evaluate occupations being practised by various members of slum households draw our attention to the fact that most of the slums house workers that labour in urban informal low-end service economies such as garbage collection, small-time retailing, or as domestic servants. About one-third of the informal workers are also self-employed. These studies have raised questions regarding the relationship of informality of work and urban poverty (Jana and Bhan 2013). Rather than poverty being related to the slum settlement, surely we have to ask whether inequalities and exclusions are not organically connected to the expanding informal economies of work

96 SUJATA PATEL

and labour being organized in contemporary India. Informal work has been described as unregulated work, it is low paid, unskilled, and flexible with long working hours, little to no social security and is segmented in terms of caste and gender (Harris-White and Gooptu 2001). Informal work is not restricted to the urban areas but is spread across the country and is enmeshed in all economic activities, be it agriculture or low- and high-end service activities. Informal work is present in large industries such as construction, quarrying, transport, hospitality, and as well as in small micro manufacturing units and also includes the self-employed. It integrates individuals in semi-independent peasant households who may have some land, but also may own small family businesses, small assets, and some household members could also be simultaneously petty commodity producers and traders and those who migrate across all these activities. These households exploit their own family members and also hire in and hire out their labour in various seasons.

Thus, it is clear that in India this economy is not confined to the urban arena and organized only within towns and cities as it is sometimes thought. Scholars argue that this economy combines some amount of regulation with extensive non-regulation in the use of natural resources, capital, technology, and labour. They suggest that informal work and labour are being reproduced as an economy that is highly competitive, mobile, driven by short-term profits combining various kinds of technologies (from primitive to mechanized to informational), relations of production together with control and discipline of labour (from unfree/bondage/slave labour to free and self-employed) and sites (households, sweatshops, small-scale industrial units, agricultural land) in variegated places. Thus, a household/family may have members doing agriculture work, fishing, home-based production, participate in sweat shops activities, and also do retailing across time and territories in so-called urban and rural areas (Patel and Jadhav 2011). In this context within India commentators have redefined the notion of urban commons. Its definition is no longer restricted to public gardens, sea faces, or clean air. Urban commons are sites such as ponds where fisher people fish or land where peasants' households grow vegetables and flowers or graze their livestock, and where they sell these products for retail marketing to supplement their everyday income (Parthasarathy 2011). These are not private areas but community areas and can be everywhere in cities and towns and also in officially designated non-urban area.

No wonder, it is suggested that informal economies promote spatialization through short-term and long-term migration as families fragment into two to three households, two to three dwellings and regroup with other labourers

THE URBAN EXPERIENCE 97

into new households or with new families. In this situation it is difficult to distinguish when the dwelling, household, and the family are separate or together. Wages remain low and segmented in terms of gender and ethnicity/caste. As a result, competitive wages and long-term work are never continuously available to all labourers.

As this is not a recognized legal system and is based on the absolute poverty of the workers, it affects the long-term stability of households as an economic unit and thus of continuity of dwellings and larger settlements, and in turn investments in housing. Also, sociologists working on these economies propose that the distinctiveness of this new economy is in the way it organizes the ideologies of pre-modern sociabilities to structure in uneven and diverse ways the processes and sites of production, distribution, consumption, and reproduction of settlements through social networks rather than legal processes. As a result, this economy creates islands/places of culturally distinct spatial systems of economy, social, and communication networks integrated to each other and yet dispersed across the country geographically having variegated networks depending on the legal and political jurisdiction it is located within.

Given its unregulated and non-legal orientation, these informal economies push labour to reproduce themselves in highly insecure vulnerable conditions of work and housing. This vulnerability represents itself as a slum in urban areas that is when these labourers construct temporary and non-permanent households built with recycled material pieces of wood, cardboard tarpaulin, and corrugated sheets. These are later defined by policymakers as slums. It is my argument that slums of urban India do not necessary represent this economy; rather it is the nature of the economy that creates such settlements, and these are to be found in both towns and cities and in villages across India.

A combination of intermediate classes controls this economy in a maze of outsourcing processes that organize production, distribution, consumption, and reproduction of commodities housing and services together with the reproduction of households and families. The flexibility of the system demands that work and living are intermittent leading to high levels of insecurity with wages and security of tenure almost never providing real-food equivalence and continuity of reproduction.

This affects most negatively the vulnerable strata of the populations: women, children, and caste/ethnic groups (Harris-White and Gooptu 2001). The conflicts in such a system are between various competitive fractional intermediate class groups who control the market of labour, commodities

98 SUJATA PATEL

(including that of consumption and services), and capital. They control labour through a combination of class and pre-modern ideologies of caste/ethnicity/religious, gender, and sexuality, thereby segmenting labour. Thus, rarely do we see in this system the classic capital–labour conflict. Rather in most instances the struggle over resources is organized in terms of ethnic or religious confrontations.

The distinctiveness of this new economy in the way it organizes the ideologies of pre-modern sociabilities to structure in uneven and diverse ways the places of production, distribution, consumption, and reproduction. As a consequence, we see the growth of both individual (gendered and caste) and collective (communal) violence in which the state (at all levels of administration) participates through acts of commissions and omissions instigating on one hand competitive politics among and between the poor and on the other pogroms by the rightist storm troopers. In the last decade individual and collective violence of this kind has increased and is taking place in all parts of the country—in cluster of villages, small towns, and medium-sized cities and in metros.

Researchers have suggested that this form of contemporary urban process has enveloped this economy and given it a distinct new identity. It is important to mention at this juncture that what we are seeing today as the urban process is not only restricted to India. On the basis of the Indonesian material, the geographer McGee (2002, 10) has called such coexistence and intensively intermingled urban and agricultural forms of land use and settlement as desakota. In this context how do we assess the economic reforms initiated by the government? Will it help to lessen spatial inequalities and unequal access to services? Does it help the state to intervene to distil segregation?

Urban Policies, Governance, and the New Middle Class

I have presented two propositions in the earlier part of my presentation: the first suggests that until recently there was an uncritical rendering of the urban experience in India by professional social sciences and whenever some effort was made in this direction, it was biased towards an analysis of India's big metropolis and megacities and towards its elite. It is only recently that we are seeing a reflective assessment of the urban outside large cities which examines small and medium towns and has been shown in the earlier sections focuses on the living conditions of the poor, the marginalized, and

THE URBAN EXPERIENCE   99

the excluded. Second, I have also suggested that policy formulations were also caught in a similar time wrap; the census is a prime example of this discourse. In this section I take a stock of the critiques made of urban policies which have been variously termed disconnected, changing continuously without any rhyme or reason, formulated in fit and starts, myopic, opaque, and chaotic and constituted through discursive incoherence (Shaw 2008).

I discuss and elaborate on three themes: first, the inconsistencies in the content of urban policies; second, paradoxes regarding decentralized governance and the impact of economic reforms; and third, the new middle class on policymaking and governance (Mehra 2017).

Urbanists have shown how during the last seven decades urban policy went through three phases of contradictory reformulations. These contradictions were related to the lack of clarity about what to emphasize and which class interest to support. On one hand, the state showed interest in developing urban pockets that benefitted the middle- and upper-income groups and simultaneously used banal and un-thought of socialist policies to cater the urban poor. This can be seen in all three phases of its development during the plan periods from 1951 to 2012.

In the first phase of the initial three plan period, the focus of the government was to create industrial towns around public sector manufacturing units and to settle refugee populations. The model that they used was that of UK's 'new town movement' wherein towns were purposefully planned to remedy overcrowding and congestion. Thus, in the early years after independence, new towns and cities suddenly emerged wherein low- and middle-class housing was promoted. Examples of this are Rourkela, Bhillai, Durgapur, Bokaro, and Faridabad (for refugees). Second, urban policy had a general mandate to provide housing and services to those sites in large cities where slums had developed. Lastly, there was an attempt to promote regional development through urban land regulation and the use of master plans to provide housing, clear slums, and rehabilitate the population.

These three discrete interventions were reorganized in the second phase which covered the fourth to the sixth plan period. In this phase, the government extended the mandate of slum clearance and combined it with balanced regional development with the goal to promote small and medium towns. This new policy however found little acceptance as it asked the state governments to initiate these changes. In this phase, the state recognizing that land had come to have a high exchange value and introduced hurriedly the Urban Land (Ceiling and Regulation) act 1976. This act was part of the populist measures initiated by the Indira Gandhi government during the

Emergency and as a consequence of pressure from the real estate lobby was later withdrawn. In the last phase that is from the seventh to the twelfth plan period the urban economy was opened to private participation and to planning mechanisms.

The state inaugurated new housing policy for the involvement of the private sector and repealed the Urban Land (Ceiling and Regulation Act. Other programmes and schemes allowed market-based regimes to be introduced displacing earlier subsidy based infrastructural projects in areas such as health and education. This is the time the state also introduced the 74th Constitutional Amendment creating mechanisms for democratic decentralization in the local bodies promoting further inconsistencies in the execution of policies and governance (Shaw 2008). The conflicts and contradictions outlined above in urban policy also found reflection in the various administrative mechanisms that governed local bodies. Available literature attests that by and large the principle of decentralization was missing in urban governance even though since the colonial period there have been attempts to transfer many functions of governance to local municipalities and corporations and after independence these rights were provided to rural India.

The colonial legacy had given power to the elite citizens, that is, those who owned land and paid property tax, and this has not changed in recent times when through the 74th Constitutional Amendment Act, for the first time an attempt to devolve powers was made. But many states have subverted the implementation of this act (Mehta and Mehta 2010). For example, except in Shimla there is no direct election of Mayors and Deputy Mayors. State governments which have always determined the functions, power, and finances of the municipalities have not allowed its implementation and have postponed municipal elections or had them when these are convenient to them politically.

Also the state and central governments have formed supra state agencies which have controlled the decision-making regarding services, such as slum boards. And sometimes the centre and the states have given powers to more than one ministry and department to handle services. For example, three ministries handle water supply in India and it is demarcated from sanitation. This has resulted in confusing, uncertain situation of governance, where penal action coexists with tolerance, service provisions exist without norms and entitlements, and institutions are expected to maintain infrastructure and deliver services without financial contribution.

Overlapping domains and the uncertain fixation of responsibility and accountability have meant that, on the one hand, the disempowerment

THE URBAN EXPERIENCE   101

of urban local governments while, on the other, a culture of politicized institutions, poor service standards, opacity, and non-accountability also thrives, resulting in apathy and alienation towards local governments (Bhide 2017). The question that we have to ask thus is how these inconsistencies do and contradictions in policy and governance play out since the 1990s when economic reforms were initiated. I would contend in the 1990s through structural reform, the India state conceptualized a coherent urban policy and put in place economic and administrative instruments to realize it. There was a vision here of what kind of India the state wanted to create and there was a clarity of the instrument that it wants to promote to constitute it—the middle class. Let me elaborate.

First, the goal of economic reforms programme was to expand the economy through an intervention in physical infrastructure, that is, roads, transport facilities, and communication, thereby encouraging the relative transformation of all areas of the country into the urban form. Second, since the 1990s, the Indian state reorganized its economic and fiscal policies to not only encourage private investment in the tertiary sector, such as in physical infrastructure, but also in construction and housing, in hospitality and tourist businesses, in professional/service sector education and health and integrated these with information and communication technologies (ICT). Third, the goal has been to ensure continuous expansion and circulation of commodities and of the money market by speeding up the information systems of this sector and thus make their use efficient and rational.

Fourth, to aid this process, the state created new institutions, changed legal instruments, introduced new policies of privatization, and created an economy of real estate and land market as also of other services, such as electricity, sanitation, roads, education, and health. Reforms have also commodified markets in natural resources which have limited circulation such as water and then promoting its privatization. If the political economy discourse during the post-1950s phase was incoherence of policy and an unstated belief that industrialization would power urbanization and development programmes would aid poverty alleviation, today it has changed radically; it is that of private consumption economies stimulating growth and a belief that this growth would alleviate poverty. As a consequence, the state's priorities have shifted. It is to encourage the growth of middle class which will fuel the consumption economy and thereby enlarge the market.

It is now recognized that the growing visibility of the 'middle classes' marks the emergence of a wider national political culture of liberalizing India. The middle classes represent the cultural symbols of the nation. Fernandes (2004)

102 SUJATA PATEL

has argued that the new political culture promoted by the middle classes shifts the earlier ideologies that promoted poverty alleviation and a form of asceticism and in urban areas allowed middle-class housing to coexist with slums to a new ideology where it represents *the* nation. She suggests that this new discourse is not about emptying places or regions but of 'forgetting' the discourses that assessed how economics and politics structure the marginalization of groups and about forgetting intellectually and emotionally the poor and the working classes. It is about sanitizing and naturalizing the Indian society and representing it as a group of people climbing the ladder of mobility; it was about being an aspiration class and leading an aspirational nation. As a consequence, this class has now built various strategies of 'spatial purification' to erase the presence of the poor from its gaze.

The new middle classes were initially created by redefining their lifestyles. The availability of commodities such as cell-phones, colour televisions, washing machines, and cars was made initially and these became status markers that distinguished this social group. Later, leisure became a critical social space for the production of such social distinctions and huge investments were made in this industry. If large dams and steel plants were the icons of Nehruvian India, that of bowling alleys, ice-skating rinks, video parlours, restaurants, malls and amusement parks, beauty salons, religious monuments are the icons of the new India of the liberalizing middle class.

This class has grown in strength and has now created for itself a political project. This has been possible because it has now identified for itself its economic, social, and cultural interests. Consequently, in various cities and towns of the country, fractions of the middle classes have evolved political strategies to control and extend its influence over the urban space. If part of the city has been taken over to install gated communities, the other part has beautification projects in public spaces and cleansing projects to remove dirt and ugliness embodied in the slums, and those represented by the pavement hawkers. This assertive middle-class identity is articulated both in public discourses and in a range of cultural and social forms such as the development of new urban aesthetics and claims on public urban space through the emergence of new civil and community organizations.

Commentators have suggested that chaotic, myopic, and opaque, incoherent state policies (which I have discussed earlier) have helped this identity formation. The ambivalences of policy and inconsistencies within governance have allowed the middle classes to use the local state bodies to take over the public spaces and privatize them, be it the sea beach, gardens, promenades, *maidans*, or streets. This collaboration between the state and the middle class has provided a critical model of 'urban livability' today that actively excludes marginalized social groups. Thus, it is no surprise to note that with the middle classes has converted themselves as the 'common man' in the public discourse. The 'other' has been variously identified as the slum dweller. For them the 'other' is the slum dweller or the poor, the illegal migrant or the Muslim minority who they argue accesses through illegal means all public services which are meant for them, the real citizens of the country.

Srivastava (2014) who has dissected this discourse for Delhi has called it postnationalist. He suggests that the middle class once it identifies itself as a common man finds it easy to use the radical language of nationalist politics designed in an earlier period to confront colonialism now in a new context. For Srivastava, postnationalism is associated with framing of the new middle class and with it a national 'family' as being a nuclear family who combines modern values with 'traditional' concerns and thus tries to project itself as the new Indian. Politically this class questions the subsidies given to the poor alleging that the poor are constantly accessing illegally public resources. In this new political culture, the slum dweller/poor/minority is perceived as a criminal and a threat. It is in this context one has to examine the new Smart City policy of the present government which aim to have completely isolate sections of the new cities for the inhabitation of the middle and upper classes of India.

Towards a Conclusion

I started this article with the suggestion that we need reorganize our sociological gaze to comprehend the ways in which urbanization is restructuring our national, regional, and local spaces in context of global dynamics. I am suggesting that even though India may not have been declared as urban in and through government statistics, the country has become urban. There are of course differences among various localities regions with the country depending on the way these inequities and exclusions are being experiences in different ways. I have argued that contemporary urbanization is creating variegated and uneven geographies and these geographies are related to the way capital accumulation, led and deepened by state policies creates *representation of spaces* which groups makes into places (settlements) through *spatial practices*. In this article I have outlined four attributes for study of contemporary urbanization: intersections of class, caste, gender, and ethnicity in the constitution of inequities and exclusions of spaces; relations of

104 SUJATA PATEL

these inequities with informalization of work, labour, and services including housing, water, and sanitation; neoliberal state policies and its discourses together with its politics through the formation of the new middle class; and lastly the growth of individual, collective, and state violence in the context of these changes.

I am also suggesting that the present policies will not decrease these spatial inequalities and its variegated geographies, it will only increase them. Any intervention for decreasing these has to specially target and include the informal labouring population and involve them in reorganizing themselves as sustainable economic and cultural communities that have opportunities to be mobile and who are not excluded and made into the 'other'. The present strategies adopted by the state and the middle classes and which have now found support in local bodies will perpetuate discourses of cleavages. Given that we live, work, and organize out lives in and through the urban habitat and have an interest in its sustenance culturally, socially, ecologically, and politically, I think we need an open, frank, and a critical discussion on these matters. We need to collectively intervene in these processes at various levels to counter the hegemonic project that is being implemented today in the name of the urban.

References

Bhan, G. and A. Jana. 2015. 'Reading Spatial Inequality in Urban India'. *Economic and Political Weekly* 50 (22): 49–54.

Bhide, A. 2017. 'Changing Trajectories of Local Urban Governance'. In *The Contemporary Urban Conundrum*, edited by S. Patel and O. Goyal, 172–83. Delhi: India International Centre Quarterly.

Dupont, V. 2011. 'The Challenge of Slums and Forced Evictions'. In *Urban Policies and the Right to City in India: Rights, Responsibilities and Citizenship*, edited by M-H. Zerah, V. Dupont and S. Tawa Lama-Rewal, 76–97. New Delhi: UNESCO.

Fernandes, L. 2004. 'Politics of Forgetting'. *Urban Studies* 41 (12): 2415–30.

Harris-White, B. and N. Gooptu. 2001. 'Mapping India's World of Unorganised Labour'. *Socialist Register* 37: 89–118.

Jana, A. and G. Bhan. 2013. 'Of Slums or Poverty: Notes of Caution from 2011 Census'. *Economic and Political Weekly* 48 (18): 13–16.

Jha, P. 2016. *Oxford India Short Introductions: Labour in Contemporary India*. New Delhi: Oxford University Press.

Kundu, A. 2009. 'Exclusionary Urbanisation in Asia: A Macro Overview'. *Economic and Political Weekly* 44 (48): 48–58.

Kundu, A. 2011. 'Method in Madness: Urban Data in 2011 Census'. *Economic and Political Weekly* 46 (40): 13–16.

Kundu, A. 2017. 'Urbanisation versus Rurbanisation in India: The Need for an Alternate Development Paradigm'. *IIC Quarterly* Winter 2016–Spring 2017: 17–27.

McGee, T. G. 2002. 'Reconstructing "The Southeast Asian City" in an Era of Volatile Globalization'. *Asian Journal of Social Science* 30 (1): 8–27.

Mehra, A. 2017. 'India's "Urban" and the Policy Discontent'. In *The Contemporary Urban Conundrum*, edited by S. Patel and O. Goyal, 161–71. Delhi: India International Centre Quarterly.

Mehta, M. and D. Mehta. 2010. 'A Glass Half Full? Urban Development (1990s to 2010)'. *Economic and Political Weekly* 45 (28): 20–3.

Mukhopadhyay, P., M.-H. Zerah, and E. Denis. 2017. 'Subaltern Urbanisation Revisited'. *IIC Quarterly* Winter 2016–Spring 2017: 28–44.

Parthasarathy, D. 2011. 'Hunters, Gatherers and Foragers in a Metropolis. Commonising the Private and the Public in Mumbai'. *Economic and Political Weekly* 56 (50): 54–63.

Patel, S. and Jadhav, V. 2011. 'Poverty Alleviation Legislations and Intersectional Exclusions: An Analysis of the Limitations of MNREGA and USSWA. CDS-ASSR Project on Social Security. Mimeo.

Rao, V. 2006. 'Slum as Theory: The South/Asian City and Globalization'. *International Journal of Urban and Regional Research* 30 (1): 225–32.

Robinson, J. 2002. *Ordinary Cities: Between Modernity and Development*. London: Routledge.

Roy, A. 2008. *Calcutta Requiem: Gender and the Politics of Poverty*. New Delhi: Pearson Education.

Shaw, A. 2008. 'Urban Policy in Post-Independent India—An Appraisal'. *Economic and Political Weekly* 31 (4): 224–8.

Sidhwani, P. 2015. 'Spatial Inequalities in Big Indian Cities'. *Economic and Political Weekly* 50 (22): 55–62.

Srivastava, S. 2014. 'Post-Nationalism: Urban Spaces, Consumerism, and Middle-Class Activism in Delhi'. In *Entangled Urbanism*, edited by S. Srivastava, 85–111. Delhi: Oxford University Press.

UN-Habitat. 2003. *The Challenge of Slums: Global Report on Human Settlements 2003*. Nairobi: UN-Habitat.

Vithayathil, T. and G. Singh, G. 2012. 'Spaces of Discrimination'. *Economic and Political Weekly* 47 (37): 60–6.

PART TWO

THE URBAN PROCESS AND NEOLIBERALIZATION

6

New Urbanism and the Remaking of Citizenship, Class, and 'Community'[*]

Sanjay Srivastava

This chapter seeks to think about some of the key aspects of urbanization and what they tell us about ideas of citizenship, relations with the state, and notions of community. It is also an attempt to reflect upon ideas of class through focusing upon certain new urban spaces and the manner in which processes of urbanization might be linked to the formation of the collective consciousness of class. The discussion will unfold through focusing upon the locality of the privately developed Delhi Land Finance (DLF) City in Gurgaon in Haryana. Gurgaon is part of the National Capital Region (NCR; population approximately 22 million).[1] According to one report, the areas falling under the recently (2008) constituted Municipal Corporation of Gurgaon (that includes DLF City as well as several other privately developed residential enclaves) contained around 1.2 million persons. However, local Residents' Welfare Associations (RWAs) dispute this estimate, claiming the true figure to be closer to 2 million. The RWAs suggested that the actual figure had been suppressed so that the 'corrupt' corporation did not have to provision for the actual number of residents.[2]

A significant strand within this discussion relates to changing relationships between the state, private capital, and citizens. Hence, I would like to begin with a brief account of some of the ways in which the state has been theorized both in general and within the Indian context. This will allow for a regionally specific understanding of Indian modernity.

---

[*] This work was supported by a National Research Foundation of Korea Grant funded by the Korean government (NRF-2017S1A6A3A02079749).

[1] In addition to Delhi, the National Capital Region consists of parts of the states of Haryana, Uttar Pradesh, and Rajasthan. The National Capital Region was formed under the National Capital Region Board Act of 1985. The board was established with the aim of encouraging and overseeing a variety of planning and economic development objectives.

[2] Sanjeev K. Ahuja (2010). For a detailed discussion on RWAs and urban politics, see Lalitha Kamath and M. Vijayabaskar (2009).

Sanjay Srivastava, *New Urbanism and the Remaking of Citizenship, Class, and 'Community'* In: *Neoliberalism, Urbanization, and Aspirations in Contemporary India*. Edited by: Sujata Patel, Oxford University Press. © Oxford University Press 2021. DOI: 10.1093/oso/9780190132019.003.0006

110 SANJAY SRIVASTAVA

Within European foundational theories of the state and subsequently in post colonial contexts, the state has been imagined as the space and the process that has banished lawlessness and wilderness through—as Max Weber famously put it—gaining the 'monopoly of the legitimate use of physical force in the enforcement of its order'.[3] The general neglect of the state in social science disciplines beyond political science has, as Fuller and Harris put it, 'contributed to the tendency in scholarship on the state to reproduce the Weberian argument that formal legal rationality eclipses substantive cultural factor, so that all modern states are substantially the same'.[4] However, 'the state is nothing like as discrete as the idea of its "actual organization" would suggest, for "the edges of the state are uncertain; societal elements seem to penetrated it on all sides, and resulting boundary between state and society is difficult to determine".[5]

After India gained independence from colonial rule in 1947, 'State planning was generally given strong support by the capitalist bourgeoisie [however] . . . the "relative autonomy" of the state's planning elite—"the body of experts"—from a range of special interests in society was very rapidly eroded'.[6] Facing a diminution in its ability to carry out development projects free from external interference, the political scientist Sudipta Kaviraj points out, '"the state elites began to seek alliances with pre-capitalist forces on a larger scale", so that it could no longer "dictate to them" and instead began to reflect their interest'.[7]

In the decades following independence, it has also been suggested, the nationalist leadership (with Prime Minister Jawaharlal Nehru as its key icon) 'failed to create the common sense legitimacy which the colonial order had necessarily lacked'.[8] Hence, Fuller and Harris go on to say, 'As Kaviraj puts it elsewhere, the elite around Nehru "neglected the creation of a common thicker we-ness . . . and the creation of a single political language for the entire polity. . . ." As the state expanded, a profound gap developed, too, between the bureaucratic elite, at home with a "modernist discourse" which often corresponded fairly well with Weberian rationality, and the personnel at lower levels, whose "vernacular everyday discourses" were not structured around principles of formal rationality at all'.[9]

[3] Veena Das and Deborah Poole 2004, 7.
[4] C. J. Fuller and John Harriss 2000, 2.
[5] Fuller and Harriss 2000, 3.
[6] Fuller and Harriss 2000, 8.
[7] Fuller and Harriss 2000, 8.
[8] Fuller and Harriss 2000, 8.
[9] Fuller and Harriss 2000, 8.

REMAKING CITIZENSHIP AND 'COMMUNITY'   111

I have outlined these perspectives on the state in some detail as not only do they have considerable currency in India-related scholarship but also provide the background to the discussion of this article. In particular, this chapter suggests that new contexts of urbanism are significant sites for understanding contemporary Indian society as well as *changing* relationships between the state, the 'people', and capital. Hence, to return to some of the observations provided earlier, this chapter seeks to ask the following kinds of questions: To what extent is it true that a modernizing elite was (and is) less corruptible as compared to a lower-level 'vernacular' officialdom? Is self-interest the dominant characteristic of only the latter groups? And, what can an ethnography of the city tell us in this regard? Sudipta Kaviraj has suggested that 'an important reason for the modern Indian state's failure to implement its policies successfully is therefore the fact that it is "overstretched", and because policies are finally implemented "very low down in the bureaucracy, they are interpreted beyond recognition."[10] The fault, in other words, is due to the 'backward' and venal nature of the lower bureaucracy. According to this line of theorizing, this aspect goes to the heart of how we should understand the nature of the Indian state and why things don't work.

This chapter argues that, in addition to the contexts aforementioned, new forms of urbanization in India also allow us to engage with another aspect of Indian society. This, as summarized by Fuller and Harris, relates to the idea that 'the institutions, disciplines, arrangements and practices associated with the post colonial state have not been supported by a modernist ideology that has found popular acceptance. The state idea, in other words, is not part of ordinary Indians' understanding'.[11] In a paper on the manufacture and circulation of fake documents—such as ration cards and identity proofs—in Delhi, I have argued that it isn't so much that the 'state idea... is not part of ordinary Indian's understanding', but rather that 'ordinary Indians' understand the state only too well, choosing to engage with it through the Nietzschean dictum 'about the long-term well-being provided by error and untruth in human and social life... [and] the injunction for us not to labor under the illusion of eliminating trickery on the assumption that there is some other world out there beyond and bereft of trickery'.[12] That is to say that the production and circulation of fake documents in Indian cities indexes a context within which the urban poor view the state as a series of processes that *lack*

---

[10] Fuller and Harriss 2000, 8–9.
[11] Fuller and Harriss 2000, 9.
[12] Michael Taussig 1997.

any sense of 'impersonal norms and values',[13] and hence, must be dealt with through entirely *ad hoc* and contingent means, of which faking is both the most elaborate and the most frequent; citizens understand the state. And the politics and practices of the city have a great deal to tell us about both quotidian practices that constitute 'society' as well as the structures which such practices confront.

To proceed with the discussion, there are two specific concepts I wish to utilize in order to explore contexts of new urbanism in India. These are 'post-nationalism' and 'moral consumption'. The next section provides an explanation of the first of these terms, whereas 'moral consumption' will be discussed in the fourth section that explores new ideas of 'the people'.

Post-Nationalism

I will utilize 'post-nationalism' as a connecting thread between the different ethnographic contexts in this chapter. To begin with, 'post-nationalism' does *not* mean to imply that the nation-state is insignificant as a context of analysis, or that we now live in a 'post-patriotic' age where the most significant units of analysis are certain 'postnational social formations'[14]—such as NGOs—that putatively problematize nationalist and statist perspectives. Further, my deployment is also different from another recent usage. Here, it is posited as 'a distinct ethico-political horizon and a position of critique' and a concept 'that can be instantiated by suspending the idea of the nation as a prior theoretical-political horizon, and thinking through its impossibility, even while located uncomfortably within its bounds'.[15] Post-nationalism, in the context of the present discussion, is the articulation of the nationalist emotion with the robust desires engendered through new practices of consumerism and their associated cultures of privatization and individuation. A fruitful way of approaching the topic—and providing concrete illustrative examples—is through a brief exploration of the contemporary politics of urban spaces in Delhi.

In 1999, soon after being elected to office, Delhi's erstwhile chief minister, Sheila Dikshit, 'called for an active participation of Residents Welfare Associations in governance'. The rationale for this was the 'failure' of 'civic

[13] Fuller and Harriss 2000, 14.
[14] Appadurai 1993, 411.
[15] M. De Alwis et al. 2009, 35.

REMAKING CITIZENSHIP AND 'COMMUNITY' 113

agencies' to carry out their normal tasks. The chief minister's secretary noted that the call to actively involve RWAs in urban governance heralded a new era, marking as it did 'the first step towards a responsive management of the city'.[16] Positing a 'moral' distinction between the state and the 'community', the secretary further noted that the 'failure' of 'civic agencies' meant that 'it's really time for the community to be given direct control of managing the affairs of the city'.[17] Subsequently, the government decided to 'empower' RWAs to 'take certain decisions on their own'. It was proposed that RWAs be given control over the management of resources such as parks, community halls, parking places, sanitation facilities, and local roads. A more direct relationship between the state and RWAs was also mooted through the idea of joint surveys of 'encroached' land—that is, land that had been 'illegally' occupied, usually by slum-dwellers—with the possibility that all illegal structures would 'then be demolished in a non-discriminatory manner'. Finally, it was proposed that RWAs be allowed to impose fines on government agencies which failed to carry out their assigned tasks.

In 2005, the Delhi state government announced that it would raise electricity tariff by 10 per cent. The Delhi Residents Welfare Association Joint Front (RWAJF) was formed in the same year in order to protest against the measure. The front consisted of 195 separate member RWAs from around the city. The increase in power rates for domestic consumers was the second one since the state-owned electricity body was 'unbundled' in June 2002 as part of power sector 'reforms'. As a result, three privately owned companies secured contracts for electricity distribution.[18] There was vigorous protest over the price rise and, in addition to the RWAJF, NGOs such as People's Action and another group known as Campaign Against Power Tariff Hike (CAPTH) joined the campaign. Individual RWAs asked their members to refuse payment of the extra amount, while RWAJF lobbied the government and organized city-wide protests. The protests gained wide coverage in both the print and electronic media and, echoing Gandhian anti-colonial strategies, the organizers were reported to have deployed 'the ideas of "civil disobedience" and "people's power"'.[19] Indeed, the parallels sought to be drawn between the Gandhian anti-colonial moment and the present times were even more explicit with the convener of the RWAJF referring to the

[16] Ojha 1999
[17] Ojha 1999.
[18] Sethi 2007; Kanbur 2007
[19] Sethi 2007, 5

114   SANJAY SRIVASTAVA

protests as 'non-violent *Satyagraha*'.[20] 'Satyagrah', made up of two words 'satya' (truth) and 'agrah' (insistence), was used by Mahatma Gandhi to refer to non-violent resistance in his struggle against colonial rule. Eventually, the Delhi government backed down and the price rise was shelved. According to Sanjay Kaul, president of the People's Action NGO, the success of the protest heralded the making of a 'middle-class revolution'.[21] Kaul is one of many who has rediscovered and deployed anti-colonial vocabulary on behalf of the 'people' at a time when the colonial era itself has become part of the sphere of mass consumption. In the wake of the 2011 anti-corruption movement led by social worker Anna Hazare, yoga guru Baba Ramdev invoked 'Gandhi in calling for a "*satyagrah* against corruption"'.[22]

The circulation of the ideas of 'civil disobedience', 'Satyagrah' and 'revolution', and the consolidation of the notion of a 'people' contesting the state occur in a context that might be called post-national. By this, I mean a situation where the original moral frisson of these terms—provided by anti-colonial sentiment—no longer holds. Indeed, in an era of post-Nehruvian economic liberalization characterized by consumerist modernity,[23] the ethico-moral universe of the anti-colonial struggle is no longer part of popular public discourse. In fact, the 'colonial ambience' is the stuff of popular marketing strategies. So, the Spencers [*sic*] department store in DLF City in Gurgaon[24] outlines its history through a series of billboard-size sepia photographs placed at the entrance. The photographs—of 'fashionable' European ladies shopping for fine goods at Spencers' stores—are from the colonial period and represent an efflorescence of colonial chic in the Indian public sphere. Other contiguous sites include the five-star Imperial Hotel in central Delhi liberally decorated with 'Delhi Durbar' series of photographs (consisting of images from a 1911 ceremony held in Delhi to commemorate the coronation of King George V) and themed restaurants such as 'Days of the Raj' and 'Sola Topee', also in Delhi. Within this new context, the earlier emphasis on the ethics of 'saving' and delayed gratification for the 'national good'—that were indispensable ideological accompaniments to 'civil disobedience' and 'satyagrah'—do not find any resonance in contemporary popular discourses on the role of the state. As I have noted above, the term 'post-national' does *not*, in my usage, mean to imply that the nation-state is

---

[20] Sirari 2006.
[21] Sirari 2006.
[22] Copeman and Ikegame 2012, 318.
[23] Fernandes 2006; Mazzarella 2003; Osella and Osella 2009, S202–21.
[24] Srivastava 2012.

REMAKING CITIZENSHIP AND 'COMMUNITY' 115

insignificant as a context of analysis. But rather, it refers to the new ways in which the nation-state relates to citizens, the contexts within which it relates to different fractions of citizens and the manner in which it relates to capital.

In light of the above and to pre-empt an aspect of my discussion, there appears to be in train a process of rethinking the state[25] such that it is increasingly imagined as a 'friend' of the *middle classes*. The post colonial state in India has most significantly been imagined as a benefactor of the poor, with 'development' as its most significant policy focus. Indeed, the 'development' focus of the state has been a defining feature of perceptions of postcoloniality itself.[26] As Akhil Gupta points out, 'development became the chief "reason of state" in independent India.'[27] Investment in 'heavy industry' was, further, seen to be an important aspect of postcolonial development[28] and this, in turn, led to a perception of the state as pro-industrialization and anti-consumption. RWA activity such as that discussed above has become a site for the reformulation of these well-entrenched notions of the state and its relationships with different class fractions. These neighbourhoods and city-level activities unfold in tandem with the broad national thrust towards 'de-regulating' the economy[29]—including a shrinking public sector and easy loans for consumer purchases—and produce a palpable sense of amity between the 'people' and the state. It is this that I refer to as characteristic of post-nationalism.

One of the most significant ways in which the post-national moment resonates within the politics of urban space concerns the repositioning of the language of anti-colonial nationalism from the national sphere to the sub-urban one. This, in turn, also indexes the move from the idea of the 'national' family to the nuclear (gated) one and the translation of the notion of nationalist solidarity to (middle) class solidarity.

Creating DLF City: From State Control to Consumerist Utopia

I begin with a brief introduction that provides a historical sketch as well as outlines some contemporary contexts of the development of India's most

---

[25] Kamat 2002.
[26] Chatterjee 1993; Gupta 1998.
[27] Gupta 1998, 107.
[28] Roy 2007.
[29] Guha 2009, 45–52; Derné 2008.

116 SANJAY SRIVASTAVA

significant private township and symbol of new urbanism, DLF City. The 3500-acre DLF City has been developed by the Delhi Land and Finance Corporation, India's largest real estate company. DLF City is located south of Delhi, immediately across the border, in the Gurgaon district of Haryana. Beginning in the mid-1980s, the city was constructed by the DLF Corporation and is regarded in both scholarly[30] and popular writing[31] as a significant site for the making of contemporary cultures of transnational urbanism in India. Its 'hyper' malls, gated residential communities, and corporate offices (occupied, among others, by call centres, Business Process Outsourcing companies and prominent multinational corporations) speak of an urban transformation that is also the making of new ideas of the modern—'middle-class'—Indian self.

The Delhi Land and Finance company was established in 1946 by Chaudhury Raghvendra Singh, a civil servant and landowner belonging to the agricultural caste of Jats (his caste affiliation was, as I show below, proved important in the context of DLFs business success). Till the mid-1950s, DLF had a significant presence in the private real estate market in Delhi. The key aspect of its business strategy was its ability to both surmount and manipulate the extraordinary layers of land and 'planning' regulations instituted by the colonial state.[32] The background to this lay in the control the state exercised over vast tracts of *Nazul* lands, viz., 'the Delhi Crown lands denoting property which has descended to Government either as successor of former Government or by escheat, in absence of heirs to legal owners'.[33] The colonial government had, in 1874, 'handed over the administration of *Nazul* estates to the Delhi Municipal Council as well as all income accruing there from'.[34] Hence, private interests in the real estate business, such as DLF, had two ways of acquiring land for their commercial activities: buying from large landholders (*Zamindars*) whose properties escaped the *Nazul* regulations, or, acquiring lands falling under the *Nazul* areas through negotiation with the Delhi Improvement Trust (DIT). The latter body was established in 1937 in the wake 'of a report by Mr. A.P. Hume (a senior civil servant)on congestion in Delhi city'.[35] In February 1938, the trust 'notified' its first (and best known) urban improvement scheme, viz., the Delhi Ajmeri Gate Slum Clearance

---

[30] King 2004; Dupont 2005.
[31] Jain 2001.
[32] See, for example, Hoshagrahar 2007; Legg 2007.
[33] *Gazetteer of Rural Delhi* (Delhi: Delhi Administration, 1987).
[34] *Hume Report* (GOI 1936, 26–7).
[35] *Annual Administration Report of the Delhi Province for 1937-38* (GOI 1939).

REMAKING CITIZENSHIP AND 'COMMUNITY' 117

Scheme.[36] Covering an area of 68.21 acres, the scheme, as Legg suggests, was produced through 'adjustments' to 'European, liberal, welfare policies to the colonial context';[37] these adjustments related to 'a reluctance to invest [in the colonized society and] a landscaping urge that sought to separate and contain the potentially threatening native population' (191).

By 1949, DLF had 'developed some of the first residential colonies in Delhi, such as Krishna Nagar in East Delhi'.[38] The social imaginary that DLF sought to conjure for its localities was one animated by a curious mixture of American and British stylistic references. A DLF advertisement from 1955 for some of its key projects is a case in point.[39] Here, in a city still pockmarked by the scars of the post-partition trauma (that created the separate nations of India and Pakistan) and regulated by the dicta of the DIT Building Manual is a vision of joyful cartoonish intensity. A man-about-town preens near a fountain in North-West Delhi, an insouciant young couple goes boating in North Delhi, a Hollywood starlet-like figure prepares to descend into a swimming pool in West Delhi, an 'Oxford' Don welcomes a school boy in South Delhi and a prosperous elderly couple surveys manicured domains in Central-South Delhi. It is a fantabulous vision of post-partition utopia wrenched from the ascetic reaches of the Five Year Plan state and distant from the messianic—'slum-clearing'—gaze of the DIT. There is a striking continuity of aspirational themes between mid-twentieth advertisements such as these and the ones for twenty-first-century gated residential communities in DLF City that show images of 'modern' men and women jogging on private tracks, swimming in private pools, and enjoying privatized educational facilities. Real estate developments in India have been a prime site for the making of the citizen-consumer and the current phase of middle-class 'activism', in the shape of RWAs, also owes much to urban spatial transformations initiated by companies such as DLF, which gained ground in the wake of economic liberalization policies put in train by the Congress party through its New Industrial Policy in 1980.[40]

The *soi-disant* dreams of an alternative spatial modernity—marked by swimming pools and buxom beauties, lakes, and carefree couples, 'flower bedecked' roads and their patrician crowds—came to end, however, in 1957. For, following a highly critical report of an enquiry into the functioning of

---

[36] *Delhi Improvement Trust* (New Delhi: Delhi Improvement Trust, 1941)
[37] Legg 2007, 191.
[38] See DLF. Available at http://www.dlf-group.com, accessed 26 July 2012.
[39] Advertisement found in unmarked file at the Delhi State Archives, Delhi. Copy in possession of author.
[40] See, for example, Dutta 2004; Sengupta 2008, 35–42.

118 SANJAY SRIVASTAVA

the DIT published in 1951, the postcolonial state promulgated the Delhi (Control of Building Operations) Ordinance of 1955, leading to the establishment of the Delhi Development Provisional Authority. The provisional authority was, in turn, succeeded by the Delhi Development Authority (DDA) in 1957.[41] The Ordinance of 1955 elaborated a magisterial vision of urban control, transcribing its writ across the erratic ambitions of the living *and* the moribund spatiality of the dead; for, not only did the DDA hold sway over all areas that fell outside the jurisdiction of local authorities (such as municipal committees) and those covered by the DIT Town Expansion Schemes, it also declared 'all graveyards in Delhi State to be controlled areas'.[42] With the establishment of the DDA, the small window offered to private developers was firmly shuttered and even 'while the DDA was in the process of preparing a Master Plan for the city, the government announced a freeze on all vacant undeveloped land within the urbanizable limits'.[43] Further, 'Establishing itself as the sole agency legally authorized to develop and dispose off land, the State left little, or no role for the private land developer'.[44]

After the closure of its real estate business, DLF undertook a series of other unsuccessful commercial ventures. From the early 1980s, however, the company refocused attention to land and under a new generation of family leadership (the founder's son-in-law, K.P. Singh), the company began to acquire land in Gurgaon in the state of Haryana. After some initial hiccups (Gurgaon was considered 'too far', there was a great deal of termite infestation and the local, mainly, rural populations were considered 'threatening' to middle-class residents), DLF's townships, gated communities, and office complexes proved an unprecedented success. Confronted with a context of small land-holdings (typically four to five acres) and multiple land-ownership patterns, K.P. Singh relied heavily on local knowledge to achieve his aims. Hagiographic accounts relate how obtaining of clear title involved securing agreements with dozens of owners, a task achieved through invocations of bucolic trust and patrimonial obligation: he frequently invoked his caste identity when negotiating

[41] The enquiry was constituted under the chairmanship of the leading industrialist G. D. Birla and the report came to be known as the Birla Report. In blunt terms, it concluded that 'the story of the Trust is the story of failure' (Birla Committee Report 1951, 7); that its record of slum-clearance had been 'meagre' (1951, 3); that the Town Expansion Schemes had merely resulted in the 'freezing' rather than 'development' of considerable land areas; that it had commissioned neither a 'civic survey' nor a 'Master Plan'; and that its strategy of selling land to the highest bidder had only exacerbated the 'housing problem' (1951, 4).

[42] Letter from the Secretary, Delhi Development Provisional Authority, 11 August 1955 File 1/142/1955/Local Self Government/Delhi State Archives, Delhi.

[43] Dasappa Kacker 2005, 72.

[44] Dasappa Kacker 2005, 72.

REMAKING CITIZENSHIP AND 'COMMUNITY' 119

with the agricultural castes who owned land in Gurgaon and with whom he had to negotiate to build up a 'land-bank' for his business. Grass-root corporatism was matched, on the other hand, by persistent lobbying of the state to change laws that militated against residential development on agricultural land. This was achieved through measures such as the reclassification of agricultural into 'non-agricultural' land. The blending of corporatist ambition with state patronage, communal bonds, and peasant cultural economy paid rich dividends, and by the mid-1980s, DLF had acquired some 3,500 acres of land in Gurgaone—much of it on credit, with promises to pay later—and was ready to transform the rural hinterland into, as its publicity later proclaimed, the 'Millennium City'.

Fields of green have, within the space of some two decades, turned into spaces of global commerce and local habitation fuelled by changes in the economy since the mid-1980s. One of the most significant of these has been the rapid expansion of the retail banking sector and the relative ease of obtaining home loans. Aggressive market forays by both state-owned and new private entrants (including foreign banks) sought to target 'young and highly educated professionals who began their careers through the 1980s, [but] could not afford to own their own homes'.[45] DLF City is famous for its shopping malls and gated residential communities. The different 'phases'— or sections—of DLF City are themselves located in 'sectors' designated by the state-run Haryana Urban Development Authority (HUDA). Phases I, II, and III mainly consist of independent houses built on plots purchased from DLF and semi-detached bungalows built and sold by it. In Phase III, the DLF built 'White Town Houses' are grouped around narrow streets with mock-Victorian street lighting, whereas in other areas, the design of the independent houses has been borrowed from the wildest reaches of imaginations. Near Silver Oaks Apartments (the first gated condominium built by DLF) in Phase I, there is a large house built in a neo-Gothic style which is in the vicinity of another with the façade of a traditional Indian mansion, the *Haveli*. Nearby, just beyond DLF Phase IV, there is an art gallery—whose exhibitions come from the private collection of an industrialist—that is housed in a startling (and recently finished) building that is designed like a massive rusting monolith, its exterior clad in metal and interiors fashioned to give an 'industrial' feel. Almost opposite this building is an under-construction hotel in red and pink sandstone that is a combination of Doric columns and

---

[45] Khanna 2007, 107.

120 SANJAY SRIVASTAVA

'Indo-Saracenic' balconies and cupolas. Next to the art gallery is a building that houses the offices of the white goods manufacturer, Whirlpool, with a swirling glass frontage that is a cross-between a space ship and a see-through washing machine.

Traffic in the locality flows along several main ('sector') roads and their tributaries, part of the infrastructure that has been constructed through a scheme of 'private–public partnership'. Beyond DLF City, about 10 kilometers further south into Haryana are two areas that are the hub of current—and feverish—real estate activity. The first of these centres on 'Nirvana Country', a three-hundred-acre apartment and villa complex being developed by another real estate firm, Unitech Builders. The main thoroughfare—entered through a gateway—is lined with semi-detached bungalows, collectively named Aspen Greens. Other areas include Birch Court, the Close, and Espace. From Nirvana Country, moving in a southerly direction, past a patchwork of agricultural land overgrown with weeds and fenced-off with the markings of their new owners—a variety of real estate companies—one encounters a highway that is crowded on both sides with a multitude of condominium and commercial projects still under construction. The traffic is joined by a seemingly endless line of trucks conveying building materials. Privately hired security personnel guard the perimeters of the building zones and long stretches of the road-side have been taken over by semi-permanent 'offices' of real estate agents. This is Sohna Road, which leads to the village of Sohna. Some prominent projects include the Nile apartments (based on an 'Egyptian' theme), the Mansionz (bungalows in a 'French provincial' style), and Vatika City, being designed by a firm headquartered in New York. In DLF City, there are gated communities with names such as Hamilton Court, Birmingham Apartments, and Windsor Court.

Gated communities such as those in Gurgaon are being constructed across 300 Indian cities and such topographical transformations are accompanied by broader discursive shifts regarding family life, state, nation, and citizenship.[46] In this context, gated communities have created new relationships between gender, consumerism, domesticity, and the morality of the markets. I will here discuss some aspects that address my attempts to outline why post-national modernity and moral consumption (discussed below) are useful in thinking about new urbanism in India and, in turn, about relationships between the home and the world.

---

[46] For South Africa, see Landman and Schönteich 2002; for China, see Pow 2007, 1539–58; and for Turkey, see Geniş 2007, 771–98.

REMAKING CITIZENSHIP AND 'COMMUNITY'   121

To begin with, the mammoth transformations of space currently underway in the contexts described above can be put alongside another similar experiment during mid-twentieth century, viz., the construction of 'steel towns' by the postcolonial state. A comparison between contemporary—private— spatial transformations and mid-twentieth century state-sponsored one's points to significant shifts in the imagination that conjures the 'ideal' citizen and his [*sic*] relationship to the state. From the late 1950s, the Indian state undertook construction of a number of industrial townships in different— usually economically underdeveloped—areas of the country that were intended to be 'exemplary national spaces of the new India'.[47] Located within the larger framework of centralized economic development (whose most public manifestation were the Five Year Plans), the townships were the state's attempts at *postcolonial* modernity where the modern citizen would work and live in an environment that 'proclaimed the birth of the sovereign nation' (138). Hence, 'apart from innovations in urban design' (143), the thinking behind steel towns also addressed itself to the possibilities of engineering *new* 'forms of subjectivities, practices, and social relations' (143) that would distinguish these settlements from the 'backwardness' of their immediate localities, as well as the stasis afflicting national life: they were to be the spatialized models of a new national culture. The townships of Rourkela (Orissa state), Bhilai (Madhya Pradesh), Durgapur (West Bengal), and Bokaro (Bihar) thus came into being. Of course, as Roy also points out, in subsequent years, the steel towns did not live up to the promise of sovereign modernity that was imposed upon them. But that is another story. Of greater relevance here are the unfolding narratives of citizenship, the state and capital that link them to the contemporary spatial transformations of a similar—or greater— magnitude. However, while both steel towns and contemporary gated communities might be located within the discursive promises of a 'new India', there are significant differences in the nature of the new in each instance. These differences also tell us something about the shifting relationship between national and global cultural and political economies, and the changing senses of being Indian.

Most significantly, the nationalist project of producing modern citizens within steel towns related to external spaces—such as town planning, streetscape, and design of shopping spaces—through which residents were expected to pass through. Surrounded by well-delineated areas for industrial

---

[47] Roy 2007, 134. Further page references are in the main text.

122 SANJAY SRIVASTAVA

activity, 'shops, schools, parks, and entertainment centres' (142), the citizen was to absorb the spatial geometry, transforming it into personal discipline across a number of areas of social life such as democratic engagement, secular belief, and industrial work practice. The belief that spaces mould human characteristics has a relatively well-established history in the annals of Indian modernity.[48] Discourses of transformation surrounding contemporary gated communities, on the other hand, shift the focus to internal spaces. So, gated communities are presented as effecting transformations that significantly relate to *domestic* (kitchens, dining areas, bedrooms, etc.) aspects of urban living. In advertisements, intimate spaces are more directly addressed, locating, as it were, the domestic sphere as the indispensable ground for the making of a global Indian modernity. It is, as if, Indian *private* life must be aligned with global standards through *public* display of the spaces where this might happen. In this way, the public exhibition of intimate spaces indexes an era where *national* dreams of modernity no longer suffice to define Indianness. For, gated enclaves posit a model of *post-national* citizenship that constitutes a particular gloss on the relationship between the state and its citizens in the backdrop of transnational consumerist modernity; the bedroom is a window to the world. The movement from postcolonial to post-national projects of citizenship also posits the journey from the 'citizen-worker'[49] to the consumer-citizen, just as it does from the spaces of national identity to those of suburban and domestic ones.

Further, unlike steel-towns, it is no longer Indian and foreign *nation-states* that contribute to spatial transformations that are the putative sites of revolutions in personality and culture.[50] Rather, it is the relationship between the state, citizens, and various forms of capital—national and global—that is seen to be fundamental to the task of remaking national life.

Creating a People

The emergence of the domestic sphere as the site of a new national (or, rather, in terms of this discussion, post-national) identity relates, as implied above, to newer models of family life. What is the family 'type' that is being imagined

---

[48] See, for example, Srivastava 1998.

[49] Roy 2007.

[50] The governments of the erstwhile USSR, Germany, and the United Kingdom were significant contributors to steel-making technologies in these towns.

REMAKING CITIZENSHIP AND 'COMMUNITY' 123

through the focus upon domestic spaces as the new crucibles of national identity? Patricia Uberoi's discussion on Indian 'bridal magazines' provides a useful entry into this topic. The magazines Uberoi takes up for discussion were mostly launched in the mid-1990s and address an imagined high-income consumer, not unlike occupants of an up-market gated community. The following quote from an editorial in the inaugural issue (1997) of the *Bride and Home* magazine captures the social terrain that bridal magazines encounter, and also allows us, via Uberoi's discussion, to think about the discourses of domesticity in a new context of consumer culture.

> Arranging a wedding in India [the editorial says] has traditionally been a family affair, and so it should remain; but it is to offer choice that *Bride and Home* steps in and gives young couples a freedom to partake in the most important decision of their lives: marriage.[51]

Bridal magazines such as *Bride and Home*, Uberoi says, seek to address young women through the neoliberal trope of 'choice' in a social context 'where descent, succession and inheritance are in the male line; post-marital residence is "patrivirilocal" . . . and authority resides with the senior males of the family or lineage' (245). And yet, within all this is the idea that the 'modern' form of marriage and domesticity—such modernity defined through an association with the good and services (including those of 'marriage planners')—is a key moment in the making of modern Indian identity. How then to address the tension between older (and very real) structures of power and the apparent promise of consumerism-led liberation? Here, Uberoi suggests, the domestic sphere becomes a site of 'adjustment' to changes on a broader scale: it is a place 'of the consolidation of this new, cosmopolitan culture of Indian kinship and marriage,' that is self-consciously both "modern" and "ethnic"' (245). Applying this insight to the present discussion, we might say that contemporary domestic-nationalism conjures a family type based around a 'couple' whose modernity is based around its 'freedom' to make choices about the goods it might consume rather than, say, 'spousal choice' (241). That is, the emerging politics of domesticity—one that gathers around the spaces of the gated community as well as ideas of intimacy and marriage conjured by *Bride and Home*—consists of reformulations

---

[51] Uberoi 2008, 239. Further page references are in the main text.

124 SANJAY SRIVASTAVA

and reinstitution of older structures of power in a new era of post-national consumerist modernity.

This is an appropriate point in the discussion to introduce the second concept I wish to utilize in order to understand new urbanism in India, viz., 'moral consumption'. I will also gesture at the relationship between moral consumption and post-nationalism within this context.

The making of moral consumption and a moral middle class is, as I have argued elsewhere, a context 'where the active participation in consumerism is accompanied by an anxiety about it and its relationship to "Indianness".[52] Moral consumption, in my usage, refers to the context where consumerist activity is accompanied by explicit and implicit discourses of the possibility of exercising control over it. This is different from viewing consumerism as a threat to established life-ways.[53] Hence, recent contexts of consumerism indicate that the long-standing cultural discourses of the sacrificing and nurturing mother that actively proscribe 'indulgent' consumption[54] are able to be encompassed *within* acts of consumerism by women. Let me provide two examples here. Firstly, women visitors to the Disneyfied (and hyper-consumerist) Akshardham temple complex in Delhi can move seamlessly between playing consumers and devoutly religious persons precisely because the same space provides opportunities for both consumerism and religiosity.[55] That is to say, the (masculine) anxiety over female consumption is 'assuaged' through a process of moral consumption whereby women take part in hyper-consumerism *and are also* able to withdraw to the realms of religiosity. And, though each realm is interpenetrative, each is imagined as separate. Hence,

> the making of a moral middle class, one that has control over the processes of consumption, and hence modernity, is, in fact, located in the processes of (surplus) consumption itself. For it is only through consumption that one can demonstrate *mastery* over it. So, one consumes a wide variety of products of contemporary capitalism—IMAX cinema, the Disneyfied boat ride, Akshardham baseball caps—in combination with 'spiritual' goods such as religion and nationalism. What differentiates the moral middle class from others is its *capacity* to take part in these *diverse* forms

---

[52] Srivastava 2011, 381.
[53] van Wessel 2004, 93–116.
[54] See, for example Donner (2011).
[55] Srivastava 2011.

of consumption, whereas a more 'de-racinated' (or 'Westernized') middle class might only be able to consume the products of capitalism.[56]

Secondly, within gated communities—where the 'street' is not the street, and, for precisely that reason, is a site of intense middle-class activity—'public' women can be both the guardian of tradition *and* take part in the sexualized presentations of the self. So, while on the occasion of the Hindu festival of *Karva Chauth* women dressed in traditional (and elaborate) Indian clothing pray for their husband's welfare, they can also be found pacing the condominium grounds on their exercise rounds dressed in skin-hugging clothing. And, unlike the constraints placed on women at public celebrations of *Holi*, at the Bacardi-sponsored *Holi* Mela (fair) at one of the gated communities, men *and* women dance together to Bollywood songs on an open-air stage. Consumerism here is the grounds for the making of a moral middle class within which women are not determined by modernity, but are able to take part in it and 'return home' when required; they can be both 'modern' and 'traditional'. Further, post-national consumerism provides the grounds for the making of moral consumption: for one must take vigorous part in consumerism in order to display one's ability to withdraw from it. One must display modernity to remain traditional. The relationship between post-nationalism, moral consumption, and the new urban spaces of gated communities also speaks to the long history of anxiety about the public woman through the question: how can the public woman belong to both the world and the home?

It will be clear that—in admittedly imprecise ways—I am gesturing at the relationship between the cultural and political economies of contemporary capitalism and urbanism that, in the Indian case, have specific spatial dimensions. There are two other aspects to the post-national moment as might be illustrated through examples of the politics of urban spaces. The first concerns the accumulating discourse on 'village India'. The 'imperial construct' of 'village India'[57] has found a new life through contemporary consumer culture. Through a number of contexts, the Indian village has become a significant site of the urban middle-class imagination. So, discourses of leisure, aesthetics, spirituality, health, and housing—among others—draw upon romanticized images of' 'village India; there are purpose-built 'ethnic villages' to experience 'authentic' rural food and entertainment,[58] 'living

---

[56] Srivastava 2011, 381.
[57] Inden 1992.
[58] Nayar 2006, 189.

126   SANJAY SRIVASTAVA

museums' to watch 'tribals' producing handicrafts,[59] clothing designed to reflect rural exuberance and gated enclaves that promise rural idyll.[60] The earlier colonial and anthropological preoccupation with the 'village India' has, more recently transformed into newer enterprises of the middle-class imagination. A significant consequence of the middle-class idealization of the 'rural' manifests in the hostility towards 'debased' villagers: the urban working classes and slum-dwellers who do not fulfill their vocation as material for the urban imagination. The slum-dwellers are, in this sense, 'improper' and 'inauthentic' villagers, out of place, threats to civic life and hence, not deserving of sympathy. Hence, the slum is not so much 'the reinvented "compassionate" village' as Nandy suggests)[61], as the site of an urban anger at the dismantling of its rural imaginary.

Secondly, there is in train a process whereby capital actively produces its own citizens such that the notion of separate and autonomous spheres of the state, citizens, and capital becomes untenable. What we are left with, in fact, is a simulacra[62] of separate spheres. Like all private developers, many services within DLF City continue to be provided by the DLF corporation. This includes water, electricity, and external security. The fees that residents pay for these are known as 'maintenance charges'. These are paid to DLF which then pays the relevant government authorities. This is a context for the relationship between citizens (in the shape of RWAs), the state, and the private capital, DLF.

In 1986, some residents of DLF City combined to form the Qutub Enclave RWA (QERWA). One of its most consistent demands has been that DLF hand-over its townships to the government. As per the Haryana Development and Regulation of Urban Areas Act 1975, a real estate company must hand over a privately developed locality to the state within five years of its establishment. QERWA mounted a considerable agitation over this issue. It filed court cases, petitioned the government, and even fought in state assembly elections. In the early 2000s, another RWA—known as the DLF City RWA—appeared on the scene. This is an umbrella body which claims affiliation from many individual RWAs in DLF City. An office holder of the Qutub RWA (the older body) described the situation as follows:

[59] Greenough 1995.
[60] Dupont 2005.
[61] Nandy 2001, 20.
[62] Baudrillard 1988.

DLF did not want to hand over its townships to the government and the government is not interested either: for as long as DLF has control it can arbitrarily can continue to use the land within its areas as it pleases by changing original planning agreements. So, it can build a commercial building on a plot that was earlier indicated on planning documents as a community centre or a medical dispensary. The government does not wish to change anything because of the massive amounts of under-the-table money that it gets from private developers. If the 'colonies' were handed over to the Municipal Corporation of Gurgaon, it would be more difficult to make money. It's easier to make money from the private sector.

The DLF City RWA was, in fact, created by the DLF corporation to counter what it perceived to be an association of residents (the Qutub Enclave RWA) that was hostile to its interests. In particular, the company was concerned at QERWA's demand that the company hands over the township to be administered by the Haryana government. The DLF-sponsored RWA has a comfortable air-conditioned office in the same building as many of DLF's corporate offices in Phase 1 in DLF City have. A Qutub RWA office holder told me that in the early 2000s, DLF initiated moves that led to the Haryana government appointing an administrator to oversee its affairs and that it currently lies dormant. The DLF-sponsored association, on the other hand, appears to be flourishing. It is headed by retired corporate executive and primarily acts (as the head told me) 'as a bridge between DLF and the residents of DLF City'. The DLF corporation has, in this way, reconfigured the relationship between the state and the market in order to produce a non-state version of the civic sphere, which simultaneously grows out of the collaboration with the state; it has created its own citizens group—and a private citizenry—through sponsoring the DLF City RWA. This too is an aspect of post-national urbanism where the idea and the body of the active citizen are produced not through political processes and debate over rights and responsibilities, but through a relationship between the state, the corporate sector, and urban real estate.

The processes of new urbanism in India—as exemplified by the privately developed DLF City—provide a fruitful entry towards an understanding of changing relations between the state, citizens, and private capital. These processes also provide a more complicated picture of the nature of the state itself: it emerges as an entity that is *part* of the informality and impropriety it seeks to banish as well as set itself apart from. These aspects can be summarized through, in conclusion, the notion of kinship capitalism.

128 SANJAY SRIVASTAVA

When DLF began to purchase land in Gurgaon, it did not have sufficient funds to pay for the purchases, its commercial activities since the late 1950s not having generated much revenue. The purchases came to fruition through two processes, both of which can be grouped under the rubric of kinship capitalism. DLF head K.P. Singh's own Jat background was, as I have suggested earlier, crucial to his negotiations with the agricultural castes who owned land in Gurgaon. The following is a quote from an interview he gave in 2005:

> I set about identifying myself with each family whose land I wanted to buy. A team of 70 to 80 people were deputed to find out everything about these people: the size of their families, how many children, who was good in studies, any family disputes . . . every little detail. I did everything it took to persuade these farmers to trust me. I spent weeks and months with their families—I wore *kurtas*, sat on *charpais*, drank fly-infested milk from dirty glasses, attended weddings, visited the sick. . . .[63]

This is how a farmer—now real estate dealer—from the nearby village of Nathupur (now part of DLF Phase 3) described the situation:

> DLF bought the smaller plots of land on cash terms and larger plots on credit. They were very considerate: if our cattle were electrocuted, DLF paid compensation. Now the younger generation of DLF owners is not like that.

DLF bought a great deal of land on credit, an aspect that was facilitated by the fact that K.P. Singh was able to invoke a sense of bucolic trust between caste-brethren into his dealings with the landowning farmers. There was another aspect: DLF also managed to convince the villagers to trust him with the money that was paid for the land they sold. It created a financial arrangement (known as 'chit-fund' in India) that offered a slightly higher rate than local banks and villagers were encouraged to deposit their money with DLF itself. Hence, it managed to get farmers to deposit money they had received from sale of their lands to the corporation into fixed deposits and utilized this money to make further purchases. There was, however, one

---

[63] Quoted from Radhakrishnan Swami 2005. Singh notes in his autobiography that 'The acquisition of land [by] Singh was meticulously done over a period of time, taking every farmer or landowner into confidence. . . . I myself came from a rural background so I knew their realities. We spent weeks and months on building a relationship with farmers whose land we wanted to buy' (Singh 2011, 99). 'It also helped', Singh points out, 'that my parents-in-law belonged to Haryana and were a leading family in the state' (101).

significant complication for the company. In most areas, while the land was in one person's name, it was actually being cultivated by and in possession of someone else. In all these situations, DLF got the land registered on a '50–50' basis: half of it was registered in the name of the person who was the actual owner and the other half to the person in possession. This paved the way for legal sale of the land to DLF without any state involvement, but within a context that was facilitated by the state. For, soon after the company began to acquire agricultural land, it lobbied various levels of government and succeeded in changing land-use regulations so that such land could be put towards urban use.

This discussion has attempted to the specific ways in which changing relationships between the categories we call 'the state', 'capital', and 'the people' are significant in the making of new contexts of urbanism in India. And, finally, I have suggested that operations upon urban spaces understood via post-nationalism and moral consumption tell us something about both the public life of the new city and the making of new urban identities in India.

References

Ahuja, Sanjeev K. 2010. '11.53 Lakh Population: The Numbers Lie, Say Residents'. *Hindustan Times*, August 10, 4.

Appadurai, Arjun. 1993. 'Patriotism and Its Futures'. *Public Culture* 11: 411–29.

Baudrillard, Jean. 1988. 'Simulacra and Simulations'. In *Selected Writings*, edited by M. Poster, 166–184. Stanford, CA: Stanford University Press.

Birla Committee Report [DIT Enquiry Report]. 1951. *Report of the Delhi Improvement Trust Enquiry Committee*, Vol. 1. New Delhi: Manager, Government of India Press.

Chatterjee, Partha. 1993. *The Nation and Its Fragments. Colonial and Postcolonial Histories*. Princeton, NJ: Princeton University Press.

Copeman, Jacob and Aya Ikegame. 2012. 'Guru Logics'. *HAU: Journal of Ethnographic Theory* 2 1: 289–336.

Das, Veena and Deborah Poole. 2004. 'State and Its Margins: Comparative Ethnographies'. In *Anthropology in the Margins of the State*, edited by V. Das and D. Poole, 3–33. New Delhi: Oxford University Press.

Dasappa Kacker, Suneetha. 2005. 'The DDA and the Idea of Delhi'. In *The Idea of Delhi*, edited by Romi Khosla, 68–77. Mumbai: Marg.

De Alwis, M., S. Deshpande, P. Jeganathan, M. John, N. Menon, A. Nigam, and S. A. Zaidi. 2009. 'The Postnational Condition'. *Economic and Political Weekly* 44 (10): 35.

Derné, Steve. 2008. *Globalization on the Ground: New Media and the Transformation of Culture, Class, and Gender in India*. New Delhi: SAGE.

130 SANJAY SRIVASTAVA

Donner, Henrike. 2011. 'Gendered Work, Domestic Work and Perfect Families: New Regimes of Gender and Food in Bengali Middle-Class Lifestyles'. In *Being Middle Class. A Way of Life*, edited by H. Donner, 47–72. London: Routledge.

Dupont, Véronique. 2005. 'The Idea of a New Chic Delhi through Publicity Hype'. In *The Idea of Delhi*, edited by Romi Khosla, 78–93. Mumbai: Marg.

Dutta, D. 2004. 'Effects of Globalisation on Employment and Poverty in Dualistic Economies: The Case of India'. In *Economic Globalisation: Social Conflicts, Labour and Environmental Issues*, edited by C. Tisdell and R. Sen, 167–185. Cambridge: Edward Elgar.

Fernandes, Leela. 2006. *India's New Middle Class: Democratic Politics in an Era of Economic Reform*. Minneapolis, MN: University of Minnesota Press.

Fuller, C. J. and John Harriss. 2000. 'For an Anthropology of the Modern Indian State'. In *The Everyday State and Society in Modern India*, edited by C.J. Fuller and Véronique Bénéï, 1–30. New Delhi: Social Science Press.

Geniş, Şerife. 2007. 'Producing Elite Localities: The Rise of Gated Communities in Istanbul'. *Urban Studies* 44 (4): 771–98.

GOI (Government of India). 1936. *Hume Report* (Report on the Relief of Congestion in Delhi), Vol. I. Simla: GOI Press.

GOI (Government of India). 1939. *Annual Administration Report of the Delhi Province for 1937–38*. Delhi: Manager of Publications, GOI Press.

Greenough, Paul. 1995. 'Nation, Economy, and Tradition Displayed: The Indian Crafts Museum, New Delhi'. In *Consuming Modernity: Public Culture in a South Asian World*, edited by Carol Breckenridge, 216–248. Minneapolis, MN: University of Minnesota Press.

Guha, Atulan. 2009. 'Labour Market Flexibility: An Empirical Inquiry into Neoliberal Propositions'. *Economic and Political Weekly* 44 (19): 45–52.

Gupta, Akhil. 1998. *Postcolonial Development: Agriculture in the Making of Modern India*. Durham, NC: Duke University Press.

Inden, Ronald. 1992. *Imagining India*. Oxford: Blackwell.

Jain, Madhu. 2001. 'Tyrannies at Work'. Seminar: First City? A Symposium on Remembering Delhi, No. 515, July.

Kamat, Sangeeta. 2002. *Development Hegemony: NGOs and the State in India*. New York: Oxford University Press.

Kamath, Lalitha and M. Vijayabaskar. 2009. 'Limits and Possibilities of Middle Class Associations as Urban Collective Actors'. *Economic and Political Weekly* 44 (26–27): 368–76.

Kanbur, Ravi. 2007. 'Development Disagreement and Water Privatization: Bridging the Divide'. Available at http://www.arts.cornell.edu/poverty/kanbur/WaterPrivatization.pdf, accessed 18 Jan 2011.

Khanna, Tarun. 2007. *Billions of Entrepreneurs: How China and India Are Reshaping Their Futures*. Boston, MA: Harvard Business Press.

King, Anthony. 2004. *Spaces of Global Cultures: Architecture, Urbanism, Identity*. London: Routledge.

Landman, Karina and Martin Schönteich. 2002. 'Urban Fortresses: Gated Communities as a Reaction to Crime'. *African Security Review* 1 (4): 71–85.

REMAKING CITIZENSHIP AND 'COMMUNITY' 131

Legg, Stephen. 2007. *Spaces of Colonialism: Delhi's Urban Governmentalities*. Oxford: Blackwell.

Mazzarella, William. 2003. *Shoveling Smoke: Advertising and Globalization in Contemporary India*. Durham, NC: Duke University Press.

Nandy, Ashis. 2001. *An Ambiguous Journey to the City: The Village and Other Odd Ruins of the Self in the Indian Imagination*. New Delhi: Oxford University Press.

Nayar, Pramod K. 2006. *Reading Culture: Theory, Praxis, Politics*. New Delhi: SAGE.

Ojha, Abhilasha. 1999. 'RWAs Will Soon Have Direct Control over Sanitation and Community Halls'. *Indian Express*, January 12. Available at www.indianexpress.com/res/ple/ie/daily/19991201, accessed 11 Dec 2011.

Osella, Filippo and Caroline Osella. 2009. 'Muslim Entrepreneurs in Public Life between India and the Gulf: Making Good and Doing Good'. *Journal of the Royal Anthropological Institute* 15: S202–21.

Pow, Choon-Piew. 2007. 'Securing the 'Civilised' Enclaves: Gated Communities and the Moral Geographies of Exclusion in (Post-) Socialist Shanghai'. *Urban Studies* 44 (8): 1539–58.

Radhakrishnan-Swami, Meenakshi. 2005. 'Building on a Dream'. *Business Standard*, March 22.

Roy, Srirupa. 2007. *Beyond Belief: India and the Politics of Postcolonial Nationalism*. Durham, NC: Duke University Press.

Sengupta, Mitu. 2008. 'How the State Changed Its Mind: Power, Politics and the Origins of India's Market Reforms'. *Economic and Political Weekly* 43 (21): 35–42.

Sethi, Aman. 2005. 'The Price of Reforms'. *Frontline* 22 (19, Sept 10, 2005): 5–6.

Singh, K.P. 2011. *Whatever the Odds: The Incredible Story behind DLF* (with Ramesh Menon and Raman Swamy). New Delhi: Harper Collins.

Sirari, Tanvi. 2006. 'Civil Uprisings in Contemporary India'. Centre for Civil Society Working Paper No. 161, Delhi: Centre for Civil Society.

Srivastava, Sanjay. 1998. *Constructing Post-Colonial India: National Character and the Doon School*. London: Routledge.

Srivastava, Sanjay 2011. 'Urban Spaces, Disney-Divinity and Moral Middle Classes in Delhi'. In *Elite and Everyman. The Cultural Politics of the Indian Middle Classes*, edited by Amita Baviskar and Raka Ray, 364–390. New Delhi: Routledge.

Srivastava, Sanjay, 2012. 'National Identity, Kitchens and Bedrooms: Gated Communities and New Narratives of Space in India'. In *The Global Middle Classes: Theorizing through Ethnography*, edited by Mark Liechty, Carla Freeman, and Rachel Heiman, 57–84. Santa Fe, NM: School of Advanced Research Press.

Taussig, Michael. 1997. *The Magic of the State*. New York: Routledge.

Uberoi, Patricia. 2008. 'Aspirational Weddings: The Bridal Magazine and the Canons of "Decent Marriage"'. In *Patterns of Middle Class Consumption in India and China*, edited by C. Jaffrelot and P. van der Veer, 230–262. New Delhi: SAGE.

van Wessel, Margit. 2004. 'Talking about Consumption: How an Indian Middle-Class Dissociates from Middle-Class Life'. *Cultural Dynamics* 16 (1): 93–116.

7

Rural Real Estate

Empty Urbanization and the Agrarian Land Transition

Carol Upadhya

While carrying out research in Coastal Andhra over the last several years, I became curious about the many stretches of fallow land that punctuate the rich landscape of green paddy fields, especially along major roads connecting regional towns such as Vijayawada and Machalipatnam, and around 'old' as well as new Amaravati (the planned capital city of Andhra Pradesh).[1] These are advertised as residential 'layouts'—large blocks of empty land created by converting agricultural land into saleable house sites which are purchased by middle-class residents of nearby towns and more distant cities such as Hyderabad, or by affluent Non-Resident Indians (NRIs) (Upadhya 2018b). The incremental transformation of agricultural land into real estate is not unique to Andhra—this process is evident across several regions of India, especially on the peripheries of large towns and cities (Gururani 2019; Verstappen and Rutten 2015). On the southeast edge of Bengaluru (earlier called Bangalore) as well, the rapidly urbanizing rural landscape—marked by high-end residential complexes and apartment blocks sprouting up

---

[1] This chapter is based partly on research in Andhra Pradesh that began in 2014 as part of the Provincial Globalisation research programme, a collaboration between the National Institute of Advanced Studies, Bangalore and the Amsterdam Institute for Social Science Research (AISSR), University of Amsterdam, supported by WOTRO Science for Global Development, The Netherlands. Between 2016 and 2019, research on the Amaravati capital city project was funded by a grant from the Azim Premji Foundation. Research on Bengaluru was carried out as part of a research project entitled 'Speculative Urbanism: Land, Livelihoods, and Finance Capital', funded by the National Science Foundation [grant number BCS-1636437]. The support of all these funding agencies is gratefully acknowledged. I thank my research associates for their valuable inputs to these projects—S. Udaybhanu and Rohith Gutta in Andhra, and Kaveri Medappa and Sachinkumar Rathod in Bangalore. I am also very grateful to my colleagues in the Speculative Urbanism project—Vinay Gidwani, Michael Goldman, Hemangini Gupta, Helga Leitner, and Eric Sheppard—for ongoing discussions on questions of land, real estate, and finance capital.

Carol Upadhya, *Rural Real Estate* In: *Neoliberalism, Urbanization, and Aspirations in Contemporary India.*
Edited by: Sujata Patel, Oxford University Press. © Oxford University Press 2021.
DOI: 10.1093/oso/9780190132019.003.0007

AGRARIAN LAND TRANSITION   133

haphazardly along rural roads—is dotted with 'illegal' housing developments carved out of agricultural land.

Numerous studies have highlighted the transformation of India's cities since the 1990s by the emergence of gated communities, luxury apartment complexes, glitzy shopping malls, and manicured office parks—developments that are usually attributed to economic reforms, the forces of globalization, the expansion of the consumption-oriented middle classes and the new service economy, the entry of foreign capital into the real estate sector, and the easier accessibility of credit for housing.[2] But the literature on neoliberal urbanization tends to overlook the more quotidian and socially embedded processes through which the city is produced—in particular, the incremental conversion of agricultural land into 'urban' forms of property. We also know little about how the assetization and financialization of land is reconstituting rural economies and societies and shaping processes of urbanization.

In this chapter I explore the transformation of agrarian land into what I am calling 'rural real estate', a dimension of urbanization in post-liberalization India that has been relatively neglected. The conversion of agricultural land to urban uses is not a 'natural' outcome of the expansion of urban settlements into their rural hinterlands, or of rational urban planning and the increasing demand for land for 'development'. Instead, with the increasing assetization and financialization of land, it becomes a key site for the production and multiplication of value and for accumulation by various actors at different scales—even when it is devoid of any 'use value'. As agrarian land gets imbricated in circuits of accumulation that earlier operated mainly in and through urban real estate markets, it is not just alienated from farmers or dislodged from the agrarian economy, displacing or dispossessing rural communities—issues that have been widely discussed in the literature on compulsory land acquisition. Rather, the ways in which this agrarian land transition is unfolding point to a significant shift in the meanings, status and values of land itself, as well as a reconfiguration of the 'rural' and the 'urban'.

This chapter is a preliminary attempt to explore these shifts, drawing on research carried out in Bengaluru as well as the new capital region of Andhra Pradesh ('Amaravati'). I argue that the current pattern of urban development in India is structured not only by 'neoliberal' state policies and the interests of the real estate industry and finance capital, but also by local and regional actors that control land markets in rural areas as well as by regional social

---

[2] See, for example, Brosius (2010); Goldman (2011); Searle (2016); Srivastava (2015).

134   CAROL UPADHYA

formations and modes of accumulation centred on land. Within this larger picture, I discuss some of the mechanisms and networks through which agrarian land is rendered into real estate.

Neoliberal Urbanization and the Financialization of Land

As cities and towns expand, they consume land—for the development of infrastructure such as roads, airports, and power installations, for housing and public amenities, and to support industrial and commercial activities. While spatial agglomeration is usually viewed as an inevitable element of urbanization, it is remarkable that *land* as such—its meanings, affordances, and transitions—has not figured centrally in urban studies or urban sociology (although, crucially, it has long been a key issue in agrarian studies).[3]

Land has entered into discussions on urbanization in India mainly in the literature on informal urban settlements ('slums'), where claims to land and housing are tenuous, giving rise to continuous struggles around the 'right to stay put' (Weinstein 2014). The massive slum evictions carried out in metropolitan cities such as Mumbai and Delhi since the 1990s as part of programmes of urban upgradation and gentrification are usually understood as an outcome of 'neoliberal urbanization'—referring to a set of policy initiatives promoted by international agencies and widely adopted by governments across the world to address the growing 'urban crisis' (Leitner et al. 2007; Parnell and Robinson 2012; Peck et al. 2009). The 'worlding' of Asia's cities (Roy and Ong 2011) is the most visible face of neoliberal urbanization, reflecting the circulation of hegemonic planning models designed to bring order to Asia's chaotic megacities and thereby make them more attractive to international capital. In India, urban reform programmes were adopted in the 1990s to improve governance and reduce 'corruption', enhance state revenues, and to promote 'entrepreneurial urbanism', all in the name of stimulating economic growth.[4] In this context, state and municipal governments have attempted to capture large swathes of occupied but 'underutilized' land for infrastructure

---

[3] Land has also been central to debates on the agrarian transition in India (D'Costa and Chakraborty 2017), but in this chapter I use the term 'transition' in a different sense, to emphasize the changing role of land in processes of accumulation much beyond agriculture.

[4] See Basu (2019); Brenner and Theodore (2002); Coelho et al. (2013); Kennedy (2014); Smitha (2017).

AGRARIAN LAND TRANSITION 135

development and urban renewal projects, as well as to monetize land to raise financial resources.[5]

Studies of evictions and displacement in India have drawn heavily on David Harvey's (2003) 'accumulation by dispossession' (ABD) thesis, which posits that global capital, in response to a crisis of over-accumulation, has entered a new phase of primitive accumulation. This framework has been invoked particularly in the context of compulsory land acquisition for 'public purposes', leading to the widespread displacement of peasant and Adivasi communities as well as slum-dwellers (Banerjee-Guha 2010). But as Levien (2013b) points out, in India the state rather than capital has been the main agent of such dispossession. This is particularly evident in the many Special Economic Zones (SEZs) that were set up across the country by state governments, which acquired land from farmers only to hand over to private sector industries and real estate developers.[6] SEZs 'became an outlet for speculative real estate capital' (Levien 2013b, 395) as well as the main focus of India's 'land wars' (Levien 2013a; Sampat 2016b). These developments show that India's 'homegrown neoliberalism' has been led not by capital but by an 'activist state' (Roy 2011b) that acquires land for infrastructure, industrial and real estate projects and outsources governance through special township policies and land pooling schemes, thereby accommodating 'different factions of the dominant coalition' (Basu 2019, 79).[7] The SEZ policy in particular represented a shift from a regime of 'land for production' (under the Nehruvian developmental state) to one of 'land for the market' (Levien 2013b, 384).

More recently, the central government's ambitious plans to build a series of 'smart cities' such as Dholera,[8] as well as massive infrastructure corridor projects (Balakrishnan 2013; Sampat 2017), are formed in the same mould. Such programmes reflect a neoliberal model of urban development that depends on private sector participation and capital investment for infrastructure development. In public–private arrangements, land usually constitutes the state's equity contribution while the private partners provide the financial resources (Kennedy 2014; Sud 2017). Land is particularly crucial to such

---

[5] See, for example Anjaria and MacFarlane (2016); Bhan (2009); Doshi (2013); Ghertner (2014, 2015); Shatkin (2014); Weinstein (2013, 2014).

[6] See Banerjee-Guha (2008); Jenkins et al. (2014); Levien (2011); Sampat (2010).

[7] The Amaravati project encompassed 217 sq. km. of land in Guntur district, of which 34,000 acres was pooled from farmers.

[8] See Basu (2019); Datta (2015); Kennedy and Sood (2016); Ramachandraiah (2015); Sampat (2016a); Upadhya (2018a).

136　CAROL UPADHYA

deals because private companies are often reluctant to invest in long-gestation infrastructure projects without solid collateral (Balakrishnan 2017).

Public–private partnerships in infrastructure and urbanization projects have been enabled by the array of financial instruments that state agencies now have at their disposal, in particular modalities of 'land-based' financing in which land is used as leverage to attract private capital.[9] In addition, and partly in response to the widespread protests against direct land acquisition, state and municipal governments increasingly employ indirect modalities of land assembly that integrate market and state mechanisms, such as land pooling. The use of market mechanisms to free up agrarian land for development in turn has contributed to the activation of land markets across the country (discussed subsequently). In such policies and programmes, land is appropriated from landowners or cultivators not so much for its use value (for industrial, commercial, or residential purposes), but because of its potential value as equity. This strategy is based on the possibility of extracting profits from land through exchange, as prices rise due to the increased circulation of money through land markets.

Another key driver of neoliberal urbanization in India was the opening up of the real estate sector in India to foreign investment in 1995. This policy shift led to a considerable flow of transnational capital (especially private equity capital) into high-end commercial and residential projects in major Indian cities such as Bangalore and Delhi (Goldman 2011; Halbert and Rouanet 2014; Searle 2016). These investments have shaped urban development in visible as well as less visible ways—underwriting the homogenous 'global' look image of commercial and residential projects that marks most Indian cities, pushing up real estate prices through 'global forms of land speculation' (Goldman 2011, 576), and by stimulating a major restructuring of the real estate industry itself. But despite this important shift, most private capital investments in land and real estate still come from domestic rather than international capital (D'Costa and Chakraborty 2017; Levien 2013b).[10] Moreover, international investors have only recently shown interest in

---

[9] See: 'Value Capture Finance Policy Framework', Ministry of Urban Development, Government of India, February 2017. Available at http://amrut.gov.in/writereaddata/3-VCF%20Policy%20Book_FINAL.pdf.

[10] Indeed, a closer look at real estate investments suggests that they emanate not just from 'national capital' but more often from 'regional capital', as in the case of Andhra's new capital city project (Upadhya 2017; cf. Sud 2017). Most real estate companies in India are very localized, rooted in particular cities, and often find it difficult to operate in a new market because they are not plugged into the local business or political networks needed to acquire and convert land; cf. Sud (2014b).

AGRARIAN LAND TRANSITION   137

property markets beyond the major metropolitan centres—yet land prices have skyrocketed in small towns and rural areas as well (Sarkar 2015). These observations suggest that we need to decentre 'planetary urbanization' (Brenner 2014) or global capital as the key agent of change in Indian cities, and pay more attention to the strategies and interests of diverse actors and circuits of capital operating at other scales.

Thus, several key policy changes through which neoliberal urbanization has been operationalized have been based on the extraction of value from land. Land is increasingly valued as an asset or a form of equity and as a site of accumulation for finance capital, rather than as a 'factor of production' or the basic substrate needed to build housing, commercial properties, or industries. This surmise is supported by the fact that private investors in an SEZ or infrastructure project often exit early, deriving their profits from the increase in the value of land rather than from whatever was (supposed to be) built on that land (Balakrishnan 2017, 274; Cross 2014, 52). Similarly, foreign private equity investors in real estate projects usually withdraw their capital much before the project is completed, as soon as the mandatory three-year lock-in period is over and often even before ground is broken. Such investors realize surplus value not from the construction or sale of real property but from the escalation in the value of land that is assembled for the project.[11]

These developments, and the policy shifts that have enabled them, suggest that land is not just becoming commoditized or 'monetized', but actually financialized. Here I follow Krippner's definition of financialization as 'the tendency for profit making in the economy to occur increasingly through financial channels rather than through productive activities' (2011, 4). The financialization framework was developed by scholars after the 2008 global financial meltdown caused by the sub-prime mortgage crisis in the US (Davis and Kim 2015; Krippner 2005), building on David Harvey's prescient writings on the financialization of housing and land markets which turned property into a 'pure financial asset' or a 'form of fictitious capital' (1982, 347). While some scholars believe that the concept of financialization should be confined to the advanced post-industrial economies, which are now thoroughly dominated by finance capital, it has been usefully applied more widely—particularly in the 'global land grab' literature.[12] As Fairbairn argues, 'the financialization

---

[11] Sources: Interviews with real estate developers and key informants in Bangalore conducted under the 'Speculative Urbanism' project; and personal communication, Michael Goldman and Sanjiv Aundhe.

[12] See, for example, Adnan (2013); Borras and Franco (2012); Hall et al. (2015); and White et al. (2013).

138 CAROL UPADHYA

of the global economy since the 1970s has opened up new possibilities for the incorporation of farmland into financial circuits . . . ' (2014, 779).

One symptom of financialization is the volatility that periodically punctures the functioning of 'rational' markets, generating higher returns than are available in the 'real economy'—such as during land bubbles (Fairbairn 2014, 780, 782). This observation resonates with the Indian experience, where one of the main effects of the planning of mega-projects (such as SEZs, infrastructure corridors, and 'smart cities') has been the creation of new land markets (and often speculative bubbles), as investors buy up cheap land around the project site in anticipation of rising prices (Cross 2015; Sathe 2011; Upadhya 2020). However, in such cases the gyrations of land markets do not reflect 'the foreignization of space' (Zoomers 2010), as in the Latin American and African examples, but rather are shaped by investments from regional and national capital.

In the following sections I explore in more depth the operations and reverberations of the activation of land markets in rural areas at the edges of growing cities and planned infrastructure projects, arguing that the financialization of land is not just an effect of land acquisition or the entry of capital into these areas, but occurs at multiple scales involving diverse actors and pathways of capital accumulation.

Financialization from Below: Tracking Rural Land Markets

Addressing calls for a postcolonial critique of urban studies and for 'new geographies of theory',[13] Brenner (2014) argues that the theoretical focus should shift from the 'city' or the 'urban' understood as a distinct spatial formation, to *urbanization* as a world-wide set of 'sociospatial processes' driven primarily by capitalist accumulation (Brenner and Schmid 2015). But such global theories of urbanization tend to 'flatten the complex sociopolitical terrain and dilute, if not obscure, the constitutive outsides like the rural and agrarian that make the urban' (Gururani and Dasgupta 2018, 42) in the postcolonial worlds of Asia and Africa. Urban scholars of the global South have pointed to the many ways in which cities and towns have been marked by their regional histories and agrarian locations (Nair 2013), reminding us that

---

[13] See Leitner and Sheppard (2016); Robinson (2006, 2016); Roy (2009).

AGRARIAN LAND TRANSITION   139

in places such as India, the 'urban question' is also the 'agrarian question' (Roy 2016; cf. Robinson 2016).

Building on these theoretical turns, an emerging body of work on the peri-urban in South Asia has documented the complex transitions that are taking place at the edges of expanding cities. Gururani and Dasgupta (2018) employ the idea of 'frontier urbanism' to capture the 'heterogeneous politics of land . . . the feverish non-metrocentric remapping of the urban–agrarian hinterland that is taking place in South Asia' (2018, 41). By studying these 'agrarian-urban edges', they suggest, we can better track how 'new geographies of capitalist accumulation are spatially fixed and how the relentless negotiations, speculations, contestations, displacements, and dispossessions produce new urban subjects and social formations' (2018, 42). Gururani (2019) proposes the concept of 'agrarian urbanism' to capture the deep entanglement of the agrarian and the urban in peri-urban sites, pointing to the centrality of struggles around land in such contexts. The politics of land is underwritten by a regime of 'flexible planning' (Gururani 2013), in which informal and formal processes and institutions are deeply interdigitated, producing the 'fractal' urban spaces (Dubey 2018, citing Roy 2011a) that are so typical of peri-urban sites. The activation of markets and the transformation of local residents into agents of the market have been documented in several studies of the peri-urban in South Asia.[14]

Another emerging body of literature suggests that the debate on land and dispossession needs to shift away from direct land acquisition by the state to document and understand the other ways in which agricultural land is appropriated from owners and farmers and turned into a financial asset. Studies from across India indicate that land alienation is increasingly taking place through the market rather than the state (Raman 2016; Vijayabaskar and Menon 2018). As noted earlier, the announcement of new infrastructure projects typically gives rise to vibrant land markets in the vicinity, as outside investors and real estate developers enter the market, tempting cultivators to earn quick money by selling out. In the case of Amaravati, the government's announcement of the location for the new capital city fuelled waves of speculative investment, driving up land prices to very high levels (both within and

---

[14] See, for example, Dubey (2018) and Sarkar (2015) on the National Capital Region, Balakrishnan (2018) on Mumbai's hinterland, Raman (2016) on Chennai, Kundu (2016) on Kolkata, and Anwar (2018) on Karachi. The literature on small towns in India similarly engages with the question of rural–urban interfaces (Denis and Zerah 2017), but the question of land is largely absent in these studies. However, see Verstappen and Rutten (2015).

140 CAROL UPADHYA

around the perimeter of the designated capital zone), leading large and small farmers alike to sell their land (Ramachandraiah 2016; Upadhya 2020). In this case, as in other examples of 'greenfield' city projects (Kennedy and Sood 2016), investors include urban middle-class professionals, NRIs (the regional diaspora), and local businessmen in search of a quick profit, as well as builders and land aggregators.[15] Similarly, on the perimeters of expanding cities, the prospect of future 'development' (i.e., real estate development) and attendant economic opportunities often attract speculative investments by 'land sharks', politicians, and regional elites. This inflow of capital drives up land prices, often creating speculative bubbles and generating windfall profits for some sellers as well as for market intermediaries and investors.

Of course, land markets are not new in India—across many regions land has long been commoditized, since at least the late colonial period. But land markets are traditionally 'sticky' because cultivators tend to hold on to their land unless faced with a crisis which requires a large sum of cash (Chakravorty 2013, 143), and land usually changed hands within the village. The difference, since the 1990s, is the large flow of investments coming from outside the local area (and from non-agriculturalists) into agricultural land. Chakravorty (2013, 161–6) argues that the high prices of land prevalent in states such as Punjab and Haryana are not based on agricultural productivity but are inflated by inflows of capital in search of a solid asset—from affluent urban residents and speculators as well as politicians and business persons looking for a safe haven for their 'black money'. Other observers too have noted a qualitative shift in the functioning of land markets since around 2000:

> The late 1990s and beyond witnessed growing inequalities of incomes in the country, which resulted in a class of wealthy individuals seeking to invest their savings in land, gold, or financial instruments . . . National actors, such as real estate firms, small and not-so-small property developers, and high net-worth individuals seeking outlets for investing their savings . . . play a significant role in rural land markets as they seek a hedge against inflation and a means to reduce portfolio risks . . . The political elite too play an

[15] Although then chief minister of Andhra Pradesh, Chandrababu Naidu, had assiduously wooed foreign investors to partner with the state government in building the new capital city, he was not very successful in attracting international capital. Most of the real estate development has taken place around the edges of the designated capital zone rather than inside it. Not surprisingly, after the victory of the opposition YSR Congress Party in May 2019 and the ouster of Naidu, the Amaravati project is in limbo and the associated real estate markets have largely collapsed.

AGRARIAN LAND TRANSITION 141

important role in boosting demand and supply. They constitute a growing source of demand given their ability to invest large sums of black money in land. (Vijayabaskar and Menon 2018, 576–7)

In their study of three villages on the outskirts of Chennai, Vijayabaskar and Menon (2018) found that the price of agricultural land had escalated mainly due to investments coming from outside the immediate area. They conclude that land values are determined more by location and attractiveness to non-rural investors than the productive capacity of the land. Here, the state has mainly played an 'indirect role in enabling land markets for rural land that transfer land from small and marginal farmers to private firms and urban elites' (Vijayabaskar and Menon 2018, 584). An analysis of data from seven states 'indicates a tenfold to twentyfold increase in rural land prices in recent years due to more attractive returns from speculative land markets vis-à-vis investments in stocks or gold' (Rajshekar 2013, cited in Vijayabaskar and Menon 2018, 576). The ballooning of land prices in peri-urban areas may be understood as a symptom of financialization, in which land is transformed into a new form of capital (Sarkar 2015, 444).

Vijayabaskar and Menon (2018) argue that the increasing alienation of land through the market represents a process of 'dispossession by neglect', stemming from the increasing unsustainability of agriculture and the neglect of this sector by the state in recent years. As in their case study of villages near Chennai, farmers in villages on the outskirts of Bengaluru complain of falling water tables, dried up irrigation tanks, and scarcity of agricultural labour—factors that have made cultivation unremunerative and the sale of land more attractive. Apart from the wider agrarian crisis that has created financial distress for many rural households, owners in areas that have been marked for urban development may be subtly or overtly pressured to sell their land by brokers, land mafias, or political operatives. But land sales are not necessarily coerced—for many, the high prices of land present an attractive opportunity to exit agriculture and cash in on their land, generating quick money that can be invested in land elsewhere or in other assets. Of course, not everyone can participate in the market in the same way. Very often, it is small and marginal landowners who are the first to sell out, at relatively low prices and often due to direct or indirect pressures, while larger landowners can afford to wait for prices to rise and so reap greater benefits from the new land market. These differences—tied to caste and class position—tend to magnify existing inequalities based on unequal access to land and social capital (Levien 2015).

142 CAROL UPADHYA

Thus, the monetization of agrarian land does not simply lead to the wholesale displacement or impoverishment of rural communities. Rather, the emergence of a speculative land market has complex and contradictory consequences—large landowners may benefit enormously while tenant farmers and landless agricultural workers lose their livelihoods as cultivation declines and land is converted to other uses. In addition, rich farmers often multiply their new wealth by becoming active agents in the land market—as brokers, moneylenders, or rentiers—further profiting from the conversion and assetization of agrarian land (Cowan 2018; Sami 2013). As Sarkar argues, 'while the state opens up a landscape for transformation through its legal and planning instruments, the actual process of commodification depends on the way the social agents—landowners, investors, and real estate developers—organize themselves and participate in this new political economy of land' (2015, 439). In some cases, such as in the Amaravati project, farmers have been persuaded to participate in this process in other ways, by pooling their land and becoming direct stakeholders in urbanization projects.[16]

Agrarian–Urban Transitions

The financialization of land is perhaps most visible on the edges of expanding and newly established cities, where the land transition is occurring at multiple scales and through diverse modalities—from large-scale real estate projects and state-led infrastructure development to small-scale and incremental land conversions. In Gurgaon, informal settlements and 'urban villages' nestle up against high-end real estate projects and shopping malls (Chatterji 2013; Cowan 2018), producing the complex social fabric described by Srivastava (2015) as 'entangled urbanism'.

On the south-eastern edge of Bengaluru, the landscape is similarly fractured. The area boasts one of the largest apartment complexes in the city, occupying over 100 acres of land purchased from farmers by a professional land aggregator, who then entered into a joint venture with a large real estate developer. This high-end gated community, occupied mainly by software engineers and other professionals who work in the nearby office parks, is located just adjacent to the village on whose land it was built—itself rapidly urbanizing as residents build up on their houses or construct

---

[16] See Balakrishnan (2013, 2019); Datta (2015); Levien (2018); Upadhya (2018a, 2020).

new apartment blocks to take advantage of the increasing demand for rental units. Yet just down the road one finds a patchwork of coconut groves, cultivated fields of ragi and maize, grape orchards, and small dairy farms, interspersed with 'international schools', open plots of barren land, luxury villas hidden behind tall fences, migrant labour camps fashioned out of blue plastic sheets, and residential layouts offering house sites for sale to the urban middle class.

Such peri-urban landscapes often seem illegible, as stretches of emptied land and under-construction buildings of varying sizes and aesthetic qualities visible along traffic-choked roads seem to tell only the standard story of 'unplanned' urban growth. Yet beneath the surface one can discern the 'power geometries' that are producing this fractured landscape—the opaque yet vibrant land markets organized by loose networks of brokers and local elites tied to shadowy but powerful politicians, who in turn are linked to land aggregators and real estate companies that control much of the city's land. New modes of accumulation and livelihoods are pursued by those who have been dislodged from the agrarian economy and are seeking a foothold in the urban—from small-scale land brokering and moneylending to tending the manicured gardens or cleaning the corridors of the new gated apartment complex as contract workers (especially women). Enterprising farmers may become experts in cobbling together parcels of land for higher-level brokers, while influential local businessmen forge connections with land aggregators by specializing in persuading farmers to sell. Narratives about the new wealth generated from brokering a single land deal abound in these peri-urban villages, where residents tell tales about a local man who prospered by creating layouts illicitly on common lands and then leveraged his money into a successful political career. At the same time, stories of dislocation and ruin linked to the declining agrarian economy are told by agricultural labourers, and by Dalits who sold their land too early and find themselves deeper in debt. These divergent experiences can all be traced to the circulation of finance capital, which is drastically altering rural and peri-urban landscapes by pushing up land values, inducing sales, and thereby entangling agrarian economies in urban circuits of accumulation.

In Bengaluru, the rapid expansion of the city into its hinterland has been enabled by professional land aggregators, who purchase land from farmers and assemble it into parcels of 25 to 100 acres for sale to developers. Even in areas far from the city, aggregators have created large 'land banks' in anticipation of future demand. The location and ownership of these parcels of alienated land are difficult to determine, for this is valuable

144 CAROL UPADHYA

proprietary information not readily shared. Moreover, land banks are rarely visible because the original owners or their tenants may continue to cultivate the land until it is required for development—a rather paradoxical situation in which financialized land continues to produce concrete yield. Land banks are assembled not so much in anticipation of a future need for development, but for the profit land can yield as it is gradually assetized and converted into urban real estate.

As Sud (2017) points out, a wide range of agents are involved in such land deals, from local brokers to land aggregators, real estate developers and an array of political and official actors and intermediaries who interface with buyers, sellers, and state agencies. In our study of peri-urban villages in Bangalore, we have mapped the chains of actors that enable the arduous process of assembling small plots of land into parcels large enough to be attractive to developers. As land passes up the value chain, from the farmer through a broker to an aggregator and then a developer, its value multiplies; some portion of this value is captured by the actors at each link that facilitate these transactions, with the largest chunk accumulating in the hands of large land aggregators and real estate companies and the smallest portion accruing to the original owner. Once separated from the cultivator, agricultural land becomes an asset which is quickly financialized as it enters the city's circuit of real estate and land capital.

Beyond the mega-projects that gobble up large parcels of land on the outskirts of the city, the agrarian land transition is occurring in more incremental and quotidian ways as well. Local upper-caste landowners have accumulated land by encroaching on village common (*gomala*) lands) or by 'grabbing' dalits lands, to form residential layouts offering house sites for sale to middleclass investors (Upadhya and Rathod 2021). Many of these layouts are unauthorized, but they are created in the (well-founded) expectation of future regularization or on the assurance by political power brokers that they will not be challenged (Benjamin and Raman 2011).[17] Indeed, the 'land grab' is a well-known appurtenance of political and caste power in Bengaluru, as elsewhere, and it plays out at multiple scales in peri-urban Bangalore as well as in Amaravati.

---

[17] Carving residential layouts out of agricultural land is not a new practice—Bengaluru is dotted with 'revenue layouts', referring to residential colonies formed on 'revenue land' (that is, agricultural land governed by the Revenue Department and listed in their records) converted into house sites. Over time these colonies have attained legal or quasi-legal status, or have been regularized through various political and legal tactics (Nair 2005).

The activation of rural land markets has ripple effects far beyond the immediate locale. For instance, farmers in peri-urban Bangalore as well as the villages of the new capital region of Andhra Pradesh have used money gained from land sales to purchase agricultural land in more distant locations where prices are much lower. This land is usually leased out to local cultivators, thereby contributing to the activation of land and lease markets in other areas. Thus, 'proceeds from land commodification [circulate] back through the rural economy as further land purchases, fuelling agricultural rentiership and land speculation' (Levien 2011, 475). Another typical outcome of the urbanization of rural spaces is the emergence of a rentier economy—farmers often use the proceeds of land sales to construct new houses or add additional floors to their existing village homes to rent out (Anwar 2018; Cowan 2019; Naik 2015; Sampat 2016a). In peri-urban locales of Bangalore as well as the new capital region of Andhra, these rental units cater to migrant workers—both informal sector workers and middle-class professionals employed in the burgeoning urban service economy or construction industry.

The injection of large sums of money generated by land sales into local rural economies sets into motion other changes—a construction boom accompanied by an influx of workers and business people from outside the local area, giving rise to a new rental economy; the appearance of novel financial instruments and institutions for the circulation and multiplication of money, together with new forms of debt; the emergence of new occupations and income opportunities linked to the property market; and the formation of wider political and economic networks that channel capital into the area, empowering and enriching some local actors who become conduits for these capital flows. These processes are evident in peri-urban villages of Bangalore as well as in the Amaravati project, leading to the accumulation of wealth and social power by some groups and the increasing impoverishment and marginalization of others (especially Dalits).

While agrarian land gets converted into urban real estate through diverse pathways, all depend on 'informal' transactions to consolidate parcels of land and to navigate the maze of legal steps and official clearances required to complete the processes of sale and conversion—procedures that are managed by multi-scalar networks of intermediaries that connect the 'local' and the 'rural' with 'metropolitan' or transregional circuits of capital. The formation of multi-scalar networks around land markets illustrates the complex entanglements of 'rural' and 'urban' on the peripheries of expanding cities. These developments suggest that India's 'neoliberal' urban transformation has been deeply shaped by regionally rooted social-political configurations

146 CAROL UPADHYA

that structure the circulation of capital through rural land markets, as financialized land has become a key site of accumulation in the contemporary moment.

***

In this chapter I have provided a broad sketch of the trajectory of 'actually existing' neoliberal urbanization (Brenner and Theodore 2002) in contemporary India, by focusing on the transformation of rural land into urban real estate. I have suggested that land should be viewed not just as a valuable commodity or a factor of production that can be appropriated by state or capital for their projects of accumulation. Instead, land is generating value in new ways as it is incorporated into multi-scalar circuits of accumulation that encompass agrarian social formations and regimes of property and power while also transforming them.[18]

It could be argued that land in India is not fully commodified and so could hardly be financialized. Land remains bound by social structures of caste and kinship and governed by complex legal structures and bureaucratic systems as well as exclusionary social and political networks.[19] Nonetheless, I suggest that the concept of financialization is helpful in unravelling the entangled current trajectories of urban development and agrarian change. The financialization of land, as discussed here, not only facilitates 'accumulation by dispossession', it also enables the interlinking of different circuits of capital and spheres of value, as capital moves through formal and informal credit and land markets and mutates between different forms of value such as real estate, financial instruments, and assets such as gold. These modalities of capital accumulation, while grounded in regional economies and caste-based configurations of power, are increasingly transnational and transregional (Upadhya 2017, 2018b)—although their transnational dimensions may not include the 'usual suspects' of global capital (Wall Street investment firms, large multinational corporations).

Within this broad framework, I have tried to map out some of the routes through which agrarian land is dislodged from rural economies as it enters urban real estate markets—a process that occurs not only on the edges of expanding metropolitan areas such as Bengaluru, Chennai, and Delhi but

[18] The concept of multi-scalar networks of value production through land is being employed in the NSF-funded Speculative Urbanism project, drawing on recent literature from geography.
[19] See, for instance Anwar (2018); De Neve (2015); De Neve and Donner (2015); Dubey (2018); Sud (2014a).

around the sites of 'new city' projects such as Amaravati, and even in more remote rural areas where land markets were till recently quite dormant. In all these places, the inflow of money seeking new sites of investment pushes up land values, which in turn encourages farmers and other landowners to sell. But because such investment is often speculative (in the sense that it hinges on the uncertain promise of future development and wagers that prices will rise dramatically), it may lead to 'empty urbanization', in which agricultural land—ostensibly purchased for other purposes—remains unoccupied and unutilized, merely a site of investment meant to generate more value each time it changes hands. Such land is not only divorced from its productive role in agriculture, it also does not fulfil any other function such as the creation of housing, industry, or infrastructure. Yet land as a financial asset is central to the contemporary pattern of capitalist accumulation, at different scales, and deeply marks the trajectory of urbanization in India today.

The production of rural real estate is accomplished through complex actor-networks that stretch across various scales and blur the traditional boundaries of state/market, rural/urban, and formal/informal, reshaping spatial forms and local economies in sometimes unexpected ways. This means that to understand how urbanization is taking place, we need to map these networks across different regions of India, documenting how value is extracted from land and through what modalities, and how it is seques-tered and deployed by different sets of actors. This exercise must also take into account the regional formations of capital, caste, and class that struc-ture the process of accumulation through land, and uncover the subterra-nean channels that link provincial places such as Amaravati and peri-urban Bangalore to other sites and forms of capital.

Finally, I have sought to show that agrarian land has become a key site of speculative accumulation not only for metropolitan elites or large real estate companies, but also for provincial capital, urban middle-class citizens, and the rural landowning classes. This development has important implications for our understanding of urbanization in India, which is not just a spatial, economic, or social transition but a ramifying mode of accumulation that builds on and mutates historically embedded social structures of property and power—with contradictory consequences for the various actors and groups that become entangled in the agrarian land transition across different scales.

References

Adnan, S. 2013. 'Land Grabs and Primitive Accumulation in Deltaic Bangladesh: Interactions between Neoliberal Globalization, State Interventions, Power Relations and Peasant Resistance'. *Journal of Peasant Studies* 40 (1): 87–128.

Anjaria, J. S. and C. MacFarlane, eds. 2016. *Urban Navigations: Politics, Space and the City in South Asia*. Delhi: Routledge.

Anwar, N. 2018. 'Receding Rurality, Booming Periphery: Value Struggles in Karachi's Agrarian–Urban Frontier'. *Economic and Political Weekly* 53 (12): 46–54.

Balakrishnan, S. 2013. 'Highway Urbanization and Land Conflicts: The Challenges to Decentralization in India'. *Pacific Affairs* 86 (4): 785–811.

Balakrishnan, S. 2017. 'Land-Based Financing for Infrastructure: What Is New about India's Land Conflicts?' In *Political Economy of Contemporary India*, edited by R. Nagaraj and S. Motiram, 260–78. Delhi: Cambridge University Press.

Balakrishnan, S. 2018. 'Seeing Mumbai through Its Hinterland: Entangled Agrarian–Urban Land Markets in Regional Mumbai'. *Economic and Political Weekly* 53 (12): 55–60.

Balakrishnan, S. 2019. 'Recombinant Urbanization: Agrarian–Urban Landed Property and Uneven Development in India'. *International Journal of Urban and Regional Research* 3 (4).

Banerjee-Guha, S. 2008. 'Space Relations of Capital and New Economic Enclaves: SEZs in India'. *Economic and Political Weekly* 43 (47): 51–9.

Banerjee-Guha, S., ed. 2010. *Accumulation by Dispossession: Transformative Cities in the New Global Order*. New Delhi: SAGE Publications.

Basu, I. 2019. 'Elite Discourse Coalitions and the Governance of "Smart Spaces": Politics, Power and Privilege in India's Smart Cities Mission'. *Political Geography* 68: 77–85.

Benjamin, S. and B. Raman. 2011. 'Illegible Claims, Legal Titles, and the Worlding of Bangalore'. *Revue Tiers Monde* 206: 37–54.

Bhan, G. 2009. 'This Is No Longer the City I Once Knew: Evictions, the Urban Poor and the Right to the City in Millennial Delhi'. *Environment and Urbanisation* 21 (1): 127–42.

Borras, S. and J. C. Franco. 2012. 'Global Land Grabbing and Trajectories of Agrarian Change: A Preliminary Analysis'. *Journal of Agrarian Change* 11 (2): 34–59.

Brenner, N. 2014. 'Introduction. Urban Theory without an Outside'. In *Implosions/Explosions: Towards a Study of Planetary Urbanization*, edited by N. Brenner, 14–35. Berlin: Jovis.

Brenner, N. and C. Schmid. 2015. 'Towards a New Epistemology of the Urban?'. *City* 19 (2–3): 151–82.

Brenner, N. and N. Theodore. 2002. 'Cities and the Geographies of Actually Existing Neoliberalism'. *Antipode* 32 (3): 349–79.

Brosius, C. 2010. *India's Middle Class: New Forms of Urban Leisure, Consumption and Prosperity*. Delhi: Routledge.

Chakravorty, S. 2013. *The Price of Land: Acquisition, Conflict, Consequence*. New Delhi: Oxford University Press.

Chatterji, T. 2013. 'The Micro-Politics of Urban Transformation in the Context of Globalisation: A Case Study of Gurgaon, India'. *South Asia: Journal of South Asian Studies* 36 (2): 273–87.

Coelho, K., L. Kamath, and M. Vijayabaskar, eds. 2013. *Participolis: Consent and Contention in Neoliberal Urban India*. Delhi: Routledge.

Cowan, T. 2018. 'The Urban Village, Agrarian Transformation, and Rentier Capitalism in Gurgaon, India'. *Antipode* 50 (5): 1244–66.

Cowan, T. 2019. 'The Village as Urban Infrastructure: Social Reproduction, Agrarian Repair and Uneven Urbanisation'. *ENE: Nature and Space* 50: 14–30

Cross, J. 2014. *Dream Zones: Anticipating Capitalism and Development in India*. London: Pluto Press.

Cross, J. 2015. 'The Economy of Anticipation: Hope, Infrastructure, and Economic Zones in South India'. *Comparative Studies of South Asia, Africa and the Middle East* 35: 424–37.

Datta, A. 2015. 'New Urban Utopias of Postcolonial India: "Entrepreneurial Urbanization" in Dholera Smart City, Gujarat'. *Dialogues in Human Geography* 5: 3–22.

Davis, G. and S. Kim. 2015. 'Financialization of the Economy'. *Annual Review of Sociology* 41: 203–21.

D'Costa, A.P. and A. Chakraborty. 2017. 'The Land Question in India: State, Dispossession, and Capitalist Transition'. In *The Land Question in India; State, Dispossession, and Capitalist Transition*, edited by A.P. D'Costa and A. Chakraborty, 16–45. New Delhi: Oxford University Press.

De Neve, G. 2015. 'Predatory Property: Urban Land Acquisition, Housing and Class Formation in Tiruppur, South India'. *Journal of South Asian Development* 10 (3): 345–68.

De Neve, G. and H. Donner. 2015. 'Revisiting Urban Property in India'. *Journal of South Asian Development* 10 (3): 255–66.

Denis, E. and M. Zerah, eds. 2017. *Subaltern Urbanisation in India: An Introduction to the Dynamics of Ordinary Towns*. New Delhi: Springer India.

Doshi, S. 2013. 'The Politics of the Evicted: Redevelopment, Subjectivity, and Difference in Mumbai's Slum Frontier'. *Antipode* 45: 844–65.

Dubey, S. 2018. 'Urban Transformations in Khora Village, NCR: A View from the "Periphery"'. *Economic and Political Weekly* 53 (12): 76–84.

Fairbairn, M. 2014. 'Like Gold with Yield: Evolving Intersections between Farmland and Finance'. *Journal of Peasant Studies* 41 (5): 777–95.

Ghertner, D.A. 2014. 'India's Urban Revolution: Geographies of Displacement beyond Gentrification'. *Environment and Planning A* 46: 1554–71.

Ghertner, D. A. 2015. *Rule by Aesthetics: World-Class City Making in Delhi*. Oxford: Oxford University Press.

Goldman, M. 2011. 'Speculative Urbanism and the Making of the Next World City'. *International Journal of Urban and Regional Research* 35 (3): 555–81.

Gururani, S. 2013. 'Flexible Planning: The Making of India's "Millennium City", Gurgaon'. In *Ecologies of Urbanism in India: Metropolitan Civility and Sustainability*, edited by A.M. Rademacher and K. Sivaramakrishnan, 119–43. Hong Kong: Hong Kong University Press.

Gururani, S. 2019. 'Cities in a World of Villages: Agrarian Urbanism and the Making of India's Urbanizing Frontiers'. *Urban Geography* 41 (7): 971–89.

Gururani, S. and R. Dasgupta. 2018. 'Frontier Urbanism: Urbanisation beyond Cties in South Asia'. *Economic and Political Weekly* 53 (12): 41–5.

Halbert, L. and H. Rouanet. 2014. 'Filtering Risk Away: Global Finance Capital, Transcalar Territorial Networks and the (Un)making of City-Regions: An Analysis of Business Property Development in Bangalore, India'. *Regional Studies* 48 (3): 471–84.

Hall, R., M.Edelman, I. Scoones, B. White, and W. Wolford. 2015. 'Resistance, Acquiescence or Incorporation? An Introduction to Land Grabbing and Political Reactions "from Below"'. *Journal of Peasant Studies* 42 (3–4): 467–88.

Harvey, D. 1982. *The Limits to Capital*. Oxford: Blackwell.

Harvey, D. 2003. *The New Imperialism*. Oxford: Oxford University Press.

Jenkins, R., L. Kennedy, and P. Mukhopadhyay, eds. 2014. *Power, Policy and Protest: The Politics of India's Special Economic Zones*. New Delhi: Oxford University Press.

Kennedy, L. 2014. *The Politics of Economic Restructuring in India; Economic Governance and State Spatial Rescaling*. London: Routledge.

Kennedy, L. and A. Sood. 2016. 'Greenfield Development as *Tabula Rasa*: Rescaling, Speculation and Governance on India's Urban Frontier'. *Economic and Political Weekly* 51 (17): 41–9.

Krippner, G. 2005. 'The Financialization of the American Economy'. *Socio-Economic Review* 3 (2): 173–208.

Krippner, G. 2011. *Capitalizing on Crisis: The Political Origins of the Rise of Finance*. Cambridge, MA: Harvard University Press.

Kundu, R. 2016. 'Making Sense of Place in Rajarhat New Town: The Village in the Urban and the Urban in the Village'. *Economic and Political Weekly* 61 (17): 93–101.

Leitner, H. and E. Sheppard. 2016. 'Provincializing Critical Urban Theory: Extending the Ecosystem of Possibilities'. *International Journal of Urban and Regional Research* 40 (1): 228–35.

Leitner, H., J. Peck, and E. Sheppard, eds. 2007. *Contesting Neoliberalism: Urban Frontiers*. New York City: Guilford.

Levien, M. 2011. 'Special Economic Zones and Accumulation by Dispossession in India'. *Journal of Agrarian Change* 11: 454–83.

Levien, M. 2013a. 'The Politics of Dispossession: Theorizing India's "Land Wars"'. *Politics & Society* 41: 351–94.

Levien, M. 2013b. 'Regimes of Dispossession: From Steel Towns to Special Economic Zones'. *Development and Change* 44 (2): 381–407.

Levien, M. 2015. 'Social Capital as Obstacle to Development: Brokering Land, Norms, and Trust in Rural India'. *World Development* 74: 77–92.

Levien, Michael. 2018. *Dispossession without Development: Land Grabs in Neoliberal India*. Oxford: Oxford University Press.

Naik, M. 2015. 'Informal Rental Housing Typologies and Experiences of Low-Income Migrant Renters in Gurgaon, India'. *Environment and Urbanization ASIA* 6 (2): 154–75.

AGRARIAN LAND TRANSITION **151**

Nair, J. 2005. *The Promise of the Metropolis: Bangalore's Twentieth Century.* New Delhi: Oxford University Press.

Nair, J. 2013. 'Is There an Indian Urbanism?' In *Ecologies of Urbanism in India: Metropolitan Civility and Sustainability,* edited by A. Rademacher and K. Sivaramakrishnan, 43–70. Hong Kong: Hong Kong University Press.

Parnell, S. and J. Robinson. 2012. '(Re)theorizing Cities from the Global South: Looking beyond Neoliberalism'. *Urban Geography* 33: 593–617.

Peck, J., N. Theodore, and N. Brenner. 2009. 'Neoliberal Urbanism: Models, Moments, Mutations. *SAIS Review of International Affairs* 29 (1): 49–66.

Rajshekar, M. 2013. 'Great Rural Land Rush: 3 to 100-fold Rise in Farm Land Prices May Not Bode Well'. *Economic Times,* November 12.

Ramachandraiah, C. 2015. 'Andhra Pradesh's Master Plan for Its New Capital'. *Economic and Political Weekly* 50 (38): 10–13.

Ramachandraiah, C. 2016. 'Making of Amaravati: A Landscape of Speculation and Intimidation'. *Economic and Political Weekly* 51 (17): 68–75.

Raman, B. 2016. 'Reading into the Politics of Land: Real Estate Markets in the South-West Peri-urban Area of Chennai'. *Economic and Political Weekly* 51 (17): 76–84.

Robinson, J. 2006. *Ordinary Cities: Between Modernity and Development.* London: Routledge.

Robinson, J. 2016. 'Comparative Urbanism: New Geographies and Cultures of Theorizing the Urban'. *International Journal of Urban and Regional Research* 40 (1): 187–99.

Roy, A. 2009. 'The 21st Century Metropolis: New Geographies of Theory'. *Regional Studies* 43 (6): 819–30.

Roy, A. 2011a. 'Slumdog Cities: Rethinking Subaltern Urbanism'. *International Journal of Urban and Regional Research* 35 (2): 223–38.

Roy, A. 2011b. 'The Blockade of the World Class City: Dialectical Images of Indian Urbanism'. In *Worlding Cities: Asian Experiments and the Art of Being Global,* edited by A. Roy and A. Ong, 259–78. Malden, MA: Wiley Blackwell.

Roy, A., 2016. 'What Is Urban about Critical Urban Theory?'. *Urban Geography* 37 (6): 810–23.

Roy, A. and A. Ong, eds. 2011. *Worlding Cities: Asian Experiments and the Art of Being Global.* Malden, MA: Wiley Blackwell.

Sami, N. 2013. 'From Farming to Development: Urban Coalitions in Pune, India'. *International Journal of Urban and Regional Research* 37 (1): 151–64.

Sampat, P. 2010. 'Special Economic Zones in India: Reconfiguring Displacement in a Neoliberal Order?'. *City and Society* 22 (2): 166–82.

Sampat, P. 2016a. 'Dholera: The Emperor's New City'. *Economic and Political Weekly* 51 (17): 59–67.

Sampat, P. 2016b. 'India's Land Impasse'. *Seminar* 682 (June): 48–52.

Sampat, P. 2017. 'Infrastructures of Growth, Corridors of Power'. In *The Political Economy of Contemporary India,* edited by R. Nagaraj and S. Motiram, 230–59. New Delhi: Cambridge University Press.

Sarkar, S. 2015. 'Beyond Dispossession: The Politics of Commodification of Land under Speculative Conditions'. *Comparative Studies of South Asia, Africa and the Middle East* 35: 438–50.

Sathe, D. 2011. 'Political Economy of Land and Development in India'. *Economic and Political Weekly* 46 (29): 151–5.

Searle, L.G. 2016. *Landscapes of Accumulation: Real Estate and the Neoliberal Imagination in Contemporary India*. Chicago, IL: University of Chicago Press.

Shatkin, G. 2014. 'Contesting the Indian City: Global Visions and the Politics of the Local'. *International Journal of Urban and Regional Research* 38 (1): 1–13.

Smitha, K. C., ed. 2017. *Entrepreneurial Urbanism in India; The Politics of Spatial Restructuring and Local Contestation*. Singapore: Springer.

Srivastava, S. 2015. *Entangled Urbanism: Slum, Gated Community and Shopping Mall in Delhi and Gurgaon*. New Delhi: Oxford University Press.

Sud, N. 2014a. 'Governing India's Land'. *World Development* 60: 43–56.

Sud, N. 2014b. 'The Men in the Middle: A Missing Dimension in Global Land Deals'. *Journal of Peasant Studies* 41 (4): 593–612.

Sud, N. 2017. 'State, Scale and Networks in the Liberalisation of India's Land'. *Environment and Planning C: Politics and Space* 35 (1): 76–93.

Upadhya, C. 2017. 'Amaravati and the New Andhra: Reterritorialization of a Region'. *Journal of South Asian Development* 12 (2): 177–202.

Upadhya, C. 2018a. 'Capitalizing on the Future: Negotiating Planned Urbanization in South India'. In *Urban Asias: Essays on Futurity Past and Present*, edited by T. Bunnell and D.P.S. Goh, 169–82. Berlin: JOVIS.

Upadhya, C. 2018b. 'A "Love for Land": Transregional Property Investments in Andhra'. In *Provincial Globalization in India: Transregional Mobilities and Development Politics*, edited by C. Upadhya, M. Rutten, and L. Koskimaki, 162–87. London: Routledge.

Upadhya, C. 2020. 'Assembling Amaravati: Speculative Accumulation in a New Indian City'. *Economy and Society* 49 (1): 141–69.

Upadhya, C. and S. Rathod. 2021. 'Becoming Urban: Land and Caste at the City's Edge'. *South Asia Multidisciplinary Academic Journal (SAMAJ)* [forthcoming].

Verstappen, S. and M. Rutten. 2015. 'A Global Town in Central Gujarat, India: Rural-Urban Connections and International Migration'. *South Asia: Journal of South Asian Studies* 38 (2): 230–45.

Vijayabaskar, M. and A. Menon. 2018. 'Dispossession by Neglect: Agricultural Land Sales in Southern India'. *Journal of Agrarian Change* 18: 571–87.

Weinstein, L. 2013. 'Demolition and Dispossession: Toward an Understanding of State Violence in Millennial Mumbai'. *Studies in Comparative International Development* 48 (3): 285–307.

Weinstein, L. 2014. *The Durable Slum: Dharavi and the Right to Stay Put in Globalizing Mumbai*. Minneapolis, MN: University of Minnesota Press.

White, B., Saturnino Borras Jr., Ruth Hall, Ian Scoones, and Wendy Wolford. 2013. 'The New Enclosures: Critical Perspectives on Corporate Land Deals'. *Journal of Peasant Studies* 39 (3–4): 619–47.

Zoomers, A. 2010. 'Globalisation and the Foreignisation of Space: Seven Processes Driving the Current Global Land Grab'. *Journal of Peasant Studies* 37 (2): 429–47.

8

Political Centrality of 'Capital' Cities

A Case of Amaravati, Gurgaon, and Rajarhat[*]

Purendra Prasad

Indian cities have been going through major transformation with the opening up of the Indian economy in the post-1990s leading to the creation of new hubs of urban growth. In this phase of neo-liberalization, cities are witnessing large-scale transformation under the influence of the expanding capital and new technologies. Several studies pointed out that this has brought about increased spatial and economic inequality, ethnic segregation, social movements, and the contested role of the state (Shaw 2012; Sharma 2013). Despite growing inequalities and segregations,[1] there is renewed interest in the last decade or so in building new cities variously labelled 'smart', 'green', or 'integrated' now accompanied by an increasing tendency to instrumentalize the urban in pursuit of economic growth and a competitive drive to attract global financial flows (Kennedy and Sood 2016).

A certain kind of neoliberal restructuring is found in the existing as well as in the newly built cities. This is evident with the urban imagination and development of new capital cities such as Amaravati, Naya Raipur that is necessitated by the formation of new states. On the other hand, greater emphasis is laid on the development of greenfield frontiers such as Gurgaon, Greater Noida (Delhi), Rajarhat (Kolkata), Electronic city (Bengaluru), and Cyberabad (Hyderabad). All these greenfield projects in India are compelling illustrations of rescaling strategies. Explaining this periodic rescaling of urban fabric, Neil Brenner (2019) pointed out

---

[*] This chapter is a revised version of the paper submitted at the 43rd All India Sociological Conference of the Indian Sociological Society entitled 'Neo-Liberalism, Consumption and Culture' organized by the department of Sociology, University of Lucknow during 9–12 November 2017. The author thanks Prof Sujata Patel for an invitation to the plenary session of the conference.

[1] A significant consequence of this urban process has resulted in 'exclusionary urban growth' (Kundu 2009); logistical city (Samaddar 2017); suspended citizenship (Jha and Kumar 2016).

Purendra Prasad, *Political Centrality of 'Capital' Cities* In: *Neoliberalism, Urbanization, and Aspirations in Contemporary India.* Edited by: Sujata Patel, Oxford University Press. © Oxford University Press 2021.
DOI: 10.1093/oso/9780190132019.003.0008

154 PURENDRA PRASAD

simultaneous concentration of the urban process in a few urban nodes as well as a general urbanization process that goes beyond the administrative and traditional borders of urban bodies, influencing the economic activities and land-use pattern in the so-called rural areas. Brenner brings up the scale question in the light of state-led production of space, showing how the 'architectures of state space and the fabric of urbanization are increasingly woven together and intermeshed through the forward motion of capitalist industrial development' (ibid, 40). Drawing from Harvey's fixity/motion contradiction, Brenner skilfully unpacks the contraction of the spatial fix as a multi-scalar process in which 'various hierarchically organized structures ... mesh awkwardly with each other to define a variety of scales' (Harvey 1978, 424; Brenner and Schmdt 2014; Brenner 2004).

This chapter attempts to explain how 'state' has become more prominent in shaping the conditions for capital accumulation and circulation especially in leveraging their control over land for certain political interests. Taking the ideas from Henri Lefebvre, David Harvey, and Neil Brenner, I will be elaborating on rescaling strategies, and the way capital city has become the critical place where one could see how physical space, political power, and the logic of accumulation play out in the neoliberal context. In terms of methodology, the chapter relied on primary data for the analysis of Amaravati, the new capital city[2] while secondary sources particularly the published material was used for analysing Gurgaon and Rajarhat. The purpose of analysing three cities is not just to compare but to explain the underlying forces that have been contributing to the current forms of capitalist urbanization. The chapter is presented in four sections: the first section provides an analysis of the way the state has been effectively rescaling the Indian cities. The second section deals with the greenfield frontiers or urban cores emerging in every Indian city with specific reference to Gurgaon in Delhi and Rajarhat in Kolkata. Third section presents the story of Amaravati, the new capital city of Andhra Pradesh that was conceived by the state[3] to be built exclusively based on private capital. However, with the change in government in May 2019, three capital cities idea came to the forefront

---

[2] Field research was conducted in and around the villages of Amaravati during three months in 2015 and subsequent follow-up visits in 2017 and 2018. Field data was also collected from another two regions in Andhra Pradesh i.e. North Coastal Andhra and Rayalaseema in the years 2018 and 2020, which helped explain the intricate relation between capital cities and hinterlands.
[3] Between 2014 and 2019 the Telugu Desam Party (TDP)-led government created huge real estate market in and around Amaravati.

AMARAVATI, GURGAON, AND RAJARHAT 155

negating Amaravati as iconic city on one hand but at the same time stimulating speculative land market in other regions by the ruling party YSR Congress Party (YSRCP) is discussed. The final section provides the summary of discussions.

'Smart' and Greenfield Urbanization: Rescaling Strategies

Capital-intensive urbanization process has been significantly altering Indian cities of various sizes in the post-2000. It was in the year 2002 that foreign direct investment (FDI) could put its capital in real estate with a caveat that it is primarily for socially productive endeavours such as new townships. In 2004 this logic was extended to special economic zones (SEZs) allowing capital to get invested in manufacturing large swathes of rural or peri-urban land (Goldman 2015). Several studies pointed out that the investors required the state to acquire land and eventually these SEZs evolved illegally into real estate projects that privileged high-end urban residential complexes over manufacturing units (Levien 2018; Goldman 2015; Jenkins et al. 2014). Sri City with 12,000 acres in Andhra Pradesh is a classic case of how SEZ morphed into real estate venture eventually tuned into privately held township.

In 2005, Government of India launched its largest post-independence urban project called Jawaharlal Nehru National Urban Renewal Mission (JNNURM[4]) with 50,000 crores aimed at developing sixty-three Indian cities into 'world class' cities. The major thrust of the mission was to build infrastructure like roads, flyovers tunnels, skyways, airports, mega commercial complexes, real estates, and open spaces for recreation all with an aspiration to achieve international standards. Swapna Guha Banerjee (2009) pointed out that JNNURM emphasized large-scale gentrification and mega-projects, the privatization of basic services and public funds, and the liberalization of land and real estate markets.

In 2015, Government of India declared 'Smart Cities Mission' with a focus on dissemination of information, communication, and technology. Smart cities may refer to new cities (Greenfields) or existing cities (Brownfield projects) made smart through investment in technology and infrastructure.

---

[4] NDA government replaced JNNURM with Atal Mission for Rejuvenation and Urban Transformation (AMRUT) in the year 2015 with additional features of digitization and Wifi zones in cities.

156   PURENDRA PRASAD

The key concern of smart cities project is to design infrastructure and public services supported by modern technology in select 100 large cities so as to attract capital from within and outside the country for realizing agglomeration economies and building cities as engines of growth. Several international agencies explicitly and implicitly proposed that the success of globalization and livelihood strategy in India would depend on the speed with which modern production, trading, and banking institutions in all urban centres can be linked with metro cities, and global values injected into the business behaviour of the former (Kundu 2016; Burte 2014). Goldman (2015) says these global city boosters highlight the inevitability of the trend: China is building 100 global cities, and several countries are putting up land for international collaborators to build eco-cities, smart cities, knowledge cities, and greenfield experimental cities.

Similar to these trends, many states in India have begun to rescale economic development policies in favour of those regions most equipped to engage with global flows, starting with the largest city regions. The constitution of land banks, through eminent domain and enclosure processes, is central to the pursuit of these policies. As Loraine Kennedy and Ashima Sood (2016) argue, the tabula rasa fantasy links the various manifestations of greenfield urbanization, namely, new city-building (Dholera, Amaravati), integrated townships (Rajarhat New Town, Bengaluru's Electronic City), and city-centric industrial growth strategies (Chennai IT corridor, Delhi–Mumbai Industrial Corridor [DMIC], Sripermbadur–Orgadam manufacturing hub). This was evident in the case of Amaravati as well, where the effort was to transform a rural area into a massive, advanced greenfield city. The Amaravati Capital Region project is part of a greater ambition to create an East Coast Economic Corridor (ECEC), stretching from Chennai to Kolkata (Mitra, Sabyasachi et al 2016). Besides the Amaravati project, ten new ports, some of which with the status of SEZs, will be developed throughout the state to boost the economy. In this way, former Chief Minister Naidu envisioned a 'sustainable double-digit growth for the next 15–20 years' for Andhra Pradesh (Rediff 2015). These are the places or names on a map institutionalized by governments, which are branded as greenfield investment corridors. Lefebvre calls the present stage of social-spatial organization as 'critical phase', the harbinger of a certain globalization of the urban. Thus, this critical phase implies an understanding of spatiality that goes beyond the urban–rural dichotomy.

AMARAVATI, GURGAON, AND RAJARHAT   157

Urban inequalities become inevitable when cities become markets and residents become buyers or sellers or both (Saha 2019). Here comes the question of labour with this kind of smart or greenfield urbanization. After the formation of two separate states, Andhra Pradesh has begun to excessively privilege unproductive capital accumulation, primarily moneylending and speculation in real estate. This can be gleaned not only from Amaravati, but also from all the thirteen districts in the state. Vakulabharanam Vamsi and Purendra Prasad (2017) argued that the new phenomenon seems to be one in which no place exists for labour even in the imagination of the new accumulators. It would seem that many of the greenfield cities have entered a phase of post-productive capitalism. Elaborating this point further, Samaddar (2016) says:

> Hundreds of projects involving construction of the special economic zones (SEZs), power plants, airports, railway corridors, highways, bridges, new towns and new buildings and houses, flyovers, information and technology parks, and other residential and commercial projects, need not only steel, cement, and aluminium but also labour, particularly in the construction and mining sectors. The construction industry is one of India's largest employers. Thousands of construction workers build new apartments and offices, while living in squalor in roadside tents along the new buildings that come up in due course. They are like the informal miners of Bellary: migrants from the decimated agricultural sector, escaping poverty and disease at home only to be sucked into an immensely exploitative labour market.

Therefore, greenfield projects are a golden goose for capital accumulation purposes since urban growth machine operates as a multi-scalar political strategy. Brenner reconceptualizes the urban not as a 'distinct, self-contained, or pre-given institutional terrain, but as a provisionally stabilized site of mediation (evoking Lefebvre's concept) for "diverse, multi-scalar political-economical processes", including "capital accumulation", "state regulation", "territorial alliance formation" and "socio-political struggle"'. In order to conceive and build greenfield projects, state governments are under tremendous pressure to create vast land banks and release it to the market to ensure the flow of foreign capital investments. As urban is the required site for political expression, how capital's relation with the cities gets (un)realized is discussed in the next two sections.

Urban Cores[5] in Indian Cities

Every Indian city is aspiring to become a global, world class, and/or smart city. In whose imagination and for what interests is a different question altogether. But the fact is, each city today has a new inner city[6] with a prefix/suffix information technology (IT), hi-tech, electronic, or financial. To mention a few such urban cores, Gurgaon and Noida in National Capital Region, Delhi, Rajarhat in Kolkata, Electronic city in Bengaluru, Hi-tech city or Cyberabad in Hyderabad, Gujarat International Finance Tec City (GIFT city). These urban cores embody a new mode of circulation of money, information, human resources, and power. As David Harvey (1978) points out that these spatial patterns of development continuously blur their distinctions, and one must focus on the relationships emerging across both the hierarchical and non-hierarchical arrangement of the settlements. For the purpose of discussion, I have chosen two urban cores Gurgaon and Rajarhat to analyse the driving forces of urbanization in the recent past.

Gurgaon

Gurgaon represented an early prototype for private urban development of this ambition and scale. Gurgaon was initially developed by DLF which constructed residential, business and commercial buildings, and now houses the headquarters of some of the most important multinationals and IT industries of the region. Although the town started as an automobile manufacturing hub in the 1980s, private players such as DLF, quickly spotted the new opportunities in the IT and business process outsourcing (BPO) sectors. It has also been the site of intense real estate activity by a number of major construction conglomerates—Ansal, DLF and Unitech—since the early 1980s. Leveraging the demand for office space on the outskirts of Delhi, private developers kick-started the development of this urban core. Among these, the DLF corporation emerged as one of the world's largest real estate

---

[5] Greenfield sites such as Gurgaon, Greater Noida, Rajarhat, Cyberabad, Electronic City have become the core or inner cities of metropolitan Delhi, Kolkata, Hyderabad, and Bengaluru respectively.

[6] In Western usage, the term inner city refers to the urban core, the area which corresponds to the first centre of the city (Naidu 1990). In this chapter, urban core or inner city refers to the prime urban space in each of the Indian metropolitan cities.

AMARAVATI, GURGAON, AND RAJARHAT   159

company which also built a 3,500 acre DLF city. In pointing out the nexus between politicians and corporate partners post-1990s and 2000s and the significance of regional capitalism, Rana Dasgupta explains the emergence of Gurgaon as follows:

> What these partnerships could deliver in terms of profits and development was seen first and most spectacularly in the village of Gurgaon. When K P Singh *real estate* developer began to acquire land in the Haryana countryside, it was a dry, inaccessible place where very little happened beyond the wanderings of goat-herders on the baked earth. There were about eight cars in the whole village and one had to book a phone call to Delhi an hour in advance. By the early 2000s, Gurgaon was the largest private township in Asia, a booming expanse of hypertrophic, high-security apartment complexes which looked down on a landscape of pure commerce. In 2007, Singh listed his company on the Indian stock exchanges, and the 2008 *Forbes* list estimated him to be the world's eighth-richest man, with a fortune of $30 billion.
>
> (Dasgupta 2014, 65, emphasis added)

What is the rationale for this urban core? In Delhi, the trick was to start a national capital region, which meant at the least, investing huge amounts of money—diverted from other areas of national priority—in developing infrastructure, removing old 'polluting' industries to the outskirts, developing land, 'checking desertification', massive tree planting and providing water supply, resulting in an astonishing rise in real estate prices.

Many services with privately developed townships continue to be provided by the developers, rather than the Municipal Corporation of Gurgaon (MCG), formed in 2008. The fees that residents pay for these are known as 'maintenances charges'. These are paid to the developer responsible for the construction of the locality—residents of 'plotted' localities constructed by DLF and Unitech pay maintenance charges to DLF and Unitech, respectively. By 2013, Gurgaon had a plethora of shopping malls, golf courses, and five-star hotels, but lacked citywide sewage, water and electricity systems (Rajagopalan and Tabarrok 2013, 5). Gurgaon is the model of private urban development now institutionalized in SEZs and special investment regions (SIRs) and the Greenfield part of the smart city policy. In other words, 'Gurgaon looks like Singapore in terms of private-sector development, but like other Indian cities lacks in terms of public-sector development' (Sood and Rath 2017).

Several studies indicated that despite its prominence as a city of shopping malls, golf courses, and five-star hotels, Gurgaon's growth has been termed a 'failed experiment', given that it could not establish city-wide services of electricity, water, and sewerage, and thereby created zones of spatial and class exclusions. Economists would read Gurgaon's maladies as a classic case of market failure, resulting from private provision of public goods and the failure to internalize the externalities associated with such private provision. To consider one example, private sewage lines in Gurgaon end up in tanks because there is no comprehensive sewage system. This sewage must then be periodically dumped, often into water sources and commons (Rajagopalan and Tabarrok 2015). The result is the pollution of these groundwater sources over the long term, disproportionately affecting the middle and lower classes. In this way, Gurgaon's sanitation crisis reflects the well-known limitations of private provision of public goods.

Commenting on this process Polanki (2012) says:

> With its shiny buildings and galloping economy, Gurgaon is often portrayed as a symbol of a rising 'new India', yet it also represents a riddle at the heart of India's rapid growth: how can a new city become an international economic engine without basic public services? Is a city that pioneered the concept of exclusive gated communities now facing a social crisis triggered by precisely its most attractive selling point? The largely private-driven development of Gurgaon and the rapid pace at which that has happened has meant a gross neglect of its public spaces.

Through her study of landscapes of accumulation, Searle (2016) narrates Gurgaon's rise (now) stagnation by rendering a specific story of how Indian real estate became a transnational commodity in the 2000s, when the actions and actors of this market shifted from government to private sector elites and land came to have a standardized value for global markets. Srivastava (2017) analysed the significant ongoing renegotiation of the relationship between the state, private capital, and citizens as 'post-national urbanism'. It is in this context the resident welfare associations (RWAs) redefined the notions of 'civil society'. And that the notions of 'ordinariness' have very specific dimensions that relate to the new cultures of corporatization of the state and the state-like transformations of private capital in India. SEZs, SIRs (Special Investment Regions), or the integrated industrial townships proposed along the Delhi–Mumbai Industrial Corridor provides glimpses of this corporate urbanism (Sood 2015).

AMARAVATI, GURGAON, AND RAJARHAT   161

In Delhi thousands of labourers building the Airport city, the national highway leading to Gurgaon, Samaddar (2017) says that these are all parables of the current phenomenon of transit labour, because these places symbolize the conjunction of infrastructure, logistics, and labour. When one looks at the construction of several fast corridors, smart cities, and SEZs in various parts of the country, one gets a fair idea of the conjunction. But these facts do not tell us a story of seamless hyper-urbanization. They tell us of a deep-seated contradiction between the two images of the city—as an engine of economic growth through infrastructural expansion, and as a site of breakdown of an integral entity called the city (Samaddar 2017, 109). With spaces carved out to suit logistical practices, Indian cities are beginning to appear as sites of continuous fragmentation and gentrification, as well as ruralization. The city in order to survive must become a logistical hub. Never before had the city been so deeply caught in the logic of global supply chains. The mad rush for land by Indian capitalists is governed by this search for surplus profit, no matter the social cost (Samaddar 2017, 111).

In terms of labour unrest, the Gurgaon model was able to split the workers into regular and contract-based 'irregular' by entering into an agreement with the regular workforce. The struggle in Gurgaon began in 2008 around a dispute over recognition of unions at two companies (Auto Rico and Sunbeam) and a three-year wage agreement at another (Honda HMSI). There are four major assembly plants, churning out two-thirds of India's passenger cars and two-wheelers, depend on more or less the same suppliers. These dynamics did give rise to unrest but it was through the strategy of fragmenting the workers that managements were able to deal with the crisis. It is quite evident with the Gurgaon model of urban development that rescaling of economic activities is primarily to do with the role of state, which in turn lead to thriving of corporate urbanism with little regard for labour and other inhabitants.

Rajarhat

Rajarhat was the government's initiative of urban development as part of the Calcutta Megacity Programme. Rajarhat was projected as an entrepreneurial city by claiming Kolkata's position and success materializing its connections to the networked global economy (Das 2019). From the 1990s, Rajarhat was mooted primarily as an industrial hub designed to lift the economy and generate jobs. On the contrary, it was conceptualized and sold to the public principally as a residential urban centre where people across social spectrum—in

162 PURENDRA PRASAD

bureaucratic language, high-, middle-, and low-income groups—would live so that the pressure of habitation in Calcutta could be eased. Since the mid-1990s, when the project was first conceptualized, there has been a massive displacement and loss of livelihoods in Rajarhat without any substantial reintegration of the displaced people into the new economy of the new township area. Forcible land acquisition, displacement, and the failure of the state to rehabilitate the uprooted have been central to India's development story since the early years after Independence (Samaddar 2017).

It was also pointed out by scientists that Rajarhat was in the centre of the East Calcutta Wetlands and it would not be prudent to set up a township there. By one description there were sixty water farms and fifty-three kinds of fishing fauna including cultivated and wild fish in the wetlands of Rajarhat. Several small farmers had property rights over these wetlands. The government denied, first that any force had been used at all and that the people of Rajarhat had willingly parted with their lands. Second, it claimed large parts of the area were low-lying land not conductive to agriculture; the parts that could be cultivated, it said were low yielding. Finally, it denied that any ecological degradation would take place because the area was not part of the wetlands. It took time to fill the empty fields of Rajarhat in a planned way with houses, roads, streets, schools, people, office units, 'green' industries, shops and malls, water pipes, lanes power and cable lines, etc. as everything was dependent on developers, land sharks, estate owners, software giants like Wipro, Infosys, TCS etc. and the general state of the economy. Neither the government nor the West Bengal Housing Infrastructure Development Corporation (HIDCO) had any capital with it. All it had was the land acquired from the local villagers, and which was sold to private players to make the dream of public-private partnership (PPP) successful (Dey et al. 2013). This observation about Rajarhat is probably true of every new urban core or city that is expanding and emerging in India.

Kundu's exploration of place-making in Rajarhat new town near Kolkata is particularly striking for the portrait it draws of the complex relationship between urban village and gated community, as both sets of residents are 'unsettled by processes of urbanisation'. In this portrait, 'village and gated communities' are not bounded spatial entities, but 'fluid and dynamic places, imbued with heterogeneity and inherent conflicts' over claims to 'housing and infrastructure' as well as 'incremental . . . . Investments in a collective associational life'. Rajarhat is an investment and not a place to live. It was pointed out 'these investors' do not live here, and neither do they have any attachment to the place. Tenants, no matter how active they are in the social and cultural life of the community are excluded from these decision-making processes regarding the material improvement of the complex. The idea of ownership of property is thus pivotal to the attachment to place.

If one looks at the social profile of Rajarhat, it is evident that over 70 per cent of the Rajarhat's agrarian society and economy were labourers who owned no land. A large majority of the rest (over 80 per cent) were marginal and small peasants. The rest can be described as middling peasants (Dey et al. 2013, 126). Ritanjan Das (2019) argues that caste remains highly visible in Rajarhat. In the villages that lay ghettoized amidst the urban settlements—hidden away from the view of the skyscrapers promising 'five-star luxury' and 'global living standards'—the multitude of caste relations is obvious. Almost a quarter of the population are Dalits (and taken together with the religious minorities—mostly Muslims—formed more than 50 per cent of the entire population in 2003 and approximately 40 per cent in 2011 (Das 2019).

The farmers, fishermen, vegetable growers and sellers, boatmen, and agricultural labour now robbed of livelihoods all roam around these marginal places, if they are not already serving the newcomers of Rajarhat with domestic labour, transportation, vegetable supply, or serving tea and sundry snacks. But those who work in the New Town in those malls, e-firms, hotels, other companies, or live in those high rises, have few reasons to visit Kolkata or these dirty marginal places. This new inner city, supposed to produce urban wealth today, is at once exterior to the city proper. It looks like a wasteland, combining virtual production with a new type of consumption, symbolized by the mall, the city centre of the North, or the giant building material depot. Commenting on this process, Gautam Bhatia (2018) says the liberalized economy of the last few decades has created two pockets of city life. One, a small exclusive elite that occupies urban space but remains cloistered and outside of its civic forces, and a majority of dispossessed who fill the empty crevices of the city with meagre possessions and rudimentary needs.

What do the new urban spaces Gurgaon and Rajarhat tell us? These two urban cores represent post-metropolis in conception and reflect a new urban form. They indicate how the urban cores have been mediating everyday urban life, how it has been creating more inegalitarian urban spaces and a new urban topology of power. According to Samaddar (2017), the contemporary neoliberal model allows the city to become an infrastructural hub by engaging in all forms of extraction and thereby accumulating capital through rent. It is logistical because it continuously extracts from the physical aspects of the city—air, water, soil, waste—and uses rent as means to accumulate.

164   PURENDRA PRASAD

Amaravati—The 'New' Capital City

The new capital city Amaravati was visualized by the state to be a world-class, sustainable and greenfield city. What does this imagination entail? The Telugu Desam Party (TDP) led Government of Andhra Pradesh had entered into an agreement with Singapore companies to prepare a master plan and develop a 'world-class capital city'. Government conceived Amaravati—starting from preparing the master plan, design, construing the city with a foreign managing partner and the financing part of it almost entirely by private capital. Amaravati was in the process of becoming the 'first outsourced capital city'[7] representing a class of 'speculative cities' (Ramachandraiah 2016) with an 'urban fantasy' (Ong 2011).

The new capital city Amaravati has been located in a sprawling area of more than 50,000 acres, comprising land from twenty-nine villages on the banks of Krishna river between Vijayawada and Guntur. Apart from being conceived as perhaps one of the largest planned cities in independent India, it is also the most expensive one, and the scale of conversion of fertile agricultural land is unprecedented. Varied considerations such as water availability, central geographical location, caste composition in the proposed area, having a glamorous waterfront, and even *vaastu* seem to have played a key role in the final decision of locating the capital city in this region. Considerations such as sustainability, lower inequality, and greater social (including regional) equity seem to have been largely ignored as recommended by the Sivaramakrishna Committee appointed by the central government. Given little or no declared support from the central government, and having no access to surplus finances, the then AP government aggressively sought investments from foreign investors in East and Southeast Asia—Singapore, China, Japan, and Malaysia among others. The strategy for financing the capital city seems to be—on the one hand, acquire/pool land from farmers, and on the other, attract capitalist investors by promising a long-term lease of huge chunks of this accumulated land (Vakulabharanam and Prasad 2017).

---

[7] Rajappa, S. 2015. 'Thus Capital'. *Statesman*, June 2.

AMARAVATI, GURGAON, AND RAJARHAT 165

Land Pooling

The Land Acquisition, Rehabilitation and Resettlement Act (LARRA) 2013 makes it mandatory to hold public consultations through gram sabhas (village councils) to acquire land. The act has a provision that each village Panchayat (village government) has to pass a resolution with at least 75 per cent of the members of the gram sabha agreeing to give away land. Realizing that the land acquisition process may result in a huge controversy, given that a large majority of landowners (90 per cent) are peasants who own small amounts of land (less than 5 acres per household), the AP government took a decision to procure land through the method of land pooling. In land pooling, individual farmers agreed voluntarily to part with their land by entering into an agreement with a single entity, in this case, the Capital Region Development Authority (CRDA). Paradoxically, CRDA, which was given absolute power to acquire, sell, transfer, grant license to, or alienate land, was created by AP government without any consent from the village Panchayats. CRDA announced that it had procured 31,000 acres between October 2014 and August 2015. This seemed puzzling to a lot of observers across the country. Since there is a preponderance of small farmers in these twenty-nine villages, how was this operation so painless and successful?

Where persuasion through economic or caste means was not successful, the state resorted to arm-twisting tactics. During the period, January to March 2015, when land pooling was at its peak, the state planted armed police camps in recalcitrant villages and communities. Informally, rumours were spread that refusal to pool land would result in acquisition. This created fear and anxiety in the minds of small peasants, forcing them to think of parting their lands under land pooling scheme. Farmers of assigned landholdings were oppositional too (Vakulabharanam and Purendra Prasad: 72). In the construction of big and greenfield cities, the state employs various methods ranging from compensation to consent production to coercive tactics to acquire land from farmers and small landowners. With the state by their side, private capitalists accumulate the land at cheaper price while small landowners anticipate the benefits through rentier economy (Levien 2018; Sampat 2016; Gururani 2013).

Dispensing with Labour

What will be the situation of small farmers, assignees without clear titles, tenants and landless workers, artisans, and petty traders after land pooling? The

166 PURENDRA PRASAD

estimates from Tulluru mandal (a key area for the capital city) alone indicated that there were about 30,000 tenants, 60,000 agricultural workers, and several traditional craftsmen, non-agricultural workers, petty traders, while landowners were about 5,000. Most of the workers and tenants belonged to Scheduled Castes (SCs), Scheduled Tribes (STs), and Other Backward Classes (OBCs). The landowners got a reasonable compensation package, but the agricultural workers were promised a mere Rs 2500 per household per month for a period of ten years. On average agricultural workers—male members earned Rs 12,000 and women Rs 8,000 per month prior to land pooling in this region, thus the compensation provided to workers was grossly inadequate to sustain a household.

Tenants from this region have faced intense problems. Discussions with them revealed that the lease price went up by 20 per cent, when they entered and started competing outside the capital city region. This is not surprising given the fact that there is a vastly increased rate of tenancy (75 per cent and more) in coastal Andhra region in the last decade. The vulnerability of tenants is evident from the fact that all the five reported suicides in Guntur district in the month of September 2015 were that of tenants. In this process, labour will not only be devalued but also degraded and fragmented in an unprecedented way (for this region), while accumulation goes on through dispossession or by appropriation of bits of the fragmented labour.

One can speculate on the ways in which work opportunities available there supported the non-working population and now stands destroyed by land acquisition. In short, Amaravati, Gurgaon, Rajarhat are a saga of space, capital, and people in the vortex of globalized time. If we follow Henri Lefebvre's (1991) philosophy of space, we must note the dialectical and historical evolution of the space called the city, and its disintegration into a heterogeneous series of spaces, each irrelevant to the other, and all in their totality representing graphically the historic and narrative logic of capital. These narratives suggest the unity of most virtual form of capital accumulation and the primitive form. In fact, Goldman (2015) argues that the global cities are being built in large part with workers wage-less labour. Consequently, the struggle between capital and labour has reached far beyond the factory and farm, to the urban commons, sites simultaneously key to the majority's survival and integral to the urban speculative project of finanicalization.

Ecological Dimensions and Its Unsustainability

The master plan admits that a large amount of the Amaravati capital city land falls in a 'medium to low flood risk zone' and talks of designing an extensive 'water-networked city'. About 10,000 acres of land had to be raised by 2 metres incurring about 223 crores to build the Kondaveeti Vagu Lift Irrigation Scheme, which was completed in 2018. This is meant to divert flood water to river/canal to avert inundation of thousands of acres of fertile lands due to flash floods and mitigate the threat of floods submerging Amaravati.[8]

The Government of Andhra Pradesh applied for clearance from the Ministry of Environment, Forest and Climate Change (MoEFCC) to divert 124 sq km of forestland to build Amaravati capital city region. While stressing on afforestation, the state government sought clearance for diversion of 12,445 hectares of forestlands spread across Krishna and Guntur districts for 'Capital City Infrastructure Projects in Andhra Pradesh Capital Region'. In effect, the state government wanted to cut down 12,445 hectares of forests in order to accommodate infrastructure projects. To just put it in a perspective, the geographical area of the Hyderabad district (not greater Hyderabad) is 210 sq km according to the Government of Telangana and the expanse of forests that the AP state government intends to divert is 124 sq km (Minaz 2017). This proposal implied little regard for communities dependent on the forest, ecological value of the forestlands, and the procedures for diversion of forestlands.

When one closely scrutinizes two new capital cities—Amaravati and Naya Raipur proposals by AP and Chhattisgarh state governments, it is quite evident that 'Land with minimum forest cover and wildlife' was one of the criteria mentioned for site selection of Naya Raipur. Those forests falling within the selected sites have been listed as one of the 'economic catalysts' by the Naya Raipur Development Plan, 2031 (NRDA 2008) and did not ask for denotification. The Naya Raipur plan seems to have a totally different approach to that of AP's ambitious Amaravati, where the main focus seems to be land and clearance of forests. Therefore, several individuals and groups have petitioned the National Green Tribunal (NGT), urging the court to look into the

---

[8] Hans India. 2018. Kondaveeti Vagu Lift Pumping Scheme A Unique Project in Itself. Available at https://www.thehansindia.com/posts/index/Andhra-Pradesh/2018-09-08/Kondaveeti-Vagu-Lift-Pumping-Scheme-A-Uniqueproject-in-itself/410747.

168 PURENDRA PRASAD

lapses, including the coming up of a city on floodplains and diversion of the forestlands.[9] E. A. S. Sarma (2015) points out:

> If the forestlands are now permitted to be diverted for non-forest purposes as proposed by APCRDA, it will amount to an outright violation of the Environment Clearance (EC) itself, which in turn will lead to revocation of the EC for the Amaravati project.

In fact, Ramesh and Kaplana (2015) argued that the ecological impact of attempting to replace a natural forest with tree plantations is twofold: one is the effect on the natural ecosystem of the forest that is being diverted, and second is the nature of the afforestation activities carried out in non-forestlands or degraded forests. The forest blocks that the state wants to divert fall under the Eastern Ghats. The Eastern Ghats are a discontinuous range of mountains, unlike the Western Ghats. The scattered ranges have strong connectivity in terms of flora and fauna. Also these Ghats are eroded and disconnected by four major rivers: Godavari, Krishna, Kaveri, and Mahanadi. Despite the reasoned arguments and petitions, NGT refused to set aside environmental clearance granted to Amaravati. In a climax of events,[10] Ministry of Environment and Forests finally rejected AP government's request to divert thousands of hectares of forest land.[11]

Therefore, the new capital city Amaravati and state's urban rescaling strategy need a careful scrutiny not merely for its economic and political visions but ecological considerations as well. Given the fact that Indian cities have been increasingly witnessing the effects of climate change, how is it justified to plan unsustainable model on the flood plains, de-notifying the reserve forest, destroying the flora and fauna in the precarious Eastern Ghats? Major Indian cities Chennai, Bengaluru, Srinagar, Mumbai have already been witnessing floods and urban crisis for the last few years. With climate change speeding up, such ecological disasters are likely to increase. In brief,

---

[9] In fact petitioners have pointed out 'Ecology condition No 10 of statutory Environment Clearance (EC) accorded for the Amaravati project', which states that the 'The Proponent (Andhra Pradesh Capital Region Development Authority or APCRDA) shall utilise natural features such as forests and hills to create regional green networks as committed'.

[10] As TDP relations with the BJP-led central government were severed for political reasons, MoEFCC finally seem to have rejected the plea of the AP state government.

[11] MoEFCC (Ministry of Environment and Forest and Climate Change). Government of Andhra Pradesh Letter to MoEFCC. 2019. Available at http://forestsclearance.nic.in/writereaddata/AdditionalInformation/AddInfoSought.

Amaravati the greenfield city in its making offers insights about state and its accumulation strategies through rescaling of the urban.

Not One but Three Capital Cities

With the defeat of TDP in 2019 elections, the current YSRCP government announced three capital cities—executive capital in Visakhapatnam, legislative capital in Amaravati, and judicial capital in Kurnool[12] on the lines of the South African model. With the announcement of Amaravati as the capital city in 2014, a whole host of real estate marketers made the land prices in the region skyrocket. As a result, the land market escalated at least thirty to forty times higher, transforming the agrarian landscape into a prime real estate market. This provided new opportunities for accumulation for a range of actors both local and outsiders. However, the announcement of three capital cities has cast a shadow on the 'iconic' capital city Amaravati conceived by the previous TDP government.

Indeed, three capital cities primarily implied shifting of capital from Amravati to Visakhapatnam. Hence, it sent shockwaves[13] to not only new urban entrepreneurs but also medium and small landowners in the twenty-nine villages of Amaravati who were participants of the land pooling. Many farmers who made profits and invested in rental housing and commercial properties from these villages got seriously affected as possibilities for rental activities got drastically reduced. As Carol Upadhya (2020) argues, the Amaravati story is much more than a straightforward 'land grab', for it is a highly risky venture with uncertain returns for investors as well as the state, which has borrowed extensively (including from the public, in the form of bonds) to finance the project. In this context, the land that has been acquired from farmers is the main asset that the state holds and on which it can trade to push forward the project.

---

[12] Nageshwar (2020) argues that development opportunities and governance certainly need to be decentralized but not the relocation of three organs of the state—executive, legislative, and judiciary at three different places, which is erroneously termed 'decentralization of development'. The three-capital plan not only entails fiscal wastage, but puts severe stress on public representatives, government machinery, and people at large.

[13] There were no large-scale protests at the time of land pooling even though land was owned by small and marginal farmers. However, there is a protest movement largely from twenty-nine villages where land pooling took place.

170 PURENDRA PRASAD

Echoing Shatkins' 'landscape of anticipation' (2011, 88), the capital city Amaravati witnessed existing agrarian relations destroyed as landowners, property developers, and state agencies all were waiting in anticipation for rents generated by the city in making. Priti Sampat (2016) from her study on Dholera points out that the destruction of existing productive agrarian relations in anticipation of rent from future investments is a developmental leap of the rentier model of growth emerging from capitalist logics of accumulation. Highlighting the role of local actors on the ground Goldman's (2015, 247) pointed out that local actors 'must become speculators of one sort or another, taking extreme risks, and must gamble on when government agents, or land brokers will tag their possessions next for acquisition, and act before it is too late'.

It is important to understand what this capital city shift actually means for accumulators. One, the investors—the class of businessmen and entrepreneurs involved in Amaravati land market have invested in Visakhapatnam land market as well. Of course one is not denying the intimate relation between political power and party funding.[14] Second, YSRCP government also has high stakes in the speculative land market which is quite evident with articulations of 'reverse tendering', 'insider trading', 'land scams', cancellation of contracts pertaining to high-stake projects such as Amaravati capital city, Polavaram Irrigation Project, South Korean Kia Car project, Adani Data Bank, and so forth. This is quite evident with the way YSRCP government facilitated building Airport at Bhogapuram to GMR Airports Ltd, 58% stakes in Gangavaram Port and 100% stakes in Krishnapatnam Port to Adani Ports and Special Economic Zone (APSEZ) in the year 2020. Third, the dream capital city idea seems to have now spread to other regions of Andhra Pradesh as well. Nevertheless, it seems to be a disaster for the farmers who parted their land as much as those who depended on agriculture. Several respondents raised whether this uncertainty would prevail with change in every government.

Towards a Discussion

The case of three Indian cities Amaravati, Gurgaon, and Rajarhat was presented to explain the role of state in accelerating the value of land and

---

[14] It was quite evident with YSRCP agreeing to give Rajya Sabha seat to Mr Parimal Nathwani—Reliance Group President of corporate affairs and projects from Gujarat.

speculative capital, intense interaction between state and private actors as well as state actors at different scales all of which characterize the greenfield urbanization in India. It creates a situation whereby the market becomes the internal regulator of the state, but the state ceases to be the external regulator of the market (Leitner et al. 2007, 3). Although Amaravati is visualized differently by the two political regimes, but the emphasis of both the regimes is about producing landscapes of accumulation whether it is Amaravati or elsewhere in other regions of the state. In brief, this chapter presents three sets of key arguments:

One, the major discussion on Indian cities till about two decades back was regarding planned, unplanned cities, metro and non-metropolitan cities, but today it is about private capital-led city development. Amaravati, Gurgaon, and Rajarhat are prototype of this private urban development falling into the category of speculative cities. Second, in all three greenfield projects, a trend towards exclusionary urbanism where cities are less accommodative of different classes of labour. Instead of learning from the experiences of Gurgaon and Rajarhat, Amaravati (or for that matter three capital cities) seems to be moving towards urban process which is more unsustainable and exclusionary urban growth perpetuating inequalities among different classes. As Samaddar (2017) rightly points out that the neoliberal envisioning of cities and the accompanying hyper-commodification of land and new forms of social marginalization have increased precarity among different classes of labour, severely impairing their ability to negotiate city space and society at large. Third, capital cities have become the political terrains created, manipulated and contested for a variety of capitals across time and space. In effect, the power of the state has been recentred on the urban scale so that urban governance 'has served as a major catalyst, medium and arena of state rescaling processes' (Brenner 2004, 174), producing new state spaces. It is hoped that the above questions in this chapter will generate informed debate on green field urbanization and state rescaling strategies.

References

Banerjee, Swapna Guha. 2009. 'Neoliberalising the "Urban": New Geographies of Power and Injustice in Indian Cities'. *Economic and Political Weekly* 44 (22): 95–107.

Bhatia, Gautam. 2018. 'Rebuilding Our Cities'. *The Hindu*, January 29.

Brenner, Neil. 2004. *New State Spaces: Urban Governance and Rescaling of Statehood.* New York: Oxford University Press.

Brenner, Neil. 2019. *New Urban Spaces: Theory and the Scale Question.* Oxford: Oxford University Press.

172   PURENDRA PRASAD

Brenner, Neil and Christian Schmidt. 2014. 'The "Urban Age" in Question'. *International Journal of Urban and Regional Research* 38 (3): 731–55.

Burte, Himanshu. 2014. 'The "Smart City" Card'. *Economic and Political Weekly* 49 (46): 22–5.

Das Ritanjan. 2019. 'Narratives of the Dispossessed and Casteless: Politics of Land and Caste in Rajarhat, West Bengal'. *Journal of Contemporary Asia*. Available at https://doi.org/10.1080/00472336.2019.1679861.

Dasgupta, Rana. 2014. Capital : *A Portrait of Twenty-First Century Delhi*. New Delhi: Fourth Estate.

Dey, Ishita, Ranabir Samaddar, and Suhit K. Sen. 2013. *Beyond Kolkata—Rajarhat and the Dystopia of Urban Imagination*. New Delhi: Routledge.

Goldman, Michael. 2015. 'With the Declining Significance of Labour, Who Is Producing Our Global Cities?'. *International Labor and Working Class History* 87 (Spring: 137–64.

Gururani, S. 2013. 'Flexible Planning: The Making of India's "Millennial City" Gurgaon'. In *Ecologies of Urbanism in Asia*, edited by Anne M. Rademacher and K Sivaramakrishnan, 119–144. Hong Kong: Hong Kong University Press.

Harvey, David. 1978. *The Urban Process under Capitalism: A Framework for Analysis*. Ipswich, MA: EBSCO Publishing.

Jenkins, Rob, Lorain Kennedy, and Partha Mukhopadhyay. 2014. *Power, Policy and Protest: The Politics of India's Special Economic Zones*. Oxford: Oxford University Press.

Jha, K. Manish and Pushpendra Kumar. 2016. 'Homeless Migrants in Mumbai: Life and Labour in Urban Space'. *Economic and Political Weekly* 51 (26–27): 69–77.

Kennedy, Loraine and Ashima Sood. 2016. 'Green Field Development as Tabula Rasa: Rescaling, Speculation and Governance on India's Urban Frontier'. *Economic and Political Weekly* 51 (17): 41–9.

Kundu, Amitabh. 2009. 'Exclusionary Urbanisation in Asia: A Macro Overview'. *Economic and Political Weekly* 44 (48): 48–58.

Kundu, Amitabh. 2017. 'Rurbanisation: An Alternate Development Paradigm'. In *The Contemporary Urban Conundrum*, edited by Patel Sujata and Omita Goyal, 17–27. New Delhi: India International Centre.

Kundu, Ratoola. 2016. 'Making Sense of Place in Rajarhat New Town'. *Economic and Political Weekly* 51 (17): 93–101.

Lefebvre, Henry. 1991. *The Production of Space*. Translated by D. Nicholson-Smith. Malden, MA: Blackwell.

Leitner, Helga, Eric S. Sheppard, Kristin Sziarto, and Anant Maringanti. 2007. *Contested Urban Frontiers: Decentering Neoliberalism*. New York: Guilford Press.

Levien, Michael. 2018. *Dispossession without Development: Land Grabs in Neoliberal India*. Oxford: Oxford University Press.

Minaz, Ayesha. 2017. 'Amaravati Threatens to March on Kondapally'. *Economic and Political Weekly* 52 (25–26): 24 June.

Mitra Sabyasachi, Rana Hasan, Manoj Sharma, Hoe Yun Jeong, Manish Sharma, Arindam Guha 2016. Scaling New Heights: Vizag-Chennai Industrial Corridor. Manila: Asian Development Bank. 1–33.

Nageshwar, K. 2020. 'Six Months of YSRCP Rule in Andhra Pradesh'. *Economic and Political Weekly* 55 (3): 2–23.

AMARAVATI, GURGAON, AND RAJARHAT 173

Naidu, Ratna. 1990. *Old Cities, New Predicaments: A Study of Hyderabad*. New Delhi: Sage.

Naya Raipur Development Authority. 2008. Naya Raipur Development Plan-20131. https://navaraipuratalnagar.com/NRDARevampTheme/upload/Section%201%20 (Chapter%201-3).pdf

NIUA (National Institute of Urban Affairs). 2015. *Exploratory Research on Smart Cities: Theory and Practice*. New Delhi: NIUA.

Ong, Aihwa. 2011. 'Introduction: Worlding Cities or the Art of Being Global'. In *Worlding Cities: Asian Experiments and the Art of being Global*, edited by Ananya Roy and Aihwa Ong, 1–27. Oxford: Wiley-Blackwell.

Polanki, Pallavi. 2012. 'The Great Gurgaon Experiment: Has It Failed?'. Firstpost.com, 24 April.

Prasad, Purendra. 2018. 'New Migrant Question: Exploitative Forms of Transit Labour in Three Regions of Andhra Pradesh'. In *India Migration Report 2017: Forced Migration*, edited by Rajan Irudaya, 188–205. London: Routledge.

Rajagopalan, S. and A. Tabarrok. 2013. 'Lessons from Gurgaon, India's Private City'. Department of Economics Working Paper Nos. 14–32, George Mason University. Available at https://mason.gmu.edu/~atabarro/Lessons%20from%20Gurgaon. pdf.

Rajagopalan, S. and A. Tabarrok. 2015. 'Designing Private Cities, Open to All'. *New York Times*, March 18.

Ramachandraiah, C. 2016. 'Making of Amaravati: A Landscape of Speculation and Intimidation'. *Economic and Political Weekly* 51 (17): 68–75.

Ramesh, Srikonda and K. Kaplana. 2015. 'Ecological Integrity and Environmental Protection for Vijayawada Region—Scattered Eastern Ghats'. *International Journal of Sustainable Built Environment* 4 (1): 109–16.

Rediff. .2015. 'How Andhra Pradesh CM Plans to Turn Challenges into Opportunities'. Available at http://www.ndtv.com/andhra-pradesh-news/amaravati-to-be-andhra-pradeshs-new-capital-751518.

Saha, Apala. 2019. 'Revisiting the City—Capital Symbiosis: Claims to `City'zenship in the Contemporary Indian City'. *Economic and Political Weekly* 65 (50): 31–40.

Samaddar, Ranabir. 2016. 'Migrant and the Neo-Liberal City'. *Economic and Political Weekly* 51 (26–27): 52–4.

Samaddar, Ranabir. 2017. 'The Logistical City'. In *The Contemporary Urban Conundrum*, edited by Sujata Patel and Goyal Omita, 104–15. New Delhi: India International Centre.

Sampat, Preeti. 2016. 'Dholera—The Emperor's New City'. *Economic and Political Weekly*, 51 (17): 59–67.

Sarma, E. A. S. 2015. 'Petition Filed in NGT against Environmental Clearance to Amaravati'. Available at www.thehindu.com/...filed...environmental-clearance... amaravati/article8041537.ece.

Sassen, Saskia. 1994. *The Global City: New York, London, Tokyo*. Princeton, NJ: Princeton University Press.

Sassen Saskia. 2014. 'Carving up the City'. Available at http://www.saskiasassen.com/ PDFs/publications/carving-up-the-city.pdf.

Searle, Guiu Llerena. 2016. *Landscapes of Accumulation: Real Estate and the Neo Liberal Imagination in Contemporary India*. Chicago, IL: University of Chicago Press.

174 PURENDRA PRASAD

Sharma, R.N. 2013. ' "Citiness and Urbanity": The Privilege of Mega Cities'. In *Small Cities and Towns in Global Era: Emerging Changes and Perspectives*, edited by R.N. Sharma and R.S. Sandhu, 58–79. New Delhi: Rawat Publications.

Shatkin, G. 2011. 'Planning Privatopolis: Representation and Contestation in the Development of Urban Integrated Mega-Projects'. In *Worlding Cities: Asian Experiments and the Art of Being Global*, edited by A. Roy and A. Ong, Chichester, West Sussex, 77–97. Malden, MA: Wiley Blackwell.

Shaw, Annapurna. 2012. *Indian Cities: Oxford India Short Introductions*. New Delhi: Oxford University Press.

Shetty, Prasad and Rupali Gupte. 2017. 'Cities and Smartness'. In *The Contemporary Urban Conundrum*, edited by Sujata Patel and Goyal Omita, 116–27. New Delhi: India International Centre.

Simone, Maliq Abdou. 2004. 'People as Infrastructure: Intersecting Fragments in Johannesburg'. Available at abdoumaliqsimone.com/files/45662107.pdf.

Sivaramakrishnan, K. C. 2009. 'Special Economic Zones: Issues of Urban Growth and Management in Special Economic Zones: Promise, Performance and Pending Issues'. Centre for Policy Research Occasional Paper, New Delhi.

Sood, Ashima. 2015. 'Industrial Townships and the Policy Facilitation of Corporate Urbanisation in India'. *Urban Studies* 52 (8).

Sood, Ashima and Sharadini Rath. 2017. 'The Planned and the Unplanned: Company Towns in India'. In *The Contemporary Urban Conundrum*, edited by Patel Sujata and Omita Goyal, 91–103. New Delhi: India International Centre.

Srivastava, Sanjay. 2015. *Entangled Urbanism: Slum, Gated Community and Shopping Mall in Delhi and Gurgaon*. Delhi: Oxford University Press.

Srivastava, Sanjay. 2017. 'Post-National Urbanism: "Ordinary" People, Capital and the State'. In *The Contemporary Urban Conundrum*, edited by Patel Sujata and Omita Goyal, 210–21. New Delhi: India International Centre.

Upadhya, Carol. 2020. 'Assembling Amaravati: Speculative Accumulation in a New Indian City'. *Economy and Society* 49 (1). Available at https://doi.org/10.1080/0308 5147.2019.1690257.

Vakulabharanam Vamsi and Purendra Prasad. 2017. Babu's Camelot: Amaravati and the Emerging Capitalist Dynamics in 'New' Andhra Pradesh *Economic and Political Weekly* 52 (2): 69–78.

9

India's Emerging Risk Urbanism

Cities, Commons, and Neoliberal Transformations

D. Parthasarathy

Indian cities, as is the case with cities world over, are increasingly coming under stress from various exogenous and endogenous risks and hazards. While urban flooding on a regular basis is the most visible of 'natural' disasters, induced in part by climate change, landslides, heat waves, sea-level rise, coastal erosion, and other environment-related hazards occur not infrequently. These add to other risks that cities are increasingly exposed to, which include mass violence, building collapses, industrial accidents, fires, stampedes, disease epidemics, and deaths due to environmental pollution and degradation (Sherly, Karmakar, Parthasarathy, Chan, and Rau. 2015).

Cities like Mumbai, Surat, Pune, Delhi, Bengaluru, Kolkata, and Hyderabad experience chronic flooding even with relatively lower amounts of rainfall. Changes in rainfall pattern, intensity, and seasonality add to the uncertainty and risk in a situation where cities find themselves chronically unprepared or underprepared to deal with such exigencies. Chronic urban flooding is exacerbated by haphazard planning, degradation, and encroachment on ecosystems which act as flood barriers and which serve to mitigate flood risks, such as mangroves, salt pans, lakes, creeks, and rivers. Poor solid waste management practices coupled with inadequate storm water drainage systems further add to the woes (Revi 2005).

Apart from deaths and destruction, there are short- and long-term health impacts on humans and animals, short- and long-term economic losses, damage to physical infrastructure, and psychological trauma due to these extreme events, which are becoming all too common (Hallegatte, Ranger, Bhattacharya, Bachu, Priya, Dhore, et al. 2010).[1] This chapter seeks to propose the idea of 'risk urbanism' as a new way of life that populations and communities, as well as state

---

[1] The nature and extent of economic, social, health, infrastructure, livelihood, and environmental risks that are emerging due to a range of factors in the Mumbai Metropolitan Region are

---

D. Parthasarathy, *India's Emerging Risk Urbanism* In: *Neoliberalism, Urbanization, and Aspirations in Contemporary India.* Edited by: Sujata Patel, Oxford University Press. © Oxford University Press 2021.
DOI: 10.1093/oso/9780190132019.003.0009

176   D. PARTHASARATHY

agencies, market forces, and capital have to get used, cope with, plan for, and adapt to. Studies within the field of climate change and disaster management and governance have attempted to theorize, conceptualize, and make empirical assessments of the relationship between hazards, uncertainty, and risk at aggregate levels of cities, regions, and countries. Sociologists such as Douglas and Wildavsky (1983, 2013), Ulrich Beck (1992, 1995), and others (Beck et al. 1994) have theorized risk society, risks arising from modern technological, environmental, and industrial transformations, and their impacts on how individuals and societies give meaning to, reflect upon, and respond to risk. As yet, however, studies on the ways in which chronic risk and uncertainty translate into everyday social action are few, as are studies which attempt to transcribe the meanings of risk and uncertainty for the urban populace. The work of Max Weber, who drew from the Nietzschean project of meaning making, is being deployed by a few sociologists working on disasters (Stallings 2002). Empirical studies are however few, especially in the Indian context (Parthasarathy 2009, 2016).

In conceptualizing and elaborating the notion of risk urbanism, this chapter draws largely from long-term field work in Mumbai,[2] a critical review of selected urban studies literature, and studies of environmental degradation and urban problems in other Indian cities such as Bengaluru. This chapter is largely framed as an analytical and theoretical work. Empirical evidence for most of the arguments may be found in previous and forthcoming papers on climate change, urban flooding, and disaster governance in the Mumbai region by this author along with other research collaborators. The focus in these projects that are the basis for this chapter has been on changing trends and patterns of precipitation, urban flooding, and the impacts of environmental degradation on urban populations and resource dependent

---

detailed in Revi 2005, Hallegatte et al. 2010, de Sherbinin and Bardy 2015, Stecko and Barber 2007, Patankar and Patwardhan 2016, Sherly et al. 2015, and Maskey et al. 2006.

[2] Some of this research has been published, including Parthasarathy 2009; Sherly et al. 2015; Parthasarathy 2015; Parthasarathy 2016; Chouhan, Parthasarathy and Pattanaik. 2016; and Parthasarathy 2018. The research projects from which I draw insights for this chapter include (1) 'Contesting the Coastal Commons: The Changing Socio-Legal Position of Fishing Populations in Tamil Nadu and Maharashtra', ICSSR-NWO Bilateral Programme (Indian Council of Social Science Research and Netherlands Organisation for Scientific Research, 2016–18, carried out by the Indian Institute of Technology Bombay and University of Amsterdam); (2) 'Climate Change, Uncertainty, and Transformation', sponsored by Norwegian Research Council, in collaboration with IDS, Sussex and Norwegian University of Life Sciences, 2015–18, carried out jointly by partners from IDS, Sussex; IIT Bombay; Norwegian University of Life Sciences; Indian Institute of Health Management Research, Kolkata; All India Disaster Management Institute, Ahmedabad; and Gujarat Institute of Desert Ecology, Bhuj. I also wish to acknowledge learning from the PhD dissertation work of Dr Hemantkumar Chouhan and Dr M. A. Sherly.

INDIA'S EMERGING RISK URBANISM 177

communities such as fishers, livestock owners, and urban farmers. As environmental activists, NGOs, social movements, fisher organizations, and researchers are increasingly tending to argue, the degradation of the urban resource commons such as wetlands, forests, lakes, and pasture is critically linked to chronic flooding and other environment related disasters. As yet, however, a consideration of the criticality of these commons for flood risk reduction is yet to be taken seriously by urban planners and urban governance agencies. Surprisingly very little of the urban studies literature touches upon the urban resource commons, their encroachment, enclosure, and degradation by forces of capital, and the neoliberal state (Gidwani and Baviskar 2011).

As cities are increasingly subjected to various stresses and shocks, their citizens begin to behave and act in ways that I define as risk urbanism. This includes (a) attitudes to and perceptions of risk, and techniques of coping with/or inability and lack of capacity to deal with risk, and (b) the associations and relationships that individuals and groups form to mitigate risk, transform urban governance and planning, and resist neoliberal transformations that create and exacerbate risk and uncertainty. The primary argument of this chapter is that emerging forms of risk urbanism in Indian cities (and perhaps in other cities exposed to similar hazards and risks around the world) need to be understood against the backdrop of the degradation and encroachment of the resource commons, which are linked to neoliberal urban transformation. In doing so, the chapter engages critically with Marxist urban studies scholarship, in order to nuance, negate, or add to previous arguments about capital accumulation and dispossession. Taking inspiration from works that urge us to critically distance oneself from Eurocentric perspectives (Patel 2014), and develop alternative 'global south' frameworks, in order to reframe globally useful analytical categories and lenses, this chapter draws lessons from risk urbanism in Indian cities to develop conceptual and theoretical arguments that can be more globally applied in New Orleans, Houston, New York, Berlin, London, or other cities of the global north which are exposed to similar hazards and risks.

In addition to the main theme outlined earlier, the chapters also attempt to make a case for understanding the ways in which neoliberal capital creates a 'risk commons', sharing and spreading risk, even as some sections of the population experience more risk than others. In some ways risk urbanism threatens and splinters capital itself, forcing sections of capital to take a more proactive and positive view on climate action strategies. However, the fractured nature of multinational, national, regional, small scale, and petty forms of capital ensures that no coherent strategy for risk mitigation obtains as part of climate

178 D. PARTHASARATHY

and disaster governance policies and institutionalized action frameworks. The chapter also throws some light on new forms of solidarities that emerge in cities, as a response to the neoliberalization of urban risk, some of these facilitated by the popularity of social media tools. From an epistemological perspective, the chapter briefly discusses the varying role and understanding of law and science in addressing risk urbanism, observed in the strategies and policies of state agencies, capital, and social-environmental movements. The rest of this chapter is organized into the following sections. The next section outlines the concept of risk urbanism, and elaborates on its specific dimensions and characteristics, as well as its usefulness for understanding emerging ways in which urban citizens in India deal with chronic uncertainty and risk. The following section engages with urban commons, their degradation, the commoning strategies implicit in capital accumulation and their consequences, and the commoning of risk in cities. Table 9.1 in this section outlines selected cases on risk and response in the Mumbai Metropolitan Region. The final section strings together arguments about risk, neoliberal transformation and commoning practices, in developing an argument against the grain of popular (Marxist) articulations, while identifying a new lens for urban studies in India.

Cities and Disaster Risk: Risk Urbanism and the Commoning of Risk

Asian cities including Mumbai consistently figure among the most vulnerable cities in the world in many global assessments, among those exposed to disasters and natural hazards (UN-HABITAT 2012, 21; GreenAsh 2013; Hanson Nicholls, Ranger, Hallegate, Corfee-Morlot, Herweijer et al. 2011; Fuchs 2010; Nicholls et al. 2007). Coastal cities which are densely populated, numerous, and flourishing economic centres are among the most exposed, considering their greater exposure to climate change related hazards such as sea-level rise, coastal erosion, coastal inundation, storm surge, and cyclones. Worldwide, Asian cities already account for a large proportion of economic losses and deaths due to disasters, especially urban flooding (Herweijer et al. 2008; Razafindrabe et al. 2009; Regional Urban Task Force 2008). Chronic urban flooding during the monsoons, and increasingly during other seasons, disrupts normal life, diverts state finances for recovery and rehabilitation, disturbs economic activities, and affects livelihoods of the urban poor. A new form of urbanism that can be defined as 'risk urbanism' emerges, wherein citizens, state agencies, the market,

INDIA'S EMERGING RISK URBANISM   179

transportation sector, and other social and economic actors, constantly need to reflect upon and incorporate risk into their everyday activities, future plans, and hedge against risk. The multiplicity of risk from diverse sources—social, political, economic, and natural, from other human beings as well as from forces of nature, from human systems including the market, state, and social groups, as well as random systemic changes at the planetary and environmental scales—these lead to the presence of a reflexive modernity, albeit one that citizens cannot always deploy owing to their social, economic, or political positions in society (Parthasarathy 2009). Disaster impacts tend to refract through existing vulnerabilities and inequalities. Specifically with reference to natural and climate-induced risk, citizens, and communities acquire a 'risk habitus'—that affect their everyday dispositions, routines, and outlooks. It may be something as simple as checking the water levels in urban lakes in Mumbai, and the dates and timing of high tides on a daily basis during the monsoon. It may involve making small-scale alterations to housing structures and neighbourhoods in informal settlements to mitigate the risk and effects of flooding. It may involve taking greater interest in urban finances, governance, and infrastructure projects to assess risks for flooding, and/or the implications of these for disaster risk mitigation. It may involve taking precautions while travelling or commuting during specific days when warnings have been given. Citizens look for and perceive warning signs of disaster risk based on perceptual cues relating to rising water levels, intensity of rainfall, flow of water in creeks and rivers, and so on.

Second, where uncertainty predominates, and has not been converted into risk through better knowledge and information, the present and the future become dynamic and fluid, unpredictable in their outcomes, such that citizens also get used to tragedies, whether these are building collapses during heavy rains, people, animals, and vehicles getting washed away in flash floods, or mass epidemics brought on by insistent rainfall and flood water stagnation. Risk assessments are made by incorporating the weather as a factor—in changing patterns of diseases and illnesses, travel scheduling, business returns and fiduciary turnarounds, finding or losing jobs and customers, informal sector livelihoods, and recreational choices.

A third kind of risk urbanism affects specific groups defined by their location in marginal and dangerous locations, ethnicity, caste, migration status, occupation, or class. These are groups pushed to the margins, living in highly hazardous areas due to discrimination in the housing and employment market, threats of violence, availability of livelihood options and jobs, and proximity to people from similar socio-cultural backgrounds (Parthasarathy

180   D. PARTHASARATHY

2009). Some of these groups are the original inhabitants of the city—*koli fishers* and *adivasis* who live of the land and the sea, and for whom ecological health is crucial for their livelihoods, but who are also most affected by disasters when ecosystems are degraded and encroached upon due to new coastal claims (Chouhan, Parthasarathy, and Pattanaik. 2016). These groups practise and follow what may be perceived as 'rural' occupations', largely resource based, and norms/patterns of resource governance that derive from older systems of common pool resource management. The rest of the groups affected are also characterized by multi-spatial households, constantly moving between the city and the village, having a simultaneous presence, and making it difficult to involve such communities in risk reduction planning, drills, and adaptation strategies.

Finally, yet another kind of risk urbanism may be identified in terms of the commoning of risk as a general process in the city. Conventional Marxist approaches on cities, climate change, and environmental degradation tend to focus on the role of capital accumulation in dispossession and displacement of the working-class poor, and rural subsistence populations (Harvey 2003; Glassman 2006). This kind of a framework however tends to ignore the larger distribution of risk among diverse sections of the population—which may include the poor, the middle class, and the rich or elites; it is a lens which neglects to account for the large-scale damage, destruction and losses to urban informal sector and petty commodity production, as well as national and multinational businesses (Hallegate et al. 2010). Risk tends to be shared, disasters become a public 'bad', and hence cities witness the emergence of a 'risk commons' where everyone at one time or the other experiences risk is exposed to the uncertainties of climate change and disasters, and become vulnerable. The sharing of risk involves the non-poor and their economic structures as well, depending on location, the specific kind of disaster or extreme event, and the spread and distribution of impacts which are mediated by haphazard and unplanned urban growth, as well as some technical strategies for flood prevention which are narrow in scope and imagination (Adam, submitted). Where the middle class, the medium- and small-scale sectors of the economy, and sometimes the elites become risk prone, this reflects the inequality in power relations wherein the politically powerful are able to privatize and spatially segregate risk management strategies, thereby displacing risk and hazards to other areas, for instance the location of dumping grounds away from elite localities in Mumbai to newer middle-class neighbourhoods (Sharma and Parthasarathy 2018). From a sociological perspective, the role of power relations and power structures in the unequal distribution of risk

INDIA'S EMERGING RISK URBANISM   181

and exposure to hazards remain understudied and under-theorized, despite pioneering theoretical work by Mary Douglas (1983, 2013).

The commoning of risk across the city is a crucial and significant sociological process since it not only draws attention to a new kind of urban solidarity which binds urban populations even as disasters like floods divide them in terms of chronicity and impacts, but it also generates new kinds of solidarities and associations that are uniquely urban in nature; these also, however, borrowed from earlier rural epistemologies and practices, and are characterized by emerging social media and information technology-based solidarities and networks (Singh and Parthasarathy 2010). A good example here would be of fisher associations borrowing from customary knowledge and practices to adapt to changing ecological, climatic, and urban conditions and pressures. Of relevance to this chapter, the idea of risk commons relates to the older idea of resource commons; the degradation and encroachment upon resource commons in urban areas and metropolitan regions constitute an important component of India's emerging risk urbanism, as evidenced by media and academic analysis as well as activist articulations across cities like Mumbai, Bengaluru, Surat, Pune, Kolkata, Hyderabad, and many other large and smaller cities and urban agglomerations.

Commons and Commoning Practices in the City: Capital, New Urban Solidarities and Neoliberal Transformation

Marxist urban studies scholarship such as those by David Harvey have linked Marx's notion of primitive accumulation to more modern processes of 'accumulation by dispossession'. This strand of scholarship has brought to light, among other processes, the enclosure of the commons, the expropriation of resource dependent groups (the 'ecosystem people' of Gadgil and Guha 1995) from their resource base largely around the commons (wetlands, forests, grassland, marine ecosystems, lakes), and the privatization of the environmental commons. Among others, writing from a global south perspective, researchers like Sujata Patel (2014) have pointed to the Eurocentric bias in such approaches which neglect colonial plunder and the context of imperialism which facilitated such enclosures and privatization on a large scale.

In this chapter, while we recognize the role of accumulation by dispossession in the encroachment upon commons, and expropriation of resource-based livelihoods such as artisanal fishing, urban agriculture, and livestock rearing, we attempt to add more nuance to the processes through

182   D. PARTHASARATHY

which sections of the population dependent on the commons are placed in conditions of extreme and chronic risk. In cities that have experienced major flooding events such as Hyderabad, Chennai, Pune, Bengaluru, Kolkata, Surat, and Mumbai, as well as cities around the world like Houston and Florida, environmentalists, activists, and academics have pointed to the rapid degradation and disappearance of resource commons such as lakes and ponds, and large-scale construction in these areas as a key factor for flooding resulting from storm surge, extreme rainfall events, cyclonic storms, and coastal inundation during high tide (Revi 2005; Nagendra and Ostrom 2014). In Mumbai, for instance, the destruction of mangroves which acted as flood barriers is an important reason for the city's inability to manage flood waters despite having an excellent storm water drainage system, which despite its colonial era origins, has a high capacity to manage rainfall intensities of up to 300mm per day (Adam et al. 2016). These commons have gradually been taken over through amendments and violations of the Coastal Regulation Zone rules of 1991 and 2011 on a very large scale (Chouhan, Parthasarathy, and Pattanaik. 2016), as well as violations of the Wetland Rules notified by the Government of India.

As Pelling and Blackburn (2014) argue the relationship between coastal mismanagement and urbanization has been vastly understudied; with economic dynamism mostly concentrated in the coasts in most countries of the world, coasts and coastal cities are increasingly coming under pressure for real estate projects, power plants, ports, recreation and entertainment, transport, and other infrastructure projects.

The Mumbai Metropolitan Region has been no exception with past, ongoing, and planned projects such as the Bandra-Worli Sealink, the Transharbour Sealink, the Coastal Road project, the Eastern Freeway, oil refineries, oil exploration and drilling, vast real estate projects, industrial estates and special economic zones, hotels and tourism, the Navi Mumbai airport, and the Jawaharlal Nehru Port Trust, all significantly encroaching upon, damaging and destroying the coastal ecosystems including wetlands, mudflats, salt pans, and mangroves. In our previous and ongoing research these risk-generating projects have been studied by focusing on selected 'flashpoints'[3]—state- or market-led infrastructure and urban development projects which have spawned resistance and counter claims are contested using a variety of legal, socio-cultural, political, economic, health, child

---

[3] The concept was jointly developed with Maarten Bavinck and Ajit Menon to study claims and contestations around coastal commons affecting artisanal fisheries in the Maharashtra and Tamil Nadu states of India.

INDIA'S EMERGING RISK URBANISM 183

rights, human rights, and environmental arguments, and mobilizations and response has involved civil society, green tribunals, economic agents, and communities subjected to increasing exposure to risks and hazards in the form of health, loss of livelihoods, environmental destruction, and economic losses. For the Mumbai Metropolitan Region, this kind of risk generation and response—conceptualized as risk urbanism in this chapter—is summarized in Table 9.1 using selected cases and flashpoints. The actual impacts of risk-inducing projects and the nature of these risks have been elaborated extensively in the literature, especially since 2005.[4]

What is missing in the accumulation by dispossession perspective, however, is that dispossession does not only take place through physical expropriation of communities dependent on the resource commons. In many cases populations continue to live in these areas with vastly decreased livelihoods and income earnings, as these commons are increasingly polluted due to dumping of construction debris, letting out treated and untreated effluents into the rivers, creeks, and mangroves, and inefficient municipal solid waste management (Chouhan, Parthasarathy, and Pattanaik. 2016). What is occurring here is not accumulation directly for capitalist production, but a specific method of waste disposal by firms which socializes risk (Sharma and Parthasarathy 2018), even as it significantly saves costs of waste disposal and treatment for small, medium, and large companies. This is seen in Mumbai, Bengaluru, Surat, Kolkata, and many other cities in India. A public 'bad' is created in collusion with state agencies, which then contributes to the commoning of risk for specific groups dependent on the resource commons. For these groups such as the *koli* fishers, risk is an ever-present danger—the risk of livelihood loss, risk of hunger, risk of customary *gaothan* land and *koliwadas* being grabbed, and risk of loss of culture and identity; for the rest of the city, the conversion of resource commons into a wasteland creates dangers during specific extreme events—such as flooding, high rainfall intensity, high tide, and storm surge. The general Marxist analytical frameworks of production, reproduction of capital, and accumulation do not adequately (or mostly not at all) capture the commoning of waste disposal functions by the city itself and by sections of capital. The error occurs because Harvey and others believe that 'the separation of producers and means of production is a common character of both accumulation and primitive accumulation.'

This does not necessarily happen as explained here, where producers can continue to have access to means of production (land or sea), but not

---

[4] For the major studies, see the references mentioned in note 1.

184 D. PARTHASARATHY

Table 9.1 Risk and Response in the Mumbai Metropolitan Region: The Contours of Risk Urbanism

Flashpoint	Risk Impacts	Response	Actors Involved
Mumbai Floods 2005[5]	Loss of life, loss of property, economic losses, health impacts, impacts on livelihoods and wage labour[6]	Changes in the city's Disaster Management Plan; Alternate Urban Development Visions by citizen groups; pressures to better implement coastal regulation and environmental laws; revamping urban governance; neighbourhood action for flood mitigation; state-led technical solutions for flood risk mitigation	Municpal Corporation of Greater Mumbai, Mumbai Metropolitan Region Development Authority, Government of Maharashtra, Environmental Activists and NGOs (CAT, Vanshakti), Peoples' coalitions, neighbourhood groups, judiciary, and academic researchers
Coastal Road Project	Potential and actual impact on coastal ecosystems, livelihoods of artisanal fishers, enhanced flood risks, and land use change in coastal zones	Protests by artisanal fisher communities (Kolis) and citizen groups; research support from academia; petitions and court filings by activists and environmentalists	Koli associations, academic researchers, environmental groups (CAT, Vanshakti), judicial actors, citizen groups
Kanjur Marg Dumping Ground	Environmental damage, health impacts on local communities	Petitions in the local courts; public protests	Neighbourhood groups, environmental activists, local political leaders
Vasai-Virar Urban expansion	Encroachment on rural and urban resource commons, loss of livelihoods, environmental destruction, flood risks, and loss of autonomy in environmental management	Public protests and marches, petitions to state agencies; court filings; political mobilization against local private and state agencies involved in risk-laden urban expansion projects	Koli fisher associations, environmental activists, local political leaders, local Panchayats

[5] While the 2005 floods constitute a landmark event, there have also been flooding events with significant loss of life, property damage, and economic losses in Mumbai which were both city wide and localized to certain municipal wards in 2006, 2007, 2017, and 2019.

[6] For details see Hallegatte et al. 2010, Parthasarathy 2009, Revi 2005.

INDIA'S EMERGING RISK URBANISM   185

Table 9.1 *Continued*

Flashpoint	Risk Impacts	Response	Actors Involved
Projects in Palghar district[7] (Industrial estates, coastal zone violations, ports, tourism projects oil exploration and oil refineries, thermal and nuclear power plants, real estate)	Coastal ecosystem damage on land and in the sea, loss of livelihood for Koli fishers, health impacts due to pollution, loss of biodiversity, encroachment on urban and rural commons	Public protests; petitions to state agencies; court filings with the judiciary and green tribunal; political action by local communities; research support from academics; community action to protect and preserve the environmental commons	Koli fisher associations local political leaders, academic researchers, environmental activists, Panchayats
Mumbai Metro Project	Deforestation, flood and disaster risk	Public protests; court filings; academic research; political action	Local adivasi groups, citizen groups, environmental activists, small-scale financial institutions, local political leaders

necessarily the resources that are attached to those means which are affected by environmental degradation, pollution, and contamination. In a sense this leads to a process of deterritorialization (Deleuze and Guattari 1983) due to a disjuncture between culturally defined livelihood patterns and loss of place that are crucial to the sustenance of those livelihoods.

The Marxist framework also crucially does not distinguish between different types and fractions of capital, which in the context of a developing country are subjected to neoliberal transformation and global competitive pressures (including in recent years from China which has been accused of large-scale dumping), and are significant since they point to capacity and power differentials in adhering to environmental norms and regulations. Hence while big capital, which includes state-owned public sector firms, does damage and degrade the resource commons through pollution, sections of big capital are aware of sustainability pressures both from the market,

---

[7] North of Mumbai, a component of the Mumbai Metropolitan Region.

and from the need to maintain profitability, and prevent damage due to extreme events; this drives *some* of them to 'climate proof' their businesses (Giddens 2009). On the other hand, small-scale industries and informal sector manufacturing also contribute to pollution on a very large scale, a large part of them located along urban water bodies in cities like Mumbai and Bengaluru. These firms and petty producers do not get state support in effectively managing their waste, are not always served by municipal service providers, and under competitive cost-cutting pressures in a globalized market place, resort to dumping their waste untreated into the urban resource commons. These then directly create risks for the ecosystem people such as fishers, livestock owners, and other resource dependent groups in the city.

It is also important to recognize that non-capitalist modes of production exist at multiple scales in countries like India, especially in the informal sector, and in resource-based livelihoods which continue to sustain on a fairly significant scale in urbanized regions even in the core of Indian cities (Parthasarathy 2011). For Harvey, non-capitalist modes primarily refer to colonialism, war, international financial systems, and fraud, oppression, and looting. The failure to recognize non-capitalist, 'rural' forms of economy in cities, adversely affects the perception and handling of risk, since these are not incorporated either into disaster management plans, or into urban planning and governance in general. Their voices and perspectives are also rarely incorporated into the design of environmental regulations and guidelines. The crucial significance of the commons for disaster risk reduction is ignored in neoliberal arguments about growth, thus impacting back on urban economies themselves, on capital itself. In the process it is the traditional commoners, the ecosystem people who are most exposed to risk. Risk urbanism is a stark, ever-present reality for such groups.

Harvey's focus on commons tends to get restricted to public goods such as pensions, welfare benefits, and healthcare rather than the resource commons. The welfare aspects of environmental commons have by now been adequately researched and evidenced and run into hundreds of millions of dollars around the world. He also tends to elaborate more about the commodification of the commons and their resources. Commodification can, however, have many forms, and the costs saved by not properly treating and disposing of industrial waste needs to be accounted for in arguments about accumulation by dispossession, and in the degradation of the commons which put millions of commons dependent livelihoods, including those in cities, at grave risk.

The literature on the commons has been somewhat celebratory, ignoring the institutional and power dependency of the success of common pool resource management, as brought out clearly in the Nobel Prize winning work of Elinor Ostrom. However, it is increasingly becoming necessary to focus on commoning practices, since capital is as likely to use the commons for production, reproduction, accumulation, and for cost cutting, through dumping waste on public land and common pool resources, in the process adversely affecting ecosystem services of environmental systems.

The politics of epistemology and legality play a role as well in commoning practices. Harvey mentions that the state has a monopoly over violence as well as definitions of legality. In Mumbai and other urban regions, we see commons being classified as wasteland as a legitimizing exercise for takeover, re-classifying ecologically sensitive no-go zone for permitting 'development' and infrastructure as well as housing projects, and resorting to obfuscatory language in government orders to subvert progressive environmental laws that are protective of the commons. In Chennai, commons have been mis-classified as *poramboke*—wasteland thus permitting the setting up of polluting industries which pollute nearby creeks, waterbodies and agricultural land, affecting fishers, pastoralists, and farmers (Parthasarathy 2017). On the other hand, citizen groups, NGOs, and peoples' movements of resistance display a greater faith in law and legal institutions, science, and technical expertise in protecting the commons from encroachment and degradation.

The idea of risk urbanism allows us to capture this public discourse and social movements around the commons in ways that allow us to conceptualize the urban through a new set of categories and analytical frameworks. Capital, capital accumulation, and capital flows constitute an important set of processes for identifying cities in Marxist and neo-Marxist urban studies scholarship as nodes, centres of production, reproduction, and accumulation, and as places of dispossession, expropriation, and pauperization. However, sociologists, social anthropologists, feminist scholars, and political philosophers have tended to focus on systems of solidarities, forms of association, the nature of institutions and legal processes and norms, as factors which distinguish the rural from the urban, the feudal from the democratic. Mumbai's resistance to effective urban governance is frequently commented upon by political leaders, bureaucrats and scholars, with a former chief minister of Maharashtra even referring to the city as 'India's Wild West'. This is also evident in popular descriptions of the city in cinema, in literature, and in well-known urban biographies such as Maximum City by Suketu Mehta (2009). In reviewing such approaches, Vyjayanthi Rao

188   D. PARTHASARATHY

(2006) uses frames such as 'city of risk' and 'city at risk' to comment on the dangers that are a constant reference point and everyday experience for its citizens. Arguably these views hark back to a rural past that threatens the city, pointing to the failure to evolve more urbane, civilized, and institutional modes of recognizing, addressing, and resolving urban problems. However, our research indicates that while the state and its elites reflect these 'wild west' strategies, ironically it is the people, the migrants, the minorities, and the marginalized, the resource dependent populations, the fishers and adivasis, and coalitions of NGOs and civil society organization—it is these who are perhaps truly representative of reflexive modernity, not in an individualistic risk management and 'coping mechanism' sense, but in a more transformative sense (Parthasarathy 2015; Adam et al. 2016). These groups perceive the risk of an unplanned, haphazard urban development process that is constantly buffeted by neoliberal ideologies and strategies, and hence form associations, do research, develop alternative visions and plans, and struggle to get these realized by using civic strategies including elections, court battles, and social mobilizations, and contribute to reframing government guidelines, rules, norms, and legislations (Parthasarathy 2017; Sundar 2014). Iris Marion Young points to the uniqueness of urban settings which permit cross-cutting alliances across groups divided by older feudal forms of identities, which use modern institutions such as courts and tribunals, and which also create new kinds of associations through for instance the use of modern information technology, and social media (Young 2011). A critical and radical departure that Young makes is to move away from a rural to an urban paradigm of community-focused idea of justice, that does not valorize the self-sufficiency and coherence of a village community (the latter, a notion that is geographically specific and subject to questioning); instead she is cognizant of the fuzziness and messiness of urban communities, the contestations and conflicts, but also the technologies of dealing with everyday urban negotiations that inter-connect communities, and evolve norms, rules and regulations for dealing with common threats and problems. This is what we see in neighbourhoods at risk which design and develop their own associations, institutions, and governance mechanisms for coping with risk. They also display a greater sensibility and intelligence in using existing state institutions including tribunals, courts, and commissions to ensure a more sustainable urban transformation rather than a neoliberal and disaster-prone transformation.

In times of disasters, in the context of state failure, it is informal associations of friends and strangers, neighbouring groups, and 'emergent groups'

INDIA'S EMERGING RISK URBANISM   189

(Stallings and Quarantelli 1985; Twigg and Mosel 2017) who come to the rescue of those at risk of danger from flooding, landslides, building collapses, or fire accidents. If risk urbanism is about the commoning of risk across the city and its population, it is also about dealing with and addressing risk, and new forms of risk management showcase the bottom-up response to increasing hazards that cities are exposed to. In the case of the 2005 floods for instance the most comprehensive, integrated, and holistic report came from a Concerned Citizens Committee, not from state agencies and research experts. For the Dharavi redevelopment project, citizens groups and activists have come up with an alternative plan that pays more attention to housing needs, and environment/livelihood objectives (Patel et al. 2010). An alternative Peoples' Vision Document for the city developed by over a hundred NGOs and activist groups coming together under the aegis of an NGO YUVA has fewer inaccuracies and greater clarity on development and welfare needs than the new development plan for the city drawn up by the state using external corporate consultants.[8] Across a range of court battles by NGOS and peoples' movements including fisher unions and associations, there is greater use of the law, legal principles, science, and technical expertise by these, than by the state which frequently resorts to legal and scientific fictions, and illegalities in supporting neoliberal projects (Parthasarathy 2017). In the evolution of laws and rules that seek to mitigate risk and protect the environment, groups located at the bottom have had more reasoned and evolved responses to offer that address justice, welfare and sustainability concerns, than agents of the state.

Risk urbanism in the above sense, by generating a new kind of collective and associational reflexive modernity (Beck et al. 1994), reflects a new epistemic moment involving knowledge co-production by alliances from below which consult technical experts and researchers, and which are rooted in an awareness of the fundamental urban value of institutions and institutional norms of problem solving. Nagendra, Sudhira, Katti, and Schewenius. (2013), in their study of governance of ecosystems in Bengaluru, state that 'involvement of community groups, corporate and public sector agencies, and NGOs is important to ensure knowledge sharing, and willingness to follow regulations'. Citing Shaw and Satish (2007), they also suggest that 'informal, loose coalitions of different social, economic and interest groups are gaining increasing influence in negotiating local-scale agreements about resource use, and in providing important links with official institutions', something that is evident in the Mumbai

---

[8] See Table 9.1 for the range of actor groups who come up with response in the context of state and market complicity in risk generation.

190 D. PARTHASARATHY

Metropolitan Region, in Pune, and Chennai as well. The greater and increased role of these coalitions and associations involving the urban poor, activists, and researchers have evolved from a greater recognition of the crucial significance of commons, including something as basic or simple as trees on roads, for large sections of the city's underprivileged and marginalized sections (Parthasarathy 2011; Nagendra and Gopal 2011; Nagendra, Sudhira, Katti, Tengo, and Schewenius. 2014).

Mary Douglas (1990) has argued that every culture 'needs a common forensic vocabulary with which to hold persons accountable and further that risk is a word that admirably serves the forensic needs of the new global culture'. The arguments about risk urbanism in this chapter exemplify the emergence of a new culture in cities, a new way of life, behaviour and attitude that gets reflected in a new vocabulary, a new epistemology, and new associational forms of action as a response to the negative aspects of neoliberal urban transformation. This risk urbanism is linked to the ongoing transformation of the urban commons, and response/resistance from a range of social actors which oppose the commoning of risk, and support restoration of the resource commons as a risk mitigation strategy. Risk urbanism is offered as a 'forensic resource' that Douglas seeks to develop, and it will be particularly useful in the study of urban commons and disasters, since commons in general, and urban commons in particular are not popular topics of research in Indian sociology. Douglas also argues that the meanings of risk constantly keep changing and evolving. Neoliberalism valorizes certain kinds of risks, especially in the financial systems (fe.g., hedging, venture capital, start-ups). The objective of highlighting processes and phenomena of risk urbanism in this chapter is the same as that of Douglas—namely to bring to the forefront of public discourse the issue of risk, that risk is a justice problem (Parthasarathy, 2018). 'Risk Urbanism' is offered as a contribution to 'public sociology' debates (Burawoy 2005) on urban disasters. Moreover, since, as Douglas (1990) has consistently argued, the 'weak', the poor, the 'sinners', and the powerless are consistently blamed for high risk in most societies, this academic exercise has a political purpose—to understand emerging cultures of risk, the diverse meanings of risk, and how it affects different sections of the population, and to bring out the larger social construction of risk by neoliberal urbanization.

There is increasing recognition by scholars, environmentalists, and activists, as well as sections of the public, that urban commons are under severe pressure from processes of urbanization and urban development (Derkzen, van Teefelen, Nagendra, and Verburg. 2017). The idea of risk urbanism helps us recognize the consequences of the loss of urban commons and/or its degradation both for specific groups directly dependent on these commons, and for urban populations and economies in general. There is continued dependence on urban commons such as lakes, forests, pasture, and wetlands by local communities for livelihoods, cultural and religious purposes, and for preventing disasters (Nagendra and Ostrom 2014; Parthasarathy 2011). The commons also offer a safety net for new migrants into the city from rural areas, which bring them into conflict with older users. Property rights are used by proponents of neoliberal urbanization to further the accumulation of capital. It is imperative, therefore, that commons be brought into the vocabulary of property rights so that a more considered debate may take place on how cities and their populations are exposed to and adversely affected by various kinds of risk.

Risk urbanism goes beyond the simple transfer of wealth that is the staple argument of critics of neoliberalism and accumulation by dispossession. The cost-cutting measure of capital leads to pauperization of others by degrading the assets of the poor, through the commoning of public bads, and the degradation of the resource commons. Extreme events, unplanned and haphazard urbanization, and geographical location combine to make cities places of high risk and vulnerability. Climate change exacerbates risk for high-density urban settlements. Cities, as Blackburn and Pelling argue, are active agents— reshaping and transforming topographies, ecosystems, polluting air and water, and affecting the micro-climate. Human beings constantly learn and adapt to ecosystems and geographies—learning to cope, survive, thrive, and compete for resources. The dynamic interaction between cities and humans in the context of climate change and neoliberal urbanization requires a new epistemology, and the notion of risk urbanism is offered as one small contribution in the effort to better understand ongoing urban processes and trends. It is at the nexus or confluence between commons governance and neoliberal transformation that one can locate and seek to understand the emerging contours of risk urbanism in Indian cities and beyond. This is an urgent task for scholars since as yet, risk is largely studied at an aggregate level, not phenomenologically, as people actually experience risk on an everyday basis.

In conclusion, we would like to argue that even as risk urbanism offers a unique perspective from the global south, it also enables us to advance the agenda that Sujata Patel (2014) has set for us. An understanding of risk urbanism will help us better understand how risk is generated, experienced, responded, and adapted to in other metropolises such as New York, Houston, or Florida, as also Berlin and London. Patel critiques Harvey for his 'analytical foreclosure' which limits his theorizing to class conflict in the city. The notion of risk urbanism enables us to bring in other kinds of conflicts—around the environment for instance, which relates to class conflict, engenders other axes of inequality (caste, ethnicity, race, and gender), and alerts us to the

192   D. PARTHASARATHY

cross-class and cross-cutting presence of risk. This analysis of risk urbanism from the global south can therefore perhaps contribute to the larger agenda of contributing to social science globally.

References

Adam, Hans Nicolai, D. Parthasarathy, Alankar, Synne Movik, Abhiram Sahrasabudhe, and Lyla Mehta. 2016. 'Climate Change, Uncertainty and Flooding: Politics and Perspectives in Mumbai'. Paper presented at session on Impacts of Droughts and Floods in Cities: Policies and Governance, World Water Week, Stockholm, August.

Beck, Ulrich. 1992. *Risk Society: Towards a New Modernity*. London: Sage.

Beck, Ulrich. 1995. *Ecological Enlightenment: Essays on The Politics of the Risk Society*. Atlantic Highlands, NJ: Humanities Press.

Beck, Ulrich, Anthony Giddens, and Scott Lash. 1994. *Reflexive Modernization: Politics, Tradition and Aesthetics in the Modern Social Order*. Redwood City, CA: Stanford University Press.

Burawoy, Michael. 2005. 'For Public Sociology'. *American Sociological Review* 70 (1): 4–28.

Chouhan, Hemantkumar A., D. Parthasarathy, and Sarmistha Pattanaik. 2016. 'Coastal Ecology and Fishing Community in Mumbai'. *Economic and Political Weekly* 51 (39): 49.

de Sherbinin, A. and Bardy, G. 2015. Social Vulnerability to Floods in Two Coastal Megacities: New York City and Mumbai'. *Vienna Yearbook of Population Research* 13: 131–65.

Deleuze, G. and F. Guattari. 1983. *Anti-Oedipus*. Translated by Robert Hurley, Mark Seem, and Helen R. Lane. Minneapolis, MN: University of Minnesota Press.

Derkzen, Marthe L., et al. 2017. 'Shifting Roles of Urban Green Space in the Context of Urban Development and Global Change'. *Current Opinion in Environmental Sustainability* 29: 32–39.

Douglas, Mary and Aaron Wildavsky. 1983. *Risk and Culture: An Essay on the Selection of Technological and Environmental Dangers*. Oakland, CA: University of California Press,.

Douglas, Mary. 1990 'Risk as a Forensic Resource'. *Daedalus*: 119 (4): 1–16.

Douglas, Mary. 2013. *Risk and Blame*. London: Routledge,.

Fuchs, Roland J. 2010. Cities at Risk: Asia's Coastal Cities in an Age of Climate Change. Honolulu: East-West Center.

Gadgil, Madhav and Ramachandra Guha. 1995. *Ecology and Equity: The Use and Abuse of Nature in Contemporary India*. Boca Raton, FL: Psychology Press.

Giddens, Anthony. 2009. *The Politics of Climate Change*. Cambridge: Polity Press.

Gidwani, Vinay and Amita Baviskar. 2011. 'Urban Commons'. *Economic and Political Weekly* 46 (50): 42–3.

Glassman, Jim. 2006. 'Primitive Accumulation, Accumulation by Dispossession, Accumulation by "Extra-Economic" Means'. *Progress in Human Geography* 30 (5): 608–25.

INDIA'S EMERGING RISK URBANISM   193

GreenAsh. 2013. 'Natural Disaster Risk Levels of the World's Largest Cities'. March 14. Available at http://greenash.net.au/thoughts/2013/03/natural-disaster-risk-levels-of-theworlds-largest-cities/, accessed 8 Apr 2014.

Hallegatte, Stéphane, et al. 2010. 'Flood Risks, Climate Change Impacts and Adaptation Benefits in Mumbai: An Initial Assessment of Socio-Economic Consequences of Present and Climate Change Induced Flood Risks and of Possible Adaptation Options'. OECD Environment Working Papers 27: 0_1.

Hanson, Susan, et al. 2011. 'A Global Ranking of Port Cities with High Exposure to Climate Extremes'. *Climatic Change* 104 (1): 89–111.

Harvey, David. 2003. 'The "New Imperialism": Accumulation by Dispossession'. *Socialist Register* 40: 63–87.

Herweijer, C., R. J. Nicholls, S. Hanson, N. Patmore, R. Muir-Wood, S. Hallegatte, J. Corfee-Morlot, and J. Chateau. 2008. *How Do Our Coastal Cities Fare under Rising Flood Risk? Risk Management Solutions*. London, England.

Maskey, M., J. S. Shastri, K. Saraswathi, R. Surpam, and N. Vaidya. 2006. 'Leptospirosis in Mumbai: Post-Deluge Outbreak 2005'. *Indian Journal of Medical Microbiology* 24 (4): 337.

Mehta, Suketu. 2009. *Maximum City: Bombay Lost and Found*. New York: Vintage.

Nagendra, Harini, and Elinor Ostrom. 2014. 'Applying the Social-Ecological System Framework to the Diagnosis of Urban Lake Commons in Bangalore, India'. *Ecology and Society* 19 (2): 1–18.

Nagendra, Harini, et al. 2013. 'Sub-Regional Assessment of India: Effects of Urbanization on Land Use, Biodiversity and Ecosystem Services'. In *Urbanization, Biodiversity and Ecosystem Services: Challenges and Opportunities*, 65–74. Heidelberg: Springer Netherlands.

Nagendra, Harini, et al. 2014. 'Urbanization and Its Impacts on Land Use, Biodiversity and Ecosystems in India'. *INTERdisciplina* 2 (2):

Nicholls, R. J., S. Hanson, C. Herweijer, N. Patmore, S. Hallegatte, J. Corfee-Morlot, et al. 2007. 'Ranking of the World's Cities Most Exposed to Coastal Flooding Today and in the Future' (No. 1). OECD Environment Working Paper.

Parthasarathy, D. 2009. 'Social and Environmental Insecurities in Mumbai: Towards a Sociological Perspective on Vulnerability'. *South African Review of Sociology* 40 (1): 109–26.

Parthasarathy, Devanathan. 2011. 'Hunters, Gatherers and Foragers in a Metropolis: Commonising the Private and Public in Mumbai'. *Economic and Political Weekly* 46 (50): 54–63.

Parthasarathy, D. 2015. 'Informality, Resilience, and the Political Implications of Disaster Governance. *Pacific Affairs* 88 (3): 551–75.

Parthasarathy, D. 2016. 'Decentralization, Pluralization, Balkanization? Challenges for Disaster Mitigation and Governance in Mumbai'. *Habitat International* 52: 26–34.

Parthasarathy, D. 2017. 'Science and Law to the Rescue of India's Disastrous Coastal Urbanism? Loss of Imagination and Reimagining a Future'. Paper presented at the conference on Resilient Cities for Human Flourishing: Governing the Asia-Pacific Urban Transition in the Anthropocene, Asia Research Institute, National University of Singapore, 2–3 March.

194   D. PARTHASARATHY

Parthasarathy, Devanathan. 2018. 'Inequality, Uncertainty, and Vulnerability: Rethinking Governance from a Disaster Justice Perspective'. *Environment and Planning E: Nature and Space* 1 (3): 422–442.

Patankar, A. and A. Patwardhan. 2016. Estimating the Uninsured Losses due to Extreme Weather Events and Implications for Informal Sector Vulnerability: A Case Study of Mumbai, India. *Natural Hazards* 80 (1): 285–310.

Patel, Sheela, Aneerudha Paul, Sundar Burra, Bindi Vasacada, Sujay Kumarji, and Kairavi Dua. 2010. 'RE DHARAVI'. *Mumbai, India: SPARC and KRVIA*.

Patel, Sujata. 2014. 'Is There a "South" Perspective to Urban Studies?'. In *The Routledge Handbook on the Cities of the Global South*, edited by Susan Parnell and Sophie Oldfield, 37–53. London: Routledge.

Pelling, Mark and Sophie Blackburn, eds. 2014. *Megacities and the Coast: Risk, Resilience and Transformation*. London: Routledge.

Rao, Vyjayanthi. 2006. 'Risk and the City: Bombay, Mumbai, and Other Theoretical Departures'. *India Review* 5 (2): 220–32.

Razafindrabe, B.H.N., G. A. Parvin,.A. Surjan, Y. Takeuchi, and R. Shaw. 2009. 'Climate Disaster Resilience: Focus on Coastal Urban Cities in Asia'. *Asian Journal of Environment and Disaster Management* 1 (1): 101–16.

Regional Urban Task Force. 2008. 'Urban Resilience and Disaster Vulnerability in the Asia-Pacific Region: Concept Note for Regional Urban Task Force'. Available at http://www.adrc.asia/events/RTFmeeting20080130/PDF_Presentations/01_Concept-Note-for-Regional-Urban-Task-Force.pdf, accessed 21 Apr 2011.

Revi, Aromar. 2005. 'Lessons from the Deluge: Priorities for Multi-Hazard Risk Mitigation'. *Economic and Political Weekly* (Sept 3): 3911–16.

Sharma, Sneha, and D. Parthasarathy. 2018. 'Urban Ecologies in Transition: Contestations around Waste in Mumbai'. In *Sustainable Urbanization in India*, 207–23. Singapore: Springer.

Shaw, A., and Satish, M. K. 2007. 'Metropolitan Restructuring in Post-liberalized India: Separating the Global and the Local. *Cities* 24 (2): 148–163.

Sherly, Mazhuvanchery Avarachen, et al. 2015. 'Disaster Vulnerability Mapping for a densely Populated Coastal Urban Area: An Application to Mumbai, India'. *Annals of the Association of American Geographers* 105 (6): 1198–220.

Singh, Binti, and D. Parthasarathy. 2010. 'Civil Society Organisation Partnerships In Urban Governance: An Appraisal of the Mumbai Experience'. *Sociological Bulletin* 59 (1): 92–110.

Stallings, Robert A. 2002. 'Weberian Political Sociology and Sociological Disaster Studies'. *Sociological Forum* 17 (2): 200–15.

Stallings, R. A., and Quarantelli, E. L. 1985. 'Emergent Citizen Groups and Emergency Management. *Public Administration Review* 45: 93–100.

Stecko, S., and Barber, N. 2007. Exposing vulnerabilities: Monsoon floods in Mumbai, India. Case study prepared for Revisiting Urban Planning: Global Report on Human Settlements, 1–14.

Sundar, Aparna. 2014. 'From Regulation to Management and Back Again: Exploring Governance Shifts in India's Coastal Zone'. *Conservation and Society* 12 (4): 364.

Twigg, J. and I. Mosel. 2017. 'Emergent Groups and Spontaneous Volunteers in Urban Disaster Response'. *Environment and Urbanization* 29 (2): 443–58.

UN-HABITAT. 2012. *The State of Asian Cities 2010/11*. Fukuoka: UN-HABITAT.

Young, Iris Marion. 2011. *Justice and the Politics of Difference*. Princeton University Press.

PART THREE

BECOMING MIDDLE CLASS, BEING DEPRIVED, AND HAVING ASPIRATIONS

10

Dalits in Neoliberal Economy

A Discussion on Most Marginal Communities

Badri Narayan

This chapter analyses the dalit interface with neoliberal economy. It traces the implication of a neoliberal economy on the livelihood of the dalits with further examining the impact of a neoliberal economy on their elements of dalit resistance, needed to accelerate their struggle for a better future.

In India, the caste system was a closed stratified structure, where a particular caste follows its traditional occupation which was followed by that particular caste from generations, with transfer of indigenous knowledge and skills from one generation to the other. This system gradually turns an occupation, as a caste occupation or we may say hereditary occupation. In the case of dalit artisanal communities these indigenous knowledge and skills become a matter of pride for a community, like the traditional skill to identify medicinal plants by Sahariya and snake charmers skilled to trap snakes, Baheliya skilled to trap birds. Most of these skills were manual skills without any space for technological intervention. These skills were known for its perfection and excellence that add pride to the community. But globalization is adversely impacting their traditional occupations. Their livelihood and specialized skills I are losing their space and glory in the global capitalistic market. Bulk production of goods with latest technology at cheap prices has proved to be a great challenge for the skills and products of all marginal communities. Neoliberal economy has opened the door for a global market that has directly impacted the traditional occupations of dalits, and made them more vulnerable than before. Dalits neither have the capacity to compete with these productions nor do they have the capacity to negotiate for an alternative to earn their livelihood. Their traditional artisan skills and indigenous knowledge are on the verge of ruin. Many scholars have argued that the link between caste and occupation is eroding because of economic liberalization (e.g. Panini 1996, 60). He has argued that economic liberalization will enhance economic competition and employers will give

Badri Narayan, *Dalits in Neoliberal Economy* In: *Neoliberalism, Urbanization, and Aspirations in Contemporary India*. Edited by: Sujata Patel, Oxford University Press. © Oxford University Press 2021.
DOI: 10.1093/oso/9780190132019.003.0010

198 BADRI NARAYAN

importance to efficiency and skill while recruiting a worker rather than their caste identity. Such studies claim remarkable betterment of life conditions of dalits in the new liberal economy setting. Chandra Bhan Prasad, an eminent dalit thinker, in an interview to *The New York Times* opined,

This is a golden period for Dalits . . . Because of the new market economy, material markers are replacing social markers. Dalits can buy rank in the market economy. India is moving from a caste-based to a class-based society, where if you have all the goodies in life and your bank account is booming, you are acceptable.

On the contrary, recent research on the formal urban labour market has demonstrated how even highly qualified dalits and Muslims face discrimination (Thorat and Newman 2010, 23).The question is not of positive or negative impact of a neoliberal economy on dalits only, but we have to understand the impact of a neoliberal economy on the life of dalit artisanal communities, who are facing serious crisis on their traditional livelihood and are not able to shift to new livelihood options for themselves due to their inability to interact with the global market. In fact, globalization has further led to the marginalization of the already marginal section of society that was unable to access education, health facilities, and was deprived of jobs (Jogdand 2002; Chandrasekhar and Ghosh 2002; Omvedt 2005; Mungerkar 2001).[1] Most marginal communities are unable to interact with the neoliberal market and become more vulnerable. This chapter mostly derives observations from my fieldwork in Uttar Pradesh (UP).

It UP, lying in the Hindi heartland in north India, is one of the largest land areas of the country, is also the most populated state. The area of UP is 240,928 sq. km. Its population is 199,581,477 (2011 Census). The percentage of SC population to total population in UP is 21.1 per cent. The state spreads from the north-west to the south-east expanse of the heartland of India. Physically it can be divided into two parts: the Gangetic Plain and the Vindhyan Hills. The Gangetic Plain is divided into two major portions in UP. These are the Upper Ganges and the Middle Ganges plains. The Upper Ganges plain lies mainly in UP while part of the Middle Ganges Plain lies in this state, the rest lying in Bihar. The Upper Ganges Plain can be roughly

---

[1] See Mungekar 2001.

MARGINAL DALITS IN NEOLIBERAL ECONOMY   199

divided into two parts at the confluence of Yamuna–Ganga in Allahabad, the point which divides the entire state into two parts—eastern UP and western UP.

In total there are seventy-five districts in this state which differ widely from each other in terms of socio-economic development. UP has witnessed a visible assertion of dalits, still, there are many small dalit groups who have not yet developed the capacity to aspire. I am trying to concentrate on a few as:

Basor/Bansphor

The word 'Basor' means 'bamboo workers'. Basor caste traces its origin from Raja Benu or Venu who ruled at Singorgarh in the Damoh region. History says that the king was so religious that he raised no taxes from his subjects; instead he earned his livelihood by making and selling different kinds of bamboo fans. 'Venu' is a Sanskrit term that means bamboo. Another legend relates that in the past there were no bamboos, and the first Basor took the snake which was worn by Lord Shiva around his neck and planted it with its head in the ground. Immediately, a bamboo sprang up on the spot and from this the Basor made the first fan. They make numerous kinds of baskets, among which may be mentioned the chujika, a very small one, the Tokni, a basket of middle size, and the iokna, a very large one. The Dauri is a special basket with a lining of matting for washing rice in a stream. The Jhdnpi is a round basket with a cover for holding clothes; the Tipanna a small one in which girls keep dolls; and the Bilahra a still smaller one for holding betel-leaf. Other articles made from bamboo-bark are the chalni or sieve, the khunkhwia or rattle, the Bdnsuri or wooden flute, the Bijna or fan, and the Supa or winnowing-fan. Bansphors are mostly distributed in the eastern part of UP and in the districts of Azamgarh, Gorakhpur, Ghazipur, Balia, Varanasi, Allahabad, and so forth. Their total population in UP, according to the 1981 census, is 18,530. They are predominantly distributed in rural areas (Risely 1891). The community is divided into sub-castes such as the Purania (the oldest), the Juthia (who eat leftover food of others), and the Deshwari (whoreside in the desh). Bamboo basket-making their traditional occupations, their main profession keeps them closely involved with the daily market economy. They sell their crafts on cash terms in the local market.

Musahar

The Musahar are also known as Banmanus, Arya, and Banjara. In the list of SCs of UP the 'Musahar' and 'Banmanus' have been listed separately, to a Musahar, Banmanus is a mere synonym. In Sultanpur and Varanasi, they are known as 'Musahar'. In Raeareli, they are also known as 'Gonr' whereas in Faizabad they are called 'Banjara'. Regarding the etymology, the people are of the belief that since they were rat eaters, hence the name Musahars. The origin of Musahar is shrouded in mystery but according to a legend prevalent in the community, Parmeshwar created the first man of each caste, and then he gave each a horse-to-ride-on tool to work with. The others took their tools and mounted their horses but the Musahar began to dig a pair of holes in the belly of his horse to fix his feet as he rode. Parmeshwar saw his folly and ordered that his descendants should live on rats which they should dig out of the earth. When Parmeshwar had finished eating, the Musahar began to lick his bar platters. Seeing this, the Parmeshwar said, 'these are low people. They shall always lick the platter, and they have been degraded ever since' (Crooke 1896, 12–37). The Musahar are settled in central and eastern UP. According to the 1971 census, the total population of Musahar in UP is 1,04,725. The language spoken by these people is Hindi and the dialect spoken is Awadhi. Among the Musahar, sects like Bhagat, Sakatiya/Saket, and Turkahia exist.

Baheliya

The Bahelias are a scheduled caste in UP. The Bahelias were described as a hunting, game-keeping, and bird-catching group. They indulged in bird-catching, extracting honey from beehives, catching animals, and picking peacock feathers to make fans. They ascribe their lowly position in Hindu society to these occupations. The Chirimar or fowler, the nearest kin of the Baheliya, is a welcome visitor in the village market or in towns, who catches birds by trapping or shooting and sells the game to people. The total strength of the Baheliya in UP is enumerated to be 41,454 according to 1971 census records. They are mainly distributed in the central and western part of UP. The main social groupings among the Bahelias are Sisodia, Gahlot, Karaul, and Aheria (Singh 2005, 112).

MARGINAL DALITS IN NEOLIBERAL ECONOMY   201

Nat

The Nat are described as a community of the so-called gypsy dancers, acrobats, and prostitutes. They wander about with their families, settling for a few days or weeks at a time in the vicinity of villages, making make-shift instruments of Sirki (reed), and for this reason all such people are referred to as Sirkibands. They are professional in animal husbandry and gymnasium. Community is distributed in the districts of UP. In UP, their major concentration may be seen in the western areas. In this state, they are included in the list of SCs and denotified communities. Their total population according to the 1971 census figures is 1,233. The Nat are divided into five sub-groups viz., Bajania Nat or Karnat, Kalabaz, Kabutar Nat, Chamar Nat, and Muslim Nat.

Kuchbandhiyakanjar

According to their traditions, they are descended from a Manu Guru and his wife Nathiya Kanjarin. Some of them claim descent from Kush. Besides, they associate themselves with the dynasty of which Maharanapratap. They are believed to have emigrated from Rajasthan to various parts of the country to escape conversion to Islam. On their migration, they were rendered homeless, so they look refuge in the jungles and consequently resorted to hunting and looting. Their total population in UP, according to the 1981 census, is 50,752. The traditional occupation of the Kuchbandhiya was hunting; they still depend on the forest, extracting roots of the Khas grass, and collecting reeds from banks of the rivers. From the stalks of the Munji grass and from the roots of the Palas tree, they make ropes which they sell in villages. The community is also involved in tanning of skins out of which drums are made and sold.

Sapera

The Sapera is a community of snake charmers. The Kalbelia of Rajasthan and Pamalu of Andra Pradesh are also snake charmers by profession. Any historical account relating to their place of origin is not known. The distribution of the Sapera is fairly widespread as they move from place to place

202 BADRI NARAYAN

performing snake shows but would come back to their permanent settlement in Shankargarh tehsil/ village of Allahabad district. They are large in number.

Sansi

The term 'Sansi' is derived from the Sanskrit word swasa meaning 'breath'. The sansi, a scheduled caste in UP with a total population of 5,626 persons as per 1971 census, are also called as Saunsis, Sainsis, Sahnsia, Bhatu, or Bhantus, but the more prevalent term is sansi. They drive their name from the Rajput ancestor named Raja sansmal who had two sons named Mahla and Beehdoo. Beehdoo had twelve sons and Mahla had eleven sons, and these twenty-three sons are the founders of the twenty-three gotra of the Sansi. They claim to have been Bhatti Rajput who was expelled from Rajasthan by Muslim invaders. They migrated to different parts of northern India and took up pastoral and predatory activities. They further relate that their ancestors came from Gajini, Bhatnar, Chittorgarh, and in UP; they are distributed mainly in the districts of Meerut, Moradabad, and Muzaffarnagar.

Older Skills and New Challenges

There are many caste groups among marginalized communities whose traditional skills have no place in the new system. Market forces are turning them as labourers but they do not wish to work as labour because they are skilled. When after 1990 the era of liberalism came in the country and the market was opened globally, free from the clutches of socialist bounds, some of us welcomed it and others opposed it. Many termed this as 'the era of market'. This market will prove 'Mina Bazar[2]' for some, and 'Maya Bazar[3]' for others. On the one hand, this market gives prosperity to a few; on the other hand it makes others realize that they are deprived. To control this contradiction, the image of a nation state was formed. Now we are approaching thirty years of completion of a neoliberal economy in India. But the question whether this relationship of state and market would increase equality and lessen the discrimination in society is still unanswered. The idea of global market

---

[2] Mina bazar is market where selling objects allures people and creates sense of greed in them. They become ready to do anything for that.

[3] An utopian concept for market that arouse aspiration and desire.

MARGINAL DALITS IN NEOLIBERAL ECONOMY 203

strengthening is yet to be fulfilled. While the numbers of service-providing institutions and civil societies are working to make the relationship of state and market less conflicting, they are struggling to make qualitative interference in this, and this is yet to be accomplished. Many of these civil society NGOs are either not understanding the relationship of market and marginal communities and the critical social structure of discrimination or they are ignoring these issues for various reasons despite understanding structural problems.

Here I would like to see the relations of dalit groups of India with relations of market in a special context. For a section of dalits, those who have acquired the strength to dream for a better life and achieve it, market has provided the way for upward mobility. They have added happiness and comfort through trade in liberal economy. Such dalit groups have equipped themselves with education and desire to established an ambitious society for themselves. Whereas a larger population of dalits is still standing on the door of market, confused and fragile. Such groups can be called 'communities in confusion'. They are unable to join themselves with new projects for different social groups of government like skill development projects, 'entrepreneurship'. Basor, Saheriya, Sapera, Baheliya, Hari, Begar, Musahar, Nat, Sarvan are such smaller dalit communities who have not been able to join the 'microfinance' projects running in the villages, in visible capacity quantitatively or qualitatively. The reach of self-help groups of microfinance has been limited to visible dalit communities living on the margins of society and backward farming communities. 'Power to save money' has not been developed in smaller dalit communities. They have to dig the well and drink it daily. Earn daily and Eat daily. Their everyday earnings are sometimes not enough to feed twice a day. Such communities have generally been dalit artisanal communities. These communities were considered artists in earlier systems. In the system of new market and modernism, their 'skills' became worthless. In the new system, arising out of economical liberalism there is no other option left for them, other than to be labourers in the expansion of market, real estate, infrastructural projects. They don't want to become labourers. They believe that they are 'skilled community' and have proud of their skills. As a result, they can't establish themselves in an expanding market. They are feeling uncomfortable in such market system (Narayan 2017).[4] Bansfor (Basore) living in

---

[4] बद्रीनारायण (2017): 'पुरानेकौशलनयेअसमंजस"लेख, हिंदुस्तान समाचार पत्र.

204 BADRI NARAYAN

different states of Northern India is such a dalit community. In the traditional system they earned their livelihood by cutting bamboo and making products of it (Singh 1998).[5] These people used to make and sell Mauni (basket) SOOP (a plate to clean cereals) for livelihood. Now, the presence of bamboo has decreased, there is an indirect restriction on cutting bamboo as well, their access to forest produce is now under question, so they have no other option than to become labourers at construction sites or other infrastuctural projects. 'Sarvan' is a community which has worked as ear cleaners (Singh 2005).[6] They used to make medicines for this from herbs and shrubs growing in villages for fungal infections. But now their skill is becoming useless. Doctors are everywhere now. There are English medicines to clean and disinfect the ear. Due to this their livelihood has become challenging. What should they do now? They consider themselves as 'skilled community' therefore they cannot accept them as petty labourers or their transformation in labourer community.

While the livelihoods of social communities like washer-man and barbers are trying to 'adjust' in the market with new technology, many social communities who are unable to make their skill technologically proficient, who know only traditional way of earning livelihoods are feeling helpless and troubled at the gates of market (Mandal Report 1980).[7] Such is the story of Sapera community. This community is spread in Bihar, Uttar Pradesh, Madhya Pradesh, Rajasthan, Punjab, Haryana, and many states of South India. This community used to catch snakes, take their teeth out, make them dance, make medicines and antidotes of different kinds from their poison (Singh 1993).[8] Now in modern social structure, under wild-life protection laws and deforestation, their livelihood is almost on the verge of extinction. Thus, this whole community is deprived of their traditional livelihood. Now they have no other option than to be labourers at construction projects or brick clans. Kuchbandhiya[9] is such a dalit community which lives in different districts of UP (Crooke 1896). They are mostly in Bundelkhand. This community used

---

[5] See Singh (1998).
[6] See Singh (2005).
[7] According to this report few traditional occupational communities declared 'Depressed Backward Classes'.
[8] See Singh (1993).
[9] According to W. Crooke (1896) kanjars are divided into four occupational and endogamous subgroups, namely, Gehar or Patharkat (workers in stone); Sirkipal (workers producing reed mats); Kuchbandhiya (workers producing hairbrushes); and Rechband (professional tortoise catchers). In the Bundelkhand region, according to people of the community they have been involved in the task of making kooch for a long time, so their name was Kuchbandhiya.

MARGINAL DALITS IN NEOLIBERAL ECONOMY 205

to make ropes of rural products like mooj, sarpat, and used to weave the beds. With the arrival of plastic rope even their livelihood is in danger. They have reservations in being transformed as labourers or shift in the structure of a smart city.

Thus, how state and its new market effectlives of dalit communities, and whether state, power, and market manage to create a 'dignified livelihood' for them is yet to be explored.

Lacking the Capacity to Save[10]

In fact, to understanding vulnerability of the most marginal community in neoliberal market, we have to dig deep their presence in state-sponsored schemes and capability to sustain in a neoliberal market. Present state-led governance is largely influenced by liberal economy. It focuses not only on big earnings but focuses on saving too, as a means of survival strategy. It claims for making innovative efforts to develop entrepreneurship among marginals and dalits.

The microfinance sector emerged in India as an important economic strategy to build 'capacity to aspire' for the poor and marginals. The microfinance developed 'swayamsahayatasamooh' (self help groups) in various parts of India. Through these networks of microfinance has enhanced social as well economic capacity to survive for the marginals. These networks got state support through various schemes like NABARD and other banks. The NGOs, Foundations, and microfinance companies and corporates came forward to support these activities for small entrepreneurs in the various parts of country. Microfinance activities expanded itself to rural areas very successfully and reached the women of deprived groups to help them to resolve their issues in life such as illness, chronic disease, children education, marriage of daughters etc. Many microfinance companies and NGOs have also entered in this fray. Few organizations who called themselves socio-cultural organizations but keep political associations such as Rajeev Gandhi foundation also started intervening social and economic realms through microfinance. Rashtriya swayam Sewak Sangh (RSS) has also established its affiliating organization Rashtriya Sewa Bharati and

---

[10] This idea has been discussed in one of my articles in *DailyO*: 'Why Microfinance schemes have failed the weakest of Dalits', 14 August 2018.

206 BADRI NARAYAN

launched a microfinance campaign called 'Vaibhavshree'. Rajiv Gandhi Mahilavikaspariyojana which works under Rajeev Gandhi Foundation made its effective presence in central and eastern UP. During my field work, I have observed that these initiatives have inculcated a sense of new assertive community identity among women. This microfinance activities not only produced a new and assertive sense of new community identities but also creating space for shattering and demolishing feudal and patriarchal dominance in rural society. This new assertive community sense and feeling is carving out an alternative space for them where they can share their pleasure-pain (sukh-dukh). It also provide them a sense of pride which emerges from their gradual acquisition of economic capacity. This emerging new identity and sense of confidence also provide them respect (izzat) within their family and village.

Such small economic support helped them to develop few livelihood activities which may contribute to reduction of social inequality at the grassroot level. It is true that these microfinance activities are contributing to their economic, social, and political empowerment in a very impressive mode. Still we cannot hope for a complete transformation, because there is still a long way to go. But if someone is to analyse the impact of these activities, one may find that these initiatives are mostly centred on women of socially visible caste and communities of backwards and dalits. During my field work, I found that women involved in Self-Help Groups (SHGs) are mostly from Patel, Yadav, Vaisya, Maurya, and Chaurasia castes. Even it is not easy to find women of MBCs communities in these SHGs.We observed that even among dalit communities of these districts, these initiatives are yet to reach to the lower fringes and till now it has been concentrated among women of only few visible and bigger dalit communities like Chamar, Pasi, Dhobi, Kori.

There are around sixty-six dalit castes under the SC category[11] in UP. During our survey I found women of only four or five visible and numerically bigger dalit castes. Near about sixty SC castes are still waiting to acquire capacity to enter in the domain of swayamsahayatasamooh (Self-help groups). When NGOs start working to form SHGs, they pick up women mostly from the communities which are easily visible or who already have acquired capacities to speak and interact with the external agencies, who came forward to mobilize others. Many of smaller dalit communities such as Mushars, Nats,

---

[11] Available at http://socialjustice.nic.in/writereaddata/UploadFile/Scan-0019.jpg, accessed 12 Aug 2018.

MARGINAL DALITS IN NEOLIBERAL ECONOMY   207

Sapera, Kuchbadhiya, Bansfor, and many MBCs such as Bhujawa have not yet acquired that kind of visibility or unable to show their confidence to become part of such initiatives.

When I discussed this issue with the activists engaged in the field of microfinance organizations and asked them why there are no women from the communities such as Mushhar, Nat, Kanjar, Dharikar, and other such groups more than sixty communities of UP. They replied, 'It is not easy to find them'. These communities are small in numbers and mostly are on the peripheries of villages and towns. Sometimes they are nomads or semi-nomads without permanent address. Musahar is traditionally a community of rat pickers, small in numbers in districts like Amethi and Raebareli but in large numbers in various districts of central UP, Eastern UP, and Bundelkhand. Now they have diversified their occupation as agricultural labourer and brick kiln labourers. Their population of around 10 lachs is now scattered in twenty-four districts of UP. They are mostly concentrated in districts like Sultanpur, Ambedkarnagar, Azamgarh, MaharajGanj, Kushinagar, Jaunpur, Varanasi, Chandauli, Sonbhadra, Mirzapur et al.

Usually their basti known as Mushhar bastis does not come under conventional boundaries of villages. They live mostly in separate and isolated areas and on the fringes of main village. Similarly, most other marginal dalit communities also have the same kind of peripheral presence. They lack the capacity to aspire for such socio-economic activities supported by microfinance yet. The groups working in this sector need to take efforts for the inclusion of such excluded communities very sensitively, in the sphere of SHGs. It is true that they are numerically smaller communities and of course number matters in democracy but democratic morality is expected from us, which asks to provide space of margin of margins in almost all democratic space.

It is my observation that those who are visible and have acquired the capacity to assert easily come on the board of SHGs but those who are still most marginal communities, invisible and are lacking the capacity to speak are not yet included even in the domain of microfinance. It is true that their entry in SHGs may provide them the capacity to aspire, which may slowly turn into the capacity to acquire. There is no doubt that these socio-economic actions may strengthen them and prepare them to develop their own politics and capacity to speak and assert for their due share in democracy.

One may find that these smaller and marginal dalit communities have not yet got proper space and visibility. They are invisible even in the BSP-led government in UP. In the BSP frame of politics which believes in—'Jiskijatanisankhyabhari, uskiutnihissedari' (numerical strength in

208 BADRI NARAYAN

democracy) they don't matter a lot. But these sixty castes together may change the face of our democracy (Narayan 2015).[12]

New Liberal Conditions and Resistance

New liberal economy produced market on the one hand, not able to sustain respectfully dignified and community knowledge and skill-based livelihood for the marginals; on the other hand this condition is not even able to evolve capacities among many marginal communities to small saving which may help to sustain them. It also diminishing resistance and dissent capacities of many poor and subaltern marginal groups which can help them to develop pressure on the state to think for their share in state-led democracy. New liberal economy produced a market in working closely with state, its advertisement strategies for selling the products are helping in the emergence of aspirational community which prefer co-option in the given opportunities rather struggle for opportunity expansion for all those who are in need.

Resistance works as a tool for the marginals and deprived social communities in society, for better social positions. It is indeed essential for social dialectics. It paves the way for the synthesis though a churning of thesis and antithesis. In the contemporary market-oriented consumerist societies, the element of resistance is either weakening or on the verge of dying. The fragmented, fractured, and dispersed elements of resistance in the social domain may form a resistance movement together, which may be further oriented towards change of the present and in the hope and desire of the future.

In the recent past we constantly perceive the weakening of social movements. Now a day's resistance movements all over the world are appearing like diffused cells of a bomb. They are losing their vigour, and their transformative impact to challenge the structures of dominance, State and Power. These are just reducing their resistance into silence, or everyday forms of resistance, as observed by eminent anthropologist James Scott.[13] Sometimes it comes out as a civil society movement in the form of short-term resistance. The resistance movement in contemporary times failed to sustain themselves as a transformative movement; rather they are being accommodated, co-opted, and adjusted with the state or other dominant

---

[12] See Narayan (2015).
[13] See Scott (1992).

MARGINAL DALITS IN NEOLIBERAL ECONOMY 209

modes against which they have evolved initially. This may be true for dalit, tribal, labour, and other movements in South Asian societies and even in other societies of the world.

The major crisis of many resistance movements is that after a certain period of time, they start to adopt values of the dominants against which they emerged. The merits, demerits, tone, and tenures of dominant slowly percolate in the resistance movements and consequently change their characters. One may easily observe how leaders of subaltern groups adopted political culture and gesture of mainstream political parties and leaders. Most of the labour movements in Mumbai or Kolkata faded away in the recent past, as their union leaders adopted merits and demerits of their sahibs and management. Overstress on economism in labour mobilizations weakened them slowly. Some of the tribal leaders slowly submerged in dominant political parties and could not maintain their culture of difference that was their strength.

In most of the cases resistance movements articulate an alternative political culture and language and claim for their identity, rights, and values. But slowly, under the influence of mainstream politics they accept those dominant traditions explicitly or implicitly against which they have started their subversion. When Kanshiram started the Bahujan movement in UP, it was an assertion for an alternative subversive political culture. But slowly their leaders started behaving in similar manner like other dominant political parties. Opportunism, corruption, self-interest crept in the everyday life of leaders of his party. This affected the second levels of its political leaders and some of its cadres who were the back bone of the mission. In the beginning, it started as a movement and mission but slowly transformed as a political party with all faults.

Aam Aadmi Party (AAP) also emerged from the womb of the mass movement led by eminent social activist Anna Hazare but further took on various weaknesses produced by the contemporary political culture proposed and followed by dominant political parties. Most of these movements failed to develop an alternative language to communicate with their followers and started speaking the mainstream language.

Sometimes resistance movements produce potential political leaders and political parties but in most of the cases these parties failed to develop their own independent politics. In the case of dalit movement, Kanshiram diagnosed this problem as 'chamachaage' (the Era of Stooges). In his famous book 'Chamacha age' he remarked that most of the dalit leaders of our time could not developed alternative dalit politics in India but worked as stooges (*chamcha*) of dominant political parties. He analysed the politics of post

210   BADRI NARAYAN

Ambedkar RPI through this perspective and dalit leaders working in coordination with Congress in the post-independent era.

Another crisis we may observe in various resistance movements was mobility of the subaltern groups in middle class, as a product of growing consumerism culture among their grassroots cadres and workers. However, middle class also has a positive impact on the resistance movement and played a progressive role in various revolutions. But this new middle class is also taking these movements towards some compromise, negotiations, and adjustments. Though the middle class showed a positive mobility in history with its progressive impact at the same time, consumerist middle classness is eroding our resilience and elements of resistance from our socio-psychological personality. Marx, Lenin, and Ambedkar, at some point in their lives, criticized the self-centredness and leisure-seeking attitudes of our middle class. The state in close coordination with the market is applying all techniques to control resistance movements and not allowing it to sustain for a longer time. We have forgotten the suggestions of eminent historian Eric Hobsbawm that 'capitalism is question not answer'. We have stopped searching answers and are happy with whatever is being proposed by the state and market. One option is left for us as suggested by Milan Kundera in 'The Festival of Insignificance' that only one possible resistance is 'not take it seriously'. We should understand the deep meaning lies in this satire.

Conclusion

I do not deny that the neoliberal economy has opened up new options for those who have acquired the capacity to respond to this very new economic situation. But I have tried to expose the threats for resistance in this neoliberal economy. Besides, it has also created a situation of crisis for the most marginal section of dalit artisanal community for their livelihood, which will ruin the possibility of any emergence of their resistance politics. The claim of evolving new skills and entrepreneurship among dalits may be true for a section of the dalit community but it is not true for the many invisible dalit communalities of UP. It has converted many artisanal dalit communities in the community in confusion in terms of their livelihood options proposed by neoliberal economy based state and market. Many smaller dalit communities are not even in the condition to assemble, or to take part in a microfinance circle, or to assert for their space. They

MARGINAL DALITS IN NEOLIBERAL ECONOMY 211

have not yet acquired even the capacity to have a smaller saving. New liberal economy evolved a life condition in which the element of resistance among marginals is eroding day by day. New liberal market in collision with the state is constantly producing aspiration which kills the element of protest and resistance among marginals and is paving the way for consumerism-led dreams and desires.

References

Chandrasekhar, C. P., and Ghosh, J. 2002. *The Market That Failed: A Decade of Neoliberal Economic Reforms in India*. India: Left Word Books.

Crooke, W. 1896. *The Tribes and Castes of the North-Western Provinces and Oudh, Volume I*. Calcutta: Office of the Superintendent of Government Printing, India.

GOI (Government of India). 1980. *Mandal Commission Report*. New Delhi: National Commission for Backward Classes, GOI.

Jogdand, Y. A. (2002). *Humiliation: Understanding Its Nature, Experience and Consequences*. England: University of St Andrews.

Mungekar, B. L. 2001. 'State, Market and the Dalits: Analytics of the New Economic Policy'. In S. M. Michael, ed. *Dalits in Modern India: Vision and Values*. New Delhi: Vistaar Publications.

Narayan, B. 2015. 'Democracy and Identity Politics in India: It's a Snake or Rope'. *Economic and Political Weekly* 1 (16).

Narayan, B. 2017. Purane Kaushal Naye Asamanjas, Hindustan, October, 23.

Narayan, B. 2018. 'Why Microfinance Schemes Have Failed the Weakest of Dalits'. Daily O, 14 August 2018.

Omvedt, G. 2005. Buddhism in India: Challenging Brahmanism and Caste. India: SAGE Publications.

Panini, M. N. 1996. 'The Political Economy of Caste'. In *Caste: Its Twentieth Century Avatar*, edited by M. N. Srinivas, 28–68. New Delhi: Viking.

Risely, H. H. 1891. 'The Study of Ethnology in India'. *Journal of the Anthropological Institute of Great Britain and Ireland* 20: 237–38.

Singh, K. S. 1993. *The Scheduled Caste*. New Delhi: Oxford University Press.

Singh, K. S., ed. 1998. *People of India, Vol. 4, India's Communities*. New Delhi: Oxford University Press.

Singh, K. S. 2005. *Anthropological Survey of India, part 1, people of India: Uttar Pradesh*. New Delhi: Manohar.

Thorat, S. and K. S. Newman. 2010. Blocked by Caste: Economic Discrimination in Modern India. India: OUP India.

11

From Social Justice to Aspiration

Transformation of Lower Caste Politics in Uttar Pradesh in the 2000s

Sudha Pai

During the 2000s, the role of the lower castes—the backwards and Dalits—who have in recent decades played a seminal role in the politics of Uttar Pradesh (UP) has undergone significant transformation. The 1990s experienced rise of political consciousness and strong social movements among the backwards and Dalits leading to dominance of lower caste parties, the Samajwadi party (SP) and the Bahujan Samaj party (BSP), and identity politics that drove both electoral and mass politics. National parties the Bharatiya Janata party (BJP) and the Congress, viewed as *manuwadi* or upper caste parties, went into decline and lower caste parties were able to form governments for the first time. The 2000s in contrast have witnessed the weakening of identity politics and in recent years the collapse, of the two lower caste parties espousing social justice, self-respect, and dignity, and simultaneously the revival and strengthening of the BJP. Underlying these shifts has been a renewed interest and desire for economic development among the lower castes.

Much has been written about the move by the backwards and Dalits towards the BJP in recent years whose impact is visible in elections since 2014 (Badri 2014; Pai 2015; Mander et al. 2016; Pai and Kumar 2018). Scholars have argued that it is due to communal mobilization by the party, and its attempt to create a single Hindu identity and support base inclusive of the lower castes against the Muslim 'other' in a key state like UP. While this is correct,[1] the focus of this chapter is on the *manner* in which this has been achieved by the BJP and its impact, visible in its successive victories in the 2014 and 2019 general and 2017 assembly elections in UP. This was possible

---

[1] This aspect has been dealt with in Pai and Kumar 2018.

Sudha Pai, *From Social Justice to Aspiration* In: *Neoliberalism, Urbanization, and Aspirations in Contemporary India*. Edited by: Sujata Patel, Oxford University Press. © Oxford University Press 2021.
DOI: 10.1093/oso/9780190132019.003.0011

LOWER CASTE POLITICS IN UTTAR PRADESH   213

because in the 2000s the BJP redefined its Hindutva ideology as *Subaltern Hindutva* and strategies based on them, to widen its Hindu social base and obtain lower caste support. Accordingly, prior to the 2014 elections it deftly wove together the promise of social inclusion within the Hindu identity and 'Vikas' or rapid economic development for the lower castes; a strategy successfully continued in the 2017 elections. In the campaign prior to the 2019 election, the BJP added its concept of Nationalism together with able marketing of government beneficiary schemes like Ujjwala and PM Awas Yojana, distributed through a huge personal and digital outreach, which gave the party the support of even larger number of lower caste beneficiaries.

Our chapter argues that these strategies have proved successful because in the 2000s, UP has witnessed a fundamental shift from the desire for *social justice to aspiration* among large sections of the lower castes. Two significant developments have been responsible: the waning of identity politics and the re-emergence of a desire for rapid economic development among all sections of the population in the state, but most particularly among the disadvantaged sections impacted by the twin forces of globalization and cultural modernization. Simultaneously, there has been socio-economic and political change within the backward and Dalit communities due to rising levels of political awareness and some improvement in literacy. Second, the revival of the BJP and its attempt under a new generation leadership to create a more socially inclusive party, which has attracted the lower castes and enabled it to capture state power. While the shift in lower caste politics from a struggle for removal of oppression and justice towards aspiration for economic betterment was first evident in UP in the 2014 elections, and has continued. The chapter shows that quiet mobilization at the grassroots by the RSS-BJP to create a unified Hindu identity and support base, had begun in the early 2000s itself. The BJP was able to use these early efforts to obtain a strong foothold in UP and capture power at the centre.

Using a framework of globalization and cultural change, the chapter attempts to understand these shifts in UP politics and how they have brought change among the lower castes and their social and political outlook compared to the 1990s. UP is a backward state and globalization and economic reform compared to states in southern and western India did not lead to improved growth because successive regimes in the 1990s and 2000s were unable to put forward effective policies for development, which impacted particularly on the quality of education imparted and failure to provide jobs. Consequently, by the early 2000s a rising aspiration for economic change and improvement became evident among the lower castes who felt left behind. The reasons lie in a new social churning within these communities, which in recent years has created internal divisions between a rising middle/lower middle class and the poorer and marginalized sections, together with disillusionment with the parties that represent them. Having achieved a modicum of political empowerment, identity and self-respect in the 1990s, the lower castes today are in search of a political party that can offer them economic betterment. These developments have made them vulnerable to mobilization by the BJP which promised them rapid economic development and welfare in the campaigns for the 2014, 2017, and 2019 elections. This has affected the political fortunes of the backward and Dalit parties—the SP and BSP—further introducing change in the role played by the lower castes in UP politics.

At the same time, sections of the lower castes particularly the smaller, poorer, and marginalized Dalit groups and Most Backward Castes (MBCs) who have recently entered the mainstream are undergoing a process of modernization in which culture plays an important role. During this process the Hindutva ideology has influenced some sections that aspire to be part of the larger identity of 'Hindu'. As a study argues 'culture matters', that is, the nature of the social structure can have an impact on 'public action', and consequently on the nature of political and economic development (Rao and Walton 2004). This is because culture is about relationality—relationships among individuals within groups, and among groups—and is concerned with identity, aspirations, structures, and practices that serve relational ends such as ethnicity. Culture is not a set of primordial phenomena permanently embedded in blood relationships, language, or culture within social or religious groups. Rather it is a set of contested attributes constantly in flux, subject to constant redefinition, but can be constructed by economic forces, social and political action, and identities can be 'invented' or 'imagined' (Hobsbawm and Ranger 1983; Anderson 1983). The process of modernization often tends to proceed unevenly, benefitting some sections more than others, leading to conflict and competition for political power, economic benefits, and social status among social groups both within and among different ethnic categories (Brass 1991).

Hence, what we are witnessing in UP is 'politically induced cultural change', the process by which political elites select some aspects of a group's culture, attach new value and meaning to them, and use them as symbols to mobilize the group (Brass 1991, 75). Consequently, identities have undergone

LOWER CASTE POLITICS IN UTTAR PRADESH 215

constant change and revision in response to the changing social and political context. The vehicle of change in UP has been political parties, mobilization both at the grassroots and during election campaigns by them of specific groups, which has affected their behaviour. Political parties have both created and exploited awareness of lower caste identities, as well as the desire for economic advancement.

From Politics of Social Justice to Aspiration among the Lower Castes

The trajectory of politics of the lower castes in the post-independence period in UP has been closely tied to two features in the state: movements for socio-economic equality and political empowerment at the grassroots, and the trajectory of economic development in the state which has affected the socio-economic position, needs, and desires of these communities.

Despite a long period of political stability under Congress rule in the immediate post-independence period, economic development in UP was very slow, industrial investment took place only in pockets, implementation of land reform was poor, and the state fell much behind states in western and southern India. This particularly affected the Dalits and the backward castes (Papola 1989; Dreze and Gazdar 1997). It was during the 1980s for the first time, there was a shift away from the agricultural to the non-agricultural sector, and UP registered a rate of economic growth higher than the national average. If the Fifth and Sixth Plans are taken together, UP's growth was around 9 per cent per annum, which was significantly higher than that of the country as a whole. The growth rate in food grain production rose to 4.92 per cent, which was much higher than in the 1970s; much of which was due to the second round of the Green Revolution that went into the poorer eastern districts, reducing some of the appalling poverty in that region (Lieten and Srivastava 1999, 48). These developments helped in improving the living conditions of the poorer and disadvantaged sections, creating potential for revolt from below. Rising literacy rates among Dalits and other weaker sections, contributed to increased awareness of their low social status, engendering a desire to improve it (Pai 2002). These changes underlay the movements by the backwards and the Dalits in the 1990s.

The 1990s: Politics of Social Justice

The 1990s in UP was the decade of dominance of lower caste radical movements and the social justice parties that represented them. UP has always mirrored change in the country and from the late 1980s experienced the collapse of single party rule, the rise of Hindutva and the Ram Janma Bhoomi Babri Masjid (RJBBM) movement dispute, backward caste movements leading to Mandal and a strong wave of Dalit assertion. Mandal empowered the backward castes under the SP, while Dalit assertion was harnessed by the BSP to create a strong Dalit party. The decline of the two national parties, the Congress and the BJP, enabled the state-level parties—the SP and the BSP—to capture power. Consequently, throughout the 1990s, caste-based identities drove mass politics. Despite the gradual waning of identity-based politics by the end of the decade, the dominance of these parties continued into the early 2000s as seen in the 2002, 2007, and 2012 state assembly elections. They were able to defeat both the BJP and the Congress by widening their social base by mobilizing support from the upper and middle castes.

Despite these electoral victories, political developments took place in the 1990s that underlay the gradual decline of these parties and the shift from the politics of identity to that of development. The 1990s despite the upsurge from below were a period of de-stabilizing change due to a collapse of single party dominance, hung assemblies, endemic political instability, and poor governance leading to high fiscal deficits and poor levels of growth (Pai 2007). The SP and BSP failed to put forward an economic vision or agenda that could introduce the required rapid economic development of the UP economy and yet at the same time deal with the specific problems of deprivation faced by the backwards and Dalits who form their primary support base. While the country experienced globalization in the 1990s bringing in development, UP remained mired in caste/communal politics. When in power both these parties followed policies of competitive populism and provided welfare benefits to their core constituency and showed little political will to mobilize additional resources, thus putting tremendous burden on public expenditure. Consequently, the treasury became empty and growth rates dropped significantly leading to fiscal crisis and economic stagnation. By the late 1990s, UP was in a debt trap, that is, in order to borrow it had to pay high interest rates. In the late 1990s, efforts were made by the Rajnath Singh-led BJP government to improve the situation; a White Paper on finances was issued and a loan was obtained from the World Bank in 2000–1 for fiscal management (Pai 2005). There was some improvement in the fiscal situation, but

LOWER CASTE POLITICS IN UTTAR PRADESH 217

the momentum of reforms could not be sustained as the required political will to put these measures into action was not forthcoming.

The late 1990s also witnessed rising economic aspirations among the backwards and Dalits in UP just when liberalization and the desire to catch-up with the better-off states began to assume importance in the Hindi heartland, though it was most visible among the smaller and poorer Dalits who felt neglected and left behind (Pai 2015). The achievement of a majority by the BSP in 2007 had heightened expectations among Dalits that the government would attempt to bridge the economic gap between them and the upper castes, and bring them into more prominent positions in society and polity. However, there are stark differences in the position of the lower and upper castes that are not easy to overcome and would take much time and effort. The Human Development Report of UP (2003) shows that Dalits own hardly 8–10 per cent of land while the upper castes hold as much as between 55–65 per cent; large sections of the Dalits are landless labourers or employed as labour in the unorganized sector where wages are very low; Dalit literacy and educational attainments are low particularly in the rural areas keeping them within low-paying sectors. In contrast, the upper castes have long formed the elite section in terms of both caste and class, reflected in their presence in politics, higher reaches of the bureaucracy, academia, and business.

Among the backwards the end of the 1990s witnessed the breakup of the backward-caste bloc, which had made the SP a dominant force and the emergence of a post-Mandal phase. Throughout the 1990s, the SP under Mulayam Singh Yadav had tried to weld the backwards into a cohesive political community. But class-based changes due to education, urbanization, rise of regional newspapers, and satellite TV exacerbated already existing rural–urban and poor–affluent divides. Consequently, by the 2000s the SP became a party of the Yadavs, the better-off sections with poorer MBCs moving away initially towards the BSP, and more recently the BJP. Another reason is the decay of the SP, a party with roots in a socialist/backward caste movement, into a family fiefdom with criminal and communal links and numerous factions, controlled by Mulayam Singh Yadav and his family. Both the SP and BSP shifted from radical social movements that mobilized against upper-caste dominance to parties interested in the capture of power that no longer mobilized downwards among the smaller and marginalized sections and in backward regions.

An important contributory reason was the deepening of the agrarian crisis in the 2000s, which since the late 1980s had affected the Other Backward Class (OBC) farming community, Dalits and Jats in western UP, making

218 SUDHA PAI

them unhappy and restive. A study in 2010 illustrates the attempts by the younger generation of Jats to deal with new challenges such as economic liberalization, the rise of the OBCs and a small educated Dalit class (Jeffrey 2010). Liberalization led some of these young people to hope for jobs in the new private sector and to believe in a particular vision of the future—the IT revolution in India—but they could not realize their aspirations. UP is an economically backward state and no government in the 2000s has attempted to promote development, and even in the better-off western districts finding professional jobs is not easy. Studies point to problems in the sugar industry in recent years that have affected small farmers in the western districts, as they have not been paid by industry with cane crushing being slow and prices low (Damodaran and Singh 2007). Traditional industries such as the brassware, leather, and lock industry are also not performing as well as in the past. In eastern UP the traditional weaving and carpet-making industry and other smaller crafts are also in decline creating problems (Pai and Kumar 2018).

Thus, by 2014 as sections of the OBCs and Dalits found themselves politically marginalized, economically neglected, and experienced a sense of frustrated opportunity, going with a dominant force such as Hindutva, provided them psychological empowerment. The promise of radical, social change that the lower caste movements of the 1990s held out to them had not materialized. This made them highly vulnerable to the new strategies of developed by the BJP to obtain their political support.

The 2000s: New Strategies by the BJP

While the revival of the BJP in UP in the 2000s was possible due to the weakening of the social justice parties and continued decline of the Congress. A seminal reason for its successful mobilization of the lower castes was generational change and new thinking among the younger leaders of the BJP. In 2009, a new leadership led by Narendra Modi replaced the older leaders/founders—Atal Behari Vajpayee, L.K. Advani, and Murali Manohar Joshi. Among the younger generation leaders in the BJP, Modi was able to take control of the party due to his three consecutive victories in Gujarat and his close association with the Rashtriya Swayamsevak Sangh (RSS). Soon after being designated the leader of the party, Modi introduced substantial change in the BJP's ideology and organization (Pai and Kumar 2015, 1).

Modi realized that for the lower castes in UP rather than identity-based mobilization, aspiration for economic advancement had become very

LOWER CASTE POLITICS IN UTTAR PRADESH 219

important. Also that winning power in UP required the support of the backwards and the Dalits who together constitute almost half the population of the state. He therefore introduced change in the party's core ideology of Hindutva and its support base. Conceived in the 1980s/90s as a socio-cultural and religious ideology, in a major strategic shift it was redefined as *non-Brahminical Hindutva* to create a more inclusive, subaltern ideology together with an agenda of rapid economic development to create a strong nation and improve the lives of all castes/communities, specially the disadvantaged. While in the 1980s and 1990s the support base of the party, particularly in north India, was the upper castes/classes, in the 2000s the attempt has been to co-opt the non-Yadav and non-Jatav sections as they are no longer attracted to the SP and the BSP (Pai and Kumar 2018).

It is important to underline that these strategies began to be used much earlier than the electoral campaigns under Modi's leadership. Fieldwork points to two stages: the first being grassroots mobilization by the RSS-BJP from the late 1990s/early2000s onwards, and the second beginning with the campaign for the 2014 national elections, continuing into the 2017 and 2019 elections (Pai and Kumar 2018). In the case of the backwards their positive interface with Hindutva, especially the non-Yadav OBCs, can be traced back in UP to the Mandal agitation in the early 1990s, when they formed the support base of BJP, and provided Hindutva leaders like Kalyan Singh and Vinay Katiyar. Further, despite large number of upper caste BJP candidates winning elections in the 1990s in UP, the party appointed non-Brahmin chief ministers—Kalyan Singh a Lodh, and Rajnath Singh a Thakur, and party office bearers—Babu Singh Kushwaha, Om Prakash Rajbhar, and Sakshi Maharaj. In 2017 by selecting Yogi Adityanath, a Thakur as chief minister, and Dinesh Sharma, a Brahmin, and Keshav Prasad Maurya, an OBC, as the two deputy chief ministers, the party leadership tried to balance the aspirations of the upper and backward castes. In contrast, the shift of a significant section of Dalits to Hindutva is a more recent phenomenon but has been quite rapid as election results since 2014, discussed a little later, show.

Early Grassroots Mobilization

Even before the selection of Narendra Modi as the leader of the BJP, in both western and eastern UP the party under the RSS had begun working quietly at the grassroots in the late 1990s to revive the base of the party and create a strong and united Hindu base. Many within the RSS and the BJP were keen to do so as they felt that the decline of the party in the late 1990s was because it had given up, particularly under Atal Bihari Vajpayee, its religion-based mobilization pursued during the Babri Masjid agitation. To this was gradually added the idea of social engineering of the party base by bringing in the lower castes (Pai and Kumar 2018).

This early mobilization was taken forward during the long and highly divisive campaign during the 2014 election. In western UP the campaign began at least two years earlier and while much has been written about the attempt to create polarization between the Hindu and Muslim communities leading to the Muzaffarnagar riots, less attention has been paid to the simultaneous successful mobilization of the backwards and Dalits. Modi's success lay in his ability to harness the early work by the RSS at the grassroots including in the rural areas and bring together the desire for development and social inclusion among the lower castes and take it forward in this region. In eastern UP, Mahant Adityanath, a non-Brahmin leader, in the Mau-Gorakhpur region from the early 2000s onwards quietly mobilized the backward and non-Chamar Dalits. Using his *Hindu Yuva Vahini*, a group consisting mainly of members from these two groups, he was able to extend his influence by 2017 to the entire *terai* (Himalayan foothills) region. Together with caste and communal polarization, his Robin Hood image of providing welfare and economic opportunities to the underprivileged in an underdeveloped region with few opportunities, enabled the BJP to make inroads into a region where the SP and the BSP earlier had strong bases (Pai and Kumar 2018).

The use of the cultural strategy during mobilization at the grassroots by the BJP in UP is not totally new as 'politically motivated communal forces' since the mid-1990s have been silently and ingenuously working among the Dalits and backwards (Narayan 2009, ix). However, it assumed importance in the late 1990s/early2000s because the smaller sub-castes particularly those situated in eastern UP began to enter the democratic arena. As Dalits are highly fragmented with competitive and conflicting relations along regional and sub-caste lines, an approach of wooing the individual sub-castes was used as each had its own ideas, heroes, and stories which could be used for the purpose of mobilization (Ibid:10). Badri Narayan argues that while reinterpretation of the past serves as a powerful cultural capital for Dalit communities, the process of modernization makes Dalit sub-castes less confident and leads them to draw smaller and smaller boundaries for themselves vis-à-vis other sub-castes: from national to regional, to caste boundary, and eventually to sub-caste boundaries (Pai and Kumar 2018, 4).

LOWER CASTE POLITICS IN UTTAR PRADESH   221

During the 2000s, local Hindutva leaders, including those belonging to organizations headed by Adityanath, have been unearthing local histories and myths by which they could link Dalits to Hindutva. In order to bring them into the Hindu identity the attempt has been to gradually build walls between them and others who had formed the composite culture of the villages (Pai and Kumar 2018). As Badri Narayan's work shows three Dalit communities—Pasis, Musahars, and Nishads—particularly targeted by linking them with the Ramayana and Ram during his sojourn in the forest of the region (Pai and Kumar 2018, 30). Similarly, in the Bahraich region, the BJP has attempted to create anxiety among Hindus against the Muslims by counterpoising the myth of Ghazi Mian as a foreign intruder and Suhaldev as a Pasi Hindu, a Dalit king, who protected the Hindus from the intruder's evil designs, which led to a small riot over this issue in 2003 (Pai and Kumar 2018, 94). These strategies proved useful in elections from 2014 onwards when the BJP attempted to capture power in UP and at the centre.

Impact of BJP's New Strategies on the Lower Castes in Electoral Politics

The BJP used a twofold agenda to implement its new strategies: developmental and cultural. Under Modi's leadership from 2010 onwards it began a long electoral campaign for the 2014 elections and once again in 2016 prior to the 2017 elections, holding numerous rallies across the state. Realizing that mere caste-calculation would not suffice, Modi contrary to his party's attempt to build caste alliances, in several rallies openly criticized the idea of caste in politics, and attacked corruption and slow growth and gave importance to good governance and development. The failure of the SP and the BSP to provide development during their period of dominance in the 1990s gave tremendous space to the BJP. Development was packaged for the lower castes by Modi as something denied by earlier governments (Pai and Kumar 2015).

Aware of the rising aspirations of the lower castes, in 2014 Modi evoked the so-called Gujarat model and promised to bring in rapid economic development so that UP could catch up with the better-off states and improve the economic status of the poorer sections. Talking about the apathy of the state governments towards the issues faced by the people, he countered it with his own credentials as an effective administrator in Gujarat and tried in every possible way to connect the solutions to all the problems of the state to Gujarat. Although Gujarat is not the prime destination of the people of

222 SUDHA PAI

UP, it does invite tens of thousands of migrant workers from the poor and backward areas of UP in search of livelihoods.[2] The BJP made excellent use of these migrant workers of UP to spread the message of good roads and availability of jobs in Gujarat in the backward areas of UP. This proved to be a beacon for many disillusioned villagers, particularly in the eastern parts, who were caught in the constant violence and gangsterism and had little hope left for getting anything from their own state. With development projected as the prime agenda, Modi assured people of being their 'sevak' and the nation's 'chowkidaar'. Similarly, prior to the 2017 elections Modi's ingenious twisting of demonetization into a class issue, which would extract black money from the rich, made him the supporter of the poor (Pai and Kumar 2015). In sum, he focused on arousing the frustrations and aspirations of voters, especially the unemployed youth.

Simultaneously, invoking the cultural aspects of the ideology of non-Brahminical Hindutva an attempt was made to create a larger or *Maha Hindu identity* and based on it, a *new Hindutva social coalition* consisting of the upper castes and sections of the OBCs and Dalits to give the lower castes a feeling of being included within the 'Hindu' fold. It is noteworthy that the backwards and the Jats have recently emerged from the ranks of the *Shudra* (Datta 1999). Both groups who have been oppressed and discriminated against by the upper castes and feel marginalized, are happy at being included by the BJP, which they view as a 'Hindu' party. In the 1990s for the Dalits and backwards the Hindu upper castes were the 'other' to be challenged. During the 2000s, the BJP has attempted to bring these groups into the Hindu fold and make the Muslim the 'other' with the aim of creating a unified Hindu cultural nation. In this attempt rather than identity, which was important in defining social relations earlier, in the 2000s social jealousies, cultural aspirations, and economic anxieties are the driving forces.

The use of these strategies does not mean that the BJP did not use its strategy of communal mobilization to create communal polarization and engineer riots to secure the Hindu vote in 2017. Modi made controversial, communal remarks such as the references to *Kabristan* (graveyards) and *Shamshan* (cremation grounds) being built in Muslim and Hindu villages, respectively, and of availability of power in areas populated by both communities to avoid discrimination. ('UP election 2017: PM talks about "Kabristan"

---

[2] Gujarat due to its industrialized and urbanized base is the third preferred destination of migration from UP after Delhi and Maharashtra. See, Bhagat and Mohanty 2009, 5–20.

LOWER CASTE POLITICS IN UTTAR PRADESH   223

and "Shamshan", we talk about laptop and smart phone, says Akhilesh', *The Indian Express*, New Delhi, 17 February 2017.) But it was combined with a discourse of development and subaltern Hindutva, which appealed to a larger section of the electorate. The communal remarks were aimed not so much against the minority community, but to consolidate its upper caste and even more particularly, the new, lower caste vote bank. The strategy paid rich dividends: the Jats, BCs, and non-Jatav dalits in western UP, and the non-Yadav OBCs and non-Jatav dalits in eastern UP voted for the BJP.

Based on these strategies, as Table 11.1 (appendix) shows, the BJP performed well in the 2014 general election, gaining 71 seats and 42.3 per cent of the votes and in 2017, an overwhelming three-quarter majority with 312 seats and 39.7 per cent of the votes cast. In 2014 the BSP and SP performed badly, the former gained almost 20 per cent of the vote but could not win a single seat. The SP which had gained a majority of 224 seats and almost 30 per cent of the votes in the 2012 assembly performed poorly in 2014 with just 5 seats all of which were won in family strongholds (Pai and Kumar 2015). Once again in 2017 the SP and BSP gained only 47 and 19 seats respectively, they retained 21.8 per cent and 22.2 per cent of votes, respectively, but could not translate them into seats.

More importantly, the impact of the BJP's strategies on the lower castes is visible in the results of the 2014 and 2017 elections. As Table 11.2 shows in 2014 the BJP gained 53 per cent of the Kurmi-Koeris 51.3 per cent and 60 per cent of the other OBCs and 45 per cent of the non-Jatav votes; in 2017 as Table 11.3 shows, it gained 56.5 per cent of the Kurmi-Koeri, 59.7 per cent of the other OBCs, and 38.9 per cent of the non-Jatav dalit votes. In 2017, among OBCs it is the Kurmis whose representation increased the most; they make up 29 per cent of the OBCs in the present UP assembly (Pai and Kumar 2015). The lower OBCs—Nishads, Mallahs, Malis Baghels, and so forth—still remain underrepresented. But this is because they consist of many small groups, the votes get divided among them and each gains only a modest amount. The Suheldev Bharatiya Samaj party won on three reserved seats, on the fourth a Rajbhar (MBC) candidate was elected. The Apna Dal (Soneylal) won 3 reserved seats and on the other 2 seats, upper-caste candidates won, while a Brahmin candidate gained the lone seat won by the NISHAD party (Giles Vernier Upper hand for upper castes in House' *The Indian Express*, New Delhi, 20 March 2017).

The defeat of the BSP over three elections—2014, 2017, and 2019—is not surprising as the party had been steadily declining. In the 2007 assembly elections, Dalits had solidly supported the BSP which obtained 206 seats and

224 SUDHA PAI

30.43 per cent of the votes, but in the 2012 assembly elections it obtained only 80 seats despite gaining over 26 per cent of the votes. Though Mayawati's defeat was largely due to loss of support of the *Jatavs* unhappy with her *Sarvajan* policy, it was also due to unhappiness among the smaller Dalit groups who moved towards the BJP. The divisions are visible in the Saharanpur protests in April/May 2017 that revealed the emergence of three separate groups: pro-BSP, pro-BJP, and an autonomous, aggressive section critical of both these parties, which formed the Bhim Army.[3] Internal changes have also eroded the Dalit base of the BSP. Since the mid-1990s it has progressively become a party interested in capturing political power; its earlier attempts to democratize the dalit movement by moving downwards and mobilizing the poorer sub-castes disappeared. It has even led to questioning of the position of Mayawati as the foremost Dalit leader in UP within the community. The accusation of corruption and amassing wealth against Mayawati, and the defection of important BSP leaders to the BJP have lowered her standing among dalits, weakening the party.

2019 General Elections in UP

The trend of decline and collapse of the social justice parties and shift of the lower castes towards the BJP has continued, and is evident in the results of the 2019 general elections. In 2019 neither the issue of 'Vikas' (development) nor communal mobilization played a central role. Rather, there was skilful use by the BJP, particularly by Modi, of the emotive issue of nationalism and skilful marketing of populist welfare schemes for the poor that ensured continued and in fact, increased support of the lower backwards and the smaller dalits.

As Table 11.1 shows, the BJP gained fewer seats in UP than in 2014, but it increased its vote share and its support among the backwards and the Dalits. The SP-BSP-RLD alliance, which had hoped to regain its position among the lower castes, did not perform well. It was based on the strategy that these parties would unite Yadavs, Jatavs, and Muslims who together add up to around 40 per cent of the state's population, thereby limiting the number of seats the Modi-led BJP could win. A number of factors encouraged this

---

[3] Sudha Pai and Sajjan Kumar, 'Saharanpur Protests Herald New Phase in Dalit Politics', *The Wire*, 24 May. 2017 Available at https://thewire.in/politics/saharanpur-protests-herald-new-phase-dalit-politics.

LOWER CASTE POLITICS IN UTTAR PRADESH 225

prospect: the combined vote share of the SP and BSP in the 2014 elections (42.98 per cent) was slightly more than that of the BJP (42.3 per cent). Second, a template existed; the two parties had managed this experiment in the Gorakhpur, Phulpur, and Kairana by-elections.[4] Third, it was felt that both parties could ensure transfer of their votes to each other in their corresponding seats; more than demographic arithmetic, it was felt that there would be positive chemistry between the workers of the three parties.

However, though the expected consolidation of the core constituencies of the alliance partners did happen: as Table 11.2 shows 60 per cent of the SP's core voters, the Yadavs, voted for the alliance, lower than in the 2017 assembly election, but higher than in 2014 when without an alliance the SP had obtained 53 per cent.The BSP fared better obtaining 75 per cent or three-fourth of the Jatav votes, which is higher than 68 per cent in 2014; but in the case of the other SCs, it gained the support of 42 per cent, while 48 per cent, preferred the BJP. But the SP-BSP-RLD alliance won barely 15 seats, despite getting 38.92 per cent vote share in 2019; while that of the BJP increased from 42.63 per cent to 49.55 per cent.

An important reason for the failure of the alliance lay in its caste calculation. It did not attempt to move beyond its own core constituency and mobilize the non-Yadav, non-Jatav, and non-Muslims. It failed to understand that Modi had effectively managed to mobilize, using development and *Hindutva*, these groups in 2014 and 2017 while the alliance had little to offer to them. The ambitious slogan *Ekbhi vote na ghatnepaye, ekbhi vote na batnepaye* (not a single vote should go waste, not a single vote should be split) put forward on 7 April, at the first rally of the BSP-SP-RLD, was a call for the mutual transfer of votes between their core support bases, but was also seen as a 'veiled suggestion' to other communities that they were not needed in this alliance.[5] This created a division between Yadavs and Jatavs versus the lower OBCs and smaller SCs, leading to a counter-mobilization by the latter, who moved towards the BJP in even greater numbers than in 2014. More than numbers, the chemistry between the allies did not work, leading to shrinking of seat and vote share, lower margins of victory, and loss of regional strongholds. As a consequence, as Table 11.2 shows, over four-fifths of upper castes,

---

[4] Sudha Pai, 'Changing Political Preferences among Dalits in Uttar Pradesh in the 2000s: Shift from Social Justice to Aspiration', *Journal of Social Inclusion Studies*, June 2019. Available at https://journals.sagepub.com/doi/10.1177/2394481119852190.

[5] 'BSP's heartland surge flattens identity politics in UP, Bihar', Ravish Tiwari, *The Indian Express*, 24 May 2019. Available at https://indianexpress.com/article/explained/lok-sabah-elections-results-bjps-heartland-surge-flattens-identity-politics-in-up-bihar-5745501/.

226 SUDHA PAI

four fifths of Kurmis and Koeris, and three-fourths of lower OBCs voted for the BJP. Along with non-Jatav Dalits, the three constitute around half of U.P.'s population. Until 2012 many of these groups had voted for the SP and the BSP.

Another important reason was that Modi through his campaign speeches, reiterated in social media, skilfully moved the discourse away from serious economic concerns towards populist welfare measures and the emotive issue of nationalism. The poor performance of the UP government since 2017, evident in the lack of development, deteriorating law and order, poor healthcare and education, joblessness and farm distress, had impacted on the lower castes particularly the lower OBCs and smaller Dalit groups. However, Modi was able to manage the anger against bad government performance[6] through dissemination of an intense nationalist discourse or 'desh bhakti' much before the 'actual' election to mark out critics of the party ranging from students, activists, and political leaders was reinforced later, by constant reference to Pulwama and the 'surgical strike' against Pakistan, in a state which is a major recruiting ground for the army. The Balakot strike, despite loss of soldier lives, strengthened already existing BJP support. It pushed opposition and regional parties to build a national narrative, set aside their entrenched differences and form anti-Modi coalitions, good example being the SP and BSP in UP.[7]

Even more important, the Modi government ably marketed the populist image of a massive welfare state for the poor and lower castes, just before the election. Beginning in 2014, the government introduced beneficiary schemes like Ujjwala and PM Awas Yojana, distributed through a huge personal and digital outreach, which connected it to, as claimed by Amit Shah, almost 22 crore beneficiaries.[8] Importantly, this economic intervention was

---

[6] Fieldwork during the campaign showed that upper castes, non-Yadav OBCs such as Kashyap/Dhimar, Saini, Badhai Lodh Kurmi, and a section of non-Jatav Dalits such as Khatiks, Valmikis, Pasis, and Dhanuks, rallied behind the BJP quite enthusiastically, citing the Modi factor as the most influential criterion and overriding consideration behind their decision to support the party. The fieldwork was conducted on 12 April 2019, part of a three series longitudinal fieldwork in Uttar Pradesh covering all eighty Lok Sabha constituencies. The study was supported by *Peoples Pulse*, a Hyderabad-based research institution and *Asiaville Media outlet*. For more details see Pai and Kumar (2020).

[7] 'View: Fundamental Shifts in India's Electoral Politics Witnessed in the 2019 Poll Battle', Pranab Dhal Samanta, *The Economic Times*, 21 May 2019. Available at https://economictimes. indiatimes.com/news/elections/lok-sabha/india/view-fundamental-shifts-in-indias-electoral-politics-witnessed-in-the-2019-poll-battle/articleshow/69417681.cms.

[8] Karishma Mehrotra, 'How BJP Marketed to a New Voting Bloc: The 22 Crore Beneficiaries', *The Indian Express*, 23 May 2019. Available at https://indianexpress.com/article/india/how-bjp-marketed-to-a-new-voting-bloc-the-22-crore-beneficiaries-5745514/.

LOWER CASTE POLITICS IN UTTAR PRADESH 227

undertaken by the government through a more flexible 'deprived category' index developed with the help of the Socio-Economic Caste Census, instead of the old below poverty line (BPL) concept. The use of *Aadhaar* to pinpoint individuals within this category, and transfer benefits electronically, allowed the government to create a class of beneficiaries that may come from different caste groups, but have a similar economic profile. While this did not remove caste affiliations, it gave value to the economic identity of smaller caste groups, which until now were hoping to corner benefits showing caste solidarity with dominant groups like Yadavs and Jatavs in UP. Thus, the Modi government created new, workable, credible options to old caste alliances by creating a new paradigm for accessing state resources.[9]

The work of data collection began soon after the 2014 victory through call centres contacting beneficiaries. The constituencies which saw the most beneficiary outreach were 19 in UP and 4 in Maharashtra, amounting to 8 lakh beneficiaries. In February 2019, under *Mera Parivar BJP Parivar* programme, workers/sympathizers visited the beneficiaries with the soft message 'Modi has given schemes to this many families in only five years. Give him another five and you can make that number even more'. This roused aspiration of many families in the selected areas, who supported the BJP irrespective of how many persons had *actually benefitted* from the schemes.[10] Thus, in UP the BSP-SP-RLD alliance had only arithmetic in its favour; emotional sentiment among the lower castes was with Narendra Modi.

***

The 2000s have witnessed a major transformation of lower caste politics in UP, a state where social and political change has been rapid over the last few decades. A key state, which has always mirrored changes taking place in the Indian body politic, UP has heralded the shift in the Hindi heartland from the politics of identity and social justice to that of economic aspiration and desire for economic advancement. The ongoing process of rapid social change in the state has compelled the BJP an upper-caste party to move downwards and build a more inclusive social coalition to include the lower castes within the ambit of the larger Hindu identity, and provide them economic advancement. To achieve this, the party leadership has attempted to intertwine communal polarization, social inclusivity, and the promise of economic advancement. Caste-based politics has not

---

[9] Karishma Mehrotra, 'How BJP Marketed to a New Voting Bloc: The 22 Crore Beneficiaries'.
[10] Karishma Mehrotra, 'How BJP Marketed to a New Voting Bloc: The 22 Crore Beneficiaries'.

228 SUDHA PAI

disappeared, but a new relationship has emerged between caste and development that has introduced change, but enabled mobilization along primordial lines to continue.

Traditionally, the backwards and Dalits did not vote for the BJP deemed an upper-caste party, and in the 1990s had supported the SP and the BSP following Mandal and Dalit assertion in UP. Part of the longer term process of democratization operating in the Hindi heartland since independence, caste-based politics had led to questioning of upper-caste domination. Consequently, throughout the decade, primordial politics of caste-based identity, dignity, and self-respect gave the lower castes and parties representing them, centrality in state politics. UP it was believed would lead the way to a radical anti-caste politics in the Hindi heartland as it had two strong lower caste parties opposed to politics of religious fundamentalism. However, the strong wave of assertion from below and the assertion against upper-caste domination in the 1990s could not fulfill the radical promise they held out for the lower castes. The social justice parties lost their legitimacy due to their lack of an economic vision for UP leading to disillusionment and the search for a new politics of socio-economic upliftment.

While the 2000s witnessed weakening of identity politics, the critical agent was the BJP which under a new leadership redefined Hindutva as *subaltern*, and transformed state politics. While the attempt to create a more inclusive 'Hindu' support base began in the early 2000s, it was Modi who recognized the desire among the lower castes for economic advancement and attempted to widen the base of the party making it more plebian than in the 1990s. Equally important, has been the delayed impact of globalization and emergence of the private sector in the Hindi heartland and cultural modernization among the poorer and smaller sections of the backwards and Dalits in the state. While the former created frustration due to backwardness and lack of opportunities in UP compared to states in southern and western India, the latter led to a desire for inclusion within the larger Hindu community due to sustained mobilization by the BJP, which under the leadership of Modi has skilfully harnessed their feelings of being left behind.

The shift of the lower castes from the parties of social justice to the BJP has opened a new chapter with immense significance for UP and national politics. The 2000s have witnessed gradual decline and collapse of the social justice parties and a growing hegemony of rightwing Hindutva ideology in UP. The base of the SP and BSP has shrunk leaving them with only their

LOWER CASTE POLITICS IN UTTAR PRADESH 229

core supporters, the Yadavs and Jatavs, respectively. Successful mobilization based on social engineering of the lower castes and capture of power by the BJP in successive elections shows that the BJP has built a massive support base among the lower castes. While the 2014 elections attempted to establish right-wing rule, in 2019 the attempt has been to consolidate its position in the country and in UP. Neither the SP nor the BSP, or the Congress party, seems to have the capacity to challenge its social and political dominance. This has led to fracturing and deep divisions in the backward caste and Dalit movement in the state. As the chapter showed this is not a sudden shift by the lower caste groups towards the BJP but a result of sustained grassroots mobilization from the late 1990s/early 2000s.

As UP is a politically important state these changes will impact on national politics. While in the 1990s politics in UP was bi-polar, with competition between two lower caste state-level parties, now with the revival of the BJP, a national party has once again become dominant in the state. The BJP today occupies the position that the Congress party did in its period of dominance in the state. UP, which does not have a regional character unlike states in southern India, has returned to its earlier situation of being controlled by the party in power at the centre. As a result federal relations have once again undergone change with centralization of power by the central leadership.

An important question which arises is will the new social coalition stitched together by the BJP by bringing together non-Brahminical Hindutva, cultural mobilization and desire for economic advancement be able to sustain itself? It is a heterogeneous coalition in which the upper castes are still numerically dominant and the backwards are jostling for space and power. The Dalits do not have a place of much significance within it. Moreover, the backwards and Dalits traditionally had an antagonistic relationship as the former constitute the direct oppressors of the latter. After the formation of a government in UP, the OBCs have emerged as a strong aggressive force under the BJP which has given them plum posts with lesser importance being given to the Dalits. Moreover, growing atrocities against Dalits in UP and in the country has made them unhappy. However, at present the BJP has been able by sustained grassroots mobilization and over three successfully fought elections, to build a strong Hindu vote bank and to establish itself as a strong political force with the help of the lower castes.

230 SUDHA PAI

Appendix

Table 11.1 Seats and Percentage of votes won by Parties in 2014 and 2019 General and 2017 Assembly Elections in UP

Party	Seats and Votes Won in 2014	Seats and Votes Won in 2017	Seats and Votes Won in 2019
BJP	71/42.3	312/39.7	62/49.4
Congress	2/7.5	7/6.2%	1/6.31
SP	5/22.0	47/21.8%	5/17.96%
BSP	0/19.6%	19/22.2%	10/19.26%
RLD	------	1/18%	--------
SBSP *	------	4/7%	--------
AD#	1/1.0%	9/10%	2/1.0%
Independents	1/18%	3/26%	1/6.73%
Total	80/100	403/100	80/100

Notes: *Suheldev Bharatiya Samaj Party. #Apna Dal.

Source: Compiled from the reports of the Election Commission of India

Table 11.2 Support to Various Political Parties across Castes in 2014 and 2019 General Elections

Castes/ Communities	Congress		BJP		BSP		SP	
	2014+ RLD	2019	2014 +AD	2019	2014	2019 MGB	2014	2019
Brahmins	11	6	72	82	5	6	5	------
Rajputs	7	5	77	89	5	7	8	------
Vaishya	-----	13	___	70	___	4	___	------
Other Upper castes	9	5	76	84	3	10	7	------
Yadavs	8	5	27	23	3	60	53	------
Kurmis/Koeis	16	5	53	80	4	14	17	------
Other OBCs	8	5	60	72	11	18	13	------

LOWER CASTE POLITICS IN UTTAR PRADESH 231

Table 11.2 *Continued*

Castes/ Communities	Congress		BJP		BSP		SP	
	2014+ RLD	2019	2014 +AD	2019	2014	2019 MGB	2014	2019
Jatavs	2	1	18	17	68	75	4	------
Other Dalits	4	7	45	48	29	42	10	------
Muslims	11	14	10	8	18	73	58	------
Others	10	1	51	50	20	35	17	------

Note: Figures may not add up to 100 due to rounding.

Source: CSDS-Lokniti Post-Poll survey. *The Hindu*, May 26, 2019.https://www.thehindu.com/elections/lok-sabha-2019/post-poll-survey-why-uttar-pradeshs-mahagathbandhan-failed/article27249310.ece?homepage=true

Table 11.3 Percentage of Votes Cast By Various Castes for BJP in UP Election 2017 Post Poll

Caste\Community	Vote Percentage 2017
UpperCase	66.1
Yadav	9.7
Kumi+Koeri	56.5
Other OBCs	59.7
Jatav Dalits	9.4
Non Jatav Dalits	38.9
Muslims	8.9
Others	0
Total	**100%**

Source: CSDS, National Election Study, Uttra Pradesh Post Poll 2017

References

Anderson, Benedict. 1983. Imagined Communities. London: Verso.

Bhagat R. B. and S. Mohanty. 2009. 'Emerging Pattern of Urbanization and the Contribution of Migration in Urban Growth in India'. Asian Population Studies 5 (1): 5–20.

232 SUDHA PAI

Brass, Paul R. 1991. *Ethnicity and Nationalism: Theory and Comparison*. New Delhi: Sage.

Craig, Jeffrey. 2010. *Timepass Youth, Class and the Politics of Waiting in India*. New Delhi: Oxford University Press.

Damodaran, Harish and Harvir Singh. 2007. 'Sugar Industry in Uttar Pradesh: Rise, Decline and Revival'. *Economic and Political Weekly* 29 (Sept): 3952–7.

Datta, Nonica. 1999. 'Jats: Trading Caste Status for Empowerment'. *Economic and Political Weekly* 6–12 (November): 3172–3.

Dreze, Jean, and Haris Gazdar. 1997. 'Uttar Pradesh: The Burden of Inertia'. In *Indian Development: Selected Regional Perspectives*, edited by Jean Dreze and Amartya Sen, 33–128. New York: Oxford University Press.

Hobsbawm, Eric and Terence Ranger, eds. 1983. *The Invention of Tradition* Cambridge: Cambridge University Press.

Human Development Report of UP. 2003. UNDP Programme. Government of India, 15 January 2014.

Lieten, G. K. and Ravi S. Srivastava. 1999. *Unequal Partners: Power Relations, Devolution and Development in Uttar Pradesh Indo Dutch Studies on Development Alternatives*. New Delhi: Sage.

Mander, Harsh, Akram Akhtar Chaudhury, Zafar Eqbal, and Rajanya Bos. 2016. *Living Apart: Communal Violence and Forced Displacement in Muzaffarnagar and Shamli*. New Delhi: DK Publishers.

Narayan, Badri. 2009. *Fascinating Hindutva Saffron Politics and Dalit Mobilization*. New Delhi: Sage.

Narayan, Badri. 2014. 'Communal Riots in Uttar Pradesh'. *Economic and Political Weekly* 69 ((37, Sept 13): 29–32.

Pai, Sudha. 2002. *Dalit Assertion and the Unfinished Democratic Revolution: The BSP in Uttar Pradesh*. New Delhi: Sage.

Pai, Sudha. 2005. 'Populism and Economic Reforms: The BJP Experiment in Uttar Pradesh'. In *The Politics of Economic Reforms in India*, edited by Jos Mooij, 98–129. New Delhi: Sage Publications.

Pai, Sudha (ed). 2007. *Political Process in Uttar Pradesh: Identity, Economic Reforms and Governance*. New Delhi: Pearson/Longman.

Pai Sudha. 2015. 'Dalit Entrepreneurs, Globalization and the Supplier Diversity Experiment in Madhya Pradesh'. In *Dalits in Neoliberal India: Mobility or Marginalisation?*, edited by Clarinda Still. New Delhi: Routledge.

Pai, Sudha. 2015. 'Uttar Pradesh: Competitive Communalism Once Again'. *Economic and Political Weekly* 18 (15): 16–19.

Pai, Sudha and Avinash Kumar. 2015. 'Understanding the BJP's Victory in Uttar Pradesh'. In *India's 2014 Elections: A Modi-led BJP Sweep*, edited by Paul Wallace, 119–38. New Delhi: Sage Publications.

Pai, Sudha and Sajjan Kumar. 2018. *Everyday Communalism: Riots in Contemporary Uttar Pradesh*. New Delhi: Oxford University Press.

Pai, Sudha and Sajjan Kumar. 2020. 'War of Perception, Brand Modi and Voters' Choice in Uttar Pradesh'. In *India's 2019 Elections: Modi-led BJP Wave*, edited by Paul Wallace, 119–137. New Delhi: Sage Publications.

Papola, T. S. 1989. 'Uttar Pradesh'. In *Economies of the States of the Indian Union*, edited by M. Adiseshiah, 63–79. New Delhi: Lancer International.

Rao, Vijayendra and Michael Walton, eds. 2004. *Culture and Public Action*. New Delhi: Permanent Black.

12

Markets and Aspirations

Aseem Prakash

The Framework to Understand Aspirations

My only dream is to be respected and earn enough to get a decent house for my family and also educate my children....

(An Uber Cab Driver in Pune, India)

The word 'aspirations' is frequently used in our social vocabulary. Aspirations have the power to motivate and persuade individuals to choose a certain trajectory towards realizing their wants, needs, expectations, targets, and thereby shape their immediate as well as distant future. Aspiration is not necessarily a dream. Ms X can have a dream to become a Bollywood star. But resources and capabilities available at her disposal—financial, individual, and social—may not be robust enough to realize her dreams. Aspirations are seen to coincide with reference points that have the possibility of realization. The reference point is not an abstract goal shaped by grand dreams but a systematic understanding of her original 'position' in the social structure (social identity and caste), the possibilities that can be harnessed through invoking agency towards achievable goals. Hence, I claim that aspirations are not merely individual goals but are rooted in the class and social location of the aspirer and her relationship with the wider socio-economic and political structure. In synergy with this line of argument, the chapter moves away from the existing frameworks for understanding aspirations of individuals that argue that individuals' aspirations are either constituted by themselves—an individual cognitive effort to shape their future—or shaped by their class location.

I argue that aspirations in the context of a market society are formed by the individual's social location and further fashioned at the intersection of state, market, and civil society. In my view, the foundation of aspirational

Aseem Prakash, *Markets and Aspirations* In: *Neoliberalism, Urbanization, and Aspirations in Contemporary India.* Edited by: Sujata Patel, Oxford University Press. © Oxford University Press 2021.
DOI: 10.1093/oso/9780190132019.003.0012

234   ASEEM PRAKASH

goals is not only reflective of original social class but is moulded by the interplay of institutions in state, markets, and civil society on one hand and the individual's relationship with these institutions, on the other. I will explain this thesis upfront while differentiating it from other viewpoints.

How Do Aspirations Acquire Roots?

Following a utilitarian argument, the representative writing of Sherwood Jr. explains that aspirational studies presuppose that individuals make efficient choices to maximize their satisfaction and minimize their dissatisfaction (Sherwood 1989). Accordingly, he invokes the metaphor of 'investment' to explain aspirations—'Individuals must act, must invest time, effort, or money to pursue their goals'. In other words, individuals assess opportunities, constraints, and risks and accordingly choose strategies for attaining the goals.

The second view point in aspirational study is represented by the economists Genicot and Ray (2017).The authors define aspirations as 'income or wealth thresholds that enter individual utility as reference points' (2017). It is explained that aspirations of individuals are determined by distribution of income which in turn is contingent on the performance of the whole economy. If the economy performs well, the individual may earn better. However, it is the individual aspirations that 'incentiv[izes] to invest, accumulate, and bequeath'. The authors argue that the best sort of aspirations are those that are at a reasonable distance from their existing class positions. Otherwise aspirations can also be a recipe for frustration. Both these representative writings illuminate but do not sufficiently dazzle with their insights. These writings fail to take into account that sociocultural institutions of caste and religion can induce formation of substantially different aspirations within the same class. Put simply, these social institutions can constrain the capability to aspire for the lower caste/minority religion while empowering the privileged castes and religion to nurture robust aspirations.

In this context, the work of Appadurai (2004), an anthropologist, acquires significance. Appadurai asserts that the capacity to aspire is specifically constrained by the social structure. The latter makes the poor subscribe to norms that further diminish their dignity, exacerbate their inequality, and

MARKETS AND ASPIRATIONS 235

deepen their lack of access to material goods and services, a condition reinforced by the lack of voice necessary to engage in civic action. It is in this sense, the capacity to aspire is a future-oriented cultural capacity through which individuals aim to contest the prevailing cultural ethos instrumental in retaining them in poverty. Appadurai's work is an important contribution persuading us to think beyond psychological-cognitive dimension on one hand and class-income lens on the other. Building on these insights, the paper goes beyond the given—constraining social structure—and invokes the agency of the aspirer who contests, negotiates, and often challenges the limiting conditions towards realizing their aspirations. Accordingly, aspirations have the following three distinct elements which are embedded in the spatio-temporal specific interplay of institutions in the realm of state, markets, and civil society and the relationship of the aspirer with these institutions.

Socially Structured: Aspirations are rooted and shaped by the initial class and social location. They acquire their wings due to the discomfort with the current situation, an anger with the available socially determined fringe opportunities, and a resentment against the marginal socio-economic existence.

Socially Situated: Aspirations are woven around the 'idea of an *aspirations window*'. The aspiration window is formed from an individual's cognitive world, her zone of 'similar', 'attainable' individuals that act as a reference point/individual group (Ray 2006). It is based on prevalent notions of success as well as consumption. It can be fashioned through emulating the social groups/individuals who are considered to be successful in similar or attainable social/class bracket.

Socially Contested: Aspirations of the marginalized and socially peripheral groups are also shaped by their claim to recognition of their dignity and entitlements to material goods (Fraser 1995).[1] These claims are often contested by the privileged groups resulting in counter assertion by the weaker social groups. There is also a possibility that aspirations are shaped and reshaped in the continuum of assertion and contestations on one hand and reassertion and strategic compromises, on the other.

The chapter, thus, argues that aspirations are incubated and sustained through original social interactions, experiences, and contestations which in turn are shaped by the context-specific interaction of state, civil society, and markets. These specific elements shaping aspirations have given rise to a distinct nature of the aspirational class. The following section elaborates

---

[1] Fraser has aptly described it as 'Recognition and Redistribution'.

236 ASEEM PRAKASH

on three specific moments in Indian postcolonial history. We will emphasize more on the last moment—the market–state moment—which has given
shape to a specific character of an aspirational class while also focusing on
the aspirational class emerging from certain under privileged social identities (religion and caste).

ASPIRATIONAL CLASS: THE THREE BIG MOMENTS

Post-Independence: The State as a Harbinger of Change

The first moment was immediately after independence where the state due to
specific postcolonial conditions dominated over civil society and markets. It
is best reflected in the famous 'tryst of destiny' speech by Jawaharlal Nehru:

> And so we have to labour and to work, and work hard, to give reality to our
> dreams. . . . To bring freedom and opportunity to the common man, to the
> peasants and workers of India; to fight and end poverty and ignorance and
> disease; to build up a prosperous, democratic and progressive nation, and
> to create social, economic and political institutions which will ensure jus-
> tice and fullness of life to every man and woman.[2]

The legitimacy of the Indian state was based on the fact that it will usher in
development while the colonial economy exploited and drained the Indian
resources for its own benefit. The state was to be a harbinger of change and
would 'wipe every tear from every eye' (Nehru). The Indian state created a
vast network of public sector institutions, intervened in every sector of the
economy and society and created tremendous hope and aspirations. The
state grew in stature and expanse and acquired tremendous power due to pe-
culiar historical reasons. All classes were expected to act in unison to usher
India on the path of equitable development. The limited market-based operations during this phase of Indian history have been best described as state
capitalism. The state created and controlled the market. Private capital was
very weak and was dependent on the state investment. The aspirations of
the poor, middle class, and the rich were all structured and sought to be fulfilled around state provided incentives and distribution of socio-political and

---

[2] Extract is from Jawaharlal Nehru's 'Tryst with Destiny' speech delivered on 14 August, 1947,
the eve of India's independence, to the Indian Constituent Assembly in the Parliament.

MARKETS AND ASPIRATIONS 237

economic resources. Special provisions through affirmative action policies were created for the historically marginalized sections to participate in the state-led development processes.

Civil Society: Articulating the Aspirations

The state's inability to fulfil the expectations and aspirations of the poor, the historically marginalized, the geographically segregated, and the weaker gender etc., translated into the beginning of a new moment from the mid-1970s onwards. Civil society became the domain through which aspirations were articulated and realized. A vibrant civil society was seen as the realm outside and against the state—a domain of (new) social movements, civil liberties movements, and various other protest formations. These movements and protest collectives were seen as the basis of a substantive democracy (Vijay and Ajay 2000), or a foundation of a creative society calling for a decentralized, participatory and accountable state (Mohanty 1998), or acting as a counter hegemonic force against the state trampling the rights of its citizens (Chandhoke 1995, 1998, 2003). The aspirations of the people, especially the poor and the marginalized, were to be realized through the active role of the civil society and people-centric institutions. The civil society was seen to empower the people and push the agenda of humane governance (Kothari 1988).

Markets: A Vehicle for Shaping Aspirations

As we attempt to understand the character of states and society in 2021, we recognize that history has not ended (Fukuyama 1992).[3] The world as a whole is not increasingly drifting towards identity and religion-based violence (Huntington 1996).[4] With Brexit, looming economic crises in several West European nations and variety of peoples' movement across Europe, the continent does not seem to as a picture of stability (Cooper 2003).[5] However,

---

[3] Francis Fukuyama declared that with the fall of the Berlin Wall democracy won the war against communism and history had ended.

[4] Samuel Huntington predicted a clash of civilizations where the world will be riddled with conflict drawn from people's cultural and religious identity.

[5] Copper argued that the emerging character of the states can be understood by the breakdown of state control over violence (ability of small groups to wield weapons of mass

238 ASEEM PRAKASH

within this tradition of grand theorization and particularly in the context of this chapter, Phillip Bobbitt's (2003) work on market-state acquires a certain significance. In his monumental work, Bobbitt argued that the nature of our constitutional order is changing from a nation state[6] into a market-state. The character of the hitherto nation state was based on the notion that it will provide for material welfare of its citizens. 'The state seems less and less credible as the means by which a continuous improvement in the welfare of its people can be achieved' (Bobbitt 2003). Now, 'the market-state offers a different covenant: It will maximize the opportunity of its people' (Bobbitt 2003). How does the market-state acquire legitimacy? Bobbitt argues that the market-state seeks to acquire legitimacy not as a provider or distributor of welfare goods and economic resources. Instead, it supports an enabling framework for the society to secure opportunities and better goods and services (Bobbitt 2003). Providing employment is not the goal of economic expansion. Instead the state is expected to provide a supportive environment and incentives to its citizen to enter and participate in the market-based exchange (for instance, Make in India and Start-up India). It is in this context where market has acquired a pre-eminent institutional space that we endeavour to understand aspirations and aspirational class.

By the late 1980s, India was in throes of economic crisis. In order to meet her financial commitments and keep the economy afloat, India sought conditional loans. This led to opening up of the economy through economic reforms described as structural adjustment programmes. In the beginning of the 1990s, the market slowly developed itself as a hegemonic institution gradually acquiring the role of architect, allocator, and distributor of resources. It reconfigured the state–society relationship. Market-led institutions were no more to be rowed by the state. The state was seen merely as steering the economy. The promise of civil society activism waned. In fact, civil society itself became a site for accumulation (Prakash 2015). If individuals are not participants in market-led growth, their dreams and aspirations cannot be realized. The coming of markets led to a tremendous expansion of the middle class where consumption (their ability to buy and demonstrate the possession of those commodities) became the hallmark of the realization of

---

destruction) on the one hand and a stable European state which does not wield sovereignty in the classical sense.

[6] The concept of a nation state may not be disputed in the context of India but the larger arguments of Bobbitt are largely valid.

aspirations (Jodhka and Prakash 2016). Unlike yesteryears, this new middle class is not the product of state expansion. They have successfully penetrated the markets and owe their socio-economic positions to it. They largely belong to the upper castes[7] and have acquired the legitimacy to speak on behalf of society (Jodhka and Prakash 2016). The active expansion of the market-state and fast and sustained growth of the middle class has translated into significant growth of a 'new economy' (referred as service sector) which in turn is populated by the new entrants to the market economy. It is in this context of a market-driven economy and society that we want to put forth our thesis on aspirational class.

The aspirational class is a group of individuals belonging to diverse social groups who have entered the market and are still fighting for their survival. Their aspirational destination is what the new middle class currently command. In an earlier work jointly done by the author with Jodhka (Jodhka and Prakash 2016), the aspirational class has been explained in the following terms.

> These 'upwardly mobile poor' are invariably young men and women who have acquired modern education through one of the hundreds of thousands of colleges spread across the country giving degree/diploma courses in information and technology, marketing, law, finance, business or tourism. Many of them have moved from rural areas to urban locations by selling their parental assets and have entered into the field of transport, manage small businesses, work as sales executives in big consumer retails or as supervisors in showrooms of a big corporates, offer utility maintenance services, perform the role of delivery agents or clerks with an e-commerce company. Countless numbers of them are employed in the new business economy of supplying goods and services to middle and upper middle-class homes.... They aspire for a place in the Indian growth story and hope to eventually climb-up within the private economy.

The aspirational class is not a homogenous social group. It is segmented by caste, religion, region, and other social identities. Social identities are important in two critical respects for our discussion. First, aspirations of individuals are shaped by their initial social location. Second, social identity mediates between the individual and her relationship with institutions in

---

[7] India has also seen a slow growth of middle class from underprivileged background.

240 ASEEM PRAKASH

the realm of state, markets, and civil society and significantly determine the outcomes in the markets.

To elaborate further on the tryst of the aspirational class with the market, we turn to our field evidences.

MARKET AND ASPIRATIONAL CLASS: THE VIEW FROM THE FIELD

Socio-Economic and Educational Profile

In order to understand everyday market entry and operations, we interviewed 120 (hundred twenty) individuals from diverse groups and sectors in the cities of Pune and Hyderabad. The same has been elaborated in the following Table 12.1. Although not a representative sample, the interviewees provided us a fair insight into the interplay of aspirations, social identity, and markets in India. These new age economic agents work and earn in two most modern cities of India—Pune and Hyderabad. The interviews were structured to elicit a detailed background account—family, education, and kith and kin network—along with a comprehensive account of their everyday life in the markets as economic agents involved in delivery of goods and services.

The sample population of the interviewees was not pre-designed. It was through a snow ball method. Every respondent gave us contact details of her friend/ acquaintance in their sector of economic activities. Alternatively, we just walked into the shops, parking lots (for cab aggregator service—Ola, Uber), congregation places (App-based food delivery services—Swiggy), booked plumbers carpenters on the web app to avail their services (instead we took their interview and paid their per hour charge). The social location that the sample throws up is purely accidental. It turned out that every second and third person interviewed were either Hindu Upper Castes (HUCs) or Other Backward Castes (OBCs), respectively. Against this dominant presence of HUCs and OBCs, Dalits and Muslims were fewer in number. Every fourth and fifth person interviewed was either Dalit or Muslim (Table 12.1).

Further, the respondents analysed for this study highlight that economic enterprises/activities which require larger initial capital investment have significantly higher presence of HUCs and OBCs. Muslims and Dalits do not seem to enjoy similar economic opportunity/spaces as the HUCs and OBCs (Table 12.1).

MARKETS AND ASPIRATIONS 241

Table 12.1 Social Demography

No. of Individuals	Sectors	Caste/Religion			
		HUC	OBC	Dalit	Muslim
40	**Transport:** (Cab Aggregators- Ola Uber)	15	8	8	9
34	**Home Service:** App-based food delivery and home plumbing and carpenter services	5	15	9	5
40	Franchise owner of courier shops (9); Owner of small eateries (8); App-based Mineral Water Suppliers (8); App Design (4); App-based delivery of organic fruits and vegetables at home (3); Patient relation officer in hospital (3); Credit card agent (2) Home-based Physical fitness instructors (2); photocopy and stationery shop (1)	17	10	5	8
6	Insurance agents	2	1		3
Total 120		39 (33 %)	34 (28 %)	22 (18 %)	25 (21%)

HUC = Hindu Upper Caste; OBC = Other Backward Caste

% figures have rounded off to nearest zero.

Source: Calculation from the primary survey conducted by the author.

More than 80 per cent of the respondents reported that the earning members of their family worked in the informal sector of the economy. However, the majority of HUC and OBC interviewees came from families having agricultural land as the primary source of income. A small proportion of them also worked at the lower echelons of government departments or as contractual employees in the private sector. On the contrary, our Dalit respondents informed that their family members either worked as agricultural labour in rural areas or wage labour in urban areas. A small proportion of them also reported that their fathers accessed government jobs through affirmative action policies. All Muslims in our sample came from urban areas and their fathers either worked as wage labour, or at lower echelons of government departments or as contractual employees in the private sector (Table 12.2).

242 ASEEM PRAKASH

Table 12.2 Family Occupation

	Agriculture-Rural Origin				Urban Origin			
	Agricultural Labour	Famer > 2 Acres	Farmer 2-5 acres	Farmer < 5 Acre	Wage Labour	Petty Shop	Class IV Govt. Employee	Private Sector Contractual Employee
HUC	Nil	2	10	14	Nil	Nil	4	9
OBC	Nil	1	11	12	Nil	Nil	6	4
Dalit	7	1	Nil	Nil	9	Nil	5	Nil
Muslim	Nil	Nil	Nil	Nil	4	11	Nil	10
Total	7 (6 %)	4 (2 %)	21 (17 %)	26 (22 %)	13 (11 %)	11 (9 %)	15 (12 %)	23 (19 %)

HUC = Hindu Upper Caste; OBC = Other Backward Caste

% figures have rounded off to nearest zero.

Source: Calculation from the primary survey conducted by the author.

It may be essentially noted that all respondents were school educated, albeit their higher education pursuits differ drastically (Table 12.3). HUCs topped the chart in our sample as far as higher educational achievements are concerned. All of them were either graduates or had acquired technical education. So was the case with OBCs. Although some Dalits and Muslims were graduates, a very small proportion of them had had access to technical education. In order to help pursue their study, HCU and OBC families were able to fund the higher and technical education of our respondents. Many of them were able to access public money (scholarships or government-subsidized institutions). Their dependence on private loans was minimal. On the other hand, the families of Dalit and Muslim respondents did not have sufficient economic capacity to fund their education. This gets reflected in the fact that very few of them can move beyond the undergraduate degree to any kind of technical education. Even to fund their college degree, Dalits and Muslims reported that they had to access private loans, often at a high interest rate. While conversing with these respondents, it was realized that HUCs and OBCs had access to better educational institutions. Most of them specifically migrated from smaller towns to bigger cities to access educational opportunities—also a reflection of better economic capacity and a social network that provided information and other support to explore academic and career opportunities. The ability of social networks to facilitate access to educational

MARKETS AND ASPIRATIONS 243

Table 12.3 Educational Background of Entrepreneurs in the New Economy and Source of Funding for Acquiring Education

	Degree/Diploma			Source of Funding for Education		
	Under-graduate	Post-Graduate	Technical [π]	Immediate Family	Loan	
					Public*	Private[♦]
HUC	20		19	25	12	2
OBC	20	4	10	22	9	3
Dalit	16		6	6	5	11
Muslim	18		7	5	5	15
Total	74	4	42	58	28	34

HUC = Hindu Upper Caste; OBC = Other Backward Caste
*Banks, Scholarships, Subsidised fee at Public Institutions
♦ Money Lender, Close relatives, Community networks
[π] Private certificate in computers, IT; diploma, engineering degree, MBA

opportunities was also a factor for Dalits and Muslims. However, Dalit and Muslim interviewees informed us that retrospectively they have realized that their social networks had weak capacity to advise and help them with their career choices and facilitate their academic endeavours. Irrespective of the social group, all respondents reported that their college education gave them sufficient exposure, and capacity to reflect on their abilities and provided them with a kaleidoscopic lens to imagine their future.

Seed Money and Market Entry

Entry into the market as self-employed or initiating a business in goods and services is one of the important initial steps towards the realization of aspirations. As evident from the testimony of a Hyderabad-based entrepreneur (mineral water supplier), a decent income is necessary for fulfilling basic human needs and lead a life of dignity.

I came into the business because I wanted to give my family three decent meals, a house and education to my children. Also, with income and ability to give education to my family, I also command some respect in society. . . .

244 ASEEM PRAKASH

However, all our respondents had various kinds of difficulties in raising finances and completing the formalities required to initiate their economic activities. The following Table 12.4 summarizes the diverse experiences of individuals belonging to different social groups when it comes to raising finances and completing registration formalities.

It is evident from our respondents that initial class and social position matter during the course of entry into the markets. The individuals belonging to HUCs and OBCs raised their finances through a diversified resource basket that included the sale of family assets, credit from formal institutions and borrowing from family and caste-based social networks. Sale of family asset is a major contributory source to raise the initial finance which helps them to lower their future transaction cost (loan interest, speed money etc). While raising money from formal and informal channels, family and caste-based social network (kith and kin relationship, caste and village associates—both overlap) were seen to be major facilitator in accessing formal credit institutions as well as informal channels of credit. These networks were also instrumental in helping them to access government offices for registration of their economic ventures. More than 80 per cent of the respondents in this group reported that they were able to save

Table 12.4 Seed Finance and Market Entry

	Sale of Family Asset	Formal Loan		Informal Loans		Registration Formalities	
		With Informal Help	Without Informal help	From Kith and Kin	From Market	With Informal Help	Without Informal help
HUC	25	21	8	17	6	28	11
OBC	28	6	13	23	11	24	10
Dalit	3	8	0	2	14	18	4
Muslim	15	14	6	8	12	18	7
Total	71	48	37	50	43	76	44

HUC = Hindu Upper Caste; OBC = Other Backward Caste

Seed Money Source: Adding up the numbers will not give the actual total for the particular social group because seed money basket can have combination of sources

Family asset means, land, gold, silver, vehicle etc.

Source: Calculation from the primary survey conducted by the author.

MARKETS AND ASPIRATIONS 245

time and paid less 'speed money' due to the social links activated by their respective social networks. The following representative statements from a Pune cab driver attest this fact.

> It is difficult to start any economic activity. . . . When I thought of buying a car to run it as a taxi, I only had dreams . . . my dreams were supported by my cousin and Uncle from my village. My cousin connected me to the banks official who was his wife's relative. My loan was sanctioned very quickly. My village uncle facilitated my car registration through his friend and I had to pay very less bribe. . . .

Individuals from the Dalit community came from a very weak class position. An overwhelming majority did not have any family assets to contribute to their initial financial requirements. Majority of them had to take loans at high interest rates from the informal market as well as pay 'speed money' for completing their official/formal registration formalities. Some of our Dalit aspirers also got loans from formal institutions especially devoted to financing the economic ventures of Scheduled Castes. A significant majority of Dalits (14/22) were denied loans by banks due to unsatisfactory credit rating. Dalits attribute the denial with subtle forms of discrimination and a lack of social links with bank officials rather than credit rating. A Dalit courier shop owner who was determined to mark his presence in the market shared:

> If I had known the bank manager or he was my relative, I would have easily got the loan. This is how the bank works. . . . However, I was determined to leave the caste profession practiced by my parent and enter the market. . . .

The loan portfolio of Muslims was also very diversified. It included use of family asset, credit from formal institutions (mostly Islamic Bank), and borrowing from informal sources. Muslims also seem to have very thick social networks which are usefully deployed in lowering transaction costs (lower interest rates for the informal credit, less speed money, and saving of time and so forth) while setting up their businesses.

Having noted the socio-economic background and market entry of our respondents, we now discuss their aspirations claims and gaps.

246 ASEEM PRAKASH

Aspirations Claims and Aspirations Gaps

Aspirations claims, shaped by initial socio-economic location, endeavour to address the perceived causes of current socio-economic marginalization, earn sufficient income, achieve social status, and a claim to dignity that is similar to a person(s) who are considered successful and respected in an individual's cognitive worldview. Although the aspirations claims are personal goals an individual considers desirable in her given social context, but these goals are shaped by the confluence of state, market, and civil society.

The distance or the gap between aspirations claim and actually realized aspirations can be termed as aspirations gap. It often translates into frustration, cynicism, vulnerability, and insecurity of the individual experiencing the aspirational gap. Each individual has their own specific understanding that explains their particular nature of aspirational gap and the reasons for the gap. Although, I have analytically separated the aspirational claims and gaps, in practice the explanation of both often overlap.

I carefully sifted through their explanations and tried to arrange them thematically. There appears to be broad convergences as well and critical divergences in the explanation of aspirations claims and why do aspirations gaps occur.

The aspirations claim of individuals from each social category who have entered the 'new' economy rests on their desire to live a life of dignity and respect. Dignity and respect are seen to be realized through both material and non-material claims. These claims are not merely a right against the state but also a claim to earn in the market and desire to be treated as equal in the domain of civil society.

All our interviewees articulated their aspiration to ensure good education and health facilities for themselves, their children, and family members. Education coupled with able body and good health is seen as a means to enter the market and earn. An HUC who works for a popular home food delivery agency argued:

Education is an investment of time and resource . . . it has given me confidence to get into my current economic activity and earn money to help me and my family to survive . . . I want to ensure good education in an international school for my children [Read English medium school with international syllabus].

MARKETS AND ASPIRATIONS 247

As noted earlier, the Dalits and Muslims tend to have higher educational aspiration than HUCs and OBCs, but lower level of facilitating resources. Facilitating resources are not only economic but also a claim for institutional spaces to promote socio-religious diversity in the realm of civil society. Both economic and socio-political resources combine to translate into lower educational achievements. A Muslim entrepreneur in Hyderabad told us:

> It was difficult for me to attend college because my father wanted to earn and support the family. However, I insisted on acquiring a College degree. . . . My College peers were predominantly from the other religion [read Hindu]. . . . I was never invited for any social events or given a representation in the college cultural bodies. I was never able to integrate myself into College life. As a result, I left going to College regularly after the first year. I only went to appear in the examination. My family was happy with the decision since they wanted an additional earning member. . . . Although I wanted to study further but then I decided to leave the College and start my own business. . . . Now, I am not in touch with any College peers. . . . I do not want the same experience for my children. I want to provide them with education in a good private college that does not discourage religious diversity.

Similar experiences were narrated by several Dalit respondents. A representative testimony from a cab driver in Pune is in order.

> College is for privileged social groups and rich . . . I never had any space to participate in the academic and cultural life of the college. . . .

However, these social groups wished for state subsidy in health and affirmative action policies in education. They want their children to go to the best of English-medium schools followed by business schools, law universities, and medical and engineering colleges. In the face of their inability to get seats in good public institutions, Muslims and Dalits aspire to get their children admitted in reputed English medium private educational institutions. Nearly 90 per cent reported that it is not possible for them to afford education in private institutions. For almost all of HUCs and OBCs, the first preference invariably was private educational institutions.

In the absence of good government schools, they want a cap on private college fees or a fellowship/scholarship by the state (OBCs, Dalits, and Muslims) to access private colleges. Nearly 90 per cent of the Dalits and 65 per cent of Muslims argued for representation in the cultural and political bodies in the

248 ASEEM PRAKASH

college in order to mark their presence, provide voice to their demands, and confront discrimination.

Similarly, respondents across social groups aspired to own material goods—upgrading their vehicle from the current two-wheeler to a better model or buying a car in the near future, possessing a new version of a smart phone, wearing branded clothes (most of them currently wear cheap imitations), latest gadgets for entertainment purpose (iPad, iPod, play stations, video games, and so on), refrigerators (or replacing the old one), fancy kitchen equipment, eating in restaurants, visiting tourist destinations, and so forth.

While discussing the aspirations claims, one particular pattern which stood out was their dissatisfaction with the current physical living conditions. Nearly 78 per cent of our respondents did not own a house. The social groups that owned their own house were largely Muslims. This was largely because they were urban settlers and had stayed in the city for several generations. However, they were not very happy with their crammed living conditions. Most of the HUCs and OBCs wanted to buy a better house in the locality where they were currently residing. The reasons being familiarity with the area and relationships and networks with neighbours. Dalits wanted to shift to a better area with improved access to roads, sanitation, and public transport. Also, it would mean not staying in a Dalit-majority area. Several respondents pointed out that the name of the locality where they lived itself revealed their caste location and therefore a new locality may (albeit not necessarily) help mask it. Muslims did not want to shift out of their current location due to their perceived sense of security and social networks.

Cutting across social groups, all respondents aspired to have a firm foothold in the market as owners of capital dealing in various goods and services. As we have noted that their aspirations claim to enter the market is to earn, acquire capabilities (health and education), own and enjoy material goods including housing. However, there are nuanced differences in the explanation given by individuals belonging to different social groups on their reasons/ aspirational claims for participating effectively in the realm of markets. HUCs and OBCs explained that a decent income provides them an avenue to move closer and eventually emulate individuals from their reference group considered to be successful. It will also give them respect amongst their immediate family, friends, and kith and kin. A full-time insurance agent belonging to OBC social category from Hyderabad explained:

A good income and established business will hold me in high position in my family. I will be treated with respect by my family members and friends

MARKETS AND ASPIRATIONS 249

who are successful. Currently all take me for granted and call me to run errands assuming I am sitting at home.... It will also help me to realise the material wants of myself and my family....

For Dalits, a decent income is not only required to access tangible goods and capability enhancing resources but also as claim to dignity in the realm of civil society. A representative testimony from a Dalit home service provider is:

In order to survive in society, enjoy the good things the market sells, and earn respect, money is also important....

Further the Dalits argue that effective market participation in the modern economy also means moving away from their caste professions, and hopefully acquiring the ability to earn on the basis of the merit and quality of the goods/services they offer, in other words autonomy from the influence of the hierarchical social order on economic outcomes.

Muslims consider the institution of the market as the only space which will not discriminate base religious location. Due to their initial weak class location, lack of any affirmative action policies on behalf of the government, perceived sense of discrimination by the institutions of the state, Muslims enter the market hoping that market will be a space where discrimination will be minimum and inclusion would be maximum. A Muslim app developer for a small business in Pune shared the following:

Business [read Markets] is the only avenue to earn and survive. We will not get jobs in the government and even if we manage one, we will be ridiculed and discriminated for our religion, dress and various cultural practices.... I want to establish myself in the market as a trusted and affordable IT solution service provider....

Markets, argued Muslims, also provide a perceived sense of space where they can harness the resources of their social networks towards market entry and sustenance.

Explaining the Aspirations Gap

As discussed, the aspirations of all our interviewees are focused on deepening their participation in the market, acquiring capabilities (health and

250 ASEEM PRAKASH

education), material goods, and housing for themselves and their family members. A premium is placed on acquiring recognition and respect by the wider society.

However, all our respondents shared the aspirations gap experienced by them. All of them spoke about their weak foundations in the markets. They spoke about the insufficiency of capital to invest, inability to carry their respective businesses on a secure footing and failure to reap a decent return in the markets. Although, the reasons for the aspirations gap differ between individuals but there also seems to be a broad convergence between individuals belong to specific social groups.

We have thematically classified the responses of our interviewees explaining the reasons for aspirations gap subsequently. It is important to note that lack of effective participation in the market is seen to be a critical vector causing aspirations gap. However, lack of market participation may also be caused due to inability to tap into the informal institutions of civil society. In other words, the aspirations gap in the perception of interviewees is significantly caused by their inability to tap into the social networks that govern market operations—entry, sustenance, and expansion. We take the same for discussion in the following pages. First, we explain what we understand by social networks in the markets.

The literature coming from the discipline of economic sociology insightfully points out that economic activities in the market require cooperative action, which finds its basis in social networks. In other words, it helps us recognize the importance of strong ties of kinship (with both immediate and extended family), community, and culture, in mobilizing resources—both economic and non-economic—in the course of market operations. Thus, the argument being that relationships in the market are embedded in social networks, built on kinship or friendship and trust or goodwill that not only sustain economic relations and institutions, but also govern economic rewards and punishments (Granovetter 2005; Burt 1983; Podolny 1993; Thorat 2008; Harriss-White 2003).

Our field evidences corroborate these analytical generalizations drawn by economic sociologists. As per the testimony of the respondents, the positive enablers that lead to better market outcomes may be arranged along four informal institutional dimensions, viz: association with market peers, relationship with state's institutions, relationship with kith and kin, relationship with wider community. These informal institutional dimensions, mostly overlap and inform us on how market participants interact with each other and influence market outcomes and hence can be understood as social networks.

The level of participation and embeddedness of the individuals in these informal institutional dimensions define their location in the social networks governing market outcomes. Absence of an optimum participation in these dimensions translate into aspirations gap.

Association with market peers can help in informal credits, access to business orders, information about business opportunities, besides offering a place in the wider socio-economic networks. HUCs and OBCs pointed out that they do have a good horizontal network formed on the basis of sectoral-specific businesses buttressed by caste locations. However, there seems to be class and sub-caste dimensions to the network too. The testimony of an OBC supplying organic fruit, vegetables, and milk through app-based service informed us:

> Caste based peers are indeed helpful, but I don't get any access to bigger business persons of my caste . . . They are the big players who have lots of business opportunities which they are not themselves able to cater, yet they don't give me any access to those clients. . . .

Likewise, an HUC private fitness instructor in Hyderabad lamented:

> The successful caste friends whom I want to emulate in the market help me in many ways. . . but do not provide me access to their business relations. . . .

Inability to access vertical social networks also brings to our attention the fault lines that are governed by sub-caste locations. Several HUCs and OBCs argued that big players in the market also belong to specific sub-castes. Over a period of time, the latter have diversified into various economic sectors because of their ability to invest and exploit the dominant network resources. Not being from the same sub-caste is also seen as a handicap in accessing vertical network resources. An OBC courier shop owner aptly described his experience in following words:

> The big players are notionally of my caste but different sub-caste, they are in the market for several generations and they tend to go the extra mile to help their sub-caste peers . . . They do help us with contacts in the government and some small help in the market, but never extend real help that can make my business grow big.

Almost all our HUC and OBC respondents attested that it was difficult for them to access the vertical social network though all of them were firmly

252 ASEEM PRAKASH

embedded in the horizonal social network emanating from their caste and village/region of their origin. The vertical social network was seen as crucial for moving their business by leaps and bounds. The resources available through horizontal social networks were limited, that is, it was helpful in the everyday running of the business—informal credit, accessing state resources like permission for licenses, concession in municipal taxations, occasional help with the local police and local political leaders, and so forth. However, the respondents were of the view that the big players (mostly coming from other sub-castes) jealously preserve their market dominance through blocking critical information and opportunities to access big contracts. Only that information is shared which will not disturb the economic hierarchy in the market.

Dalits and Muslims perceived being extremely discriminated in business dealings—in both vertical and horizontal linkages—whereas for Muslims religion is an additional vector. Dalits have very insignificant horizontal networks since most of the business peers in their sector belong to different caste/social location. Access to the state's resources is mostly through speed money. They do not have any access to vertical social networks. Most of the Dalits reported that their interaction with other business peers—horizontal and vertical—is invariably mediated through their caste identity which strongly disfavours any equal and level playing field. A Dalit plumber in Hyderabad shared:

> I am not able to get access to any big housing society because the caretaker of the society only favours his caste and village people. Once they have the entry to the society, they only give extra/surplus business to their friends who are generally from their caste. The sanitary shops in our area are mostly controlled by Raos [a title for higher caste-mostly Kammas], who mostly prefer to give business information to their caste people. . . .

Muslims also perceive an intense discrimination due to religious location. However, the nature of discrimination experienced by them in everyday business practices and in the vertical and horizontal social networks is slightly different from Dalits. A representative testimony of a Muslim owner of a small 'lunch home' (hotel) in Pune throws light on the same.

> The food cooked at my lunch home is liked by all non-vegetarian and vegetarian eaters irrespective of their religion. However, many Hindus look at me through an eye of suspicion assuming that I may be against them, their

MARKETS AND ASPIRATIONS   253

families and larger Hindu society. Although many of the Hindu family eat at my lunch home regularly, they do not give me big catering orders at their private parties . . . my rates are very competitive and even less. . . . it appears they don't want the wider society to know that their celebration dinner/lunch has been cooked by a Mulsim. . . . this may also be the reason that my regular Hindu clients have never recommended me for any big catering. . . .

As reflected in the above testimony, Muslims are alienated and feel that they are not part of the same socio-economic ecology of business activities. There seems to be a perceived sense that their economic interaction with the wider community is narrowly defined at the terms set by Hindus.

However, Muslims have a very strong horizontal network within their community facilitated by family and kith and kin ties. A cab driver in Hyderabad who migrated from a nearby district told the author:

My Uncle and a distant cousin brother helped me with the finances to buy the car, facilitated the registration process and connected me to other drivers who guided me in my initial days. . . . I never felt as an outsider in this new place of work and residence. . . Despite having friendly community friends, I am not able to earn enough to help my family stay comfortably and my son acquire a good education. . . .

Likewise, a small bakery owner in the old city who has started a photocopy and stationery shop in new part of the city spoke appreciatively of the help extended by his extended family and but is hugely disappointed by non-accessibility of the vertical social network and discrimination in the domain of civil society. He pointed out

I required some resources—both financial and physical space—to open a relatively bigger shop. . . . I was not able to get any resource from big business people in my community . . . they all advised me to restrict myself to the old city, although all of them have a business outlet in the new city . . . I am still not able to hire a house on rent near my new business. . . no Hindu flat owner is willing to rent his house to me. . . . I have to travel long distance every day. . . my children are also not able to study in a good English medium schools which are mostly located in the new city. . . .

254 ASEEM PRAKASH

As explained above, the sense of not being included due to class location and thereby denting their aspirational claims runs across all social groups. Caste identity helps HUC and OBC acquire some footing in the horizontal social network. However, it is not perceived as sufficient to take their business to the next level in terms of scale and profit. Dalits and Muslims perceive that they are not merely excluded but their exclusion is reinforced by values of discrimination born, nurtured, and sustained in the domain of civil society. The values governing discrimination adversely impact business outcomes since they raise transaction costs in the markets and make state officials 'unfriendly' and 'inaccessible'.

***

As outlined clearly in the above discussion, the respondents feel that aspirations claims and aspirations gaps are shaped by two critical factors:

First, the initial socio-economic location and their constraints construct a corresponding reference point that the aspirer wants to realize in the immediate future. Second, this initial social location determines their interaction with the formal and informal institutions in the domain of state, markets, and civil society. The respondents shared in no uncertain terms that the aspirations gaps are overdetermined by the market outcomes. As discussed in the previous sections through several narratives (and scores of them which are not documented here) that the outcomes in the markets are shaped at the intersection of state, market, and civil society. This nature of intersectionality translates into two social patterns. First, the values associated with the ideology of caste, religion, class, region as present in civil society are reflected in institutions that constitute the state and market. This mirroring of values results in the blurring of boundaries between state, market, and civil society. Second, the intersection and interaction between state, market, and society creates a unique domain that transcends the original character of each, and has its own set of norms, rules, and behavioural patterns, different from and contradictory to the assumed rationalities of markets and state policies.

The argument of intersectionality is crucial because it helps us analytically contest the artificial binaries of state–markets, state–civil society, and market–civil society. More important to note is the interconnectedness of various institutions that interact with and shape each other, and often act simultaneously in sustaining some form of exclusion and discrimination against the aspirer. Further, it also helps us to differentiate between exclusion and consequent marginalization due to class location,

MARKETS AND ASPIRATIONS   255

and discrimination and consequent socio-economic maldistribution due to caste, religion, and regional location. Lastly, and more importantly, the intersectionality argument helps us to appreciate that there can be possible spaces beyond the intersection that may not governed by the informal norms and logic of intersection spaces under a specific combination of the socio-economic context.

References

Appadurai, Arjun. 2004. 'The Capacity to Aspire: Culture and the Terms of Recognition'. In *Culture and Public Action*, edited by V. Rao and M Walton, 59–84. Palo Alto: CA, Stanford University Press.

Bobbitt, Phillip. 2003. *The Shield of Achilles: War, Peace and the Course of History*. New York: Anchor Books.

Burt, R. 1983. *Corporate Profits and Cooptation*. New York: Academic.

Chandhoke, Neera. 1995. *State and Civil Society. Explorations in Political Theory*. New Delhi: Sage.

Chandhoke, Neera. 1998. 'The Assertion of Civil Society against the State'. In *People's Rights: Social Movement and State in the Third World*, edited by Manoranjan Mohanty, P.N. Mukherjee, and Olle Tornquist, 23–41. Delhi: Sage.

Chandhoke, Neera. 2003. *The Conceits of Civil Society*. New Delhi: Oxford University Press.

Cooper, Robert. 2003. *The Breaking of Nations: Order and Chaos in the Twenty-First Century*. London: Atlantic.

Fraser, Nancy. 1995. 'From Redistribution to Recognition? Dilemmas of Justice in a "Post-Socialist" Age'. *New Left Review* I (212, July–August): 374–82.

Fukuyama, Francis. 1992. *The End of History and the Last Man*. London: Penguin.

Genicot, Garance and Debraj Ray. 2017. 'Aspirations and Inequality'. *Econometrica* 85 (2): 489–519.

Granovetter, Mark. 2005. 'The Impact of Social Structure on Economic Outcomes'. *Journal of Economic Perspectives* 1: 33.

Harriss-White, Barbara. 2003. *India Working: Essays on Society and Economy*. Cambridge: Cambridge University Press.

Huntington, Samuel P. 1996. *The Clash of Civilizations and the Remaking of World Order*. New York: Simon & Schuster.

Jodhka, Surinder and Aseem Prakash. 2016. *The Indian Middle Class*. Oxford University Press: New Delhi.

Kothari, Rajni. 1988. *State against Democracy: In Search of Humane Governance*. Delhi: Ajanta.

Mohanty, Manoranjan. 1998. 'Social Movement in Creative Society: Of Autonomy and Interconnections'. In *People's Rights: Social Movement and State in the Third World*, edited by Manoranjan Mohanty, P. N. Mukherjee and Olle Tornquist, 63–78. Delhi: Sage.

256 ASEEM PRAKASH

Podolny, J. 1993. 'A Status Based Model of Market Competition'. *The American Journal of Sociology* 4: 829–72.

Prakash, Aseem. 2015. *Dalit Capita: State, Markets and Civil Society in Urban India.* New Delhi: Routledge.

Ray, Debraj. 2006. 'Aspirations, Poverty and Economic Change'. In *Understanding Poverty*, edited by edited by Banerjee. A, Roland Bénabou, and Dilip Mookherjee, 409–22. New York: Oxford University Press.

Sherwood, Richard A. Jr. 1989. 'A Conceptual Framework for the Study of Aspirations'. *Research in Rural Education* 6 (2): 61–6.

Thorat, S. K. 2008. 'Caste, Social Exclusion and Poverty Linkages—Concept, Measurement and Empirical Evidence'. Mimeo, Indian Institute of Dalit Studies, New Delhi.

Vijay, G. and G. Ajay. 2000. 'Civil Society, State and Social Movements'. *Economic and Political Weekly* 18 (24, March): 1035–6.

13

The Muslim Middle Class

Structure, Identity, and Mobility[1]

Tanweer Fazal

Historians have alluded to the migration-pattern in the aftermath of Partition to explain a substantial shrinking in the size of the middle class among Muslims. The salaried class, or the salariat, a term used by Hamza Alavi, having acquired modern education moved into new professions such as law, medicine, journalism, or bureaucracy. Its political orientation was exclusivist as it advocated Muslim separatism while in terms of its cultural-ideological framework, it betrayed an uneasiness with the *ulema* and their conservatism. Largely drawn from among the *ashraf* elite, a substantial section of the middle class from northern India, it has been argued, shifted to Pakistan where it successfully entered into the high rungs of the army and the bureaucracy. For Alavi, Muslim ashraf in terms of their ideological and political orientation could be divided into three types: the Muslim landlords who were loyal to the British; the *Ulema* who rose in revolt against the British and were actively involved in anti-British campaigns; and the Muslim salariat, the educated ashrafs who depended mainly on careers in government employment and the professionals.[2] The salariat faced stiff competition from the Hindu educated elite who fared better in securing government jobs. Muslim exclusivism that eventually led to the demand for Pakistan was the outcome of this instrumental need of the Muslim salariat. Mushirul Hasan too holds the view that the Muslim league primarily represented the fears and aspirations of the newly emergent professional groups, and on Partition, much of this middle class shifted to Pakistan.[3]

---

[1] This chapter draws from field data collected as part of the UPE 2 project on the 'Muslim Middle Class'. I thank Dr Amir Ali, CPS, JNU and Co-PI of the project and Shaunna Rodrigues, research assistant, for sharing their views and extending support in the collection of data. I also express my gratitude to Dr Srinivas Goli, CSRD, JNU, and Rajeev Kumar, IIPH, Delhi for help in tabulating NSS figures.

[2] See Hamza Alavi 2002.

[3] Mushirul Hasan 1988.

Tanweer Fazal, *The Muslim Middle Class* In: *Neoliberalism, Urbanization, and Aspirations in Contemporary India*. Edited by: Sujata Patel, Oxford University Press. © Oxford University Press 2021.
DOI: 10.1093/oso/9780190132019.003.0013

258   TANWEER FAZAL

Of late, the Muslim middle class—its size, politics, and ideological orientation—has been a point of public discussion in a variety of contexts. The most dominant mode of thinking about the Muslim middle class is to try and account for its absence. Its absence or diminutive size is lamented upon to explain the conservative turn in Muslim politics. The ascendancy of religio-cultural leadership, its politics centred on symbolisms and identity assertion, and evasiveness on questions of gender and status-based intragroup inequalities, is partly attributed to this eternal crisis—the timidity of the middle class. Of late, developmental studies have relied on the migration patterns and the 'missing middle class' to explain the impoverished condition of Indian Muslims and their sluggish economic mobility.[4] In particular, their gross under-representation in public and private employment, absence from centres of higher and technical education, low enrolment levels in schools, minimal presence in mass media and civil society organizations is cited as both, the symbol and cause of the Muslim decline.

Middle Class and Sociology in India

The question of the definition of what constitutes middle class has variegated implications. An expanding middle class for the market economist is a sign of the success of structural adjustment programmes as well as an expanding consumer market which could further multiply investments. The size of middle class is in essence the size of the consumer market. Therefore, income and expenditure indicators, expanding asset holdings and consumption patterns become critical to the assessment of the size and economic behaviour of the middle class. For the Marxist theorist, however, the middle class posits itself in a fundamentally different way, leading to two kinds of questions. The first pertains to the origin of the middle class, and whether it represents relations of production or consumption. And secondly, if the middle class is an ally of the proletariat or the bourgeoisie in the impending class struggle. While this was the dilemma for early theorists, in more recent years the neo-Marxist tendency is either to include them among the proprietary or the ruling classes on account of their possession of human and social

---

[4] The argument that Partition-related migration disturbed the human development profile of the Muslim population in India hardly holds true when faced with empirical data. As Basant and Shariff (2010) point out, most of the migration between India and Pakistan was within 50 km of the borders. Given the thin spread of out-migrants from other parts of India, the human development profile of other areas did not change. See Basant and Shariff 2010, 6–7.

MIDDLE CLASS STRUCTURE AND IDENTITY   259

capital[5] or to view it as a separate class, that in the final analysis, functions to reproduce the ideological domination of the capitalist social relations.[6]

In contrast, the Weberian perspective on middle classes held that the white-collared workers formed a class distinct from the working class in terms of their market capacity, work situation, and social status (Lockwood 1989; Giddens 1981).[7] Influenced by Weber's *magnum opus, The Protestant Ethic*, sociologists have also tended to study middle-class values and moralities that define their class location. However, the task of uncovering the defining characteristics of the middle class often left the sociologists perplexed. As a class located between the two extremes of the propertied and property-less, as a hegemon in terms of ideas and values, it wavered on a range of subjects such as politics, culture, and morality. This led some sociologists to think of it as a class 'vacillating' in terms of public opinion, 'unfocused and discontinuous in their actions' and 'worried and distrustful': 'They may be politically irritable, but they have no political passion. They are a chorus, too afraid to grumble, too hysterical in their applause. They are rear guarders.'[8]

For most sociologists, the formation of the middle class is judged fundamentally in terms of middle-class values: the duality of modernity versus tradition, the forging of class identities through consumer practices and inter-class relations. With the expansion in the middle class over the years, studying middle-class values have helped sociologists in making a distinction between the 'old' and the 'new' middle class. Alan Wolf discerns a cultural war between the two middle classes in American society. Speculation has replaced savings, production is passé and career is the new middle-class norm. The amalgamation of faith and secular modernity that old middle

---

[5] For Pranab Bardhan, the middle-class professionals including white-collar workers constitute one of the three proprietary classes in India. See Bardhan 1994 and Rudra 1989, Rudra sees the intelligentsia and not the entire middle class as co-opted into the ruling class which is otherwise constituted of the big industrial bourgeoisie and the big landlords. Although the intelligentsia is diverse, it constitutes a class because along with the other two ruling classes, it stands in a contradictory relationship with the rest of society.

[6] For instance, for Poulantzas, white-collar workers are the new petty bourgeoisie. As they are engaged in unproductive labour, they are separate from manual labourers. They play the role of supervisors and managers and reproduce the ideological domination of bourgeois social relations, see Poulantzas 1975.

[7] According to Lockwood ([1958] 1989), white-collar workers are different from the working class on account of their market profile, work situation, and status—the three components of class location.
Anthony Giddens argues that class position is determined essentially by the market capacity for which ownership of means of production is not the only requirement. It also derives from educational and technical qualifications and manual labour power. A difference in market capacity for white-collar workers distinguishes them from the working class (Giddens 1981).

[8] See Wright Mills 1951, 353.

260 TANWEER FAZAL

class was adapted to is replaced by a noticeable rise of fundamentalism and evangelism. Politics takes a rightward shift with a sense of personal entitlement overwhelming the idea of universal good or a concern for the underprivileged.[9]

In India, a renewed interest in studying the middle class follows the introduction of the neoliberal reforms in the early 90s. The restructuring of the economy prompted the emergence of new industries such as the software, triggered the rise of the service sector, and flooded the market with consumer goods. Unlike the old middle class that largely depended on public employment, the newer one owed its origins to the policies of economic liberalization and purportedly remained its principal cheerleader. A new middle class, its shifting role in social and political process, together with its imprints on changing attitudes, lifestyles, and consumption practices, has increasingly come to demand the attention of sociologists. Beyond the obsession with size, proportion or affluence, sociologists tend to inject a degree of complexity to the simplistic formulation of the economist and the demographer. Several questions have followed: Is the new middle class entirely new or does its origin lie in the earlier middle class? Does the expansion of the middle class suggest the rise of new social groups hitherto outside the frame? In what ways is the new middle class different from the older one in terms of its social attitudes, cultural practices, and ideas of politics?

Arguments are both, for and against. A study of its structure indicates continuity rather than change. Its historical and social roots, according to one view, are traced to its predecessor, the older middle class that owed its existence to the state-driven economy. Accordingly, the 'newness' of this middle class barely indicates an upward social mobility among lower strata of Indian society. In terms of its social composition, it is suggested, the post-liberalization middle class is drawn largely from the 'English speaking urban white collar segment' of the society and therefore replicates the homogeneity of the past. The middle class is not 'new' in terms of its structural or social basis. In other words, its 'newness' does not refer to upwardly mobile segments of the population entering the middle class—rather its newness refers to a process of production of a distinctive social and political identity that represents and lays claim to the benefits of liberalization.[10]

---

[9] See Wolfe 1993, 49–64. Other commentators too highlight the difference in values between the old and the new middle class. Varma for instance took the new middle class to task for 'materialistic exhibitionism' and abandoning social responsibility towards the poor (see Varma 1998).

[10] See Fernandez 2006, xviii.

MIDDLE CLASS STRUCTURE AND IDENTITY 261

Jaffrelot and Van der Veer too found that two of the major 'mainstays' of the Indian middle class, the 'petty bougeoisie' and the 'intelligentsia', along with other components came from the upper castes.[11] This caste commonness of the middle class made them more cohesive in terms of shared values. Nonetheless, theoretically, it is not a sealed off category, the underlying assumption being that other groups could potentially join in. For instance, Upadhyaya noticed that a large majority of the software professionals were from small towns but from upper caste and affluent families though a 'significant minority' came from middle castes or OBCs.[12] This turns the middle class into an aspirational one, with others imitating it in the hope of attaining social mobility.

A counter view holds that the rise of new professions and expansion of the service sector that liberalization prompted, offered opportunities of mobility to individuals and groups who were able to change their fortunes and join the middle class. In contrast to its earlier avatar, the new middle class is thus proposed to be a heterogeneous one that includes diverse religious, ethnic, and caste groups. Beteille drew attention to the heterogeneous social composition of the Indian middle class, internally differentiated along the axes of language, religion, and caste, as well as stratified on the basis of income, occupation, and education.[13] Sheth, based on a Centre for the Study of Developing Societies (CSDS) survey conducted in the initial years of liberalization, observed how members of the lower castes had entered the middle class in sizeable numbers, which had prompted change in the character and composition of the old middle class which constituted entirely of English-educated upper castes. His conclusion: 'the new middle class . . . is becoming . . . politically and culturally more unified but highly diversified in terms of social origins of its members'.[14] Sridharan too noticed the entry of 'non-twice born' dominant castes' as also the OBCs, SCs, STs, and religious minorities, in the middle class though the Hindu upper castes continued to be disproportionately more compared to their share in population.[15]

Studies on middle class are either fixed on assessing its size or are obsessively absorbed with consumption patterns and practices. The centrality accorded to consumption, in both estimating its size and determining its distinguishing features, usually obviates the central role of morality and

[11] Jaffrelot and van der Veer 2008, 17.
[12] Upadhyaya 2011, 172.
[13] Béteille 2018, 79.
[14] Sheth 1999, 2510.
[15] Sridharan 2008, 39.

262   TANWEER FAZAL

middle-class values, or for that matter, the politics of the middle class. In contrast, Van Wessel's middle-class informants of Baroda city constantly moralized against the conspicuous consumption and crass materialism that had become the hallmark of middle-class identity for certain sections.[16] Fernandes sees the rise of the new middle class as 'a political process of group formation' that involves a range of 'aesthetic, spatial and civic practices' that create cultural and social boundaries to differentiate from subaltern groups.[17] Thus consumption practices are not merely responses to advertisements or rise in income levels, but a strategy of upward mobility and boundary formation.

The Muslim Middle Class: Some Questions

An expanding middle class, arguably, represents the success story of the process of liberalization. Various kinds of evidence are cited to buttress this point, such as declining poverty ratios, increased preference for English education and the mushrooming of private schools, boosting of entrepreneurship, new social groups in the middle class and diversity in the social origins of the members etc. The National Council of Applied Economic Research (NCAER) based its estimates on the household income survey and discovered that the size of the middle-class households swelled nearly three times from 10.7 to 28.4 million between 2001–2 to 2009–10.[18] Krishnan and Hatekar (2017) calculated the middle class on the basis of per capita daily expenditure (between 2 and 10 $ a day) and recorded an 'astonishing change' in India's class composition. In absolute size, the middle class nearly doubled: from 304 million (30 per cent) in 2004–5 to 604 million (50 per cent) in 2011–12. While there was marginal increase in all sections of the middle class, the bulk of the expansion was led by the lower middle class counted between 2 $ and 4 $ a day per capita expenditure. The social composition of the new middle class was set for a massive overhauling too. While the upper castes continued to dominate the middle class, there was a significant entry of the lower castes and the Muslims in the changing class composition, they concluded.[19]

---

[16] See van Wessel 2004, 93–116.
[17] Fernandes 2006, xxx–xxxii.
[18] Shukla 2010, 100.
[19] Krishnan and Hatekar 2007, 42–3.

Critics of free market economy have on the other hand pointed towards how retrenchments in the public sector, stillness in the manufacturing units, increasing mechanization and so on have led to an actual impoverishment of sections of the middle class. Using an asset-based assessment of the middle class in India, Krishna and Bajpai present a rather dismal picture. The growth of the middle class in the initial decades of liberalization could be 'tapering off' in more recent years. Thus, it is 'fragility and volatility, rather than stability or continued progress', which characterizes the new Indian middle class, Krishna and Bajpai argue.[20] The social composition of the middle class too showed little to celebrate: the upper echelons of the middle class continued to be disproportionately populated by the Hindu upper castes while OBCs, SCs, STs, and the Muslims showed greater tendency to be in its lower rungs.

As we come to comprehend the impact of these changes on the Muslims of India, several questions follow. To what extent have the Muslims in free India been able to enhance their economic status and enter the ranks of what could be called a middle class? Apparently simple, the problem is intricate. For one, the middle class is itself multilayered with managerial-level white-collar workers presumably benefitting the most out of the free market economy. By all accounts and empirical studies, Muslim presence among them is miniscule. Their presence even at the clerical level, to a certain extent, remains inadequate. A large section of the Muslims however, as the Sachar Report (2006) and other empirical studies confirm, depend on self-employment for their living. Do the new recruits into the middle class depend on self-employment and skills of entrepreneurship? Outside the formal spaces of economic activity, is self-employment a matter of choice or a result of structural constraint? For instance, across swathes of rural India, deprived of landholdings, Muslims are largely self-employed in non-agricultural activities. As a result, self-employment is scarcely income generating or stable enough to ensure a sustained presence in the middle class.

The subject allows for yet another exploration, one pertaining to the social composition of India's Muslim middle class. In a caste differentiated Indian Muslim society, while the colonial and much of the postcolonial middle class comprised the ashraf nobility is the new middle class socially diverse that embodies the middle-caste *ajlafs* and the lowest, *arzals* thus suggesting a process of upward social mobility? A correlation therefore needs to be built

---

[20] Krishna and Bajpai 2015, 76.

264 TANWEER FAZAL

between self-employment, caste-based occupational pattern and opportunities that market-driven economy has facilitated. What constitutes the Muslim middle class is a subject to be probed, but beyond that, in what ways is the structural composition of the Muslim middle class different, needs to be examined.

The middle class, as recent advances in sociological and historical literature suggest, is not merely an economic category to be determined by indicators such as monthly consumption indicators, income levels, and educational achievements. An analysis of its cultural makeup, ideological framework, and political orientation is far more critical in understanding the middle-class identity and the constituting behaviour pattern. The erstwhile north Indian Muslim elite prided itself on being proponents of the great tradition of Urdu culture. The middle class entrenched in such a cultural milieu sought to preserve it as a signifier of its Islamic identity. How does the new middle class culturally define itself? Apart from north India, substantial Muslim population is to be found in the non-Urdu-speaking belts of the East consisting of Bengal and Assam, and in the southern Indian states. Presumably, therefore, material and cultural constituents of Muslim middle class have regional specificities. This paper though does not for the moment enter into regional segmentation. It does ask, however, if despite its segmentation along multiple planes of language, caste, and regional planes, does the cultural constitution of the middle class demonstrate any commonality of action and purpose? Or do the multiplicity of cultural identifications fragment the middle-class identity among Muslims?

The middle class being invariably attributed with historical agency, what does the emergence of a new middle class among Muslims hold for the community, and for politics in general? Does it signify a shift from isolationist and identity-centric mobilizations to those aimed at addressing material deprivations, educational advancement, women's empowerment etc.? And what will be the vehicles of that politics: old-style political mobilizations or the new and apparently apolitical/non-state associations through which a middle class participates as socially unmarked citizens? Further, a new religiosity, centred around individual salvation and without the encumbrances of the conventional systems have historically fascinated middle-class adherents. Is there a reimagining of the ways in which to be a Muslim?

Social origins apart, the question of heterogeneity emerges in terms of the old and the new as well as between different layers of the economic category— the upper, the middle, and the lower middle class. What kind of 'classificatory practices' are deployed to maintain social distance and symbolic boundaries

MIDDLE CLASS STRUCTURE AND IDENTITY 265

between old and the new, the affluent and the subaltern as well as between different sections of the middle class? Does the middle-class formation among Muslims therefore follow the material and the symbolic practices that tend to be associated with new Indian middle class?

In short, the following questions become critical in the analysis and assessment of the nature and social character of the Muslim middle class:

1. Has the restructuring of the economy prompted a rise or expansion of the middle class among Muslims? What are the routes of middle-class formation among Muslims?
2. In what ways is the new middle class different from its earlier form? Is it more socially diverse thus embodying the middle-class ajlafs and the arzals?
3. Does the cultural constitution of the middle class demonstrate any commonality of action and purpose? Or do the multiplicity of cultural identifications fragment the middle-class identity among Muslims?

The questions highlighted above warrant the employment of a mixed method strategy that depends on the triangulation of quantitative data sets with narratives gathered through select interviews. The periodic household consumption data is relied here to assess the size of the middle class among Muslims. To approximate the size, expansion, and distribution of middle class population by social groups, I particularly use the estimates computed by Krishnan and Hatekar (2017) based on three rounds of NSS viz; 55th round conducted in 1999–2000, 61st round in 2004–5, and the 68th round in 2011–12. Krishnan and Hatekar (2017) use 2–10 dollars per capita daily expenditure as a benchmark for measuring the size and its variations over the years which also helps them in further disaggregating the category into upper, middle, and lower-middle class.

Apart from this, an ingenious usage of monthly per capita expenditure (MPCE) data cross-tabulated with religion and social groups has helped in tracking middle class formation among Muslims belonging to OBC and non-OBC populations. Comparison between different rounds of NSS survey gives us a picture of the nature and social character of the middle class over the years. It also aids in comparing and contrasting middle-class formation among diverse religions and caste categories such as OBCs, SCs, and STs.

Computed on the basis of daily per capita expenditure, Table 13.1 shows the size of different economic classes in India by the social groups to which

266 TANWEER FAZAL

Table 13.1 Size of Different economic classes by social groups

1999–2000	Poor	Middle class	Affluent
SC	83.8	16.1	0.1
ST	86.8	13.1	0.0
OBC	75.5	24.3	0.2
Hindus	71.3	28.3	0.4
Muslims	75.7	24.2	0.2
2011–12			
SC	59.1	40.4	0.5
ST	70.5	29.2	0.4
OBC	48.7	50.3	1.1
Hindus	48.1	49.9	1.9
Muslims	54.0	45.1	0.9

Source: Krishnan and Vatekar 2017.

they belong. In the first decade of liberalization, up till 1999–2000, a little less than a quarter of Muslim population could be considered as middle class.

By 2011–12, however, the middle-class proportion among Muslims along with those among SCs, OBCs, and Hindus in total swelled significantly. Notably, though, the percentage increase among Muslims (20.9 percentage points) was much lesser when compared with SCs (24.3 percentage points) and OBCs (26 percentage points). Still, by 2011–12, a little less than half of the Muslim population could be counted among the middle class.

As we tend to unpack the middle class in terms of lower, middle, and upper middle class, the scenario appears rather grim. Bulk of the middle class is confined to the lowest rung—that which survives on per capita expenditure of a paltry 2–4 dollars a day. Among Muslims, and so is true of other social groups such as SCs, more than 80 per cent of the middle class could be bracketed in its poorest segment. As we juxtapose social categories against emerging class structure, the predominance of Hindus over Muslims and upper castes over lower castes in the middle and the affluent classes was not much altered.

Much of the Muslim middle class, prior to its most recent expansion, was considered predominantly upper castes with those in white-collar jobs and

MIDDLE CLASS STRUCTURE AND IDENTITY 267

Table 13.2 Upper, middle, and lower middle class by social groups

1999–2000	Lower MC	Middle MC	Upper MC
SC	14.6	1.2	0.3
ST	11.6	1.2	0.3
OBC	21.2	2.4	0.7
Hindus	23.1	3.8	1.4
Muslims	21.0	2.4	0.8
2011–12			
SC	33.1	5.4	1.9
ST	24.9	3.1	1.2
OBC	39.0	8.2	3.1
Hindus	36.9	9.0	4.0
Muslims	36.5	6.1	2.5

source: Krishnan and Hatekar 2017

professions occupied by different ashraf castes. However, the new middle-class expansion among Muslims has a different story to tell. It is largely led by Muslim OBCs albeit majority of them remain would fall in the lowest middle class. Table 13.3 is computed by merging the MPCE quintiles of NSS 68th round (2011–12). Going by these indicators, by 2011–12, nearly half of the Muslim OBCs fell in the middle expenditure quintiles, while the Muslim others (non-OBC) outscored them in the affluent quintiles. Recent developments in middle class formation among Muslims hold implications

Table 13.3 Distribution of Classes by social groups among Muslims

Classes	OBC		Other		All	
	1999–2000	2011–12	1999–2000	2011–12	1999–2000	2011–12
Poorest	42	32	46	38	44	35
Middle	42	48	39	40	41	44
Affluent	16	20	15	22	15	21.0

Source: NSSO, MPCE data, 1999–2000 and 2011–12

268 TANWEER FAZAL

for the stratification system at large, more so, for the course of Muslim politics.

Before we rush to celebrate the arrival of the Muslim middle class in the consumer market, a caution is advised. During 2004–5 to 2011–12, the period that accounted for a 'phenomenal' growth in the Indian middle class, the rise of monthly per capita expenditure for Muslims of all social standing has been the least compared to any other social category. When contrasted with Hindu others (121.7), the escalation in Muslim MPCE, both Muslim OBCs (64.2) and Muslim others (66.2), was abysmally low. The figures only confirm that middle-class formation among Muslims continues to be weak.

The statistics presented above point to the following: there is definitely an expansion of the Muslim middle class, but this expansion is largely in the lowest rung of the middle class and their share declines as we move up the ladder. Among the new entrants into the middle class are the Muslim OBCs, the bulk of whom remain in the lower middle-class category. Across the board, the rise of expenditure levels remains the least among Muslims. If the rise in income and expenditure levels among Muslims remains insignificant, is there a possibility of inter-generational decline or dispossession that sections of Indian Muslims could be facing? A recent survey on occupational mobility in the state of Uttar Pradesh noted significant inter-generational decline among the state's Muslim population. In three generations, Muslims showed far greater tendency to move into unsecure and less remunerative

Table 13.4 Difference in MPCE by Religion and Caste

2004–5 to 2011–12	
Hindu ST	68.8
Hindu SC	73.4
Hindu OBC	89.1
Hindu Others	121.7
All Hindu	93.0
Muslim OBC	64.8
Muslim Others	66.2
All Muslims	59.7

(at constant prices, 1987–88)

Source: Post-Sachar Evaluation Committee Report, 40

MIDDLE CLASS STRUCTURE AND IDENTITY 269

occupations such as self-employed petty trader/skilled non-agricultural labour and unskilled non-agricultural labour categories. Primarily owing to their initial advantage, the generational decline was significantly more noticeable among Muslims who claimed upper-caste status.[21]

Survey data, though not exact, offer comparative figures of Muslim presence in the middle class. They also give us an indication of a plausible reconfiguration in the Muslim class system. However, this leaves us with some pressing questions regarding formation of class identity, prevailing ideology and value system that Muslim middle class adheres to. Does the cultural constitution of the middle class demonstrate any commonality of action and purpose? Or do the multiplicity of cultural identifications fragment the middle-class identity among Muslims? These are questions that require a descriptive analytical frame. We turn to narratives captured from variegated middle-class homes located in metropolitan Delhi and its suburbs.

The interviews referred to here were conducted in 2016 and 2017 and were set in the backdrop of an inflamed social and political atmosphere with news of lynching of Muslim individuals, suspicions regarding their patriotism and religious profiling of terrorism, proscriptions on food choices, and livelihood options, reported denial of housing in mixed middle-class colonies dominating public discourse. Many of these group prejudices and cultural stereotypes, dormant earlier, came to the fore with the ascendance of a government with a pronounced supremacist ideology at the centre and many Indian states. Needless to say, our discussions during the course of the interviews frequently lapsed into fears and trepidations of the respondents. The names of the respondents are changed here to maintain confidentiality.

First, a brief biographical sketch of the respondents. Tasneem and Rashid (name changed), both in their 40s, are a couple who live and work in multinational corporations in Gurgaon. They have lived in the US for close to four and a half years, and in Gurgaon, live in an upscale apartment complex. They have degrees in management from premier management institutes, and have studied in elite Jesuit schools in Ranchi, where they spent their childhood. Tasneem's father was officer in charge of sales department of a public sector unit. Rashid's father, a college professor, came from a landed family of Katihar. His decision to move to Ranchi and take up college teaching as a profession enabled an entire generation of his relatives to gain education and enter professional lives. Ties with land in the village are still retained by the

[21] Trivedi et al. 2016, 120.

270 TANWEER FAZAL

family. Both Tasneem and Rashidare upper-caste Syeds, and their families are known to each other for years. Their total household income ranges between 30 and 40 lakhs annually.

Farzana Anjum (name changed), in her late 30s, belongs to the second generation in her family with formal education. Her father is from Bihar but worked as an assistant engineer in Haryana all his life. Her caste is Ansari, a relatively prosperous one among the Muslim middle castes. She does not retain any connection with the village from where her father came. She was educated in a private school in Gurgaon and finally graduated with an MCA degree. She quit her job as software professional to join her husband, Shaaz Qamar's (name changed) business. Shaaz, also in his late 30s, did hotel management but after working for a few years in a corporate firm, quit his job and is now a motivator and speaker on spiritual issues for corporates, and trains people in spirituality and 'mindpower'. Shaaz is a Sheik Siddique from Lucknow. His father was an MSc and his mother a BSc graduate. His grandfather was an Urdu poet. Both Shaaz and Farhana together earn in the range 15–30 lakhs a year.

Anwar Moradabadi (name changed), 54, is an Urdu journalist, author of several books, and the chief editor of a daily and a fortnightly. He is also a columnist for a large number of Urdu dailies in the country. A Pathan by caste, he moved to Delhi in 1977 from Moradabad, a town in western UP Moradabadi had a maternal uncle in the city who helped him in the initial years. To fulfil his brother's wishes, he went to a Madrasa to learn Arabic and Persian for three years, where he also learnt calligraphy. Subsequently, he earned an MA degree in Urdu from Rohilkhand University and *Adeeb Kamil* (degree in Urdu) from Jamia Urdu, Aligarh. He learnt English after he was able to persuade one of his teachers to teach him the language.

Moradabadi comes from a family with an illustrious history of participation in the public life of India. His *Nana* (maternal grandfather), used to publish an Urdu magazine, and according to Moradabadi, was a close aide of Maulana Azad. His father was a bus driver, and son of a freedom fighter. Moradabadi seemed to have a deep sense of gentle entitlement about his family's role in public life, and the freedom movements that were shaping India before her independence. But after independence, the family fell in bad times. His father was employed in UP railways and sustained a family of ten on a salary of 500 rupees. Moradabadi said that though his family was poor, they were instructed about moral values (*tarbiyat) at home*. He also grew up in a religious environment, reading the Quran with the *jamaat* (congregation) everyday.

MIDDLE CLASS STRUCTURE AND IDENTITY 271

Forty-eight-year-old Rihad Ashraf (name changed) works as a lower division clerk at Delhi's Jamia Millia University. A Syed by caste, his ancestors moved from Sirhind in Punjab to Shahjahanpur on receiving zamindari from emperor Shahjahan. Part of the family moved to Delhi during the World War II when they settled down in Old Delhi. In 1989, Ashraf and his brother decided to move to Jamia Nagar, a Muslim middle-class colony in south-east district of the capital. According to Ashraf, over time, the family sold off their land and all the shops that they owned in the village in order to maintain their lifestyle. Therefore, after independence, they preferred taking up government jobs as a secure source of income, and probably also to maintain status. Like him, his father, mother, and his brother, all took up government employment.

Yaqub Khan (name changed), 52 years of age, belongs to the Saifi caste that specializes in carpentry and iron work. Soon after his class eight, he came from Meerut to Delhi to work with one of his acquaintances who ran an iron welding and fabrication shop. For the next ten years Yaqub worked in his shop as a welder till he started his own unit. There are five members in his family including three adolescent children. Yaqub has managed to send all of them to one of the English medium schools that have come up in the neighbourhood. Over the years, Yaqub bought a plot of land and built his house in Chhattarpur village of Delhi. Along with him, many of his friends as well as kinsmen have come to live in the same neighbourhood.

Twenty-five-year-old Farah Hassan (name changed) is an environmental researcher and lives with her parents in an upmarket colony of South Delhi. Her father was from Aligarh who had inherited land from his family in parts of Punjab and Haryana. His ancestors reportedly served in the Mughal army and received Zamindari in return. As much of the inherited land lied on the Indian side of the border, the family decided to stay back during Partition. That her grandfather was a prominent Congress leader at Aligarh Muslim University was another plausible reason that led the family to arrive at this decision. Farah comes from a prominent family that took to higher education early on, men since the last 4–5 generations and women in the last 2–3 generations. Around the time when Farah was born, her parents moved to Delhi. Initially, they settled at extension area of the city, and later to New Friends Colony, where they have been living since the last eight years. The decision to shift a colony close to Jamia Nagar, a Muslim concentrated area was taken following an incident in which the neighbours at South Extension hounded the family. Moving to Delhi was a matter of adjustment for her father as coming from a conservative city like Aligarh, the new place appeared

272   TANWEER FAZAL

completely different. But over the years, Farah notices that her father has become far more conventional than he was. However, her mother, who along with her Shia faith also practises Buddhism on the side, could exercise her freedoms and choices in ways that would never have been possible, and be considered blasphemous, in Aligarh.

Raziuddin Ahmad (name changed) is 48 years old and works with a unit of the Home Ministry, Government of India. At the time of the interview, he held the position of Deputy Commissioner of Police. He insisted that we put down his caste/biradari as Syed, Sunni Muslim. After completing his BSc Honours in Botany, Ahmad did his post-graduation in Industrial Management from Patna University. He comes from a family, which once prominent in Bihar, fell on hard times after independence. His grandfather was a barrister trained in London. His family began to witness dispossession after the death of his grandfather—his relatives took over all the property. His father was a middle-level government officer in Patna and was able to educate all his four children to complete their Masters. He moved to Delhi after having been selected for the Home Ministry job in 1991. Having lived in different parts of Delhi, Ahmad recently purchased and moved to a new apartment in east Delhi. The society in which he lives is a mixed one and Muslims are very few among the apartment owners.

With these biographies in mind, we turn to investigate middle-class values among Muslims. As with all social categories, middle-class values tend to differ among Muslims. What emerges most starkly in interviews with the respondents belonging to various different sects, genders, regions, and social strata is their eagerness to move from the particular to the universal. However, unlike what enlightenment modernity prescribes, the particular is not dispensed with in pursuit of the universal, but seeks adjustments with it. The particular and the universal remain in a fraught relationship, expressed in different ways in different individuals. Tasneem and Rashid consciously disavow the choice to live in what they see as Muslim ghettoes, imagined by them as dens of prejudice and backwardness, preferring more heterogeneous neighbourhoods. Their choice of upscale suburban housing is articulated in terms of their identification of themselves as cosmopolitans. Shaaz Qamar, our other respondent, who lives in one of those 'downmarket apartments', felt how the community concentrated areas were rather unsafe as they come to be easily stigmatized. In case of a confrontation with members of other religions, he feared that Muslims might force him to be on their side.

Moradabadi attached a positive value to living in Taj Enclave, a predominantly Muslim gated colony in East Delhi. Also active in affairs of the

MIDDLE CLASS STRUCTURE AND IDENTITY   273

residents' welfare association, he was pleased with the exposure to Islamic ethics and culture his children received, as well as the influence *Tablighi-i-Jamaat* wielded in the area, and over his son. It is interesting to note that to him, it was Old Delhi—another, much older concentration of Muslims—that held negative connotations. Inhabitants of old Delhi, in his words, were not truthful and honest, and Taj Enclave represented an escape. Over the years, choices of neighbourhoods are also determined by factors such as security, affordability, proximity and the fact that mixed neighbourhoods are increasingly becoming closed for Muslims. So when Rihad Ashraf and his brothers decided to shift out of Old Delhi, their next choice was Jamia Nagar, another Muslim locality. Farah's family, given their cosmopolitan taste, opted to initially stay in South Extension, an upscale locality in Delhi. On being forced to leave the place, their next option was New Friend's Colony, another upmarket neighbourhood, but adjoining Jamia Nagar. Similarly, Raziuddin Ahmad found virtue in living in a religiously diverse apartment complex; however, he ensured that it was adjoining Taj Enclave, a predominantly Muslim housing society. *Apna mahaul* (our environment), as Laurent Gayer (2012), found while researching Muslim settlement patterns in Delhi, could be another such reason among a combination of factors that determined Muslim residential choices.

More than, middle-class locations—whether in professions, software industries, self-employed, and entrepreneur—it is social capital, cultural networks and the historicity and route of middle-class formation that plays a significant role in the shaping of values and norms. Thus, for Tasneem and Rashid, now for several generations into the middle class, their values are a legacy of what can be described as the 'old' middle-class values formed in much more stable, secure, and less aggressive world of government service and old aristocracy. This is evident in their cautious consumerism that detests frequent visits to malls, expensive restaurants and their aversion to flashy home décor. Irrational and conspicuous consumption is not what shapes their class identity as it speaks through their comfort with English language, literary taste, convent education, IIM graduation, and high managerial level positions. On a similar plane, advertisements were not something that seemed to have influenced Farah's decision-making. Her choices of artefacts in the consumer market were determined more by her class location—a sense of cultivated grace and elegance reflected in consumer choices that were not so ostentatious.

In contrast, Farzana and Shaaz, now only second generation into middle-class status, have had a different route to identity formation. It depends on

274   TANWEER FAZAL

everyday symbolic assertions—their choices dependent on advertisements, brand consciousness, and performances. The connection with the past, in this case, is not so profound and rarely referred to. Moradabadi's obvious pride in his past derives not from any purported noble descent, but from his family's participation in the freedom movement, as a result of which his grandfather was also once jailed. It is this that defines his cultural identity and politics. His invocation of *tarbiyat* (a *sharif* value par excellence), which he was taught at home, his struggle from a calligraphist to an editor of a newspaper, his insistence on work ethic and honesty remind one of Margalit Pernau's analysis of the rise of middle class in mid-nineteenth-century North India, which in differentiating itself from nawabi decadence on the one hand, and menial classes on the other, emphasized precisely these values. Adherence to values of individual achievement, hard work, husbanding of resources, and concomitant behaviour led to a process she describes as *ashrafization*' whereupon those who were not necessarily noble or well-born could stake a claim to a higher social status.[22]

Moradabadi is embedded in older forms of patronage networks (the help, for instance he received from the politician Azam Khan to set up his newspaper, or his relations with other leaders as evident in his numerous photographs with political leaders from Hamid Ansari to Manmohan Singh and Arjun Singh in his office) and state institutions such as Urdu Akademi (run by Delhi government), whose relevance seems to be fast receding. While the patronage networks represented earlier forms of social mobility, appointments in bodies such as Urdu Akademi correspondingly signalled the rise in his status. Unlike other respondents, Moradabadi is wholly involved in community activities (president of the Urdu press association, the secretary of the All India Urdu Editor's Conference, and the general secretary of the All India Muslim Majlis-e-Mushawarat) and he articulates his concerns from that vantage point. He is an actor in the field of 'Muslim politics'. Lacking the skills which might allow him entry into a cosmopolitan middle class, he detests it and clings onto more familiar, older ways.

Foy Yaqub, setting up his own welding unit freed him from the bondage of the employer and also enhanced his social status among relatives and friends. In his locality, Yaqub is active in the local RWA, has been its president twice, and takes keen interest in its elections. This also has enabled him to establish contacts with local state functionaries and the police. He asserts his rising

---

[22] Pernau 2001, 21–41.

MIDDLE CLASS STRUCTURE AND IDENTITY 275

class status through the Santro car he drives, the annual health packages he buys and the claims of having stayed in upscale middle-class colonies in the past. Nonetheless, at the level of values, Yaqub disparages the atomized and isolated existence of middle-class neighbourhoods and instead emphasizes his strong *biradari* and community ties.

The classification struggles, according to Bourdieu (1996), determine symbolic boundaries; define taste in culture and consumption so as to maintain social distance. However, this struggle does not take place only in the context of the dominant and the dominated, the two polar opposites in class system. It acquires much more complex and nuanced form among individuals and groups placed broadly within the same class location, here in our case, the middle class. This symbolic struggle is very much discernible, as Alan Wolfe found in the case of America, in the form of cultural war or war of values between the old and the new middle class. To be sure, this everyday form of maintaining social distancing is not unique in the case of the Muslim middle class alone.

Dispossession as much as upward economic mobility informs the Muslim presence in the middle class. Rihad Ashraf, the clerk, insists on recreating a past glory and grandeur of his ancestors—whether real or imagined. In his telling, one of his ancestors, originally from Sirhind in Punjab, was made a Hakim during Shahjahan's time and granted a zamindari over three villages in Shahjanapur. Over time, the family sold their land in order to maintain their lifestyle and charitable works such as a mission school, which he still treats as his family legacy. According to him, most of the family properties —but for a haveli—have been sold. Therefore, he says, after independence, they preferred taking up government jobs as a secure source of income. This is reiterated to affirm that he is not a new arrival but part of an older elite, albeit one that has fallen on bad times. The past—long gone—is both an aspiration and a resource to claim higher social location.

The respondents, torn between pulls of modernity and tradition, have worked out their own resolutions that compete to shape middle-class identity among Muslims. Tasneem tried wearing the Hijab, initially in order to protect her falling hair, and discovered that she received immense respect from others. However, she found it too cumbersome to continue. Islam is fiercely personal for her, a matter of choice, a world of spiritual quest, and largely non-conflictual. Anwar Moradabadi is deeply religious and so is Ashraf, but this has not stopped the latter from occasional indulgences such as eating out at restaurants serving halal food. One of Anwar's sons, a *tabligh*, on the other hand frequently dissuades him from conspicuous consumption. Consumption is not simply an economic behaviour, a response to aggressive

276   TANWEER FAZAL

marketing strategies, or a means to status enhancement—it is also culturally determined. This relationship between culture and consumption needs far more serious investigation than there has been. It is not market alone that determines and dictates consumer conduct, but culture too limits and restricts the market. Middle-class Muslims sometimes resent the limited choice that the market enforces upon them. There are fewer restaurants serving halal food, swimming pool for Tasneem and Rashid is a waste of resources, limited availability of Urdu teachers can be a problem. Raziuddin Ahmad and his wife requested the Convent school where their two children are enrolled, to teach Urdu instead of French and German as Urdu was deemed to be part of their cultural inheritance. Their request was not entertained on grounds that there were not sufficient number of students opting for Urdu. Muslim parents collectively hired a Madarsa teacher who could teach their wards the language at home. Interestingly, however, this nostalgia for the lost cultural inheritance squared little with their everyday practices. On probing further, Ahmad and his wife stressed that they subscribed to English newspapers alone and preferred English language news channels on television.

One of the key features of the new middle class, according to Fernandes, is the acquisition of a 'new suburban aesthetic identities', which though 'coded in terms of representative citizenship' are in practice 'often defined by exclusionary social and political boundaries'. These middle-class practices transform citizenship into a category that is marked by exclusions based on social markers (such as caste and class) that delineate the identities of the urban poor.[23] While this could be certainly true of the upper levels of the new middle class, it is worth asking if a Dalit middle class, or in our case, a Muslim middle class, or the lower regions of the middle class populated by social groups hitherto excluded from this category, may exhibit identical aesthetic, spatial, and civic practices that distinguish, in Fernandes' view, the new middle class. Let us, for example, take the activism most associated with this class: the arena of resident welfare associations. Both Moradabadi and Ashraf are active in their local associations in Taj Enclave and Jamia Nagar, respectively; Yaqub Khan is president of the Residents' Welfare Association of Chhattarpur, New Delhi. And yet they do not participate by erasing social markers, indeed these markers are precisely what are foregrounded. Ashraf's participation rests on the recognition that Jamia Nagar being a Muslim locality has been discriminated against and denied civic amenities; Yaqub Khan's involvement is to safeguard the interests of his *biradari* vis-à-vis the civic administration.

[23] Fernandes 2006, 23.

MIDDLE CLASS STRUCTURE AND IDENTITY   277

Class location and values associated with caste origins very often coincide; they do so in the case of Muslims as well. However, upward-class mobility of hitherto impoverished castes as well as dispossessions that a section of Muslim aristocracy has come to face over the years makes the situation far more knotty. In terms of taste, cultural preferences, education, and distance, Tasneem and Rashid, Anwar Moradabadi and Rihad Ashraf, are 'classes apart', though of similar caste backgrounds. As our data demonstrate, much of the new arrivals in the middle class are Muslims who are officially categorized as among other OBCs. Does their arrival lead to a ready acceptance by those already entrenched? Empirically, we did not find much support for this assertion. However, neither did we find any effort on the part of the new arrivals to appropriate the symbols, lifestyles and cultural tastes of the entrenched. The lower middle class, represented by Yaqub Khan, and also Rihad Ashraf to some extent, was busy setting its own standards and even displayed a degree of disdain for the more affluent for their atomized existence and disregard for the community and the neighbourhood. Middle-class values in India, says Beteille, 'are marked by deep and pervasive antinomies' by which he means 'contradictions, oppositions and tensions inherent in a set of norms and values.'[24] This holds true of the Muslim middle class too.

References

Alavi, Hamza. 2002. 'Social Forces and Ideology in the Making of Pakistan'. *Economic and Political Weekly* 37 (51, 21–27 Dec): 5119–24.

Bardhan, Pranab. 1994. *The Political Economy of Development in India*. Delhi: Oxford University Press.

Basant, Rakesh and Abusaleh Shariff. 2010. *Oxford Handbook of Muslims in India: Empirical and Policy Perspectives*. Delhi: Oxford University Press.

Béteille, André. 2018. 'The Social Character of the Indian Middle Class'. In *Middle Class Values in India and Western Europe*, edited by Imtiaz Ahmad and H. Reifeld, 73–84. Delhi: Social Science Press.

Bourdieu, Pierre. 1996. *Distinction: A Social Critique of the Judgment of Taste*, 8th edn. Cambridge: Routledge and Kegan Paul.

Fernandez, Leela. 2006. *India's New Middle Class*. Delhi: Oxford University Press.

Gayer, Laurent. 2012. 'Safe and Sound: Searching for Good Environment in Abul Fazl Enclave, Delhi'. In *Muslims in Indian Cities: Trajectories of Marginalisation*, edited by Laurent Gayer and Christophe Jaffrelot, 213–36. London: Hurst and Co.

Giddens, Anthony. 1981. *The Class Structure of the Advanced Societies*, 2nd edn. London: Hutchinson.

[24] Béteille 2018, 74.

Hasan, Mushirul. 1988. 'In Search of Identity and Integration: India's Muslims since Independence'. *Economic and Political Weekly* (Special Number, Nov): 2467–78.

Jaffrelot, Christophe and Peter van der Veer, eds. 2008. *Patterns of Middle Class Consumption in India and China*. Delhi and London: Sage.

Krishna, Anirudh and Devendra Bajpai. 2015. 'Layers in Globalising Society and the New Middle Class in India: Trends, Distribution and Prospects'. *Eçonomic and Political Weekly* 50 (5, Jan 31): 69–77.

Krishnan, Sandhya and Neeraj Hatekar. 2017. 'Rise of the New Middle Class and Its Changing Structure'. *Economic and Political Weekly* 52 (22, June 3): 40–48.

Lockwood, D. 1989. *The Blackcoated Worker*, 2nd edn. Oxford: Clarendon.

Mills, C. Wright. 1951. *White Collar: The American Middle Classes*. New York: Oxford University Press.

Ministry of Minority Affairs, Government of India, Post-Sachar Evaluation Committee Report, 2014.

National Sample Survey Organisation (NSSO), Ministry of Statistics & Programme Implementation, Government of India, NSS 55th Round, 1999–2000.

National Sample Survey Organisation (NSSO), Ministry of Statistics & Programme Implementation, Government of India, NSS 68th round, 2011–12.

Pernau, Margalit. 2018. 'Middle Class and Secularisation: Muslims of Delhi in the Nineteenth Century'. In *Middle Class Values in India and Western Europe*, edited by Imtiaz Ahmad and H. Reifeld, 21–41. Delhi: Social Science Press.

Poulantzas, N. 1975. *Classes in Contemporary Capitalism*. London: New Left Books.

Rudra, Ashok. 1989. 'Emergence of Intelligentsia as a Ruling Class in India'. *Indian Economic Review* New Series, 24 (2, July–Dec): 155–83.

Sachar Report (Prime Minister's High level Committee). 2006. *Social Economic and Educational Status of the Muslim Community of India: A Report*. Delhi: Cabinet Secretariat, GOI.

Sheth, D. L. 1999. 'Secularisation of Caste and Making of New Middle Class, *Eçonomic and Political Weekly* 34 (34/35, 21 Aug–3 Sept): 2502–10.

Shukla, Rajesh. 2010. *How India Earns, Spends and Saves: Unmasking the Real India*. Delhi: NCAER-CMCR and Sage.

Sridharan, E. 2008. 'Political Economy of the Middle Classes in Urbanising India'. ISAS Working Paper No. 49, 22 September, National University of Singapore.

Trivedi, Prashant K., Srinivas Goli, Fahimuddin, and Surinder Kumar. 2016. 'Identity Equations and Electoral Politics Investigating Political Economy of Land, Employment and Education'. *Eçonomic and Political Weekly* 51 (53, 31 Dec): 117–26.

Upadhya, Carol. 2011. 'Software and the "New" Middle Class in the "New India"'. In *Elite and Everyman: Cultural Politics of India's Middle Classes*, edited by Amita Baviskar and Raka Ray, 167–92. Delhi: Routledge.

Van Wessel, M. 2004. 'Talking about Consumption: How an Indian Middle Class Dissociates from Middle-Class Life'. *Cultural Dynamics* 16 (1): 93–116.

Varma, Pavan K. 1998. *The Great Indian Middle Class*. Delhi: Viking.

Wolfe, Alan. 1993. 'Middle Class Moralities'. *The Wilson Quarterly* (1976–) 17 (3, Summer): 49–64.

Index

Aam Aadmi Party (AAP), 209
'accumulation by dispossession' (ABD) thesis, 135, 146, 181, 183, 186, 191
Adityanath, M., 220
adivasis, 180
advertisements, 34
Agarwala, R., 7
agrarian land transition, 133, 136, 142–6
  exchange value, 19
  land appropriation for private use, 19
  monetization of, 142
  processes of sale and conversion, 145–6
  use value, 19
agrarian urbanism, 139
Aiyer, S., 52
Akshardham temple complex, 124
Alavi, H., 257
Amaravati project, 20, 139, 142, 144–5, 147, 153, 155–6, 164–71
  compensation package, 165–6
  ecological dimensions and its unsustainability, 166–8
  land pooling and land acquisition process, 164–5
Andhra Pradesh, 145, 154, 156
anti-colonial nationalism, 115
anti-*Padmaavat* protests, 39
anti-poverty programmes, 10
Appadurai, A., 234–5
artisanal fishing, 181, 184
Asian cities, 178
aspirations of individuals, 233–6
  civil society, role of, 237
  claims and gaps, 246–55
  elements, 235
  field study, 240–3
  of marginalized and socially peripheral groups, 235
  markets, role of, 237–40
  owning of material goods, 248
  steps towards realization of, 243–5
aspiration window, 235

Babri mosque demolition, 10, 17, 66
Bahujan movement, 209
Bahujan Samaj Party (BSP), 9, 21–2, 207, 212, 214, 228
  performance in electoral politics, 230–1
Balakot strike, 226
Banerjee, S. G., 155
bank nationalization, 3
Bengaluru/Bangalore, 175–6, 181, 183, 186
  peri-urban villages of, 144–5, 147
Béteille, A., 261, 277
Bharatiya Janata Party (BJP), 7n7, 9–10, 22, 38, 212–14
  performance in electoral politics, 230–1
  strategies in electoral politics, 221–7
  strategy of communal mobilization, 220–2
Bhatia, G., 163
Bhilai, 121
black money, 140
Bloom, D. E., 50, 52–3
Bobbitt, P., 238
Bokaro, 121
Bots, 29
Brenner, N., 138, 153–4, 157
Brexit, 237
Bride and Home magazine, 123
business communities, 7

Calcutta Megacity Programme, 161
Canning, D., 50
capital accumulation, 20, 103, 138, 146, 154, 157, 166, 177–8, 180, 187
Capital Region Development Authority (CRDA), 165
caste and tribe discrimination, 94–5
caste parties, 212
Chakravorty, S., 140
Chamacha age (Kanshiram), 209
Chandra, K., 6–7
Chaudhury, M., 16
Chennai, 141, 146, 187, 190
Chennai IT corridor, 156

280 INDEX

Chile, 1
China, 156, 185
chit-fund, 128
chronic flooding, 175, 178
citizenship, 109, 120–2, 276
citizen-worker, 122
city at risk, 188
city of risk, 188
civil disobedience, 114
civil society, 237
Coastal Andhra, 132
coastal cities, 178, 182
Coastal Regulation Zone rules of 1991 and 2011, 182
commoning of risk, 178–92
commons and commoning practices, 181–92
   role of politics of epistemology and legality, 187
   for specific groups, 183
   waste disposal functions, 183
common sense, 34, 36, 41–4
communications
   approach to populism, 31
   communicative abundance, 29, 33, 42
   instant access and unequal knowledge, 30–1
   modern communications media, 33
   relationship between public participation and, 31
Concerned Citizens Committee, 189
Congress Party, 9, 212, 229
   performance in electoral politics, 230–1
Connell, R., 1–2
consumption patterns and preferences
   migration impact, 86
   Uttar Pradesh, 77–80, 83–4
contract labour, 8
corporate urbanism, 20
Covid 19 crisis, 11, 14
crony capitalism, 67–8
Cuaresma, J. C., 51
Cyberabad (Hyderabad), 153, 158

Dados, N., 1–2
Dalits, 21–2, 143–5, 197
   atrocities against, 229
   Bahelias, 200
   Basor/Bansphor, 199, 203–4
   discrimination of, 245, 252
   impact of a neoliberal economy on, 198
   Kuchbandhiya, 204

   Kuchbandhiyakanjar, 201
   literacy rates among, 215
   livelihood activities, 203–4
   microfinance support for, 203, 205–7
   mobilization of, 220–2
   movement, 9
   Musahars, 200, 207, 221
   Nat, 201
   Nishads, 221
   Pasis, 221
   politics, 208–10
   relationship of market and, 202–5
   Sansi, 202
   Sapera, 201–2
   Sarvan, 203–4
   state-sponsored schemes for, 205–6
Das, R., 163
Dasgupta, R., 139, 159
Deleuze, G., 34–5
Delhi, 111, 146, 158, 175
   Smart City policy, 103
Delhi Ajmeri Gate Slum Clearance Scheme, 116–17
The Delhi (Control of Building Operations) Ordinance of 1955, 118
Delhi Development Authority (DDA)/Delhi Development Provisional Authority, 118
Delhi Improvement Trust (DIT), 116–18
   Town Expansion Schemes, 118
Delhi Land & Finance (DLF Limited), 116. See also DLF City
Delhi-Mumbai Industrial Corridor (DMIC), 156, 160
Delhi Municipal Council, 116
democracy, populist vision of, 31
democratic politics, 36–8
demographic changes, 48
demographic dividend, 48–53
   accounting benefit, 50
   adult population, 50
   behavioural forces, 50–1
   benefits, 51–2
   child population, 49
   educational attainment and, 51
   effect on per-capita growth rate of income, 53
   ratio of working to non-working age population, 50
   relationship between economic progress and, 51–3
deterritorialization, 185

INDEX 281

Dharavi redevelopment project, 189
Dholera, 135, 156, 170
dignified livelihood, 205
disaster governance, 176, 178
disaster risk, 178–81, 186
disasters and hazards, 21, 168, 175–8, 180–1,
   188, 190–1
DIT Building Manual, 117
DLF City, 18, 109, 114–22, 126, 158
   gated communities, 118, 120
   in Gurgaon, 118–20, 128–9
   land purchases, 128–9
   Near Silver Oaks Apartments, 119
   residential colonies in Delhi, 117
   RWA, 126–7
   scheme of 'private- public partnership,' 120
   White Town Houses, 119
Douglas, M., 190
Durgapur, 121

East Calcutta Wetlands, 162
East Coast Economic Corridor (ECEC), 156
Eastern Ghats, 168
economic growth, relationship between
   demographic changes and, 51–3
education
   dividend, 51
   social-group attainment of, 81
Electronic city (Bengaluru), 153
empty urbanization, 20, 147
English-educated upper castes, 12–13
English language television, 32
entangled urbanism, 142
ethnic villages, 19

Facebook posts, 29, 32, 38–40
Faizal, T., 22
fake news, 41
family-based dynasties in politics, 7
female labour force participation, 48–9,
   51, 53–7
   reasons for poor, 57
   relationship between fertility transition
      and, 53–7
   trends, 54–5
   U-shaped relationship between economic
      changes and, 56–7
Female Work Participation Rate (FWPR), 16
Fernandes, L., 12–14
fertility transition, 48–9, 53–7
   total fertility rate (TFR), 49

financialization of housing and land markets,
   134–8, 142, 146
formal and informal employment, 8
Fraser, N., 33
free market perspective, 1
frontier urbanism, 139

Gaddis, I., 56
Gandhi, I., 3–4, 32, 99
Gandhi, Mahatma, 31, 114
Gandhi, R., 4, 12, 32
garibi hatao program, 3
gated communities, 11, 90–1, 102, 118, 120–2,
   125, 133
gender dividend, 57–9
Genicot, G., 234
global capitalist system, 2
global financial crisis, 2008, 137
globalization, 31, 66, 77, 85–6, 133, 156,
   198, 213
Goldman, M., 156
Greater Noida (Delhi), 153
'greenfield' city projects, 140
greenfield frontiers, development of, 153–4
greenfield projects, 157
Guattari, F., 34–5
Gujarat International Finance Tec City (GIFT
   city), 158
Gupta, A., 115
Gurgaon, 142, 153–4, 158–61
   Aspen Greens, 120
   Birch Court, 120
   DLF township, 118–20
   Municipal Corporation of Gurgaon
      (MCG), 159
   Nirvana Country, 120
   real estate companies in, 120
Gururani, S., 139

Harvey, D., 2, 135, 137, 154, 158, 186, 191
Haryana Development and Regulation of
   Urban Areas Act 1975, 126
Haryana Urban Development Authority
   (HUDA), 119
Hasan, M., 257
Hazare, A., 114, 209
Heller, P., 14
Hindu identity, 212–13, 221
Hindu majoritarian movement, 15
Hindu nationalism, 14, 31
Hindutva ideology and movement, 9, 213–14

282 INDEX

Hindutva project, 14
Hindu upper-caste communities, 15, 240, 242, 244, 247–8, 251, 254
Hinglish, 32
Hobsbawm, E., 210
Holi, 125
horizonal social network, 252
Hume, A. P., 116
Hyderabad, 22, 175, 181

ICT-oriented service industries, 11, 101
identity politics, 22
Imperial Hotel, Delhi, 114
India
  communicative abundance, 29
  economic classes, 265
  female labour force participation, 54–5
  gender dividend, 57–9
  middle class, 258–62
  neoliberalism in, 3–14
  real estate developments, 117
Indian economy
  bank nationalization, 3
  dismantling of government's controls, 5
  economic reforms, 101, 213
  flexible exchange rate regime, 5
  foreign direct investments, 5
  garibi hatao program, 3
  ICT- led industries, 4
  Indira Gandhi regime, 3–4
  labour reforms, 7–8
  privatization of public sector entities, 5–6
  Rajiv Gandhi regime, 4
  regulatory frameworks of governance, 6
  structural adjustment programme, 3
  system of licenses and permits, 6
  trade policy, 5
Indian languages television, 32
Information and Communication Technologies (ICT), 2, 4
Instagram, 29
instant access and unequal knowledge, 30–1
interactive media, 30
Internet, 31, 33
IT and business process outsourcing (BPO) sectors, 158

Jaffrelot, C., 261
James, K.S., 16–17
Jatavs, 229

Jawaharlal Nehru National Urban Renewal Mission (JNNURM), 155
Joshi, S., 12–13

Kanshiram, 209
Kaplana, K., 168
Karva Chauth, 19, 125
Kaviraj, S., 110
Keane, J., 33
Kennedy, L., 156
kinship capitalism, 127
Klasen, S., 56
Klein, Naomi, 2
knowledge about, 42
knowledge by acquaintance, 42
Kohli, A., 3–4, 6, 11
koli fishers, 180, 183
Kolkata, 175, 181, 183
Kondaveeti Vagu Lift Irrigation Scheme, 167
Kriesi, H., 31

Lahoti, R., 56
laissez- faire economic principles, 1, 36
Land Acquisition, Rehabilitation and Resettlement Act (LARRA) 2013, 165
land banks, 143–4
Lefebvre, H., 154, 156, 166
liberal democracy, 36–7
liberal education, 37

Madhav, R., 44
Maha Hindu identity, 222
Maharashtra, 7n7, 76, 176n2, 182n3, 187, 222n2, 227
  Employment Guarantee Scheme, 10
  fertility rate, 55
maintenance charges, 126
Mandal Commission, 9
marginal communities, 21, 197–8, 203, 205, 207–8. *See also* Dalits
Marxist analytical frameworks of production, 183, 185
  power differentials, 185
Maximum City (Mehta), 187
Mayawati, 67, 81
McGee, T. G., 92, 98
media
  and academia, 42–5
  role in majoritarian politics, 32
  as social institutions, 45

INDEX   283

Menon, A., 141
Mera Parivar BJP Parivar programme, 227
Merton, R., 45
microfinance activities, 203, 205–7
middle class, 102, 115, 126, 180, 214, 258–62
    consumption patterns and practices, 261–2
    growth, 263
    Muslim (*see* Muslim middle class)
    new, 12–14, 260
    resistance movements and, 210
    social composition of, 263
    solidarity, 19
    values, 259
    Weberian perspective on, 259
migration
    in-migration, 91
    out-migration, 91
    role in consumption patterns and
        preferences, 86
    seasonal migrants, 92
modernization, 214
Modi, N., 226–7
    BJP's campaign, 32
Mody, A., 52
moral consumption, 19, 112, 124, 129
Mumbai, 175–6, 181, 183, 186–7, 189–90
Mumbai Metropolitan Region, 175n1, 178,
    182–5, 190
Muslim middle class, 22–3, 258, 262–77
    ajlafs, 263
    arzals, 263
    expansion of, 268
    household income, 262, 270
    nature and social character of, 265
    per capita daily expenditure, 262, 265, 268
    self-employment, 263
    social composition, 262
    social groups, 267
    values, 269–75
Muslims, 247
    ashraf elite, 257
    consumption level, 84–5
    discriminated in business dealings, 249, 252–3
    exclusivism, 257
    identity, 23
    land ownership, 80–1
    loan portfolio of, 245
    OBCs, 23, 86, 267–8, 277
Muslim salariat, 257
Muslim separatism, 257

Nagendra, H., 189
Naidu, C., 20
Narayan, B., 21
Nathupur, 128
nationalist solidarity, 19, 115
National Rural Employment Guarantee
    Act, 10
Naya Raipur Development Plan, 2031, 167
Nazul lands, 116
Neff, D., 56–7
Nehru, J., 236
neoliberal citizenry, 37
neoliberalism, 15, 35, 64, 190
    consequences of changes towards, 5
    and democratic politics, 36–8
    as a development strategy, 2
    East Asian experiment, 4
    Global South *vs* Global North, 1–2
    in India, 3–14
    labour, 7–8
    nature of state, 6–7
    organizational forms, 3
    power of, 44
    and regional divides, 11
    by 'stealth,' 3
    urbanization process, 11
neoliberal restructuring, 153
neoliberal urbanization, 20, 134–8, 190–1.
    See also urbanization
new liberal economy, 198, 208–11
News As Knowledge, 42
Nietzschean project, 176
non-Brahminical Hindutva, 219, 222, 229
non-capitalized production systems, 21, 186

Ostrom, E., 187
'other,' 38, 103, 212, 222
Other Backward Castes (OBCs), 9, 22, 80–4,
    240–2, 244, 247–8, 251–2

Papanek, H., 17
Park, R., 42
Parthasarthy, D., 20–1
Patel, S., 18, 191
patronage-oriented governance system, 10
patronage system, 7
Peoples' Vision Document, 189
peri-urban village, 139, 141, 143–5, 147, 155
planetary urbanization, 137
PM Awas Yojana, 213, 226

284 INDEX

Polanki, P., 160
politics after television, 31
populism, 30, 35
  communications perspective, 31–3
  distinctions between democracy
    and, 44–5
post-nationalism, 112–15, 125
Prakash, A., 21–2
Prasad, C. B., 198
private-spatial transformations, 121–2
productive age group, 48
pro-market strategy, 4
The Protestant Ethic, 259
public-private partnerships, in infrastructure
    development, 135–6, 162
public sphere, 33
Pulwama strike, 226
Pune, 22, 175, 181, 190

Qutub Enclave RWA (QERWA), 126

Rajagopal, A., 31
Rajarhat, 161–3
  agrarian society and economy, 163
  displacement and loss of livelihoods
    in, 162
Rajarhat (Kolkata), 153
Rajeev Gandhi foundation, 205–6
Rajiv Gandhi Mahilavikaspariyojana, 206
Ram, K., 9
Ramdev, B., 114
Ramesh, S., 168
Ram Janmabhumi, 32
Ram Mandir, 66
Ranjan, R., 67
Rashtriya Sewa Bharati, 205
Rashtriya Swayam Sewak Sangh (RSS), 205
Ray, D., 234
Reagan, R., 2
real estate development, 117, 136–7
  foreign private equity investors in, 136–7, 155
Reddy, J., 20
resident welfare associations
    (RWAs), 126–7, 160
resistance movements, 208–10
  failure of, 208–9
rhizome, concept of, 34–5
  characterization of Web as, 35
risk urbanism, 21, 175–8
  affecting specific groups, 179–80

from climate change and neoliberal
    urbanization, 190–1
  commoning of risk, 178–92
  as a 'forensic resource,' 190
  in Mumbai Metropolitan Region, 184–5
  risk assessments, 179
  sharing of risk, 180
Rourkela, 121
Roy, A., 95
rural real estate, 19, 133
  actor- networks, 147
  land markets, 138–42
rurbanization, 91

Sachar Report, 263
Samaddar, R., 157, 161, 163
Samajwadi Party (SP), 212, 228
  performance in electoral politics, 230–1
Sampat, P., 170
Sapera community, 204
Sarma, E. A. S., 168
satyagrah, 114
Searle, G. L., 160
self-employment, 21
self-help groups, 21, 205–6
74th Constitutional amendment act, 100
Sheth, D. L., 261
Shimla, 100
Singh, A., 67
Singh, C. R., 116
Singh, K., 67
Singh, K. P., 118, 128
Singh, M., 67
slum settlements, 93–4, 97, 103
smart cities project, 135, 155–6
social media, 29–30
Sohna Road, 120
  Mansionz, 120
  Nile apartments, 120
  Vatika City, 120
Sood, A., 156
spatial inequalities, 94–5, 98, 104
spatial purification, 102
Special Economic Zones (SEZs), 135, 137–8,
    155–6, 161
speculative cities, 164, 171
speculative investment, 139–40, 147
speculative land markets/real estate, 135, 138,
    141–2, 147, 155, 170
Sri City, 155

INDEX 285

Sridharan, E., 261
Sriprumbadur-orgadam manufacturing hub, 156
Srivastava, R., 17–19, 67
Srivastava, S., 20, 103
statutory towns, 92
Stiglitz, J., 2
Subaltern Hindutva, 213
subaltern urbanization, 91
sub-prime mortgage crisis, 137
Sud, N., 144
Surat, 175, 181, 183
Swaminathan, H., 56

Thatcher, M., 2
three capital cities, 168–9
'Tiranga Yatra' motorcycle rally, 39
Twitter, 39

Uberoi, P., 123
Ujjwala scheme, 213, 226
UK's 'new town movement,' 99
unemployment, 11
Unitech Builders, 120, 158
Upadhya, C., 169
Upadhyay, R., 39
UPA regime, 10
upper- caste middle classes, 18
urban inequalities, 157
urbanization, 11, 18, 20, 89–93, 111, 133, 154.
    See also DLF City
economy of real estate and land market, 18
employment structure, 95–8
growth of gated communities, 91
in India, 134
inequalities and exclusions, 93–5
modernity and, 95
physical infrastructure, 18
public-private partnerships in, 135–6
and rise of new middle classes, 101–3
segregation of religious minorities, 95
settlement agglomerations, 92
slum settlements, 93–4
spatial inequalities and segregation, 94–5
spatial spread, 91–2
subaltern, 91
urban policies and governance, 98–103
Urban Land (Ceiling and Regulation) Act 1976, 99–100
urban livability, 103

urban policies and governance
contradictions and inconsistencies in, 99, 101
decision-making regarding services, 100
growth of middle classes, 101–3
mandate of slum clearance, 99, 117
new housing policy, 99–100
phases of development, 99
principle of decentralization, 100
Uttar Pradesh, 9, 15, 17, 22, 39, 214–15
area and population, 198
atrocities against Dalits, 229
average monthly per capita expenditure (MPCE), 78, 83–4
BJP government, 66–7, 86
under BJP rule, 218–9
BSP government, 68, 81, 86
Congress government, 65n2, 66
consumption levels, 83–4
Dalit communities of, 206–7
Development Council, 67
employment situation, 74–7
Gangetic Plain, 198–9
government programmes, 68–9
growth performance under neoliberalism, 69–72
industrial growth, 66–8, 73–4
inter-group inequity in secondary school education, 81
land transfers and land ownership, 80–1
level and pattern of consumption, 77–80
lower-caste radical movements, 216–18
neoliberal agenda, 66–9, 85–6
OBC reservation issues, 66
political economy, 65, 69
scams, 67–8
social group equity, 80–5
social justice parties, 228
SP-BSP-RLD alliance, 224–5, 227
SP government, 67–8, 86
trajectory of politics, 215
2019 general elections, 224–7
Vindhyan Hills, 198
white collar jobs among SCs, 82

Vaibhavshree, 206
Vajpayee, A. B., 220
Van der Veer, P., 261
vertical social networks, 251–2
Vijayabaskar, M., 141

286 INDEX

village India, 125–6
Visakhapatnam land market, 170

Weber, M., 110, 176
Wetland Rules, 182
WhatsApp messages, 16, 29–30, 32, 38–42
   end-to-end encryption, 40
   role in communal clashes, 39
   spread of anti-Muslim hysteria, 38–9

spread of fake news through, 41
users in India, 40
working of, 40
white collar jobs among SCs, 82
Wolf, A., 259
woman's contract work, 8, 143
working age population, 48

Yadavs, 229
Young, I. M., 188